Field Works, Their Technical Construction and Tactical Application

Charles Booth Brackenbury

Nabu Public Domain Reprints:

You are holding a reproduction of an original work published before 1923 that is in the public domain in the United States of America, and possibly other countries. You may freely copy and distribute this work as no entity (individual or corporate) has a copyright on the body of the work. This book may contain prior copyright references, and library stamps (as most of these works were scanned from library copies). These have been scanned and retained as part of the historical artifact.

This book may have occasional imperfections such as missing or blurred pages, poor pictures, errant marks, etc. that were either part of the original artifact, or were introduced by the scanning process. We believe this work is culturally important, and despite the imperfections, have elected to bring it back into print as part of our continuing commitment to the preservation of printed works worldwide. We appreciate your understanding of the imperfections in the preservation process, and hope you enjoy this valuable book.

MILITARY HANDBOOKS FOR OFFICERS

AND NON-COMMISSIONED OFFICERS

VOL. VII.

FIELD WORKS

UNIFORM WITH THE PRESENT VOLUME.

Fifth Edition.

MILITARY SKETCHING AND RECONNAISSANCE.
By Colonel F. J. HUTCHISON and Major H. G. MACGREGOR, Garrison Instructors. With 15 Plates. 4s.

'That officer must be dull indeed who cannot learn, by its aid, to read the details of ground on a military map, and to produce a readable and fairly accurate sketch of ground, accompanied by a "reconnaissance report."'
UNITED SERVICE GAZETTE.

Sixth Edition.

THE ELEMENTS OF MODERN TACTICS PRAC-
TICALLY APPLIED TO ENGLISH FORMATIONS. By Lieut.-Col. WILKINSON SHAW. With 25 Plates and Maps. Small crown 8vo. 9s.

'The exercises are thoroughly practical and not mere theoretical diagrams. The book is thoroughly adapted to the use of Volunteers, Militia, and Yeomanry, as well as regular troops, and needs nothing beyond an ordinary knowledge of drill for the full comprehension of its lessons. We are glad to congratulate him on having produced a work which cannot but add to his professional reputation as well as to the general information of the service.' TIMES.

Third Edition.

FIELD ARTILLERY: Its Equipment, Organisation, and
Tactics. By Major SISSON C. PRATT, R.A., Professor of Military History at the Royal Military Academy. With 12 Plates. 6s.

'Some excellent illustrations and plans serve to elucidate the writer's remarks, and a most successful effort has been made to produce a really useful and fairly exhaustive manual on a subject which, though of the greatest importance, seldom meets with the attention it deserves.'
TIMES.

ELEMENTS OF MILITARY ADMINISTRATION.
FIRST PART: Permanent System of Administration. By Major J. W. BUXTON. 7s. 6d.

'It is difficult to over-rate the industry and ability which Major Buxton has brought to bear on the subject. He has really presented the army, for the first time, with as clear, continuous, and systematic an account of British military administration, as the nature of the topic permits.'
UNITED SERVICE GAZETTE.

Third Edition.

MILITARY LAW: Its Procedure and Practice. By Major
SISSON C. PRATT, R.A., Professor of Military History at the Royal Military Academy. 4s. 6d.

'The object of the manual under notice is to afford officers and non-commissioned officers some assistance in overcoming the many difficulties which attend the study of the legal part of their profession. It is well calculated to perform that office in all respects, particularly so from the method of arrangement which has been adopted.'
ARMY AND NAVY GAZETTE.

CAVALRY IN MODERN WAR. By Colonel F. CHENEVIX
TRENCH. 6s.

'The clear and independent mode in which the first chapter of this essay has been treated can scarcely be too highly praised. The author's style is incisive; his facts are marshalled with clearness, and the conclusions he arrives at are natural and consistent with common sense.'
ARMY AND NAVY GAZETTE.

London: KEGAN PAUL, TRENCH, & Co., 1 Paternoster Square.

FIELD WORKS

THEIR TECHNICAL CONSTRUCTION AND

TACTICAL APPLICATION

BY

COLONEL C. B. BRACKENBURY, R.A.

DIRECTOR OF THE ARTILLERY COLLEGE

WITH APPENDICES AND NINETEEN PLATES

BEING THE SEVENTH VOLUME OF

Military Handbooks for Officers & Non-Commissioned Officers

EDITED BY

COL. C. B. BRACKENBURY, R.A.

LONDON

KEGAN PAUL, TRENCH, & CO., 1 PATERNOSTER SQUARE

1888

(The rights of translation and of reproduction are reserved)

PREFACE.

This book has a double object. In the first place, it is intended, like the rest of the series, for the use of that numerous body of Englishmen, including the Militia and Volunteers as well as many persons in civil life, who care to study different branches of the military art without going deeply into technicalities; in the second place, it is a humble attempt to fill a gap in our military literature by adding to the elaborate treatises on the fortification of localities and positions in the field, some help as to the best methods of attacking and defending such localities and positions. A considerable amount of attention is now paid to the technical details contained in the first five chapters, which may be passed over by those skilled in such work; but it may, perhaps, be found that the number of officers and non-commissioned officers who are thoroughly conversant with the arts of attack and defence, irrespective of the construction of the works, is rather limited.

The form in which the book is cast—namely, a

volume with two plates of examples in a pocket, and a separate appendix which contains the technical plates and some information of a specially technical character, is designed for the comfort of those readers who interest themselves more in tactics than technical details; but even those trained to the execution of works may, perhaps, find one or two points new to them: for instance, the principle that the first defence of a village should commence a mile or two in the direction of the enemy, and the second defence should be fifty yards outside the village. Such rules as these and others are plainly indicated by the facts of modern war, but have not yet been worked into a system, as I have now endeavoured to do.

All the reasoning in the following pages is based on certain principles which are stated again and again, and to which all details are subordinated. It appears to me that if we take a young man of average intelligence and cram him with facts and formulæ only, we run a risk of disgusting him by charging his memory to the brim with a mass of material which it will soon throw off. But if, on the other hand, the vital principles of the military art are insisted upon and illustrated by examples from history, especially the history of our own times, there is a possibility of developing the faculties which may be called military instincts, and disposing the mind to swallow facts and, what is infinitely more important, to digest them. Acting on this idea, I have selected and analysed a large number of modern instances bearing on the subject of the defence and attack of positions large and small. My own opinions have been fully stated, but those students who feel inclined to question either statements of facts or opinions will gain much more by frank denial and argument than by blind belief. The only way to acquire the military instinct is by the exertion of the intellect and the judgment. To cram a few rules in order to pass examinations is of no practical use whatever, and I have tried to make this volume as unattractive as possible to those who have only that evil purpose in view, though I trust the book may be of some value, however small, to real military students.

The appalling dulness which characterises almost all books on fortification has heavily oppressed me during those leisure moments which, for many months, have been devoted to this work; and I shudder to think that this book may be found as dull as any. But, at least, any ordinary reader can master its contents; among which he will find no mysteries, real or pretended. Thus he may learn not only how to delay the march of an invader, but even how to make the villages and towns of England mere graves for that famous invading army of 100,000 men which certainly may, and probably will be some day landed on our shores.

The reader will observe a constant reference to two principles, which are really the mother ideas of the whole military art. They may be thus stated :—

First, soldiers are not machines, but human beings with legs, and stomachs, and nerves, and a moral sense. To obtain success in war it is necessary to develop their muscles, but not to over-fatigue them; to fill their bellies before asking hard work from them; to quicken their nervous energy, while taking care not to exhaust it; and to raise their moral tone by every possible means, while depressing, as far as may be, that of the enemy. I have seen strong men faint, die, and even weep in war from pure exhaustion; and there are many steps between absolute failure and perfect condition. The moral sense is equally capable of many stages, from heroism to collapse of courage, and the quality of a good officer will be shown by his power of keeping his men in good heart and strength as long as possible, while he knows how to bow down the spirit of the enemy.

Second, the whole art of strategy and tactics is summed up in the principle to be superior to the enemy at the right time and place. The superiority may be either that of greater numbers, superior skill, better physical condition, or higher moral tone. Superior armament will also tell, but in a less proportionate degree. Some of these advantages must be gained by the leader at the time; others can be prepared in peace.

The improvement in modern weapons has greatly enhanced the destructive effect of infantry fire on life, and of artillery fire on both life and material. Tactics have had to accommodate themselves to the altered conditions.

Instead of masses of men, called columns, or stiff but thinner bodies, in what we call line, manœuvring on open ground close to each other, we now find armies extremely flexible, using every means to cover themselves, whether at rest or in motion, from the deadly fire of the enemy. We have to expect in future wars a great development of the use of entrenching tools both in attack and defence. It is even probable that two equally skilled antagonists will each both attack and defend at different points of the battlefield, and it is certain that the new style of fighting will bring both responsibility and opportunity much lower in the military hierarchy than was the case in the battles of the past. In the fighting of to-morrow, officers of the higher grades will be unable to retain the direction of the combat; subalterns and even corporals will often have to judge for themselves. A good judgment in emergencies can never be the property of the ignorant or the thoughtless, and if this small volume adds ever so little to the knowledge and the capacity for thought of the many who wear the Queen's uniform, its object will have been achieved, even if it never contributes a single additional mark to a candidate's score in an examination.

C. B. BRACKENBURY.

July 1888.

CONTENTS.

CHAPTER I.

ELEMENTARY.

Field fortification does not imply weakness—Elementary ideas—Main objects to be aimed at—Cover—Exposure of enemy—Obstacles to enemy, retaining him under fire—Communications—General description of means for gaining these objects . . 1

CHAPTER II.

THE ARMS IN USE.

Details of defence must vary with variation in weapons—The modern rifle, its rapidity, range, and penetration—Question of long range fire—Soldiers' energy to be economised—Machine guns—Artillery, its range, penetration, and rapidity of fire—Different kinds of fire—Proportion of losses in different wars, chiefly influenced by tactics—Comparative effect of infantry and artillery fire—French experiments at Bourges . . . 8

CHAPTER III.

COVER AGAINST THE ARMS IN USE.

Nature of defensive works governed by time available, and amount of fatigue to men which can be afforded—Conditions of a good parapet and ditch—Definitions of terms used and requisite qualities of various parts—Defilade—Simple rule for defilading a work—Choice of ground should avoid necessity for defilade—

Splinter-proof field casemates—Tiers of fire, their value—Restrictions on their use—General idea of perfect field work when plenty of time and men available 19

CHAPTER IV.

HASTY ENTRENCHMENTS AND REGULAR FIELD WORKS.

Hasty cover can be made without engineers—Valuable in attack as well as defence—Qualities of the shelter trench, and principles for its use—Charger and gun pits or epaulments—Artificial shields—Horses to be sent out of fire—Remarks on details—Dangerous tendency towards too much cover—Evil results from yielding to it in the field—The Volunteers and hasty entrenchments—Skobeleff and the spade—Regular field works—More the business of engineers, but principles simple and within grasp of all—General principles—Plevna as much a warning as an example—Field works good servants, bad masters—Shelter trenches often preferable—Traces of field works—Definitions, explanations, and criticisms—Elaboration of details necessary for complete protection—Disadvantages of salient angles—Effect of them on the men—Names of works and their parts, with criticisms on them—Redoubts—Advice concerning them—Garrisons—Never place artillery in redoubts if it can possibly be avoided 28

CHAPTER V.

ACCESSORIES AND OBSTACLES—USE OF ACCIDENTS— CLEARING THE GROUND.

Field casemates—Tiers of fire—Supply of ammunition—Head cover—Loopholes—Revetments—Embrasures—Cover for guns—Platforms—Stockades—Tambours—Caponiers—Keeps or reduits—Blockhouses—Traverses and parados—Magazines—Entrances—Definition and use of obstacles—General rules—Abatis—Entanglements—Wire entanglements—Chevaux de Frise—Crow's-feet—Military pits—Palisades—Fraises—Fougasses—Inundations—Barricades—Use of accidents—Hollows—Walls—Hedges—Cuttings—Embankments—Roads—Clearing the ground—Principles 45

CHAPTER VI.

DEFENCE AND ATTACK OF WOODS AND DEFILES.

Woods, various in kind—An average wood supposed—Organisation of the edge—Clearing the ground—Obstacles—What to begin with—Salients—Parapets or shelter trenches—Entrances of roads—Interior organisation—Artillery defence—Position of guns—Some pushed to front at first—On flanks—Within wood—Interior retrenchment—Communications—Organisation of defenders—Division into sections—Chain of responsibility—Rear edge of wood—Behind wood—Conduct of attack and defence—Advance of assailants—Action of defenders—Attack of the retrenchment—Counter attack—Further defence—Assailants at far edge—Defiles—General remarks—Definition—Specialities of defiles—Defence of defiles—In rear—Measures to be taken—In front—Measures to be taken—Within—Measures to be taken—Attack of defiles—On rear position—Measures—On front position—Measures—On position within—Measures . . . 64

CHAPTER VII.

DEFENCE OF HOUSES, FARMS, AND VILLAGES.

Still necessary in war—Examples—Defence of a house—Order of work—Details of house defence—Step by step—Defence of a farm—Principles—Exterior defences of first importance—Details—Number of garrison—Use of shelter trenches—Second line of defence—Defence of villages—Old rules affected by modern weapons—Prominence of artillery—*Pros* and *cons*—Actual cases suggest certain principles—Exterior failure need not involve fall—Cases of prolonged interior defence—The first danger—Bombardment by artillery worse than formerly—Reply by outer shooting line and inner organised defence by 'the garrison'—Reserve artillery on flanks as formerly—Summary of principles 84

CHAPTER VIII.

DEFENCE OF VILLAGES (*continued*)—DETAILS AND THEIR REASONS.

Individual soldiers important—Different shapes of villages—Circular best—Arrangement of successive defence—First position of defenders—Delaying action of artillery—Noisseville—Infantry to be kept back at first—Under cover from bombardment till enemy's infantry advances to assault—Second position of defenders—Artillery on flanks, infantry in shooting line—Garrison still under shelter—Division of village into independent sections—If enemy carries a point, isolate it—Enemy sure to envelop—The principal keep—Machine guns—The reserve and its functions—Counter attack—Rules deduced from modern instances and progress of weapons 96

CHAPTER IX.

DEVELOPMENTS OF DEFENCE OF VILLAGES—QUESTION OF REDOUBTS.

Different cases arranged under three headings—First, to cover detachments—Second, advanced posts in the field—Third, posts in the line of battle on front or flanks—These cases detailed—Opinions of Frederick the Great—General Brialmont's opinions—The three cases considered as to their treatment—Special differences—Illustrations from wars—Necessity for information—Typical cases considered (Plates)—Treatment of defences with regard to nature of village—Front defences—Flank defences—Rear of village—Supplementary defences—Spaces—Freedom for counter attack—Barricades—Supports to outer line—Interior reserve—Keep—Defence of houses—Exterior reserve—Retreat of shooting line—Counter attack—Prolongation of front—Same details in other typical cases—Notes to General Brialmont's remarks—The question of redoubts: their use and abuse, and whether they should be occupied by both infantry and artillery, discussed in conversation between A. and B.—Summary of opinion—New type of British redoubt 108

CHAPTER X.

ATTACK OF HOUSES, FARMS, AND VILLAGES.

Reconnaissance, its methods and points to be observed—Means of procuring information—Best way to deal with fortified post is to let it alone if possible—The attack of advanced post—example faults at Tashkessen—Always have strong advanced guard to deal with advanced posts—First action of artillery and first artillery position—First infantry advance—At what range com-

mence fire—Question of long-range infantry fire discussed—
Points of agreement and disagreement—Cases in modern war—
St. Privat checked but did not rout Prussians—Gorny Bougarovo, Turks repulsed and ruined at short range—General principle, use artillery to save infantry both in defence and attack
—Therefore avoid long-range fire—Formation of the attack—
General principles—Modern attack formation—General Dragomirov's modification for attack of work adopted here—Avoid
lifeless formula—General rules for details of attack—Artillery
fire—First infantry advance—Further infantry advance—Chain
closes to about 200 yards—Main body over it—Vulnerability
of different formations—Attack pushed home—Destruction of
obstacles. 138

CHAPTER XI.

ATTACK AND DEFENCE OF VILLAGES (*continued*).

Artillery preparation—Objects to be fired at—Ranges—Artillery
defence—Further remarks on infantry attack—By front and
flank—Reserves in flank attacks—Strength for frontal attack—
Action by groups—New French infantry attack—Its principles
—The group—Ranges at which fire is to be opened—Half
sections, sections, &c.—The company—Details of formation
and advance—Defence by an isolated company—The battalion
—Application of its first formation—*Formation de combat*—
Fighting patrols—Rules for the march—Fire effect—Dismounting of officers—Phases of the combat—First phase—Second
phase, in two periods—Third phase—The battalion isolated—
Defensive—Brigades and divisions—German instructions for
magazine rifles—Instruction of the soldier—Instruction of the
company—Instruction of the battalion—Four principal cases for
magazine fire—Economy of ammunition—Artillery support . 161

CHAPTER XII.

COMBAT WITHIN VILLAGES.

Information required—Importance of good interior defence—Defence of first houses—Counter-attacks—Interior attack—Columns
of attack—Organised advance—Flanking fire of defenders—Defence not always complete—Advance through houses—Artillery

in street fighting—Attack of the keep—Traversing streets under fire—House to house fighting—Underground passages and mines—Provision against counter-attack—Completion of the capture—Night work—Action of the turning columns—Extinguishing fire—Recapitulation of Defence—General considerations —General dispositions—Barricades—Artillery—Stores—Minor keeps—Land torpedoes—House to house defence—Incendiarism —Counter-attacks—Recapitulation of Attack—First entrance— Press attack—Artillery—Gradual progress—Main keep—Completion of capture—Surprises—Ought to be impossible—Outposts—Gitschin—Troops for surprise must be good—No noise— Previous knowledge—Time for surprise—Night—Precautions on the march—Night march in Balkans—Before Tel-el-Kebir— Houchard's escape—The attack—Rendezvous—Defence . . 184

CHAPTER XIII.

EXAMPLES OF ATTACK AND DEFENCE OF LOCALITIES IN MODERN WAR—CAMPAIGN OF 1866 AND 1870–71.

Campaign of 1866—Austrian defects—Affair of Podol—Night attack—Battle of Königgrätz (Sadowa)—Village of Chlum unprepared—Farm of Rosberitz also—They become turning-points in defensive battle—Battle of Custozza—Farm of Cavalchino— Campaign of 1870–71—Battle of Weissenburg—Château of Geissburg—Description of château—Prussian attack bloodily repulsed—Arrival of artillery—Garrison yields to bombardment— Battle of Wörth—Elsasshausen—Fröschwiller—Battle of Spicheren—Stiring Wendel—Battle of Gravelotte—St. Marie aux Chênes—Farms of St. Hubert and Moscow—Position of St. Privat (see Chap. X)—Lessons of St. Privat—Blockade of Metz—Battle of Noisseville—Villages of Noisseville, Servigny and Poix—Attacks and defences—Lessons—Affair of Peltre— Design—Failure—Affair of Ladonchamp—'Aggressive spirit'— Marshal Bazaine—Lesson to us in English defence—Battle of Sedan—Bazeilles—Bavarian attack repulsed—They organise centre of village—Struggle in main street—Turning movements—Final street fight—Lessons of Bazeilles—Army of Orleans—Châteaudun—Coulmiers—Ladon—Beaune-la-Rolande —Capture of Juranville by cavalry—Lesson that all arms should work together—Patay—Blockade of Paris—Basis of German arrangements—Affairs of Chevilly, Thiais, and L'Hay

—General principle of defence—Would not suit all cases—French attacks—On L'Hay—On Thiais—On Chevilly—All repulsed—Remarks—Affair of Clamart, Bagneux and Châtillon—Attack on Bagneux succeeds—That on Châtillon fails—Remarks—Le Bourget—Its importance—First capture by French—Their preparations for defence—Disposition of garrison—Ineffectual bombardment—German attack on October 30—Capture of the entrance—Inner attack and defence—Faults of defence—Capture by Germans—Their preparations for defence—French preparations to attack—Attack of December 21—Failure of attack—Remarks—Lessons of other village fights—Champigny — Villa Evrard — Buzenval — Bapaume—Villersexel—Questions raised by civilisation 204

CHAPTER XIV.

EXAMPLES—ATTACK AND DEFENCE OF LOCALITIES.

Saragossa, 1809—Special enthusiasm of the people—Their commander, Palafox—Their preparations and defence—French devices for attack—Further Spanish arts of defence—Twenty-six days for 400 yards—Suburb on left bank—First attack—Second attack—Third and final attack—Observations—Zaatcha, 1849—Preliminary remarks—Description of village—First defensive preparations—Insufficient reconnaissance for attack—Attack of July 16 and repulse—Further Arab preparations—New expedition in September—Immediate assault fails—Fresh preparations for attack and siege works—Assault October 20 again fails—Arab sortie—The attack becomes prudent—Lively sorties by the Arabs—Arrival of reinforcements—New energy on both sides—Vigorous Arab sortie repulsed—Council of war and change of plans—Mines, batteries and breaches—Arab resistance—Decision to assault—Preliminary arrangements—Assault of November 26—Character of interior fighting—Final success of French—Losses in final attack—Remarks—Lack of reconnaissance, insufficient provision of means—Divided responsibility—Lesson of the final success—Conduct of the Arabs—Russo-Turkish campaign, 1877—False conclusions drawn—Turkish errors—Sistova—Nicopolis—Tirnova—Kezanlik—The Shipka Pass—Plevna and Lovtcha—Gorni Dubnik—Telisch, first attack—Second attack—Capitulation after bombardment 242

CHAPTER XV.

EXAMPLES OF FORTIFIED POSITIONS—TORRES VEDRAS AND PLEVNA.

PAGE

Passive defence to be avoided when possible—Wellington and Torres Vedras—Torres Vedras an exceptional position—Troops available—Colossal works—The position and works—Elements of success at Torres Vedras—Repeated in position before Constantinople—Elements of success wanting at Plevna—First attack upon Plevna—Further preparations for defence—Second battle of Plevna—Russian errors of plan—Krudener's attack repulsed—Schakovskoi's attack repulsed—Remarks—Turkish attack on the Shipka Pass—Feeble Turkish attack from Plevna—Application to defence of London—Operations on the Lom—Lovtcha captured—Plevna defences developed—Russian preparations and bombardment—Elaborate plans upset by accidents—Third battle of Plevna—Attack on Gravitza Redoubt—Attack near Radischevo—The redoubts on Lovtcha road—Skobeleff's preparations—Russian carelessness in reconnaissance—Skobeleff seizes Third Knoll; skirmishes follow—Position at 2 P.M. September 11th—3 P.M. attack—Checked and reinforced—Skobeleff uses his last reserves and carries works—Condition of Skobeleff's force 4.30 P.M.—Turks attack left flank; repulsed by counter-attack—Artillery and Cossacks occupy attention of Krishin Redoubt—Russians carry Eastern Redoubt—Situation at nightfall—Problem now before general staff—Want of unity in army command; Skobeleff not reinforced—General Zotof's orders—Condition of Skobeleff's troops on morning of 12th; Turkish attacks—Turks, not pressed elsewhere, combine troops against Skobeleff, who retires slowly—Losses on both sides—Observations on third attack of Plevna—On unity of command—On necessity of reconnaissance—The best troops cannot succeed without good leaders—Tactical skill necessary—Plevna a warning, not an example 267

CHAPTER XVI.

EXAMPLES OF FORTIFIED POSITIONS—ARDAHAN, ZEVIN, AND ALADJA DAGH.

Russian plan of campaign in Armenia—Operations of third column and of second column—Capture of Ardahan—Operations of fourth column—Position of Zevin—Detailed description—Outposts—First line—Right wing—Centre—Left wing—Second line—Principles of construction for whole—Russian attacking force—Unprepared frontal attack—Russian advance—Left column—Right column—Artillery—Retreat and losses—Turks fail to pursue—Remarks—Violation of principles—Effect of the battle on the campaign—Battle of Aladja Dagh—Previous movements—Russian plan of attack—Distribution of troops—Movement of turning column—Orders for attack—Attack on Avliar—Lazareff's attack on Vizinkioi—Attack on Aladja Dagh—General result and losses—Remarks 305

CHAPTER XVII.

DEFENCE AND ATTACK OF LARGE POSITIONS.

Physical advantages of defence—Of attack—Moral advantages and disadvantages of defence—Of attack—Balance favours attack—Initiative the habit of great generals—Final results must be counted—Moral effect on campaigns—Comparative value of artillery—Occupation of vital points—Guns can defend their own front—Should be able to concentrate their fire—Infantry can act anywhere—Probably more than one position for artillery—Unity of command for artillery masses—Preliminary active defence—Points to be occupied or abandoned—Produce the greatest fire effect possible—First line—Second line—Reserve—Zevin a useful type—Modifications of Zevin type—Choice of time for counter-attack—Cases of counter-attack—Should points be connected by lines?—Particulars of average case—First line—Second line—Reserve—Flanks—Weak points of such a position—Measures if time is doubtful—The holding back system—The attack—Principles—Reconnaissance—Preliminary—Four types: Russian—German of 1870—Frederick's—Probable coming type—General ideas—Action of field artillery—High explosives—Action of infantry—The coming type—Attack should entrench a rallying position—Question of position guns with armies in the field—Night attacks—Chain of responsibility and nature of orders 325

LIST OF PLATES.

PLATE
I. SECTIONS OF PARAPETS . . . . *To face p.* 24
II. TOOLS . . . . *In Appendix*
III. SHELTER-TRENCHES, VARIOUS . . ,,
IV. HASTY WORKS—ARTILLERY . . ,,
V. TRACES OF FIELD WORKS . . . ,,
VI. PLEVNA REDOUBT, HEAD COVER, LOOP-HOLES, FIELD CASEMATES, REVETMENTS . . . . . ,,
VII. FIELD CASEMATES, ACTIVE GUN BLINDAGE, STOCKADES . . . . ,,
VIII. TAMBOURS, BLOCKHOUSES, ENTRANCES . ,,
IX. OBSTACLES . . . . . ,,
X. DEFENSIBLE WALLS . . . . ,,
XI. DEFENSIBLE HEDGES, CUTTINGS, EMBANKMENTS . . . . . ,,
XII. WOOD PREPARED FOR DEFENCE . . ,,
XIII. FORTIFIED HOUSE . . . . ,,
XIV. DEFENCE OF A FARM . . . ,,
XV. DEFENCE OF VILLAGES . . . ,,
XVI. NEWER TYPES OF VILLAGE DEFENCE . ,,
XVII. NEW FRENCH INFANTRY ATTACK . . ,,

XVIII. Attack and Defence of Villages—L'Hay, Chevilly, and Thais; Le Bourget; Château and Park of Buzenval; Bazeilles; Chatillon and Bagneux; Zaatcha; Lovtcha . *In Pocket*

XIX. Attack and Defence of Positions. Torres Vedras, Plevna (Third Attack); Zevin; Aladja Dagh; also British Fort of Newest Type . *In Pocket*

Appendix I.—Clearing the Ground.
Appendix II.—Shelter-trench Exercise.

FIELD WORKS.

CHAPTER I.

ELEMENTARY.

Field fortification does not imply weakness—Elementary ideas—Main objects to be aimed at—Cover—Exposure of enemy—Obstacles to enemy, retaining him under fire—Communications—General description of means for gaining these objects.

(*References to Plates V., VI., VIII. and IX.*)

THE art of Field Fortification in one form or another is probably as old as mankind, for it is difficult to conceive of man otherwise than as a fighting animal; and the brain which, in its developed state, has designed the great fortresses of the present day must, in its early condition, have sought some rough means of obtaining advantage over an enemy. In this elementary book, fortification will be treated only as required in the field, and will always be considered, not as implying weakness on the part of those who make use of it, but as a means of adding strength both to the weak and the strong. Self-defence forms part of the instruction in the use of every weapon, and to make use of field works is only another form of the same principle which causes boxers to defend as well as attack, and swordsmen to study guards as carefully as cuts and thrusts.

In order to get at the most elementary ideas of field fortification, let us first imagine two men armed with some rough means of throwing projectiles, if only a sling and stone, and also capable of close combat, if only with clubs. Let us place ourselves in the position of one of them, and think what he will wish to do to protect himself and obtain advantage over his enemy.

His first instinct will be to conceal himself, while keeping his enemy well in sight, or, if he cannot conceal himself, he will hide as much of his body as he can from the enemy's missiles, and he will select, if possible, a place where his enemy must be plainly visible for some distance when advancing. He will also be glad if the enemy can be forced to advance over any objects which may detain him within reach of missiles, and he will wish to have easy means of advance or retreat for himself.

Here are four distinct conditions to be obtained if possible. They are such as would occur to any man, and they are the four great principles of field fortification. All other rules are mere refinements of detail. The main objects which underlie every system of field fortification are, then, these four :—

1. Cover for the defender from the enemy's fire.
2. Exposure of the enemy when advancing.
3. Hampering the enemy's movements by obstacles.
4. Retaining freedom of movement for the defender by what are called in military phraseology 'communications.'

If we now go a little into detail with regard to each of the four objects to be attained, the first question will be, 'What sort of cover?' The answer evidently is, 'Any sort of cover which will stop the missiles of the enemy without preventing the defender from using his weapon, whether it be sling, or stone thrown by the hand, or bow and arrow, or rifle.' The principle is the same for the savage as for the most elaborately drilled and armed soldier of the nineteenth century. A tree, a fallen log, a mound of earth, a heap of stones, a low wall, or, if none of these exist naturally, as much earth as can be scooped out and thrown up to form a mound. This last is, in fact, the modern shelter trench of which examples are given in the Appendix. But no such mound, or heap, or wall must be so high as to shut out all sight of the enemy; otherwise the second principle would be violated, which demands that the enemy should be kept in full view. To the use of early weapons such as the sling, a high wall or mound would be fatal unless the defender procures something to stand upon which raises him sufficiently to see over his defences. For more modern weapons, crossbows, muskets, and rifles, or field guns, holes can be made which are called loopholes or embrasures (Appendix, Plate VI.). But the principle remains the same.

Now let us multiply the number of men, and suppose a small party on both sides. The defenders will now have to meet a new danger. Some of the enemy may show themselves in front, others may steal round and rush in from the flank or even rear. To guard against this it becomes necessary to arrange the defences in some other shape than a straight line, and such forms as the redans, lunettes, and forts of different shapes (Appendix, Plate V.)[1] are naturally suggested. As such a method of attack would divide the enemy's force into two parts at least, there will be an opportunity for the defenders, if strong enough, to rush out on one portion and destroy it before it can be succoured, and this is the best means of meeting such an attempt. This counter-attack is like a quick return in fencing when the enemy has exposed himself. The right seizure of such moments is one of the most necessary and most difficult operations in war. If the defenders are very weak, and are yet bound not to retire, they will have more cause to fear flank and rear attack, and will arrange their defences so as to cover them all round. Thus will be formed some sort of redoubt or fort, but the important rule—namely, *to be always able to sally out against the enemy*—will have to be violated or at least partially neglected. In such cases the defence can only last for a certain time. The defenders must yield in the end unless reinforced.

On the chance of having their line of defences carried,

[1] But see later the effect of modern firearms in simplifying such forms. *See* Chap. IV. &c.

the defenders will form some inner work as a sort of citadel. It may be an interior retrenchment or a block house (Appendix, Plate VIII.). A portion of the force will garrison this to support, from a safe place, the efforts of the garrison.

But, supposing all this is done, the enemy may refuse to make a direct attack on any portion of the work. He may keep his distance, and, concealing himself as well as he can, in his turn may throw his missiles, not against the faces of the defenders, but from the flank of any one of the sides of the work. This is called 'enfilade fire,' and places the defenders in the condition of receiving a permanent, though slow, flank attack. The missiles would then not only have a better chance of striking, but might kill or wound more than one man each. In fact a heavy missile thrown by a large engine might bound all down the line and kill many in its course. The obvious precaution is to place some small defences across those already erected and inside them. These are called 'traverses.'

Then, in the case of a weak force which encloses itself for defence against a strong one, the enemy may postpone attack and endeavour to overwhelm the defenders by a long-continued shower of missiles. This is called a 'bombardment,' and in anticipation of it the defenders should build some kind of overhead cover for themselves sufficiently strong to resist the kind of missiles likely to be directed against them. The simplest and perhaps best form of shelter is to excavate a gallery just behind or under the main line of defence. So we come to the 'field casemate,' which was used with such advantage by the Turks at Plevna that no amount of bombardment by the Russians was of any effect to turn them out of their forts (Appendix, Plate VI.).

By a common-sense process we have started with the ordinary precautions of savages and reached the main features of modern field fortification. All other details are but developments of these features to meet particular cases, or to give additional strength according to the means available in time, number of men, and kind of material that can be used.

To recapitulate, the main features are—

First. Some kind of cover which exists or can be constructed artificially, but must not be of such a size and construction as to hinder full view of the enemy.

Second. Such a general shape of the work as will guard against flank attacks.

Third. A citadel of some sort to prevent a partial capture of the work from being necessarily permanent.

Fourth. Protection from enfilade fire by means of traverses.

Fifth. Complete protection for all the garrison not wanted at the time for fighting purposes. This is secured by field casemates, which are generally so arranged that the men can sleep in them.

So much for the first object, obtaining cover for the defenders.

We now pass to the second object to be attained—namely, 'exposure of the enemy when advancing.' The savage gains no advantage by getting behind a tree if his enemy can do the same, and field works will be of very little use if the enemy can advance under cover close up to them. It is therefore important to clear away everything which impedes a full view of the enemy, and for the same reason it is well to have the works raised a little above the level of the surrounding country. All timber which could hide the advancing foe should be cut down, and all hedges, walls, or banks which run across in front of the works; but they may be left if they run from the defenders in the direction of the enemy, because then they do not hide him, but divide his attack into fractions. In some cases even these must be levelled if they prevent flanking fire, or are likely to embarrass counter-attacks. On the whole a perfectly smooth field of view is generally best, and if there is any doubt the decision should be to level.

The third object to be attained is 'hampering the enemy's movement by obstacles.' This is not so much intended to prevent him from coming to close quarters at last as to keep him as long as possible in the open, exposed to the fire of the garrison who are concealed or partially covered. There are many obstacles which can be placed in the way, and the nature of them must depend upon the time and means at disposal. The main principle is that they should hamper the enemy and check him under fire without preventing the garrison from seeing him and firing at him. For instance, 'abatis'—that is, trees cut down and with their chief branches pointed and turned towards the enemy—form an excellent obstacle, but may, if the defences are low, prevent to a certain extent the defenders from having a clear view. But any hollow in front may be filled with abatis to great advantage, because the defenders' view will not be interrupted and the hollow cannot then be used by the enemy for shelter. Various forms of obstacles are given in the Appendix (Plate IX.), but one of the most useful, though most difficult to arrange under ordinary circumstances from want of material, is that called 'entanglements,' and especially 'wire entanglement.' It is the artificial imitation of tropical creepers or bramble-bushes, and is formed by half cutting down brushwood, or driving stakes into the ground and stretching interlaced boughs or wire between them. The wire entanglement has the great advantage that, even when broken up by artillery fire, the wire still coils about the feet of the attacking enemy. Land torpedoes will probably be one form of obstacle, rather moral than physical, employed in future wars, but their use will be more common in the rare case of passive defence, because their known presence cannot but hamper counter-attack. This is the weak point of all obstacles, and the presence of these aids to defence will generally prove that the defenders consider themselves weaker than the assailants, at least temporarily.

The fourth object to be attained is freedom of movement for the defenders by means of 'communications.' There is one great principle, seldom noticed in treatises on fortification, a principle which every military student should make a very prominent part of his mental equipment. It is this, that the whole intention of fortification, as of tactics and other branches of the art of war, is not so much to kill numbers of the enemy while saving our own side, as to produce the greatest effect of moral depression on the survivors of the enemy and put our own troops in the highest spirits. A long continuous passive defence will never do this. However successful it may be, the weaker spirits will be depressed by it, and the enemy encouraged to act with growing boldness bred of frequent immunity from return attack. It is therefore most important that every garrison, strong or weak, should make sallies and counter-attacks against the enemy, and for this purpose there must be good communications for advance, retreat, and for taking the enemy in flank. There may be cases when a small body of men has instructions to show their quality of tenacity to the end, and to accept death or capture rather than yield an inch to an overpowering force of the enemy. But this can only last for a short time, and there will be the great moral stimulant of self-devotion for the common good. Even then there may be opportunities for sorties. But, speaking generally of defensive works, one of the first thoughts of the designer should be how the troops can get out of them to attack the enemy. Otherwise the army which makes free use of them will certainly become subject to demoralisation. It is necessary to insist on this principle, because the tendency of all works, whether field or permanent, is to teach habits of inactivity which would soon become fatal. The danger is so real that it is a question whether, in peace manœuvres, troops should ever be allowed to construct and occupy field works without teaching them at the same time how best to advance out of them.

In arranging communications, the principles which should govern the designer are, that there should be space enough for the troops to issue in force, that they should not open to the enemy a view of the interior of the work—this can always be secured by traverses—and that the communications should be covered by the fire of the garrison, flanking or direct. If the enemy can be prevented from seeing the exit and entrance of the troops, so much the better. Sorties and counter-attacks will thus be made more sudden, and therefore more impressive.

CHAPTER II.

THE ARMS IN USE.

Details of defence must vary with variation in weapons—The modern rifle, its rapidity, range, and penetration—Question of long range fire—Soldiers' energy to be economised—Machine guns—Artillery, its range, penetration, and rapidity of fire—Different kinds of fire—Proportion of losses in different wars, chiefly influenced by tactics—Comparative effect of infantry and artillery fire—French experiments at Bourges.

THOUGH the main principles of fortification, like those of all military arts, must remain the same so long as man remains an earth-walking animal, the details must vary with the progress of weapons. The simple stockade of the savage is protection enough from spears. Defence against rifled muskets and cannon which will hit the smallest work at distances of from one to two miles requires much more elaboration. It is, therefore, necessary to understand clearly what different firearms are capable of performing.

It is usually stated that the Martini-Henry rifle will fire 25 unaimed, or 12 aimed shots in a minute; but this must depend upon the skill of the soldier, the clearness of the mark, and the readiness of the ammunition. As an average the result would be less than is given, especially for the aimed shots. Magazine guns or quick-loading arrangements may improve this in the future, and troops behind works, on the defensive, may be supplied with an almost unlimited stock of ammunition. They may, therefore, commence fire earlier, conduct it with greater rapidity, and, by placing tiers of men at different heights, one above another, as the Turks did at Plevna, produce a greater mass of fire at any given moment than is possible for infantry advancing in the open, dispersed in extended order, unable to fire while in motion, and obliged to economise their ammunition.

The possible effective range of modern rifles may be said to be 3,000 yards, and at that range, Martini-Henry bullets have penetrated 9 inches of damp sand. But all the experience of war is against long range infantry fire. It may annoy an enemy, but it will never produce decisive effects. In attack it would be absolutely useless in most cases, and the defenders will generally be better employed in eating their breakfasts and smoking their pipes under cover, than in expending their nervous energy by exposing themselves to the enemy's fire, either from rifles or artillery, without doing any work which will materially add to their chances. It is now generally recognised that each man has a fund of nervous energy, which should be economised like food or ammunition, but, unlike them, it cannot be replenished in a moment. The necessary alteration of sights is apt to be neglected in an engagement, and, on the whole, it is better not to commence fire at ranges over 800 yards, and then only with great care and under absolute control. The most deadly work will be done at ranges of 600 yards and under.

The following table gives the thickness of material which may be considered proof against rifle bullets of existing service arms at any range.

Earth	2 feet
Iron Plate	$\frac{3}{8}$ inch
Steel Plate	$\frac{1}{4}$,,
Fir { In log	12 inches
{ In 3-inch planks	6 planks
Oak { In log	6 inches
{ In 2-inch planks	3 planks
Gabions filled with earth	1
Sandbags filled { Crossways	2
{ Lengthways	1
Rope mantlet	6 inches
Loose cotton	4 feet
Compressed cotton in bale	2 ,,

Machine guns may be used by the defence at somewhat longer ranges, because the number of men exposed to produce a given effect is much less, and the weapons are not so much affected by the nervousness of the men as rifles are; though it should be added that infantry defending works can generally deliver a steadier fire than in the open, not only because the men are less exposed, but because they can rest their rifles on the parapet or walls in front of them. Machine guns in the English service give rather higher penetrative effect than the Henry-Martini rifle, but not greater than new experimental rifles which will probably be introduced.

The range of modern rifled artillery, of siege and field calibre, may be said to be fully 6,000 yards for shells with percussion fuses, and instances have occurred in which such long range fire has been useful. For instance, in 1864, the Prussian batteries of rifled 24-pounders and 12-pounders established on the Broagerland bombarded and partially burnt the town of Sonderburg, the nearest part of which was about 5,000 yards distant, and Danish batteries were silenced at distances of from 2,500 to 3,500 yards. Yet these guns were decidedly inferior in power to those of the same calibre which now exist.

Generally speaking the conditions favourable to such long range fire will not be found, for the Prussians were firing over an arm of the sea, and could not approach any nearer with an equally good field of view. Artillery should not waste ammunition any more than infantry, but it has the advantage over infantry of seeing where its shells strike, and correcting the aim accordingly. At the battle of Gravelotte the range varied from a maximum of 5,000 paces (say 4,000 yards), down to case range; and though the long range fire of a single battery may be of almost no value by itself, instances of long range are likely to occur, where batteries far away on the flanks may assist others firing from the front at shorter range. At extreme ranges common shell only would be used, and it is most effective against buildings, &c., at any range. Shrapnel is used at all ordinary ranges, and is the best man-killing projectile. The penetrative force of the bullets is on an average less than the penetration of rifles, but that of pieces of shell is much greater in most cases. Case shot is only used at close ranges against troops.

The following table, extracted from the 'Manual of Elementary Field Engineering,' and brought nearer to date, gives some details of the penetrative effect of guns. The figures, however, refer to pieces which have in many cases been superseded by others of higher power.

A single 16-pounder shrapnel shell contains 128 bullets, and a 13-pounder shrapnel 116 bullets. Two rounds per gun can be fired per minute, including laying the piece, except at long ranges, when the laying is more difficult and the time will be proportionately longer.

Thus a 16-pounder firing shrapnel can discharge 256 bullets per minute, besides pieces of shell. Some machine guns can fire as many as 400 bullets per minute if no hitch occurs, but have no projectiles capable of dismounting a field piece, and the difficulty of correcting the aim restricts their efficacy to shorter ranges. Their chief advocates do not claim for them the power of contending in equal terms with field artillery in the open, but for defence of positions they will be of great value.

Artillery fire as to its direction with reference to the horizontal plane is said to be either *front* or *frontal*, *oblique*, *enfilade*, or *reverse*.

Front or *frontal* when it strikes the front of a visible object, or is delivered straight to the front.

Oblique, when the object aimed at is struck in front, but not perpendicularly.

Enfilade, when the fire is directed along a rampart or line of troops.

Reverse, when it strikes the parapet or line in rear.

Again, artillery fire as to its trajectory may be either *direct*, *curved* or *indirect*, or *high-angle fire*.

Direct, from guns with service charges at all angles of elevation not exceeding 15°.

FIELD WORKS.

Nature of Gun	Mean Penetration of Shell at 1,060 Yards			Extreme Penetration of Shot or Shell	Thickness of Parapet in Feet	Remarks
	Into a Natural Butt		Made Earth (Clay) well rammed			
	Natural Concrete	Sand, Clay, &c.				
	ft. in.	ft. in.	ft. in.	ft. in.	ft.	
Newhaven Experiments, 1863. { 7-inch B.L. rifled gun	7 9	12 11	18 3	21 11	25 to 30	In cases in which the works might be exposed to artillery fire for some time, it would be advisable to make the parapets the full thickness given in the last column; in works of a more temporary nature the smaller thickness would suffice.
70-pr. " " "	6 4	—	14 3	17 0	25 " 30	
40-pr. " " "	6 1	—	11 8	16 4	18 " 25	
20-pr. " " "	—	7 0	10 8	13 8	15 " 18	
12-pr. " " "	3 10	3 2	4 0	—	6 " 9	
10-inch S.B. gun	3 6	—	11 0	12 0	15 " 18	
8-inch " "	4 0	7 6	11 5	12 9	15 " 18	
68-pr. " "	2 8	5 8	14 10	21 6	25 " 30	
32-pr. " "			9 5	14 0	18 " 25	
Lydd-ness, 1885, 1882. { 9-pr. M.L. rifled			4 ⎫		(Sand, 9ft. Medium soil, 12ft. Clay, 15ft.)	
16-pr. " "			6 ⎬	—		
13-pr. " "			7 ⎭			
Shoe-bury { 12-pr. B.L. rifled			17[1]			
22-pr. " "		No data at disposal.				

[1] Six shells planted on the same spot were required to breach this thickness. About three times that number would be required to do the same work in sandy loam.

N.B.—The shells for the new B.L. guns are of steel.

Curved or *indirect*, from guns with reduced charges and from howitzers and mortars at all angles of elevation not exceeding 15°.

High-angle fire, from guns, howitzers, and mortars at all angles of elevation exceeding 15°.

The following table, showing the proportion of wounded by different arms in modern war, is extracted from the *Revue Maritime et Coloniale*.

In 1864	Danes		84 per cent.	by musketry fire
			4 ,,	sabre and bayonet
			10 ,,	artillery
			2 ,,	unknown
In 1866	Austrians		90 ,,	musketry fire
			4 ,,	sabre and bayonet
			3 ,,	artillery
			3 ,,	unknown
	Prussians		79 ,,	musketry fire
			5 ,,	sabre and bayonet
			16 ,,	artillery
In 1870	French		70 ,,	musketry fire
			5 ,,	sabre and bayonet
			25 ,,	artillery
	Prussians		88 ,,	musketry fire
			2 ,,	rifle and bayonet
			5 ,,	artillery
			5 ,,	mitrailleuse

It is interesting to observe that in 1866 the tactical handling of the Austrian guns was superior to that of the Prussians, who learned a lesson in that war which taught them boldness in the use of field artillery. Their new and bolder tactics were practised in 1870 with the material result that 25 per cent. of the French losses came from the German guns, while the French, still clinging to the old tradition of taking care of their artillery, lost battles and artillery together, and only inflicted on the Germans 10 per cent. of losses from artillery and mitrailleuse fire together. In the Russo-Turkish campaign of 1877–8 the artillery was inferior and used in a timid manner. The result was again small comparative effect of artillery, and most bloody repulses of infantry attacks. *While, therefore, superiority in the shooting of individual pieces will influence the losses to a certain extent, superiority in position and tactical handling, especially in the direction of boldness, will have a much greater influence, not only on the losses, but on the result of engagements, which is infinitely more important than a mere production of a higher or lower per-centage of wounded.*

Comparative Effect of Infantry and Artillery Fire.

There has been so much controversy on the comparative effect of infantry and artillery fire, and the statements on either side have generally been so difficult to reconcile, that the results of a trial in France, carried out with the intention of arriving at definite results, can hardly fail to gratify all who seek for truth rather than the support of a preconceived opinion. The facts were published in 1880, and are detailed in General Brialmont's 'Formations de Combat, &c.,' which was published in that year.

To represent infantry fire there were 100 men of the 95th regiment occupying 100 metres[1] of frontage; for the artillery a battery of six 90 millimetre guns occupying an equal space. The duration of fire was the same in every case for each arm, ten to fifteen minutes. In some cases the distance of the targets was unknown. In others it was first ascertained by the artillery and communicated to the infantry before the comparative firing began. Both sides then fired together. The targets were exactly alike, in each case two rows 48 metres long and 1 metre 80 centimetres high, one row being 150 metres behind the other to represent shooting line and support of infantry. We need not trouble ourselves about the likeness of the targets to what they professed to represent. The present question is only what was the comparative effect of infantry and artillery occupying the same frontage? The conditions

---

[1] For rough calculation 10 metres may be taken as representing 11 yards.

were rather against the artillery, because no allowance was made for the fact that it sometimes knocked down portions of the target by its shells, and had thereafter a smaller mark to fire at.

The infantry fired sometimes independently, sometimes by volleys from half-sections. The artillery fired projectiles—shell and shrapnel—usually giving 150 fragments per projectile, and on one occasion a form of shrapnel which gives only 100 fragments.

The ranges were 800, 1,050, 1,100, 1,200, 1,300, 1,350, 1,600, and 1,800 metres. It is to be regretted that the experiments did not extend to shorter ranges.

Taking as examples the firing at 800, 1,300, and 1,800 metres, we find the results given in the following table.

Arm	Range	No. of Rounds	Hits
	metres		
Infantry	800	4,500	410
Artillery	,,	50	820
Infantry	1,300	10,417	163
Artillery	,,	68	795
Infantry	1,800	3,650	149
Artillery	,,	84	1,000

Thus we see that, in the same time and with the same frontage, the results of artillery fire were at 800 metres double, at 1,300 metres nearly five times, and at 1,800 metres more than six and a half times as great as those of infantry.

Taking into consideration the whole of the results, the following conclusions were arrived at.

First. Starting from 800 metres and up to extreme ranges, the killing effect of artillery is always superior to that of infantry, rising from double at 800 metres to sevenfold at 1,800 metres.

Second. It is most important for artillery to use projectiles giving a large number of pieces.

Third. It will be very advantageous on the field of battle for the artillery to communicate to the infantry the ranges which it obtains, if the infantry has to fire at the same object.

Fourth. It appears from the experiments at Bourges that infantry cannot deliver a very rapid fire (*un feu violent*) for more than five minutes, either because the men are fatigued, or because the smoke prevents good aim, or because the heating and expansion of the barrels diminishes the force (? accuracy) of the bullets.

Fifth. The nature of the experiments does not furnish answers to tactical questions. Each chief of a unit must judge for himself what he has to expect from fire under the circumstances, and decide whether the probable results to be obtained are worth a given sacrifice of ammunition. It appears, however, that the following observations may be laid down as correct (*on puisse formuler*).

Volleys by infantry are more efficacious than independent fire (*feux de tirailleurs*).[1]

Infantry cannot, without great danger, attack artillery in open ground.[2]

Infantry should moderate its fire at great distances.

Artillery, with its flanks protected and a clear view in front of it, can protect itself against the attacks of infantry advancing from far.

At 1,000 or 1,200 metres the man-killing effect of the four divisional batteries is about equal to that of the infantry division, whether estimated by the number of rifles which the division can at a given moment put in line, or the amount of ammunition carried by the infantry and artillery respectively, as shown by the following calculation.

The division, generally fighting with four battalions in the first line, and each battalion occupying a frontage of 300 metres, might bring about 1,200 rifles into the shooting line. But a battery produces at 1,000 or 1,200 metres three times

---

[1] This must depend on the coolness of the men. Experience in war tells that infantry in the open field and at short distance from an enemy cannot be brought to fire volleys steadily. Perhaps they may from behind cover.

[2] Of course this means frontal attack.

more man-killing effect than 100 infantry. Therefore four batteries will produce about the same effect as the 1,200 rifles of the shooting line.

Again, if we consider the ammunition carried directly by the troops, the infantry soldier having on his person 78 rounds, the division will have about 750,000 cartridges, reckoning 800 men to a battalion. The batteries of 90 millimetres having 154 rounds per gun, the four batteries have with them 3,696 rounds. But, according to the Bourges comparative experiments, less than 60 shells produce three times as much effect as 4,000 bullets. Therefore one shell has more effect than 200 cartridges, and the 3,696 shells more than $3,696 \times 200 = 780,000$ cartridges, that is to say, the ammunition carried by the men of an infantry division.

In the comparative experiments the 100 infantry have generally fired 4,000 cartridges in ten minutes, or 40 rounds per man. Thus each man might expend the whole of his ammunition in twenty minutes. At the rate of fire generally used by the guns during the experiments—namely, rather less than one round per gun per minute—a battery would take nearly three hours to expend its 154 rounds per gun.

N.B.—In presenting the above experiments and opinions to English military readers, the author would only add that the comparatively large proportion of losses in battle by infantry fire is simply due to two facts :—

First. That the greater part of the artillery fire is directed either against guns which have few men to kill, or at infantry which for the time gets under cover of some sort.

Second. That the average range at which artillery engages is vastly greater than the average for infantry.

It is clear by the above experiments that if the artillery of a division can be brought into action with its division at 800 metres, it will enormously increase the fire effect of that division. Similar comparative experiments for short ranges are much wanted.

The statement which is often made that artillery cannot remain in action against infantry at short range was often contradicted by facts in the war of 1870 ; and the power of guns to do so would be immensely increased by providing them with light steel shields, as proposed long ago by the author. The idea has been accepted widely among English artillery officers and is especially suitable for our army, which cannot afford to expend life with the freedom which prevails in Continental nations. Some day our successors will wonder why the adoption of shields was so long delayed.

At the present moment a very large advance is being made in the power of shrapnel fire. The two tables which follow show—First, the improved accuracy of the new B. L. guns, the 12-pounder and 22-pounder; and second, the increased number of bullets contained in each shrapnel shell. Taking the two tables together, it will be seen that the power of the 12-pounder B. L. is nearly double that of the 9-pounder M. L.; and the 22-pounder B. L. has, in both accuracy and number of bullets, more than twice the power of the 16-pounder M. L.

Range and Accuracy.

Nature of Gun	Elevation	Range in Yards	50 per cent. of the rounds should fall within a rectangle —— yards
9-pr. M. L.	5°	2114	54 × 4
16-pr. ,,	5°	2240	50 × 4
16-pr. ,,	9°	3390	90 × 5·5
12-pr. B. L.	3°	2040	30 × 2·5
12-pr. ,,	5°	2900	36 × 3·5
22-pr. ,,	3°	2400	28 × 2·1
22-pr. ,,	5°	3384	35 × 3·5
22-pr. ,,	9°	4857	50 × 4·2

Shrapnell Shell.

Nature of Gun	Material of Shell	Contents of Shell	Total Bullets
9-pr. M. L.	Cast Iron	28 of 18 to lb. / 35 ,, 34 ,,	63
16-pr. ,,	,,	72 ,, 18 ,, / 56 ,, 34 ,,	128
12-pr. B. L.	Steel	216 ,, 33 ,,	216
22-pr. ,,	,,	385 ,, 34 ,,	385

CHAPTER III.

COVER AGAINST THE ARMS IN USE.

Nature of defensive works governed by time available, and amount of fatigue to men which can be afforded—Conditions of a good parapet and ditch—Definitions of terms used and requisite qualities of various parts—Defilade—Simple rule for defilading a work—Choice of ground should avoid necessity for defilade—Splinter-proof field casemates—Tiers of fire, their value—Restrictions on their use—General idea of perfect field work when plenty of time and men available.

(*References to Plate I. in text, and V., VI., and VII. in Appendix.*)

HAVING now arrived at some general ideas of defence, and being acquainted with the arms which have to be resisted by our works, let us think for a moment what sort of physical obstructions the defenders will wish to create, as cover against the enemies' fire; not forgetting that the fire must be returned, and that there must be a possibility of sallying out for a counter attack, except in the cases, rare on the field of battle, when a weak garrison has to hold its position as long as possible against greatly superior numbers and with no probability of succour.

And first, for the sake of simplicity, we will suppose the ground to be open, level and of medium consistency. It will be necessary to create the cover, and the defenders must dig. But digging causes a certain amount of physical fatigue, and abstracts just so much from the strength of the men. It is, therefore, important not to spend more vital energy in digging than is sufficient for the purpose in hand. For instance, a portion of an army held back for a time may suffer from the enemy's fire, but know that it is to advance later on. A little shelter may be worth making, but the force of the soldiers must be husbanded. They would spend their strength for nought if they tried to make a Plevna. Again, there may be little time to spare, or the men may already be tired and likely to be attacked before they have had much rest. All these considerations must be thought of. Two questions then must be mentally answered before the work is commenced.

First. How much time have we at disposal?

Second. How much fatigue is worth while?

No book can answer these questions, nothing but the individual intelligence of the commander, who should be able to judge the tactical situation correctly, and to keep touch on the moral pulse of his men. But, to assist the student, the Plates of this book have been arranged in progressive steps, showing first what can be done in a short time, and afterwards, more completely if advisable, in a longer time.

Neglecting for a moment the questions above, which lead to complicated calculations, let us now try to get at the sort of thing which we should wish to construct out of the earth before us with the ordinary tools which troops have at their disposal—namely, picks, shovels, spades, felling axes, billhooks, and crowbars, supposing there is time enough.

The ground, we have said, is level. Clearly, what we must do is to throw up a mound of earth thick enough to stop the projectiles of the enemy. The earth required must be dug up, and as we require protection for the men from the enemy's fire, the height of the mound above the place where the men are to stand when under cover must be more than their height, because the bullets or shells have a curved flight and drop rather behind our mound. Again, we know that the earth must be from 12 to 15 feet thick to resist field artillery, so that the mound must be of considerable size. Where is the earth to come from? Evidently we must dig a ditch either in front or behind the mound, or two ditches, one in front and one behind. The advantage of making the ditch in front will be that the enemy cannot carry the mound with a rush, but must descend into the ditch first and then climb up the mound. But if the ditch is broad and level at the bottom, the enemy can pour into it in great numbers and assemble there, ready to make a rush over the mound in strong force. To prevent this we should have the bottom of the ditch as narrow as possible. We get then some such form as Fig. 1, Plate I., where the dotted line represents the line of the ground. It will be found necessary for easy working to leave a small portion of level ground between the ditch and the mound, on which some of the men can stand to shovel up the earth on to the mound. In technical language this is called the 'berm,' and it might help the enemy to climb the mound if it is not afterwards cut away. We have now acted on two principles :—

First, to make the mound thick enough.
Second, to make the mound high enough.
But we must fulfil a third.

Third, the form of the mound must be such that the defenders may use their arms to the best advantage.

They cannot do so if it towers up above their heads, for then they could not see the enemy any more than he could see them. The simple way to carry out the third principle is to cut some sort of step or steps in the mound, on which the men may stand and see over it. They will then find that other cutting and trimming is advisable, and so we arrive by degrees at the form of what is called the 'parapet,' that is, the mound put into good shape. Both to save time by using as many men as possible and to enable infantry to collect in safety close behind the parapet, it is well to dig a portion of the earth required, from a trench behind, leaving also a 'berm' there. Stiff soil will stand at a steeper slope than loose soil, and we can now show the 'profile' of two typical forms, which the student should master thoroughly, as they form the basis of all field fortification. (Plate I.)

Definitions and Qualities of Parts.

Plane of Site.—The level of the ground, or technically, a plane generally tangent to the ground, is called the *plane of site.*

Terreplein.—The surface of the ground within the work is called the *terreplein*.

Commencing from the left there are the—

Glacis.—Made with surplus earth from the ditch; is a protection to the *escarp* from artillery fire, and brings the enemy well in a line with the fire of the defenders over the parapet.

Escarp, Counterscarp.—The sides of the ditch, made as steep as the earth will stand well at. *Escarp* (or *scarp*) has usually a greater slope than the *counterscarp*, because it has to sustain the weight of the parapet and is exposed more or less to artillery fire.

Ditch.—The bottom of the ditch is often pointed, to prevent the enemy assembing there. It cannot be deeper than eight feet without putting a great strain upon the men to throw up the soil. Its width depends on the amount of earth required. If the bottom is too broad, leave the glacis till after the parapet is made, and then form the glacis out of earth gained by deepening and pointing the ditch. Sometimes sharp stakes may be placed at the bottom of the ditch, but this costs extra time and labour.

Berm.—The space between ditch and foot of parapet, left for convenience of the workmen. If the ground is loose the berm may have to be left, or the parapet might slip. In stiff soil it is better cut away.

Exterior Slope.—Left at the natural inclination of the soil, generally $\frac{1}{1}$ or 45°. The *exterior* and *superior slopes* are the parts of the parapet seen by the enemy, and it is important that they should look as much as possible like the natural ground in the neighbourhood, so as to afford as bad a target as possible.

Superior Slope.—Is the top of the parapet. Should be at such an angle, that the men firing over it see the crest of the glacis, or at least any enemy on the glacis. For this purpose the line of fire should not pass more than three feet above it. To make the angle greater than $\frac{1}{4}$ would weaken the parapet.

Interior Slope.—The height of the *interior slope* should be such that a soldier standing on the banquette can easily fire over the crest of the parapet at an enemy on the glacis. The height will be from 4 feet 6 inches to 4 feet, according to the slope of the ground. The inclination of the *interior slope* is generally great, about $\frac{4}{1}$, and in that case it should be revetted if possible, but the most modern idea is to leave it at the ordinary slope of ground 45° and without revetment. (Appendix, Plate VI.)

Exterior Crest.—The intersection of the exterior and superior slopes is called the *exterior crest*.

Crest or interior crest.—The intersection of the superior and interior slopes is called the *interior crest*, or more commonly *the crest*.

Command.—The height of the *interior crest* over the plane of site is called the *command*. The word *command* is also commonly applied to the height of the crest of one work over another, or over any given point within range.

Relief.—The height of the interior crest above the foot of the escarp is called the *relief* of the work.

Tread of Banquette.—For the men to stand on when firing. A double rank of men would require a breadth of 4 feet, but there will seldom be a double rank exposed now that breech-loaders are used. The second rank will be better in the trench, ready to fill up casualties. For a single rank a breadth of 3 feet, or at a pinch, 2 feet will be sufficient. The *tread* should have a slight slope to the rear, about 2 inches to drain off rain.

Slope or Steps of Banquette.—To enable the men to step easily upon or from the tread of the banquette. If there are materials for revetment and time enough, it is better to have steps revetted. (Appendix, Plate VI.) Steps may have a rise of 9 inches to 18 inches, and a tread of 12 inches to 18 inches. If a slope is necessary it should be one of $\frac{1}{2}$.

Rear Trench.—To afford good cover. Whenever time permits, and anything like a long occupation is expected, this trench will be used for the construction of *field casemates* (Appendix, Pl. VII.), where the defenders may be sheltered from long range fire.

The figures which have been given represent parapets on

level ground, but the shape will have to be altered if the enemy stands higher or lower, or if the ground rises or falls behind the parapet. The interior of a work must be screened more or less according to circumstances, and this screening is called *defilade*. If the ground falls to the rear, a lower parapet will be required. If it rises, a higher is necessary. In an enclosed work the interior can seldom be sufficiently covered from the enemy's fire by the parapet, and it becomes necessary to build *traverses* or *parados* or both. The parados is only a large traverse built inside the work to cover the defenders who stand on the faces or flanks furthest removed from the enemy's fire (Appendix, Plate V.).

Scientific defilade is an elaborate business requiring much calculation, but it all comes practically to this, that the enemy should not see from his position any part of the interior of the work nor even the men in it. A very simple method of arranging this, is to place men at the point or points most exposed, and let them look towards the enemy's probable position. Raise upright rods or bandrols at intervals along the line where the interior crest of the parapet is to be; mark on them points where the line of the men's sight directed on the enemy's position cuts into the rods; add 4 feet 6 more for the height above the ground of the rifles firing at you. The points so found on the rods will give the necessary height of the parapet to prevent the enemy from hitting your men, supposing him to be near at hand, about 200 yards. But as his bullets follow a curved line in their flight, a little more height of parapet must be allowed for moderate ranges, and a great deal if protection against long range fire is necessary.

Defilade ought seldom to be necessary in field works. A good choice of positions will give the advantage required, with great saving of time and trouble.

It is practically impossible to defilade the interior of a work against shrapnel fire, especially at long ranges. The drop of a nine-pounder shell at 3,000 yards range is nearly one in five. This alone would oblige the defender to raise his parapet four feet for every twenty feet to be protected behind it, and

PLATE I.

STIFF SOIL

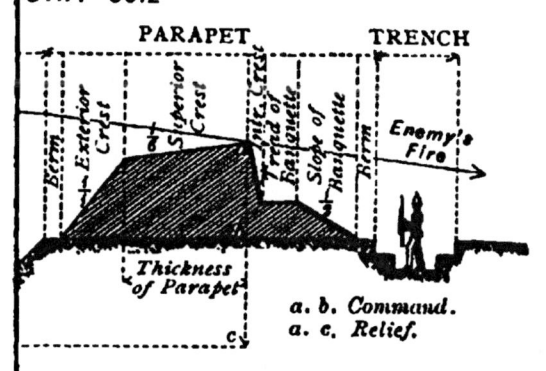

PARAPET — TRENCH

Berm — *Exterior Crest* — *Superior Crest* — *Interior Crest* — *Tread of Banquette* — *Slope of Banquette* — *Berm* — Enemy's Fire

Thickness of Parapet

a. b. Command.
a. c. Relief.

VERY LOOSE SOIL

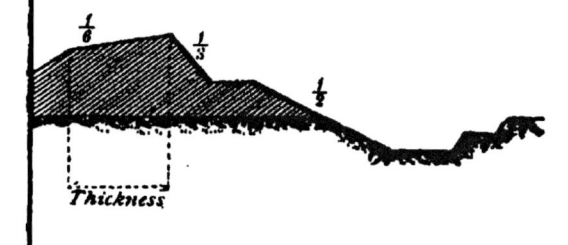

$\frac{1}{6}$ $\frac{1}{3}$ $\frac{1}{2}$

Thickness

SECTIONS OF PARAPETS.

there is in addition the burst of the projectile, which deflects many of the bullets still more downwards. Even long range infantry fire would cover the interior of the work. Some better means of protection than defilade is therefore required.

This is found in the construction of splinterproof 'field casemates,' as they are called, different forms of which are given in the Appendix (Plate VII.). These should be made whenever there is any probability of a lengthened occupation. In one form or another they have entered into all well-known successful defences of earthworks, as at Sebastopol and Plevna. They have the enormous advantage of preserving all men, not actually required at the moment, from that drain of nervous energy which the enemy desires to produce before attacking. We read of shaken and unshaken troops. The difference is that the former have had heavy calls made on their stock of nervous energy while the latter have not.

It is impossible to exaggerate the importance of husbanding nervous energy to the last moment possible. After a fever or long fasting the bravest men are sometimes reduced to such nervous prostration as to start at the slightest noise and even weep at the merest trifles. Between that condition and a full stock of energy there are many stages. No troops can bear more than a certain amount of exposure to fire without suffering in moral force, which is but another word for one form of nervous energy. Northern races such as English, Germans, Russians, are cooler, and therefore do not expend nervous energy so fast as southern, but the best of us all must yield at last. Economy of nervous energy is even more important than economy of food or ammunition. We shall frequently have to refer details to this great principle. In the meantime we may recollect with advantage how completely the use of field casemates at Plevna prevented the Turks from being shaken by the long-sustained bombardments of the Russians. During the bombardments most of the Turks sought shelter. On the commencement of the assault, they poured out of the casemates entirely fresh and ready, behind their ordinary parapets and in various tiers of firing ranks, to shake the Russians, who, being in the open, were then exposed to the demoralizing influence of the fire from the works.

In the different forms of field casemates given in the Appendix it will be seen that some are intended to be constructed at the same time as the parapet, others are later additions executed when it has become clear that there is sufficient time for them. As a general rule construct them if the troops are likely to remain in the position. The nervous energy expended will be amply filled up in a few hours during the freedom from wear and tear secured by the protection which the casemates afford.

About 8 or 9 square feet per man should be allowed, and if the occupancy is to be prolonged, a raised wooden platform for the men to lie upon will conduce to health. There should be occasional practice in turning out rapidly and manning the parapets. If you find delay or confusion enlarge the means of exit.

We have now arrived at a sort of typical parapet, with shelter behind it to save the men's nervous energy. But supposing them turned out for action to repel an assault, are we to be satisfied with the rank, single or double (generally single in these days of breechloaders), which stands immediately behind the interior slope? This must to a great extent depend upon circumstances. If the ground to be covered is large in comparison with the number of troops, a single rank only can be spared and will deliver a heavy fire. But if the works form part of the protection of an army standing on the defensive, as in the case of the Turks at Plevna, there will be men enough and to spare, and it will then become advisable to add to the intensity of fire by placing the men in different tiers. In the former case, every available space will be occupied by 'obstacles' of one kind or another. In the latter case the obstacles will be living men, with their rifles and bayonets. The advantage of obstacles is that they are always there, day and night, and have no nerves; their disadvantages are that they have no active power, that they may be gradually ruined by the fire of the assailants, and that they are generally in the way when a counter attack should be made.[1] The advantages of the men in tiers are that the defence is more active, that the enemy suffers more, and that there is always a good opportunity for counter attack, so that a repulse may be turned into a rout. The disadvantages are that an appreciable amount of time is required to send the men into the advanced places, so that if the enemy be close, a sudden rush may prevent the formation of the tiers at all, while the men of the advanced tiers cannot be kept permanently in them on account of their comparatively great exposure to artillery fire from a distance. They are therefore more valuable when the enemy is still at a distance than when he has approached near at hand, by means of zigzag trenches, as the Russians ought to have done at Plevna but did not.

On the whole, considering that different tiers of fire do not prevent the placing of obstacles further in advance, add greatly to the intensity of fire at the moment of assault and facilitate counter attack, *it will be well to use them whenever the supply of men is plentiful*, as in the case of a comparatively large force defending a narrow front—for instance, in entrenched camps like that of Plevna or Metz.

The general idea of a perfect field work, supposing that there is time enough and that plenty of men are available, will, therefore, include—

A parapet and ditch more or less like those given Plate I., Figs. 2 and 3.

Splinterproof field casemates behind the parapet so constructed that the men can rush out of them quickly to repel an assault.

Arrangements for tiers of infantry fire, so long as the distance of the enemy is such that the various ranks will have time to take their places before the work can be attacked. Tiers of fire require of course some elevation of the work over the ground in front of it.

[1] An interesting example of the advantages and disadvantages of obstacles occurred lately at Khartoum, where the Arabs were kept away by means of land torpedoes which, after hurting them on some occasions, ended by establishing a nervous dread of them. But accidents happened through their means to some of General Gordon's own people.

CHAPTER IV.

HASTY ENTRENCHMENTS AND REGULAR FIELD WORKS.

Hasty cover can be made without engineers—Valuable in attack as well as defence—Qualities of the shelter trench, and principles for its use—Charger and gun pits or epaulments—Artificial shields—Horses to be sent out of fire—Remarks on details—Dangerous tendency towards too much cover—Evil results from yielding to it in the field—The Volunteers and hasty entrenchments—Skobeleff and the spade—Regular field works—More the business of engineers, but principles simple and within grasp of all—General principles—Plevna as much a warning as an example—Field works good servants, bad masters—Shelter trenches often preferable—Traces of field works—Definitions, explanations, and criticisms—Elaboration of details necessary for complete protection—Disadvantages of salient angles—Effect of them on the men—Names of works and their parts, with criticisms on them—Redoubts—Advice concerning them—Garrisons—Never place artillery in redoubts if it can possibly be avoided.

(References to Plates III., IV. and V.)

HAVING once mastered the general principles of earthworks, and the shapes of parapets prepared carefully according to those principles, the descent to hasty entrenchments is easy. It is seldom that complete earthworks will be built without the presence of trained engineers; but every lieutenant or even non-commissioned officer may have to improvise cover which may increase the power of the little force he is commanding. The full value of hasty cover has not even yet been fully demonstrated in the practice of modern war, but every successive campaign brings the use of improvised cover into a clearer light.

Passing by the evident value of shelter trenches, as constructed by the defenders in almost every field manœuvre at

Aldershot and elsewhere, passing also the zerebas and so forth used daily in the Soudan for defence, there is a further use which has hardly yet been illustrated at all—namely, the use of shelter trenches by the attacking side.

The chief problem of modern tactics is how to attack an enemy posted in a strong position and with flanks secured— that is, how to make a frontal attack when none other is possible. The present writer believes that night attacks will in many cases be attempted, and that such solutions of the problem will be much more numerous than they have been in the past. But, supposing that an attack by day is chosen, how is it to be carried out? The enemy will have shelter trenches at least, perhaps field parapets and some obstacles. To attack steady troops at any point with equal numbers would be suicidal, yet the advance of heavy masses is almost equally so in the face of modern firearms. We have then of necessity as conditions a thin advance, but a concentration at some point whence the final assault is to be delivered. Nothing seems more suitable than the establishment, one after another, of small bodies pushed near the enemy, whose outposts must be first driven in. Such parties will throw up what protection they can, and gradually accumulate a force which may be capable of overpowering the enemy's thinner line by direct attack, with or without a previous bombardment.

At the same time, supposing the forces equal or nearly so, it will be necessary to occupy the attention of the enemy along his whole line. This can only be done weakly at parts; and here again the spade will be necessary to support the weaker detachments or the thin line as the case may be.

We see, then, that, whether for defence or attack, the spade —using the word as signifying entrenching implements generally—is likely to play a more prominent part in the wars of the future than it has done for centuries past in Europe. The reason is that the firearms both of infantry and artillery have been developed both in range, accuracy, and speed of firing to such an extent that a direct approach to contact with an equal enemy is now almost impossible without cover, natural or artificial.

Different forms of the shelter trench and the shelter pit[1] are given in the Appendix (Plate III.), but there are some points which require special notice.

First. The shelter trench is hardly at all an obstacle in itself to the advance of an enemy. It only affords a certain amount of cover to the body of the soldier in situations where there is no natural cover. It is in no respect a fortification intended for permanent occupation.

Second. Therefore soldiers should be taught to construct shelter trenches as rapidly as possible, to occupy them only as they would occupy a hedgerow for temporary purposes, and always to expect the order to advance from them.

Third. But it is possible that the position may have to be occupied for a lengthened period, in which case more complete defence may be constructed. Hence shelter trenches should begin with the shortest unit of time allowed to construct the minimum of cover, and be then developed, if required, through the forms of more protective shelter trench up to that of the field parapet with its ditch. But such development spoils the work as a shelter trench exactly in proportion as it forms an obstacle.

Fourth. One of the most valuable uses of the shelter trench is the steadiness of fire which results from the possibility of resting the rifle on the little earthen mound. It is most important to remember that the main use of the pure shelter trench is not to form an obstacle to the enemy's advance, but to increase his losses from fire while diminishing your own. Your bullets are to stop him, not your works.

Fifth. The shelter trench has one great advantage. It has no ditch in which an enemy could find shelter even for a moment, and therefore requires no flank defence and no salient angles, which are always weak points. You have only to develop good frontal fire, and the trace cannot be too simple.

Sixth. In all field-works, especially shelter trenches, avoid like poison all neatness which takes time and makes a better target.

[1] Shelter pits can be united by a slight trench.

Cover for Horses and Guns.

It is usual in books on fortification to treat charger pits and gun pits or epaulments as analogous to shelter trenches for infantry. Now this is all very well if we take for the unit of the shelter trench the French *retranchement expéditif*, which takes an hour and a half to construct, or even their *tranchée-abri*, or our 'half-hour trench,' which cost half an hour per man covered, and are not proof against artillery fire. But an infantry soldier can place himself out of sight of the enemy, and at least screened from musketry fire, in five minutes (Appendix, Plate III.); whereas the shortest time given in our text-books for the artillery epaulment is one hour for a working party of six men. If so much time and labour as this are expended in covering artillery, one is, so to say, anchoring the guns, and that is exactly what no tactician wishes to do in these days, either for artillery or infantry in the advanced line. A charger pit requires half an hour, and chargers are out of place in a line of skirmishers or a 'shooting line.' No officer should be present in such lines unless he is as active as the men.

The best rapid cover for guns would be found in artificial shields carried with them, which could be raised as quickly as infantry can extemporise the smallest cover, and would protect against what they have most to fear, namely, infantry fire and shrapnel bullets. This subject is gradually being investigated in England, but is only likely to arrive at final solution when the importance of not allowing guns to be driven away by scattered infantry sharp-shooters is accepted as a first principle in tactics, and this may require another great war. *The English army has never met in the field an enemy provided with well-served rifled artillery, nor has good shrapnel fire from rifled guns in large numbers ever yet been seen on a field of battle.*

Leaving steel shields aside for the present, it would seem that, while chargers are out of place in a shooting line, gun pits and epaulments are designed for artillery which is likely to remain a long time in position, otherwise the time and the fatigue are not worth while. But if the guns are thus to be placed in battery, why not unhook the teams and send them out of fire? It would be absurd to waste time and energy on constructing works which cost an hour at least unless you are also to take trouble against having to evacuate them at two or three minutes' notice; and surely the teams will suffer less by being placed out of the way, and only brought up when it is decided that the guns are to retire.

The same is to be said for the officers' horses and a portion of the gunners. Half of each detachment might be kept out of fire, and all the officers' horses. The enemy will then have a much smaller mark to fire at, and you will not only be able to supply casualties with fresh men, but husband that nervous force on which everything depends in critical moments. The same rule applies in even greater degree when the one-hour epaulments are run into each other so as to form a battery (Appendix, Plate IV.). Such a battery should be unassailable in front, but must be supported on the flanks by infantry if there is no shooting line before it.

In the absence of artificial shields, and if guns are to be in the same line as the infantry in shelter trenches, leave the natural soil behind the little mound of earth which should come from a trench in front. Keep the guns well separated —forty or fifty feet apart; and use any spare time and energy in making traverses, however small, every twenty feet or so between the guns. It will be well to form little caves in the parapet or traverses to hold a few rounds of ammunition, but beware of being led into expenditure of too much time and energy.

General Remarks on Shelter Trenches.

Certain technical matters are worth carrying in the head. Before deciding on the line for a shelter trench, or the character of cover for guns, remember that neither the eye of the rifleman nor that of the gunner will be on the same level as yours is when you are standing erect. Therefore in both cases place yourself in the position which the men will occupy, and then decide whether the view of the ground in front is satisfactory. If there is a choice, it is better not to sink either guns or riflemen below the ground level, unless the weather be dry and the soil of a hard and binding character. A soldier lying in a puddle, or a gun digging its wheels and trail deeper into soft soil every time it is fired, is certainly not placed to the best advantage. For this reason epaulments are usually better than gun pits, and a slight bank of earth, such as that supporting a hedge, is better than a shelter trench. It has also the advantage of being more natural, and attracting little attention till the men discover themselves by firing. Imitate the natural appearance as well as you can by hiding all freshly turned soil with branches, leaves, or grass; in short, copy the character of the surrounding ground. So will you give a less definite target to the enemy.

There will always be a tendency to err in the direction of too much cover. A clear distinction should be made between the slight shelter trench, and the work designed to stop the enemy by its own difficulties. In the former case your own men are free to advance at any moment, and should have the idea that they will advance. In the latter you throw difficulties in their way as well as in that of the enemy, and begin to inculcate a feeling of the enemy's superiority. This is not so much the case at night, when the men will sleep all the better if they feel that there are physical difficulties to an approach of the enemy. The tendency to improve the shelter trench till it becomes a fortification is apparent in all our text-books. Even in that admirable little book, the 'Manual of Elementary Field Engineering,' one finds such statements as this:—'In all cases where men are required to fire from a shelter trench or over a breastwork they should have cover for their heads.' It then proceeds to give various excellent devices for creating such cover; but they all, whether bullet-proof logs, or brushwood loopholes, or sand-bag loopholes, add considerably to the time required, and instead of being used in 'all cases,' will probably not be used in nine cases out of ten where shelter trenches may be profitably constructed.

It has been said above that 'if there is a choice' neither men nor guns should be sunk below ground; but against the chance of avoiding such sinking must be set the advantage of showing as low a target as possible to the enemy's artillery, and of rendering the mounds of earth as invisible as may be.

The examples of shelter trenches given in the Appendix, and the slight improvements of them which may be necessary or useful, should be familiar to every officer and soldier in the army, and equally so to Volunteers, who might be extremely valuable as light troops in front and on the flanks of an army in the field. There is no operation of war except actual marching in which hasty entrenchments may not be useful. General Skobeleff armed the whole of his force with large spades after the siege of Plevna, and so fully had the men become convinced of the value of that tool, that they made no difficulty about carrying their spades during their struggles through the snow-laden passes of the Balkans. In all their fatigues the spade was the last article they would part with after their rifles and ammunition, and those heavy tools were carried to the gates of Constantinople. Yet Skobeleff's column was an eminently active and aggressive force.

Having said so much against overdoing defensive works for the use of active armies, it is only fair to give what has been written by a well-known authority, Baker Pasha,[1] concerning the opinions held by the Turks. It will be remembered that while the defence of the Turkish army was occasionally obstinate, it failed signally in attack, could not recapture the Shipka Pass, and lost the campaigns both in Bulgaria and Armenia. Baker Pasha says, 'The system of shelter trenches adopted by the Turkish army varied as they gained experience. The common trench with the earth thrown up in front of it, adopted in the little instruction imparted to the English army, was soon abandoned for a

[1] *War in Bulgaria*, vol. ii. p. 855.

more practical and useful profile, which gave cover from artillery as well as from infantry fire. It was singular to note the extraordinarily small loss suffered by the men when occupying trenches of the latter type, even if exposed for hours to a continuous and heavy fire of artillery. The same system was used for guns with an equally good effect, and gun pits sunk almost to the level of the earth were found to be most practically useful.' Unfortunately no dimensions were given in the diagram, but it is manifest that, 'improved' or not, they are all shelter trenches only, not regular field works. The type had not in it any improvement worth reproducing here. One peculiar feature was a slope downwards towards the front, like the cover for abatis in Plate IX., Fig. 5.

Regular Field Works.

The construction of regular field works hardly seems within the scope of this book, which is not designed for the use of engineers so much as for the army and auxiliary services at large. Cases will, however, occur where more purely defensive earthworks are required, and no engineer officer is at hand to design them. A few words on the subject may not be out of place, and various forms of parapets, earthworks and batteries are given in the Appendix.

The chief differences in principle between regular field works and shelter trenches are—

First. The field parapet and ditch with its various additional defences constitutes in itself an obstacle to the enemy, but also an obstacle to sudden advance of the defenders. The shelter trench is no obstacle to either.

Second. The height of the crest of the parapet over the bottom of the ditch in the case of regular field works leaves a place of temporary shelter to the enemy once arrived at the foot of the escarp. Therefore the direct fire of the defenders is often supplemented by flanking fire, and this requires either constructions in the ditch for that object, or elaborately angled lines, or both. Every salient angle is a source of weakness, as will be explained later. Shelter trenches require no flank defence, and no elaboration of line. *Wherever men would be well arranged, if not covered at all, a shelter trench is in its right place.*

Third. Regular field works require a considerable time for their construction, and occupy the services during that time of a considerable number of men. Thus the greater protection given by them is bought at a heavier cost, and even then the obstacle presented to the enemy is really trifling unless the earth slopes are supplemented by other obstacles to be described later (Chap. V.); and these may be added to shelter trenches where there is time enough.

Fourth. The one great advantage possessed by the field work, when completely built with casemates and flanking defences, is that it affords complete protection to the garrison against both infantry and artillery fire provided the men avail themselves of the cover. The defence of Plevna is only one instance out of many to show that no amount of bombardment can drive out a garrison which has bomb proof cover, and sticks to it until the enemy's columns appear for the assault.

But Plevna is as much a warning as an example. A considerable army was, in the end, absolutely swallowed up there. We have, therefore, to remember that *all field works which can be turned are liable to be surrounded, and the garrison starved out with little loss to the enemy. They are too often traps for the troops which use them on a large scale. The number of battles lost in defensive positions is astonishing.*

On the other hand, a line secure on both flanks and open in rear—as, for instance, the lines of Torres Vedras, the lines of Gallipoli, or those in front of Constantinople, which rest their flanks on the sea—might be usefully and wisely fortified by a weak army which is forced for a time to stand on the defensive. What is called the siege of Sebastopol was really the defence by field works of such a position. Yet even Sebastopol fell at last.

Perhaps the best attitude with regard to field works is that they may be good servants, but are bad masters. It is bad for the tone of troops to be shut up in them long, and the general who bases the plan of his campaign on a large use of regular field works is sure to lose it. But in isolated cases they are very useful, especially if you are prepared to sacrifice the garrisons for the sake of delay. In most such cases permanent works would be better if they could be constructed in time. In short, regular field works are allied to permanent fortifications, shelter trenches to movable armies.

The following paragraph is extracted from the authorised 'Text-book of Fortification' used at the Royal Military Academy. The words are so true that all soldiers would do well to commit them to memory.

'With regard to the nature of the fortified supporting points, strong earthworks require much time and many men for their construction, furnish very little fire in comparison with the labour expended, and do not admit of obstinate defence until completed. For these reasons the defensive *localities*[1] before mentioned are generally to be preferred to them, provided they are favourably situated, and do not require too large garrisons; no time, however short, need be ill expended in their preparation, and every additional hour's work renders them stronger. The defenders, however, being more scattered, unity of action is more difficult.'

The last sentence is perhaps a concession to a craving which needs to be controlled in these days of dispersed formations and struggles for positions. The modern method of meeting the difficulty is explained hereafter in the chapters on defence of woods and villages.

Traces of Field Works. (Plate V.)

In speaking hereafter of defensive works applied to a field of battle the occasion will arise for discussing their functions and position. At present a short description of the different forms in use may serve to fix them in the mind of the student.

---

[1] Such as villages and woods.

Whatever may be the profile of a work, the governing line is that from which the fire proceeds, namely, the interior crest of the parapet; and this line, with all its ramifications laid down on paper or the ground, is called the 'trace' of the work.

Closed works are those which, being exposed to the artillery fire of the enemy on all sides, must have thick parapets everywhere. They are only used in isolated situations, or for flanks of a line or reserved works, and give the least facilities for counter attack.

Half-closed works are such as are only partially exposed to artillery fire, but may be attacked in flank or rear by infantry. A portion only of this parapet will be thick, the rest slighter. Even stockades or shelter trenches may suffice in parts, and there is the advantage that if the enemy captures the work, it remains open to the artillery fire of the troops in rear.

Open works are such as are not liable to any attack in rear. They can be left completely open there, and can be commanded by the infantry as well as the artillery fire of the troops behind them.

Gorge.—The unexposed side is called the gorge.

Faces.—The sides of the work are called faces; except—

Flanks.—Those sides specially intended for flank defence.

Salients.—Angles pointing outwards.

Re-entering angles are those which point inwards.

It is not proposed to enter into the details of constructing field works, these being rather elaborate, and involving a considerable amount of drawing and calculations, but some principles and general rules may be useful to all.

All designs should be based on the ascertained fact that the tendency of infantry soldiers is to fire either straight to their front, and therefore at right angles to the parapet, or even slightly inwards. Infantry in the open almost always fire rather inwards.

Undefended Space.—In a field work it has been found that the greatest inclination of fire outwards which can be obtained is about 30°. Therefore any space not covered by such fire is a place of comparative safety for an advancing enemy, and is called an '*undefended space.*'

Undefended spaces must occur in front of all salient angles, unless they have flanks nearly perpendicular to the faces.

Dead Angle.—In the re-entering angles of works there will often be parts of the ditch not seen from the crest of the parapet either of the face or flank. These are called dead angles, and are advantageous to the enemy.

Caponiers.—Dead angles can only be avoided by having some kind of flank defence in the ditch. Small erections for this purpose are called *caponiers*.

Traverses.—If the reader will draw a line upon paper including salient angles and their flanks, he will be struck by the fact that some at least of the faces or flanks must be exposed to the grazing or 'enfilade' fire of the enemy. To stop the bullets there must be traverses, that is, small erections across the work breaking the line of the men firing. These have the disadvantage of taking up space, slightly impeding communication, and diminishing the amount of fire on a given length of parapet.

Parados.—Again, to protect the rear of the work from being struck by fire from the front, a large traverse across that fire will often be required. This is called a 'parados.'

Field Casemate.—Again, for men not employed, bombproof covers called 'field casemates' have to be provided in various forms shown in the Appendix. But see now to what elaboration of secondary structures we are arriving, the moment we begin to break the simple line opposite the enemy used in the shelter trench, and transform it into field works of the ordinary type, such as are shown in trace (Appendix, Plate V.). It is well to think twice or thrice before occupying a defensive position which needs to be so strengthened, and which may carry with its fall the capture of a whole army.

Salient angles are the weakest parts of a line, and the more salient the weaker. Bearing in mind what was said above concerning infantry always firing towards the front, it will be clear that the more front there is the better will the fire be. Even a blunt salient angle—the very bluntest—begins to turn the fire of the men away from an enemy attacking the angle, and as the angle grows sharper the defending fire decreases, so that before long the only fire brought to bear on the enemy would be that of a man or two, or of a gun stationed in the angle itself. All defence is then left to the flanks, which be it remembered are farther from the enemy than he is from the angle he is attacking. So he brings a close fire against the garrison which can only reply with a distant fire.

There is, however, one advantage of breech-loading small-arms which may be made use of where salient angles exist. The soldier need never lift his rifle or move it from a direction once given as it lies on the parapet. Therefore the aim of the weapon is more under control of officers and non-commissioned officers, and a number of soldiers can be made to arrange their rifles in a given direction, and keep them there as long as all are firing coolly. It has even been proposed that, for long range firing, grooved planks should be laid on the parapet for the rifles to lie in. But whatever plan may be adopted, its efficacy will cease when the enemy approaches and the fire tends to become hurried. Then, whether because of the smoke or because men uncover themselves more by shooting otherwise than straight to their front, the general tendency will again be to fire at right angles to the crest of the parapet.

There is another tendency little less hurtful. Finding themselves debarred from replying to the direct fire of the enemy, men leave their places in the face and rush to the angle, with the result that they are uselessly huddled together there, a mark for the enemy without much increased fire of their own. The spaces which they have deserted thus become easy of capture to the enemy. For instance, at the battle of the Tchernaia in 1855, the Russians captured a lunette from the French through this natural fault.

On the whole, it may be said that the old redans, lunettes, and so forth, with their sharp angles and ill-defended ditches, are now becoming obsolete, and that, where field works must be used, we shall have more traces composed of straight lines fronting the enemy, possibly provided with caponiers at long intervals corresponding with the increased range of firearms. The flanks of such lines must either rest upon obstacles or be strengthened by redoubts having very flat angles.

In the Appendix (Plate V.) will be found the usual forms of field works given in English text-books. A few definitions are, however, given here.

Open Works.

Single line is a line of parapet facing the enemy, unbroken by flanks.

Redan or Flêche.—Two faces forming a salient angle not sharper than 60° at least, preferably much blunter; 120° gives a moderately good frontal fire, but not so good as that from the single line. Redans have sometimes their faces broken by small flanks.

Blunted Redan.—Three faces, one of which fronts the enemy.

Lunette.—Four faces, two forming a salient angle, the other two capable of flanking another line, but not the faces of the salient. The French call these subordinate faces 'flanks.' A salient not less than 120° is the best. Used chiefly for flanking other lines.

Blunted Lunette.—Five faces, one of which fronts the enemy. Used in more important and more isolated positions. Approaches the nature of a closed work.

Half-closed Works.

Any work may be half closed at will. The blunted lunette, for instance, would become half closed by forming a sixth face to close the gorge by shelter-trench, stockade, or any other slight defensive construction.

Closed Works.

The general principles explained above being mastered, closed works of almost any form may be constructed. They are usually called redoubts, when in the most common forms.

Square redoubts are simple in construction, but the space outside their angles is undefined. This may be obviated by placing machine guns there if there are any available. *It may be said, once for all, that regular field artillery is better placed outside redoubts on the flanks.* All the ditches of a square redoubt are undefended. *It is questionable whether it is worth while to defend the ditches of ordinary field works by caponiers. Only in important works designed to hold out for a long time is the caponier worth the trouble of making.*

Tenaille Trace.—Alternate salient and re-entering angles intended to flank each other. Very weak, as explained above generally. Frontal fire sacrificed; subject to enfilade and reverse fire from enemy; interior space restricted, especially when the work is on a small scale. Undefended spaces and dead angles.

Star Trace.—Simply a tenaille trace applied to a circle. Very bad.

Bastioned Trace.—Would require long description, and is not worth it. Even the French, formerly its great advocates, have practically abandoned it, but many examples still exist in that country. It is an elaborate attempt to gain flank defence and has many weaknesses. 'Too complicated, and requires too much labour to be practical as field works,' says the engineer school at Versailles.

Forts.—Works, the parapets of which flank the ditches, are called forts.

Redoubts.—Otherwise half-enclosed or closed works are generally called redoubts.

Having given the foregoing explanations as to the various kinds of works considered with reference to their trace, the author believes that he would be sustained by the whole intelligent military opinion in Europe in the advice to all students not professedly military engineers: *Do not confuse yourselves with any of these elaborate arrangements of times gone by, with their flank defences and calculation of angles. Two forms will be enough for practical purposes—the straight or 'single' line, and the redoubt.* There will be plenty to say of accessories hereafter, quite easy of comprehension and recollection; but we may sweep away at one stroke all the old forms of traces, and adhere to those just named. The great superiority of modern fire has at least done this for us.

What is a redoubt? Here, again, let us not allow ourselves to be bound too strictly by technical rules. In the French 'Travaux de Campagne,' a very good elementary book published for the engineer school at Versailles, it is said, 'The only closed work habitually employed in field fortification is the redoubt, of which the faces are often very irregular, their number and their dimensions depending upon the position and the importance of the points to be struck. . . . The only rule to lay down for their trace is as follows: Adapt the work to the forms of the ground, and develop as much fire as possible in the directions by which the enemy may advance against the work, always avoiding too much exposure to enfilade and complication of trace.'

That is to say, get principles fixed in your mind, and the redoubt will almost shape itself in accordance with them. The worst fault would be adherence to any particular form.

Speaking generally, it will be found that the garrison will conveniently vary from two to six English companies, and there is a sort of typical English design for a redoubt with a garrison of a half-battalion. It comprises many useful details, but the student must beware of imagining that it will fit all occasions. It is good to learn one form, and then modify it according to circumstances. Beware also of supposing that because embrasures and other arrangements for guns are shown in it, therefore artillery would be well placed there. On the contrary, the best place for guns is wholly detached from the redoubts, assisting them by flanking fire, attracting from them the enemy's artillery fire, and, in case of their capture, making their interior too hot for the enemy to remain within them.

If there are no such positions for artillery, and it must be with the redoubt because it can be nowhere else of any use, at least keep it separated from the infantry by prolonging the faces and forming new wings for the guns.[1] Such cases may also occur where emplacements for guns are to have infantry defenders—for instance, where guns are defending the flanks of a village, or the mouth of a defile. The worst possible place for guns is within a redoubt which has a garrison of infantry. The two arms will only hamper each other, and many a commanding officer wishing to save his guns by ordering them to retire as the enemy closes will lose guns and redoubt too by the bad moral effect of the guns' retreat. On the other hand, machine guns would be well placed in redoubts. They must stand or fall with the infantry, and will help to encourage the garrison, by the moral effect which they produce.[2]

[1] This is the French system, shown in Plate V., but it may be questioned whether there should not be infantry on the outer flanks of the guns. In some cases, as when a redoubt commands a long defile, the guns should be in the centre and infantry on the flanks.

[2] For a new and excellent form of redoubt, the most modern earthwork with which I am acquainted, see the latter part of Chap. IX. and Plate XIX.

CHAPTER V.

ACCESSORIES AND OBSTACLES—USE OF ACCIDENTS—CLEARING THE GROUND.

Field casemates—Tiers of fire—Supply of ammunition—Head cover—Loopholes—Revetments—Embrasures—Cover for guns—Platforms—Stockades—Tambours—Caponiers—Keeps or reduits—Blockhouses—Traverses and parados—Magazines—Entrances—Definition and use of obstacles—General rules—Abatis—Entanglements—Wire entanglements—Chevaux de Frise—Crow's-feet—Military pits—Palisades—Fraises—Fougasses—Inundations—Barricades—Use of accidents—Hollows—Walls—Hedges—Cuttings—Embankments—Roads—Clearing the ground—Principles.

(*References to Plates VI., VII., VIII., IX., X. and XI.*)

Field Casemates.

THE most important addition to the field work, considered as an enclosed space surrounded with a parapet and ditch, is cover for the garrison or such portions of it as are not for the moment necessarily exposed.

Field Casemates.—In addition to traverses and parados, field casemates should be constructed in all works intended for serious defence. Several examples are given in the Appendix. They give bombproof cover for the garrison within which all men not obliged to expose themselves for the moment can rest, eat, and sleep in safety. However slight they may be, they at least give protection from infantry fire, shrapnel, and the pieces of burst shells. There will seldom be time to arrange field casemates in works rapidly constructed by an army on the field of battle, but the possibility of doing so should be considered in all cases where the defence is likely to be long. When a Russian force first appeared before Plevna, the Turks had only just arrived and commenced to fortify themselves. If at that moment the Russian commander had made a desperate effort, he might have carried the slight entrenchments by a *coup de main*. His attack was feeble and not sufficiently concentrated. The result was that, instead of his capturing a commanding position before Plevna, the Turks had time to throw up that series of forts and entrenchments which changed the face of the campaign. The strategical effect of the defence of Plevna will be discussed later during the examination of wider questions. At present we have only to point out how great was the influence of field casemates on that defence. There were several bombardments by a vast number of field guns; even siege artillery was brought across the Danube and placed in position against Plevna; yet whenever the Russians assaulted, they found the Turks ready to meet them with great numbers of fresh undismayed men, who had found in their field casemates complete rest to body and nerves. On the first sign of an attack they lined the parapets and two trenches in the glacis, so as to bring a triple tier of fire against the Russians advancing in the open. About 100 paces behind the redoubts were reserves, also sheltered in field casemates. These formidable preparations, based on abundant supply of men and ammunition, kept at bay all direct assaults which were made without the precaution of making approaches and assembling Russian troops close to the works. The attack was unscientific, and Plevna held out till provisions began to fail. The shape of the redoubts was not worthy of imitation. One of them is, however, shown in Plate VI.

The main strength of the defence consisted in three features :—

First. Large use of field casemates.
Second. Multiplication of tiers of fire.
Third. Abundant supply and use of ammunition.

The first has now been discussed, and it only remains to say with regard to it that a point of almost vital necessity is to attend to the drainage of field casemates, either by drains through the parapet into the outer ditch, or by digging pits into which the surface water may be conducted. Otherwise there will be sickness, with its attendant misery and depression of spirits.

The use of well-drained field casemates will render frequent changes of garrison unnecessary—a great advantage.

Tiers of Fire.—With regard to the multiplication of tiers of fire, it is evident that if rows of men can be established so as to fire over each other's heads, every row will add to the intensity of the defensive fire action. The most favourable condition is—the establishment of the work on a rising ground not too high, at the foot of which is a plain. Under such conditions there is no danger in one line firing over another; but on flat ground, or even on a long slope over which the enemy must advance, nothing but a very high parapet and steeply sloping glacis will give the required power. In short, if there is no such hill on the natural ground, an artificial mound must be created at the expense of much time and labour. Another favourable condition for tiers of fire is when the enemy has to show himself coming downhill to a work which stands on the level. But the fire is not so grazing.

Supply of Ammunition.—Tiers of fire cause the expenditure of much ammunition in a given time, but all the tendency of modern tactics is in the direction of *economy of fire at long ranges, intensity of fire at decisive ranges.* At Plevna the supply was practically unlimited. If there is any question as to the sufficiency of cartridges, the men must be made to reserve their fire till the enemy is near, and then give it him hot. In addition to what the soldier carries on his person, boxes or bags of cartridges should be distributed along the parapets or outer trenches under cover. General Todleben stated, in a letter to General Brialmont, that each Turk in the Plevna works had on his person 100 rounds, and close beside him a box with 500 more.

Head Cover.—In all works where sufficient time has been given, arrange cover for the men's heads (Appendix, Plates VI. and X.). A log of wood supported at intervals, or arrangements of sand-bags or any other materials that are at hand, will give protection and prevent a fault which is very common, especially among nervous troops. Men with exposed heads are too apt to dip under cover and fire their rifles in the air. This is very bad. They should be carefully trained to feel that, whatever may be the strength of the works, it will be of no avail without accurate shooting of the defenders. *Every wasted bullet should be considered as equal to a shovelful of earth taken from the parapet and thrown into the ditch.*

Loopholes.—Different forms of loopholes are given in Plate VI. and other plates. While necessary in some cases, such as defence of houses, stockades, and high walls, do not forget that to make a hole in such structures as walls is to weaken them.

Revetments.—Earth is not to be trusted to stand at a steeper slope than $\frac{1}{1}$, that is 45°. All steeper slopes must therefore be 'revetted,' that is held firmly in their place by stiffer materials. Different revetments are given in the Appendix, Plate VI.

Do not use materials liable to splinter if you can help it. That is a golden rule. And do not be particularly anxious if your revetments crumble under the enemy's fire. The old rule applies : It is not the works which keep the enemy out, but the fire of the defenders.

The effect of artillery fire upon an earthen parapet is thus given in the 'Woolwich Text-book of Fortification' :—

'The crest is shot away, and the superior slope receives indents and irregularities which interfere with the fire from the parapet. The exterior slope and upper portion of the escarp are shaken and covered with holes, which serve as footholds to the assailant, the earth falling into the ditch and reducing its depth. Sharp angles and slopes finally disappear, the parapet becomes a shapeless mass, and much earth collects at the foot of the escarp and banquette. The glacis is covered with furrows three or four feet long, and about one foot deep. The destruction of an earthwork does not, however, practically go beyond certain limits, and the thickness at top would probably not be diminished by more than a couple of feet, nor the crest reduced in general height more than a foot or eighteen inches.'

Well, if this be all, no great harm has been done. If the parapet becomes shapeless, that is only what the most experienced modern soldiers recommend to be the state from the beginning. The furrows spoken of in the glacis do but represent that 'undulated' or 'ribbed' surface which an Austrian officer, Captain Tilzer, has recommended as the normal construction of superior slopes for all field parapets. The earth in the ditch can be quickly shovelled out again, and indeed matters little if it stays there. The defences are as strong as ever, practically, if the men remain in good heart.[1]

Revetments should, therefore, not be used for parts of the work exposed to the fire of artillery. It is better to leave the earth there at no greater slope than that at which it will stand naturally, and where revetments are used they should be of materials which can be easily replaced.

Brushwood made into hurdles is good, but requires anchoring to the parapet. The same made be said of fascines. Gabions are excellent and can be easily replaced. Any kind of a material which exists in or can be woven into cylindrical shape will do for gabions. It is the earth within them, not the exterior, which resists. Sods are very good in damp places, in mild winters, and in spring. Sand-bags—that is, any strong bags filled with earth—are much used. Timber and stones have the objection of splintering. Heather is simple and good.

Perhaps the best advice to the class of military students for which this book is intended would be—Do not trouble yourselves about revetments at all for infantry, and only for artillery just so far as they are necessary to enable the guns

[1] The reader must remember that only field guns are here supposed to be present in the attack. The whole case is altered if large rifled howitzers can be brought up, as in sieges. Heavy shells with bursting charges of 20 lbs. of powder soon cut down all earthen parapets, whether revetted or not, and the new high explosives will do still more.

to be run up close to the parapet, or in the case of overhead cover referred to below.

If it be said that the interior slope must be revetted because it is steep, the answer is that there is no necessity for having it steep. An angle of 45° would enable the men to lean against it, and to mount rapidly on the parapet to repel an assault.

Embrasures.—Avoid embrasures altogether. They form excellent targets for the enemy, and are soon knocked to pieces by his artillery; the earth which falls into them will prevent the laying of the guns. A slight depression in the parapet is far better when there is no overhead cover.

Cover for Guns.—On the other hand, overhead cover for guns, even of a very slight description, will be of great service to protect the gunners against shrapnel bullets and the fire of infantry. The great principle with regard to it is that it should be as little as possible raised above the parapet. Where gun blindages are used to fire from, it is a good plan to raise the parapet on each side of them up to their height, or even to set up small screens or mock blindages in other places. Remember that, at least during an important period of the artillery action, the enemy will be so far off that trifling artifices may deceive him. *It is of primary importance that you should conceal the exact spot whence each gun is firing as long as possible.* Wood ten or twelve inches thick, with four or five feet of earth on it, will give protection even from field guns firing common shell. The example given in Plate VII. shows cover for a gun or gatling which is kept in active use. Passive blindages are more suitable for machine guns than field guns. Machine guns are of little use for distant work, but of immense value at close quarters, and may therefore be kept under cover till wanted. Field guns under such conditions would waste their best power.

Platforms.—If the surface of the ground is soft, as it generally will be if you have disturbed it at all, platforms must be laid for the guns. Complete platforms take time, and require skilled labour for their construction. In default of them, three planks sunk in the ground will be useful—one for each wheel and one for the trail. Take care that those for the wheels are on the same level. This can be managed by making a rough plummet level such as bricklayers use. You will find something of the sort in nearly every village.

The recoil of modern field artillery is great. It will be wise, therefore, to give your platforms or planks a rather steep rise to the rear, especially at the end of the recoil. Do not be alarmed at the idea of the gun coming into sight of the enemy; *at the moment after firing it is concealed by its own smoke.*

If there is no overhead cover, guns are sometimes allowed to run back to a lower level; but beyond it there must be some means of checking the recoil.

Stockades.—Usually made of upright timber six inches to fourteen inches thick, driven firmly into the ground close together, and having horizontal ribands of wood nailed to them inside to give added strength. They should be pointed at the top, and a few nails with points sticking out there will make them more difficult to climb over. Stockades may be made of anything that will stand firmly and stiffly upright, and should be loopholed, half the loophole to be cut in each of two adjacent uprights. A small ditch on the outside will give earth to throw up at the foot, and perhaps to make a small glacis.

Stockades are useful for closing the gorges of works when covered from artillery fire by parados, &c., but they require some skill to make satisfactorily.

Stockades made of fascines, and especially bundles of bamboo, and well supported by struts, have the advantage that they are less easily destroyed by gun-cotton or other rapid explosives. Gunpowder is better but in large charges. Artillery fire also has less effect on bamboo than on timber stockades. Different forms are given in the Appendix, Plate VII.

Tambours, Plate VIII., are simply small erections of triangular or rectangular shape, made of any materials and roofed. They are placed outside, but touching stockades, walls, &c., either for flank defence only, or, in addition, to cover the means of exit and ingress. *Keep them if possible out of the reach of artillery fire.* They are closed to the enemy, and usually entered by the defenders through underground passages.

Caponiers.—May be of any form and materials. Used for defence of ditches or walls when time is no object.

Retrenchments.—Lines of parapet separating large works into two parts for purposes of second defence.

Keeps.—Separate enclosures within the outer enclosure of field works, villages, &c. Usually commanding all interior. For rallying points and second defence. Indispensable for defence of villages.

Reduit.—Another name for keep.

Block-houses.—Worth more consideration because of their almost universal application. They may stand alone for the defence of a handful of men against savages. They may give flank defence to almost any frontage, and they may be erected as keeps to small works. They may be of any form and of almost any material. If there is a chance of artillery fire being brought to bear on them, keep them as low as the ground will admit. Be very careful to drain them either into lower ground or artificial cesspools, but remember that stagnant water accumulated in the latter may breed fever and other sickness. Different forms of block-house are given in Appendix, Plate VIII., and the student should take some pains to get into his head general ideas about them, and examine any that may be within his reach erected for educational purposes.

Traverses and Parados.—Already discussed; may be of various sizes according to time and necessity. Traverses are sometimes erected hollow to hold a few rounds of ammunition.

Magazines.—Only to be considered when there is plenty of time and skilled labour. As a rule the most useful method of keeping ammunition near the guns is in small hollows under the parapet or in the traverses.

Entrances.—It stands to reason that the entrance of a work should be at the part least exposed to the enemy, and as far as possible covered from his fire and even observation.

ACCESSORIES—OBSTACLES—CLEARING GROUND.

The gates, if there are any, should be bullet-proof and loopholed.

Entrances are sometimes covered by small *flèches* outside, and sometimes made in curved or zigzag forms. Common sense will dictate all that is necessary.

MILITARY OBSTACLES. (Plate IX.)

The use of the word obstacle is rather arbitrary. A parapet and ditch, or even a wall, might be fairly called an obstacle, but by general consent a narrower technical sense is given to it. Military obstacles are not 'field works,' but *artificial obstacles of any kind so arranged as to check or embarrass the march of the enemy, and detain him under the fire of the defenders at a convenient distance*. A convenient distance is generally stated to be within 300 yards—that is within close range; but numberless cases occur when the range is not close, and even where there is no direct defence at all. None the less are the defences classed as obstacles.

Obstacles are generally used in such positions as the following :—

In front of field works.

In ditches.

In gorges of open or half-closed works.

Round fortified houses, farms, villages, or woods.

Between two works to prevent the enemy from forcing the line.

To block any defiles or passages by which the enemy may advance.

To render ground impassable by cavalry.

Obstacles are of greater value now than in the past, because, however short be the time during which they detain an assailant, he will suffer much more severely during that time because of the rapidity and accuracy of modern fire. For one volley which was formerly possible several can now be delivered. It is very difficult to break through good obstacles over a wide front; and the small passages usually made through them oblige the advancing troops to form column, a formation involving almost certain destruction under the fire of breech-loaders. Even the slightest obstacles are, therefore, of high value for passive defence—for instance, in front of redoubts constructed as pivots of manœuvre on a battle-field, or in such cases as the nightly zarebas of mimosa in the Soudan, which were rather obstacles than works.

A large number of articles might be used as obstacles—for instance, harrows, ploughs, rough wood in any form, such as roots and stumps, wheels. Any of these or like objects strewn on the ground or at the bottom of ditches or in hollows of the ground will form obstacles of more or less value, and be probably sufficient for places sheltered from artillery fire; the gorges of works, and so forth.

Obstacles are all more or less destructible by artillery fire, and should therefore be sheltered from it if possible.

They have the disadvantage of hampering the defenders almost as much as the enemy, and must, therefore, be omitted on ground over which a counter attack is likely to take place. This is their chief drawback. Another rather serious disadvantage is the length of time required for their construction. But neither of these disadvantages applies to cases where no forward movement is contemplated, and the force is to sit long in comparative inaction—for instance, the lines drawn by a besieger round a fortress. Examples — Paris and Metz.

The following rules are extracted, with some modifications, from the 'Manual of Field Engineering.' The modifications soften the rather hard and fast rules laid down in the manual. 'Should' is substituted for 'must,' and the last paragraph is altogether modified. There are many cases, and the author has seen some of them in actual war, where the first necessity is to hold the enemy back at the spot where the obstacles are used. Counter attack will come later from another direction. Such cases will happen when a long thin line has to guard itself against being penetrated while its reserves are concentrating. The blockade of an entrenched camp or fortress surrounded by detached forts is a case in point. On the other hand, the garrison of such a fortress should always retain the power of sortie everywhere.

'(a) They should be placed under the effective fire of the defender, afford the enemy no cover, and, if possible, be sheltered from his artillery fire.

'(b) They should be under easy observation, otherwise they may be rendered useless during the night.

'(c) They should be difficult to remove or surmount, and will be most effective if special appliances, not usually carried by troops, are required for their removal.

'(d) Those obstacles are most economical which require little special material, and are improvised from natural sources.

'(e) They should interfere as little as possible with counter attack.'

The technical details of obstacles will be found in the Appendix, Plate IX., but a few general remarks may be made upon them here.

Abatis.—Trees felled and placed preferably in several rows, with their branches pointed and directed towards the enemy, the stem being held in its place, either having never been cut entirely through, or having been artificially fastened in the assigned position. If the trees are too large use their branches instead.

It is evident that where such trees exist in woods, orchards, parks, and so forth, they form a natural and manageable obstacle, either by half cutting them through and pulling them down where they stand, or by felling them completely and dragging them away. In many cases they should be cut down as a mere precaution in clearing the ground.

But wood is brittle, and abatis yields to a continuous artillery fire. Therefore conceal it as much as possible, either in ditches, hollows, or behind any natural feature, such as a bank of earth, or behind a glacis purposely constructed. The usual size of tree or branch is about twelve or fifteen feet long, because these are more manageable, but much larger sizes may be used if the trees are felled on the spot. Note also the use of smaller branches in several rows. In the German lines round Paris some woods were prepared with a portion of the trees left standing, the rest made into abatis and into—

Entanglements.—Which are small trees and brushwood cut half through, bent down, and interlaced with the help of pickets which fasten them to the ground.

Wire Entanglements.—The best of all obstacles is the wire entanglement, which can be used everywhere when wire is procurable. The higher it is and the more wire the better. In woods the trees and bushes will form support for the wire, and it has the advantage of remaining in coils about the feet of an enemy, no matter how long his artillery may have played on it. The only way to defeat wire entanglement is to lie down and crawl through it or cover it over.

Chevaux de Frise.—Well known and purely artificial. Hardly available in the field.

Crow's-feet.—Same remark as above. Broken glass bottles and crockery thickly strewn are also capable of laming horses.

Military pits, deep and shallow, are of some use in open ground, but the large ones, called also *trous de loup,* take long to construct, and the smaller are soon rendered innocuous. Altogether this obstacle is hardly worth a thought unless no other is possible. They are conical holes with a sharp stake in the centre.

Palisades are practically open stockade work, and are used for many purposes, such as in ditches and gorges of works. They differ from stockades chiefly in not being of themselves defensible on account of the openings.

Fraises.—Palisades used nearly horizontally. Brialmont recommends them strongly to be used from the counterscarp of field works. He considers this position better than the escarp, because the assailants attempting to destroy them will be more exposed to the fire of the defenders, while the *fraises* themselves will be less exposed to bombardment. Abatis placed in this position or on the berm of the escarp become *fraises* in technical language.

ACCESSORIES—OBSTACLES—CLEARING GROUND. 57

Fougasses.—Quantities of stones either sunk in an inclined hole or built up in heaps, but always with a charge of powder behind them to be ignited by electricity or quick match. They have fallen out of fashion in this country, partly because we have a clumsy pattern. On the Continent they still retain favour for the defence of salients. They produce great moral effect. General Gordon used them at Khartoum. A simpler form than the English is given (Appendix, Plate IX., Fig. 20). Always hide them with earth, branches, rubbish, &c.

Inundations.—The only remarks necessary are to use as a nucleus something solid—as, for example, a bridge; and to have deep ditches under the water wherever it is not out of a man's depth.

BARRICADES.

In order not to mislead students preparing for military examinations, it is necessary to say that *barricades* are included among obstacles in English text-books, though it would appear that they hardly meet the usual conditions, being rather of the nature of field works, designed to stop an enemy and be defended by a body of men acting for the time as a garrison.

They may be made of any materials, preferably earth, and will be all the better for a ditch in front of them. They are used for street fighting and to close roads. They should either be in two portions, one covering the passage round the end of the other, or be erected where a house set back from the rest leaves a space for passage round the end of the barricade. Remember that stone is a bad material if artillery can be brought against it. Barricades should be flanked by fire from the houses (Appendix, Plate IX.). A second barricade behind the first should be at not less than 100 yards from it.

USE OF ACCIDENTS IN DEFENCE OF POSTS.

Any feature which breaks the level of the ground may be called an accident, and the student of military history cannot fail to notice the frequent use of such accidents. They may be used either for concealment or defence. In ordinary works on fortification they are only noticed with regard to their capability for defence. Concealment is, however, such an important feature, both for attack and defence, that a few words upon it will come well within the scope of this book.

Visitors to German autumn manœuvres are generally struck by the fact that, on arriving in the neighbourhood of a large force prepared for battle, they see hardly anything of it, though the ground appears to be nearly level. It is astonishing how many depressions occur even on large plains; and if to these be added such features as hedgerows, walls, strips of plantation, and so on, a large army may easily be hidden from view. In the same way the advance of infantry and even cavalry may be made without attracting notice, and thus will be gained the great moral advantage of surprise. Any reader fond of hunting will know how completely and suddenly the hounds and whole field disappear if he has to pull up for a cast shoe or a lame horse; and this happens even if he is on the crest of a moderately sized hill.

It is impossible to provide entirely against such concealed advance of a well-trained enemy. In dry warm weather clouds of dust may arise, but in damp or cold weather there will be none. The best provision against surprise is to be found in what are called contact squadrons of cavalry, which hang on to an enemy and never let him out of their sight.[1] Second to this come cavalry patrols and vedettes. Fixed vedettes may be deceived, but a combination of vedettes and patrols far out in front of a defensive line should let no movement take place without observation.

Hollows, or the reverse slopes of rising ground within easy range of a defensive position, will inevitably be used by an advancing enemy as halting and gathering places for his

---

[1] See an admirable pamphlet, *Conduct of a Contact Squadron*, by Captain R. de Biensan, translated by Major Bowdler Bell, 8th Hussars (Mitchell & Co.). Every cavalry officer should study this interesting work.

troops if you permit it. It is certain that you cannot hold all these without scattering your strength. If, therefore, you have plenty of time and means, such places should be filled with obstacles. If this cannot be done, make up your mind that the enemy will assemble there, and, after giving him a little time for the purpose, drop shells and rifle bullets upon such spots. You will have previously ascertained the exact range. Make the enemy feel that he is safe nowhere.

The progress of civilisation may produce *accidents* hitherto unknown, but they will probably fall into groups typified by one or other of the features given below. Make these familiar, and you will never be at a loss. The principal groups may be headed—

Walls, including bullet-proof banks, &c. Objects which both conceal and protect against infantry fire at least.

Hedges, including all objects which screen without protecting.

Cuttings ..⎫ on roads, railways, canals, in artificial
Embankments⎭ pleasure-grounds, &c.

Walls (Appendix, Plate X.).—Here we have a class of objects which are extremely useful for defence, but they have the disadvantage that they may be of equal use to the enemy if left as they are when the defenders retire from them. Also, that if penetrable by shells, they will burst the shells exactly in the right place for their action, and create great destruction both by fragments of shells and splinters.

On the other hand, they are perfect defences against infantry fire and shrapnel bullets, that is, the projectiles most destructive to life.

The first principle is that the defenders may be partly covered and *have rests for their rifles,* by using any low wall just as it is. Between 4 and 5 feet high will suit men standing, and if a little higher the top can be notched. Lower walls will do for men kneeling or lying down, but will not cover others standing behind them. Supports can dig trenches for themselves or lie down. Provide, if possible, head cover for the defenders lining the wall. *Remember that if there is no head cover, the men will be tempted to crouch down and fire their rifles in the air. There will always be this tendency if complete protection from the enemy is possible, and no head cover is given.*

If there is time, you can kill two birds with one stone by digging a ditch outside, near the wall but not touching it, and throw the earth so obtained against the face of the wall. More resistance to artillery fire will be obtained by this means; and if you are driven from the wall, it will not be instantly available for the enemy, or at least he will be more exposed by having to stand on the far side of the ditch. In the case of low walls a trench is sometimes dug behind them, and the earth thrown over to form the mass in front. Higher walls have sometimes a trench and banquette behind, the banquette serving for the defenders to fire from, the trench containing the supports. The higher walls are, the more they are exposed to destruction by artillery fire.

But it often occurs that high and solid walls exist where they must be utilised. In that case it is possible to have two tiers of fire by making artificial stages to support the men who form the upper tier, and loopholes for those below to fire through. Loopholes weaken a wall very much, and stages are both inconvenient and demoralising. *Experience shows that high walls with double tiers are not liked by soldiers, nor defended as tenaciously as low ones.* They also give more cover to the enemy if he takes them. Loopholes should be vertical for long ranges, and horizontal for short ranges.

Another fact is worth remembering. If the enemy succeeds in placing charges of gun-cotton or dynamite against a wall, an earthen raised banquette behind it, though not preventing the fall, will make the débris higher and more defensible. Soldiers should all be taught that in such cases of explosions they are quite safe if they stand against the wall at 15 to 20 yards from the charge, and if they lie down they are safe even nearer. There is therefore no excuse for failure to defend breaches so made.

Walls will frequently be flanked outside by tambours or

block-houses, which should be concealed from the enemy's artillery fire. This flank defence is not so necessary as it used to be, because the frontal fire of breechloaders is so powerful.

Walls are among the most necessary objects to be cleared away from the front of a position, if parallel to it and not to be defended.

To sum up :—

Low walls are the best for defence.

Head cover the first artificial work to be undertaken.

Then ditch in front, and earth thrown against the wall.

A banquette of earth is better than loopholing walls, which latter process, combined with stages, is demoralising.

Hedges.—The hedge is, in the first instance, a screen. It only needs a little artificial cover, such as a bank in front or rear, to make it very defensible. For long defence high hedges can be cut down and made into a sort of abatis. Hedges considered as screens may also be useful to attract the enemy's artillery fire, from which the defenders may find complete shelter. The thicker the hedge the better obstacle is it to the enemy, but thick hedges are difficult to fire through except just at the roots.

If hedges are defended, but likely to be evacuated, remember to make them useless to the enemy if you can.

Hedges, like walls, should be cleared away from the front of a position if they run parallel to it.

In the Appendix, Plate XI., will be found examples of hedges made defensible. The student should invent other cases, and arrange them for defence according to the principles which should now be familiar to him.

Cuttings.—A cutting is nothing but a big ditch with escarp and counterscarp. It can be defended either from the near or the far side or both, according to circumstances (see Appendix, Plate XI.).

Embankments.—A small embankment can be cut into a parapet. A large one can have a parapet or shelter trench made upon it either in front or rear.

Roads are so various that there is nothing special in their character. According to the case they run in cuttings or on embankments, on the level, on a slope, &c. They have generally walls or hedges on either side, and almost always ditches. Roughly speaking, it is well to have obstacles on the far side, and defences on the near.

Clearing the Ground.

In all cases, and with reference to all arms, a clear space for their action is to be desired. Only selection of ground can give this advantage to cavalry and artillery, because the sweep of their action is so wide. But the most telling fire of infantry takes place at short ranges, and the fire of infantry soldiers is, or ought to be, more deadly the shorter the range, especially when they are under cover. In their case, then, the clearing away of all cover for ever so short a distance round them will materially assist their fire.

When artillery is posted and in action, it has most to dread the fire of an enemy's sharpshooters established under cover at moderate but chiefly short range. Therefore any cover which may conceal an enemy is annoying and even demoralising.

These considerations show that the ground should always be cleared of everything which can afford cover to an enemy *for as wide a space as is consistent with the time and labour available.* In hasty defence little can be done; at least do that little, even if it be to clear a space of fifty yards round the most important points. If there are country people about, use them for this purpose rather than any other. They will then have nothing to tell the enemy.

Many rules might be given, but they are all summed up in two :—

1. Clear away anything that may assist the enemy to concentrate for attack and to conceal himself.

2. Leave all that may tend to disperse his attack.

Thus, as has been said more than once, you will clear away walls, hedges, &c., parallel to the line of defence, but leave those perpendicular to it, because they tend to separate the enemy, and you can flank them by your fire. Also leave no tree stumps or brushwood or long grass or banks. Harden your heart even against vineyards or rose-gardens. Throw down cottages, even if they be ideal seats of bliss, and what is more, raze everything close to the ground. A very little cover and a rush from it unexpectedly may cause a panic, and ruin the best planned defence.

In Appendix I. will be found the usual advice to engineers as to the accomplishment of this clearing, but if neither tools nor sappers are present, you can still manage a great deal with the tools carried by the infantry and artillery, and such as you find in the neighbourhood. You have to make a smooth surface by levelling the high and filling up the low. In case of doubt decide for destruction. *The point of greatest importance is to have the enemy completely within your vision for as long a time as possible.*

Sometimes common sense will tell that to throw down a tall object without carrying it away would give more cover instead of less to the enemy. In that case leave it till you are sure of time to make away with it. You must take the lesser risk. This is often the case with large trees, &c.

CHAPTER VI.

DEFENCE AND ATTACK OF WOODS AND DEFILES.

Woods, various in kind—An average wood supposed—Organisation of the edge—Clearing the ground—Obstacles—What to begin with—Salients—Parapets or shelter trenches—Entrances of roads—Interior organisation—Artillery defence—Position of guns—Some pushed to front at first—On flanks—Within wood—Interior retrenchment—Communications—Organisation of defenders—division into sections—Chain of responsibility—Rear edge of wood—Behind wood—Conduct of attack and defence—Advance of assailants—Action of defenders—Attack of the retrenchment—Counter attack—Further defence—Assailants at far edge—Defiles—General remarks—Definition—Specialities of defiles—Defence of defiles—In rear—Measures to be taken—In front—Measures to be taken—Within—Measures to be taken—Attack of defiles—On rear position—Measures—On front position—Measures—On position within—Measures.

(*Reference to Plate XII.*)

N.B.—For first advance of attack towards fortified positions see Chapters X. *et seq.*

Woods have at all times, since the use of firearms, occupied a high place in the annals of war, because they constitute in themselves an obstacle both to the view and the fire of an enemy. On the other hand, they are not, like villages, an obstacle to his advance in deployed formation, unless there is an exceptionally thick brushwood. After capture of the edge the further advance is easy or difficult according to the nature of the undergrowth. For instance, larch woods are generally clear of brushwood, while some others are apt to be filled with it; and, in tropical climates, strong creepers grow so luxuriantly as to form an obstacle no less complete than an artificial entanglement. In the last case it is evident that the defenders have little more to do than defend the roads and paths. They should, however, push out narrow paths in the direction of the front and flanks, and place scouts at the ends of them to listen for attempts to outflank them. The enemy cannot advance without cutting paths, and thereby making a noise sufficiently loud to cause detection.

For exceptional cases exceptional remedies must be provided. In treating the general case we shall suppose average circumstances, that is to say, trees of moderate size, and sufficient brushwood to make movements of troops in formation difficult, though not impossible, so that communication by means of roads and paths is important.

Organisation of the Edge.

An average wood will probably have some kind of fence round it to keep out cattle, often a bank and ditch, which form a ready-made shelter trench, in which, however, there is no shelter obtained from the trees. As you move back through the wood, looking outwards, less and less daylight is perceived through the stems, until at last nothing is perceived *near the ground* but tree trunks and bushes. You are then absolutely protected from infantry fire and shrapnel except at long ranges. On the other hand, you cannot see the enemy outside, and therefore cannot prevent him from capturing the edge of the wood. Here, then, is a good position for supports or reserves, but not for the shooting line. It is also clear that an enemy once in the wood is on equal terms with the defenders. We may start, then, with the principle that *the most important place for defence is the edge of the wood.*

Clearing the Ground.—Going back to first principles, we have to remember that, for all defence, the object is to keep the enemy in the open as long as possible under fire from the defenders under cover. This will be best done by clearing the ground in front and placing obstacles. Here the words 'in front' mean wherever the enemy is likely to attack. He is certain to attempt to envelop the defence if

F

the wood is of manageable size. *If it is not, you cannot defend all of it, and must clear a belt round the part you choose to defend. The part so chosen will then be treated as if it stood alone.* The belt should not, if you can help it, be of a less breadth than 300 yards, so that an enemy advancing over it may be exposed for as long as possible to infantry fire. Evidently such a belt should be swept by the fire of your guns from the far end of it. Note that a large tree may give the enemy less cover if left standing than if cut down.

Obstacles.—The obstacles nearest to hand will be abatis, because you have the trees on the spot. Entanglements may also be useful, especially at parts which you cannot well occupy. Wire entanglements, or even single wires stretched along the edge or among the bushes, are also admirable means for checking and demoralising an enemy; but these suppose means which may not be available, while abatis can be easily constructed. Experiments in France showed that engineers, arranged so as to have from two to three men per metre of frontage, could form a strong abatis in an hour. In Austria a regiment using its own tools as lately supplied, in a wood where the trees averaged 7 or 8 inches in diameter, constructed abatis 45 metres in depth in three hours, with about one man to two English yards of frontage. The Woolwich 'Text-book on Fortification' gives, however, six hours to twenty men to make two rows of abatis 30 yards long. Perhaps this slower work includes an amount of neatness which is not necessary. In both cases the trees were small. Half-cut abatis are the best.

It will generally be impossible to construct abatis over the whole frontage at once. *Begin with the angles, salient and re-entering, that is, the weak and flanking parts; next will come the entrances of roads* (see below), *then other places where the enemy may be likely to attack, having regard to his position, and the facilities afforded by the ground. Then, if there is time, finish the rest.* If the trees are very large leave them standing, and make abatis of their branches.

Salients.—It is probable that the wood will have salient angles of its own, and these will give flank defence. If not, do not as a rule create them artificially—they would be sources of weakness. If there is some special necessity for flanking fire, construct small lunettes well protected by abatis, and separate them from the general line of defence.

Parapets.—As soon as you begin to fell the trees the ordinary fence can no longer be used. It is well to make a rough and low parapet or shelter trench behind the abatis, beginning as before with the most important points. Earth thrown on the trunk of the rear line of cut-down trees is a good plan; and, if you have time to lay heaps of small branches, to peg them down and then throw earth over them, a very tough parapet will be made. Earth is difficult to dig in a wood because of the roots of trees.

Entrances of Roads.—There are three ways in which the entrances can be treated, without preventing their subsequent use by the defenders.

First. Place a row of abatis a few yards in front of the general line of the edge, and, leaving thus an easy exit round the ends of this detached obstacle, carry the regular abatis of the wood's edge back some distance, say 30 yards, along each side of the road.

Second. Construct a detached lunette in front of the entrance, placing abatis in front of it and along part of the road as in previous arrangement. Exit round the flanks of the lunette.

Third. Bring your regular edge defence up to the road on each side, clear a space behind it where the road passes through, throw back abatis as before along the edges of the space, place a barricade in the centre of the space across the road, and again some abatis on each side of the road behind the space. Thus nothing will show outside to attract the enemy's fire, but if he penetrates the edge, he will find himself in a *cul de sac* with fire on all sides. In this case the exit will be round the flanks of the barricade.

N.B.—From what has been said in the chapter on Earthworks it will be seen that the lunette is not the best form, and that, if used at all, its angle should be as little salient as possible.

INTERIOR ORGANISATION.

Garrison.—For all this work and defence of the wood afterwards, a garrison of from two to three men per yard of the edge to be defended will suffice, including the reserves. But woods are famous for the amount of men they can swallow up by degrees on both sides. This ought to be in favour of the defence. The wood of Masloved was held by the Prussians for several hours in 1866 against an Austrian force four times greater than the garrison. If your garrison is so restricted that you cannot occupy all the edge, select some of the re-entering angles which are well flanked, and construct there a very deep abatis, 80 or 100 yards deep, as a passive defence which will only need to be watched. The disposition of the garrison will be treated later.

ARTILLERY DEFENCE.

Position of Guns.—Putting aside the question of the comparative merits of artillery and infantry fire, it should never be forgotten that artillery enjoys the advantage of superior mobility, and may therefore be risked as detachments further away from the main body than is advisable for detachments of infantry; always provided that it be escorted by cavalry, which would have the task of watching the country so as to prevent the possibility of surprise. A flying detachment of artillery, pushed out in front of a wood to the distance of a mile or more, will assist in discovering the nature and number of the enemy by forcing him to deploy before he would otherwise do so. Deployment in a country which is at all close involves delay and embarrassment. The artillery so pushed forward should choose a commanding position, and open fire at long range on the enemy's columns. It should retire as soon as its object has been attained, or if it begins to suffer sensible losses. On such occasions it is not necessary that the whole of the gunners should be present. The guns should travel as lightly equipped as is consistent with efficiency. Either no waggons, or at most one with an extra pair of horses, should be taken to the front.

The subsequent position of the guns will depend upon circumstances. It is usual to say that they should be on the flanks of the wood, somewhat retired, but this supposes that the flanks are not occupied by other troops, nor yet liable to surprise. *Whenever artillery is placed on the flanks of an isolated position it should be protected on its outer flank by detachments of infantry, and the ground for a full mile radius should be watched by cavalry.*

If the flanks are secured by other parts of an army, and the communications within the wood are good, it will often be found advisable at the first stage to place some of the guns on the border of the wood, but slightly retired, generally upon or near the roads, both because they will be better able to see the approaching enemy and force his columns to early deployment, and because their line of retreat will be more directly open. Infantry will if beaten retire among the trees, because the cover for individuals is better there. The roads will remain open to the artillery. In such a position the artillery will open the combat and delay the enemy as long as possible. *The infantry need not during this first stage occupy the edge of the wood at all, and should certainly not be placed near the guns to form a double target.*

The artillery will only retire when the enemy has established himself so close that the losses are not compensated by the effect of the guns. If the road is fully exposed to the view of the enemy the guns should retire at first through the trees: a tree cut down here and there will leave a practicable way through most woods.

Interior Retrenchment.

Second Position.—A second position will be organised if possible, in which case a strip of wood should be cut down in front of it, so as to give an unrestricted view if only for fifty yards. A stream or ravine should be utilised if possible. Openings must be left for the retirement of the first line. Outside, on the flanks of the retrenchment, epaulements armed with guns may be useful to keep back the enemy's flanking columns.

COMMUNICATIONS.

Communications.—These are of the utmost importance. One of the chief difficulties in wood fighting is to reinforce at once the points of the edge most in danger. Supports and reserves will in the first instance be placed near existing roads, but this is not enough. Other radial communications must be established. Where brushwood exists such ways can be easily arranged by clearing away the bushes; in other cases branches can be cut down and trees blazed at frequent intervals. Place sentries at cross-roads to show the way, and establish at such spots barricades across the roads, so that the enemy can be checked there if he penetrates the wood. Take care also to have easy communication all round the edge. You cannot give too much care to the arrangement of communications.

ORGANISATION OF THE DEFENDERS.

Division into Sections.—If the difficulty of holding troops in hand in the open field is now the *crux* of tactics, how much more difficult is it in a wood! Commanding officers of battalions, for instance, could not even be seen by their men if the battalion were in closed line and he in front of it. Moreover, the noise in a wood is startlingly loud. Tree echoes to tree the crack of the rifles, and the sound of artillery is greatly intensified. Control is soon lost, especially after the enemy has once pierced the first line of defence. Yet, if left to themselves, the men will wander anywhere, fall into frightful confusion, and perhaps leave large spaces undefended for want of direction.

The best way of providing against a difficulty is to begin by recognising it frankly. Grant, then, that a battalion commander must lose his men, and let the responsibility fall on the captains of companies or double companies; with them the colonel will have some chance of being in communication. Whatever be the unit, it should have a definite task, and we would divide the responsibility somewhat as follows:—

Suppose the wood to be occupied by a brigade. Then the brigade commander should divide it into sections, and confide each section to the care of a battalion commander, with orders to organise his part of the edge and clear the ground in front of it. The general of brigade will then select his second line of defence, decide the direction in which each battalion is to retire, and send the information to all the colonels. Then he will go round to each of them in turn, observe what they are doing, and explain his intentions, taking this opportunity for correcting misapprehensions, and bringing the whole into harmony with his general design. On their part the colonels will divide their sections as seems best among the captains, and set them to work at the clearing and preparation of the edge. They will then study their own sections, and be ready to decide on the necessary communications as soon as they know the general plan of defence. It is much better that each battalion should have its own strip of edge and furnish its own supports and reserves, a general reserve being held back. In this way the mingling of battalions will be postponed as long as possible, while the general, the colonels, and the captains will have, each in his own sphere, definite responsibilities. The reserves of the first line should be in or near the retrenchment, and be specially charged with its defence. A general reserve—about a third—will be held in hand for any requirements, especially watching the flanks.

Rear Edge of the Wood.—The rear edge of the wood will often form a third defensive position, in which case it should be treated as the second position was. Take care to clear a belt of trees. The enemy, mixed and out of hand with his struggle inside, will arrive in small detachments, and should find a new line of defence, with its garrison cool and ready to continue the fight. The flanks are here the weakest spots. Take care to guard them carefully.

Behind the Wood.—If the wood has been part of a line of battle, it may be that other troops are collected behind it. Or a wood may be too large to occupy, and a position in rear has to be taken up. In such cases form abatis along the rear edge pointing inward, so as to limit the openings by which the enemy can issue. If there are straight roads through the wood, place artillery on their prolongation, and your infantry commanding the point of exit at a range not greater than 600 yards. In short, make the wood into a defile as well as you can, and defend the exit (see page 76). *It is not at all impossible to shut the enemy up in a wood after he has captured it.*

Conduct of Attack and Defence.

The exterior movement of the troops will be treated hereafter (Chap. X. *et seq.*) in general application to the attack of fortified positions, but we may give here the interior work of attack and defence peculiar to wood fighting.

Assailants' First Measures.—Suppose the assailants to have carried a portion of the edge, which will probably be at a salient angle. The defenders endeavour to drive the enemy back again by a concentrated counter attack, perhaps by a portion of the general reserve brought up when the defences seemed to be yielding. The assailants hold their ground and pour troops in at the opening, driving the defenders from the whole of the edge with the aid of other attacking units, which are ready to press in as they see the defenders giving back under enfilade fire.

Advance of Assailants.—The first advance of the assailants will be by forming a chain of infantry in dispersed order. We postpone for the present its exact constitution. The important point is to follow the defenders quickly before they have time to recover their spirits and their organisation. Supports and reserves follow the chain more closely than they would in the open. Columns march along the edge of the wood right and left, to support the flanks of the chain and outflank the defenders. Other columns follow the chain, taking care to have communication with each other by means of detachments. Drive back the enemy as quickly as possible, outflanking any parties which resist steadfastly.

Action of Defenders.—During this combat the defenders will hold their own as well as they can by individual fighting from tree to tree, and will also endeavour to make counter attacks by concentrated bodies. If they feel that they cannot resist long, the reserves of the first line will occupy the retrenchment, the general reserve especially guarding its flanks.

Attack of the Retrenchment.—The assailants will endeavour to carry the retrenchment both by rushing it on the heels of the retreating defenders and by turning its flanks, where they will bring their flanking columns in collision with the defenders' reserves. At this stage the guns of the attack may be useful by bringing the defending reserves under a flanking fire from outside, arrangements having been made previously for signals showing the general state of the flanking advance.

Counter Attack.—Just when the assailants are assembling for attack on the retrenchments, and before they are ready for the assault, is a good moment for counter attack.

Further Defence.—Suppose the retrenchment carried, the defenders will not retire by the main roads, which should be already barricaded, but by narrower paths, bordered by trees already half cut down, and only requiring to be pulled over. The spaces of wood between these paths should have been made impassable by entanglements, &c. A wood thus defended ought to hold out for a long time.

Assailants at Far Edge.—After perhaps many hours of fighting, the assailants, weary and probably hungry, arrive at the far edge, to be met there by another line of abatis, beyond which, in the open, the defenders are ready to repulse, with both infantry and artillery fire, any attempt to issue from the wood. This is a critical moment, and all may be lost to the assailants if they push on. The rule then is, not to attempt to issue from the wood under such conditions until the edge has been organised for defence against the former defenders. And, if opportunity serves, a flank attack should be made on the defender's position by outside troops, rather than an attempt to issue from the defile.

Other questions which may occur in wood fighting will be answered by the general tactical knowledge of officers. Many surprises may occur, which cannot be formally provided against. Catch the spirit of tactics, and the details will come of themselves when required. If you have not the spirit, forms will only embarrass you.

DEFILES.

General Remarks.—There is little that is peculiar in the attack or defence of defiles, and nothing that common sense ought not to teach to any student who has mastered the general principles of tactics. Still, as crude ideas on the subject are too often to be seen in print, and as, on a large scale as well as a small one, the defence of defiles may be an important duty for British troops over the sea, if not at home, a page or two may be allotted to this part of tactics.

Definition.—A defile may be defined to be any form of ground, natural or artificial, which obliges troops to relinquish their proper fighting formation and adopt a formation with a narrow front in order to traverse it. Thus narrow valleys when the hills on either side are impassable, bridges or fords over rivers, dykes over marshes, and even to a limited extent roads passing through close and difficult country, may be considered as defiles.

Specialities of Defiles.—It is evident that the length and breadth of a defile must have a great influence on its defence or attack, and that the increase of range of modern arms almost abolishes the influence of certain short defiles which might have been important when 1,500 yards was a long range for guns, and 200 yards for rifles. The nature of the ground at the entrance and exit of a defile is also important, as well as that within the defile itself. Thus the form of ground might possibly be such as to upset reasoning deduced from general principles, and so influence affairs as to modify considerably the argument contained in the following paragraphs.

Defence of Defiles.—A defile may be defended in order to allow the passage of an army either advancing or retiring, or to deny its passage to an enemy, or to engage the enemy under circumstances unfavourable to him. Under any of these suppositions, into which we cannot here enter carefully, the defenders may take up a position either—

A. In rear of the defile.
B. In front of the defile.
C. Within the defile.

A real student will do well to shut the book here and think out for himself which of these three attitudes will be most accordant with our invariable rule—namely, to be stronger than the enemy at the right time and place.

In Rear of the Defile.—Putting aside for the moment all complicating circumstances of ground or special occasions, the student should by this time be able to decide for himself that the position in rear presents the greatest number of advantages, and that those advantages are very important in themselves. He will also perceive that the greater the scale of the defile as to length, and the greater the forces engaged, the more will the advantages of the rear position stand out. Of all possible advantages, the greatest that we can have tactically is to oppose a broad front of fire to a narrow one of the adversary. It was the advantage of the oblique attack of Frederick the Great, of his attack on the head of the allied marching columns at Rossbach, and of all attacks on a flank. To await an enemy at one's own end of a complete defile is to force him to be, as it were, all flank, while you yourself have none ; that is, he is obliged to expose to you his narrowest and therefore weakest formation, while he cannot reach your weak parts without passing in front of your well-established force, and at exactly the range that you have chosen beforehand. By a perfect defile I mean one that keeps the enemy to a narrow front, and is long enough, or presents obstacles enough, to prevent the action of the enemy's artillery on your chosen field of battle altogether, or at least makes it of very little power compared with your own. If the defile is straight and exposed, like a dyke over a marsh, or the road running along the side of a lake with precipices above it, there will be the further advantage that the narrow column of the enemy will be long exposed to your fire before he issues from it. Then, supposing our enemy repulsed, what a disastrous condition is his, driven back on the crowded defile, up to the very mouth of which you can pursue his flying crowds! Thus the enemy has all the disadvantages, while you may count as advantages to yourself the avoidance of those disadvantages which a retreat through a defile brings with it, after the disadvantage of having been exposed to an enveloping attack.

Measures to be taken.—The defender should aim at two objects: 1st, to damage the assailant as much as he can on approaching and crossing the defile; and 2nd, to envelop and destroy him when issuing from it. If the defile be long and not exposed to your fire, do not attempt to attain the object by risking your own troops too much forward. The nature of the defile must influence your conduct; but avoid, above all things, allowing your own troops to mask those of the assailants when they come within range of your artillery or infantry. If, on the other hand, the defile is short and exposed, as in the passage of a moderately sized river, you should so dispose your troops as to bring the enemy under fire from first to last, even by pushing troops across if necessary, though not compromising their easy retreat; but, at any rate, by opposing any possible material obstacles to his advance. Your troops on the near side of the defile will be disposed so as to envelop the head of the assailant's column.

Disposition of Defending Troops.—Whenever it is possible, as in mountain passes, for example, line the sides of the defile with sharpshooters, and here and there place guns on strong points, taking care, however, that they can eventually retire without entering the defile. Supports should have the task of feeding the shooting line. In some cases it will even be possible to have a few men and guns in the defile to check the enemy, but they must never come to close quarters with him. No absolute rule can be laid down except this: Do the enemy as much damage as you can consistently with never giving him a chance of mingling with your troops, or following them very closely so as to be masked by them. Outside, also, your formation must depend on the ground; but a normal condition of things would be a crescent, concave side towards the enemy; a strong shooting line in front well covered, with supports and reserves; artillery and cavalry on the wings, the former behind cover, and not to act unless the enemy gets out in considerable numbers. If the assailants push some guns through, the defenders' artillery will engage them to draw their fire, but forsake them for infantry masses if any such get out. If the defenders have heavy pieces, their best place will be in front of the defile, and some 800 or 1,000 yards from it, behind epaulments. Your infantry should not be further from the mouth of the defile than four or five hundred yards, so that they may be able to advance to attack if their concentric fire has not checked the assailants. The cavalry on the wings should not be exposed to infantry fire, but be able to charge the enemy in flanks and rear if he issue. The defenders should have a second line, and a reserve rather closed up, but that will depend on the nature of the ground. The second line will occupy localities for defence, if possible, and the bulk of the cavalry should be with the reserve, which has especially to guard against turning movements of the attacking force.

In Front of the Defile.—Though the position in front is hardly ever advantageous, there are occasions where there is no choice: for instance, when the advanced guard has to cover a defile while the main body is passing through it, or when a rearguard covers the retreat of the main body and then has to retire; or if the ground at the exit from the defile is such that no advantageous position can be found, as would be the case if the ground sloped steeply down from the mouth of the defile on the defenders' side. It is possible that there may be such a great difference in favour of the position in front as to outweigh all the general reasons against it. In tactics, as in other branches of knowledge, there are exceptions to every rule in matters of detail as distinguished from general principles. The elements of a good position in front are—

1st. A good convex position, with strong points on which to rest the flanks.

2nd. Strong defensive posts within the position.

3rd. Room enough for the troops to manœuvre and carry out an active defence.

4th. A very strong locality or defensive point just outside the defile, and capable of being used as a sort of keep, which may be occupied to the last by infantry and artillery.[1]

Measures to be taken.—Push forward cavalry and horse artillery to force the enemy to deploy prematurely. The horse artillery should then take post on the flanks, and be ready to retire rapidly to the centre, getting away in the defile as soon as possible. Dispose the field batteries in a position in front of the defile, so that their retirement will be by the shortest line. The cavalry may as well retire altogether after the preliminary stage, or at least join the reserve near the entrance to the defile. The infantry and field batteries should form a convex line of defence, with a strong reserve of infantry posted near the entrance to cover the retreat. A village or a wood, if existing there, should be strongly occupied and defended. It is evident that such a general position supposes eventual retreat, and is not intended to be defended to the last, because troops tumbled headlong into a ravine or upon a causeway, &c., with the enemy at their heels, would be in a bad case. This is one of the reasons why defence in front of a defile is morally a mistake if it can be avoided. The retreat should begin from the wings inwards, and, if possible, be preceded by an offensive movement. If it be at all possible as a

---

[1] *Traité de Tactique Appliquée*, translated from the German of General Paris, by Muzio Rix and Capt. Timmerhaus, of the Belgian army. But any first-rate text-book gives much the same rules.

Plate XVII

...ack, the Battalion is in Brigade
Battalion from 400 to 200 Mètres

| ...subdivision ...ight of the 350 to 300 Left advances | A reserve subdivision pushes the right of the chain from 300 to 250 mètres, the left advances with it. | A reserve subdivision pushes the left from 250 to 200 mètres, the right advances with it. The 4 companies are now all in shooting line. |

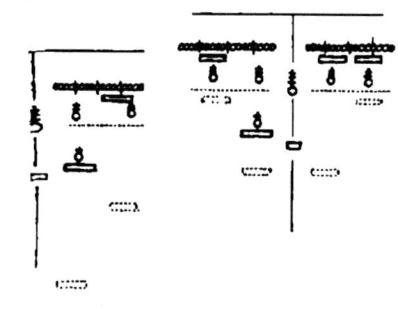

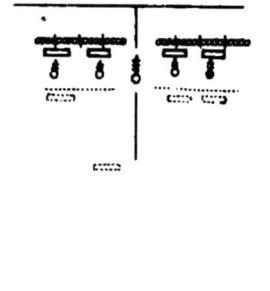

Battalion from 600 to 400 Mètres

End of the 2nd rush, the two leading companies are in line, the companies are in echelon

Battalion from 1500 to 600 Mètres

The chain opens fire, 1st reinforcement; 6 sections in the chain

chain deploys by ...ps

question of time, barricade the entrance behind the defenders.

Within the Defile.—This form may be used in combination with either of the preceding, but is usually confined to cases of very long defile, such as raised roads over extensive marshes or mountain valleys. If, as sometimes happens, a number of raised roads or mountain valleys radiate from a central point towards the assailants, that point may be defended with advantage to prevent the concentration of the enemy's columns. It is, however, to be remarked that any interior defence is liable to be turned. Example—the Turkish defence of the Shipka Pass, turned by General Gourko.

Measures to be taken.—The defence will generally have to be by small detachments of infantry, with a small proportion of guns, and only a few cavalry scouts. The infantry will occupy fortified positions, and in the case of a steep valley fill the sides of the hill with sharpshooters, furnished with supports. The reserves will be at the points of bifurcation, but the chief stress of the combat will be borne by small infantry detachments, under officers of junior rank. All the more reason for such officers to be familiar with the whole subject of tactics.

Attack of Defiles.—Here, again, the nature of the defence must determine that of the attack, and the first object is to know what the defence is, and for that purpose, as for all purposes in war, good reconnaissance is necessary. As such reconnaissance is usually made by cavalry, to save time, and also because cavalry can get out of a scrape by the speed of their horses more quickly and certainly than foot soldiers can, it is very important that cavalry officers should be skilled in all such knowledge as this book attempts to provide; for what information can be given by any officer who cannot recognise means of defence, nor the value of them? So far from cavalry officers being regarded as requiring little technical knowledge, as seems to be the idea in this country, it would appear that the 'eyes and ears' of an army need exactly the same sort of training that eyes and ears generally do; that is, they should not be mere conduits of sensation, but intelligent workers with the brain. To see anything properly is impossible unless one can recognise its quality. How can an officer report anything accurately which he does not understand?

Attack on Position behind a Defile.—This is so difficult that it should not be undertaken if the position can be turned; and if no turning movement can be made, resort should be had to surprise if possible. Difficult as night marches are, they are now being assiduously practised everywhere, because they seem to be the only means of neutralising the effect of that long range now possessed by all kinds of firearms. But supposing the attack has to be made by day, the most favourable conditions will be where, as often happens in mountain passes, the defile enlarges greatly at its exit, and the hills are passable by artillery or even by infantry. It has been said above that the defenders should occupy a position concave towards the enemy, and the converse of that is true for the assailants, who should manage, if possible, to issue with a front convex towards themselves, concave towards the defenders. By such means it may be possible to gain the advantage of a cross fire in front of the main column when issuing from the defile. This maxim applies with great force to the crossing of a river, which is exactly the same case as any other defile. Select a place where the bend of the river is convex towards the assailant, concave towards the defending enemy, and so protect the issue of the main column.

Measures to be taken.—The general principle of the attack will be to reverse as soon as possible the favourable condition of the defender's broad front by gaining a still broader front of your own if you can. For this purpose it is important to know all those paths in a mountain pass which are generally used as short-cuts from villages in the plains over the lower hills to the interior of the defile. Make them practicable for guns. It is astonishing how much can be done in a short time by bodies of mounted engineers. A mountain sheep track was made passable for the whole of

General Gourko's force by a couple of squadrons of Cossack pioneers sent two days in advance, though the path was so bad that the Turks never thought of defending it. Then push out guns so as, if possible, to outflank the defenders, or, at any rate, to take their position obliquely, and threaten the flanks with infantry attacks. The first troops which issue from the defile, whatever it may be, should spread out at once and push forward in the shape of a fan, even recklessly, to clear the mouth of the pass, or bridge, or dyke, or whatever it may be; and if there be any obstacles, as there ought to be if the defenders are wise, send working parties at the very heads of the columns, only protected by skirmishers, but using no arms themselves. The artillery will take up any possible positions, and try to distract the attention of the enemy's artillery; for the great point is, at any sacrifice, to save the heads of the columns from annihilation. Always remember the principle of obtaining a wider front than the defence, and take care that every movement is made with great rapidity and dash, so as to keep the exit clear. Other measures must depend on circumstances. Rapid extension of front, great boldness, and using the best quality of troops for the final assault, are the elements of success. If foiled, do not make the attempt again soon with the same troops.

For a well-conducted passage of a river read the Russian passage of the Danube in 1877 in Lieut. Greene's book. It is the only one of the kind since the time of breechloaders and modern artillery, and may be counted as a partial surprise.

Attack on Position in Front of a Defile.—Here we have an easier problem, the principle being to envelop the position and attack with the greatest vigour. The assailant should aim at getting as close to the defenders as possible, so as to follow them up in the defile. All the advantages are with the attacking side.

Measures to be taken.—In this case the most successful stroke would be to force the defender's centre before his wings retire; but almost the same result may be obtained by forcing one wing, and so causing a hurried retreat of the whole. The attack need not be fully described, as it is so like the attacks on all other positions, instances of which are given in Chapters XV. and XVI.—enveloping movement to begin with, deployment of as many guns as possible, then concentration of their fire on a particular point where your attack will be delivered. For the attack, roll on one wave of men after another, not letting one wave wait till the former one is spent. Troops with a defile behind them will be morally affected by that circumstance. Count on that moral effect, and act with great boldness and decision. Storm everything. If you can, send some guns to any commanding position, from which they can play on the retiring defenders. The main idea is to keep the enemy going with your sword in his reins. Your reserve should stand fast till there is no more chance of a counter attack. If possible, have small flanking columns to protect your own flanks.

Attack on a Position within a Defile.—Here it is to be presumed that the position cannot be immediately turned, nor attacked in flank, but there are cases where it can, as at the Shipka Pass, which was turned by the Russians, and later attacked on both flanks by the Turks.

Measures to be taken.—This case is one in which the assailants are likely to suffer great losses. There is nothing special in the attack, except that a flanking movement is almost impossible. The artillery must prepare the way by destroying works and obstacles, for which a more powerful explosive, as bursting charge of shells, is greatly needed. The guns may also support the infantry, but the attack itself devolves wholly on the infantry. You should hold in hand a reserve both to guard against counter attack, and to take advantage of the smallest success. If circumstances permit, always send flanking columns to threaten the flanks and rear of the defenders.

The measures recommended in the three cases suppose that the position, wherever it may be, is attackable. This is the case with nearly all mountain passes, whatever be the quality of the enemy; but, again, there are very few such that cannot be turned. Long dykes across marshes, long bridges across rivers, where the curve is unfavourable, and all other defiles perfectly exposed to the fire of well-trained enemy in good heart, may be said to be unattackable except by surprise, for the principles of which see further on, in the discussion of attack on villages, Chapter XII.

CHAPTER VII.

DEFENCE OF HOUSES, FARMS, AND VILLAGES.

Still necessary in war—Examples—Defence of a house—Order of work—Details of house defence—Step by step—Defence of a farm—Principles—Exterior defences of first importance—Details—Number of garrison—Use of shelter trenches—Second line of defence—Defence of villages—Old rules affected by modern weapons—Prominence of artillery—*Pros* and *cons.*—Actual cases suggest certain principles—Exterior failure need not involve fall—Cases of prolonged interior defence—The first danger—Bombardment by artillery worse than formerly—Reply by outer shooting line and inner organised defence by 'the garrison'—Reserve artillery on flanks as formerly—Summary of principles.

(Plates XIII., XIV., XV.)

THE defence of houses or farms has on many occasions figured conspicuously among the details of great battles, and there are hardly any important modern fights in which the attack and defence of buildings does not more or less influence the result. It is true that the increased range and power of artillery render the defence of exposed houses much more difficult than it used to be, and suggest demolition in many cases where occupation and defence would formerly have been useful. But the cases where even an isolated house is concealed from artillery fire at all but close ranges are very numerous, and, as soon as we come to groups of houses, some of the buildings are sure to be covered by the rest. As a general rule, houses, farms, and villages are so situated as, if fortified, to prevent the use of certain roads. This may be useful, even though only a temporary defence can be made. It may be said that the occupation and defence of military posts, such as houses, farms, and villages, have lost none of their value, but the choice of such posts has been somewhat restricted by modern developments of armament.

Examples.—In the first battle of the war in 1870, at Weissenburg, the château on the Geisberg resisted all the German attempts to storm it throughout the day, and only yielded at last when artillery was placed round it. On comparison of the number of defenders with the losses of the Germans during the various attacks, it is clear that each defender must on an average have killed or wounded at least one of the attacking force.

In the last great battle fought by the French regular army—Sedan—the village of Bazeilles sustained a long combat with the Bavarians, chiefly, it is said, because they attacked it without having sufficiently prepared the way by artillery fire ; and, throughout the whole campaign, the attack and defence of small military posts formed a marked feature of the struggle. At Gravelotte there was much fighting of this character, but it may suffice to mention the village of St. Privat and the farms of Montigny-la-Grange, Moscou, Point-du-Jour, Leipsic, and Saint Hubert.

Against savage nations almost any kind of a building can be held. The gallant defence of Rorke's Drift by Lieutenants Chard and Bromhead will occur to everybody. It probably saved Natal from invasion, and certainly raised the credit of British arms. But for more serious affairs, in which an enemy has to be met who is provided with modern arms, an isolated house should be of masonry to save it from being set on fire, with a roof which is also uninflammable. Brick houses are better than stone, because they splinter less. A large house is better than a small one, not because the garrison is larger —that might in some cases be a disadvantage—but because the garrison will be safe from the effect of artillery fire in the rooms which are retired from the enemy. When the infantry attack begins the artillery fire must cease, or nearly so. Then the garrison can reoccupy the side next the enemy. Flat roofs with parapet walls—such are common in the East

—and houses with projecting offices, porches, bow-windows, and the like, which furnish flank defence, are best. The ordinary builders' cheap house, as run up in the neighbourhood of great English towns, is the worst possible, both in form and structure.

Defence of a House.

Now let us suppose that the time is probably short before the enemy is likely to approach. The work to be done will come in the following order:—

Order of work.—
 1. Make the house fairly defensible.
 2. Clear the ground round it (see page 62).
 3. Provide means of communication and retreat.

N.B.—It need hardly be said that if sufficient labour happens to be available, the three portions of the work can be carried on at the same time. The Woolwich 'Text-book on Fortification' puts clearing the ground first.

*Details of House Defence.—*In perhaps the majority of cases there will be doubt as to the length of time likely to be allowed before the enemy's attack. It is only common sense to begin the preparation of the house with the most necessary work, namely, prevention of the enemy's entry, and, as far as may be, that of his projectiles, without hindering the fire of the garrison. For this purpose the ground-floor openings should be barricaded as solidly as possible, including doors, windows, and cellar gratings. To effect this, use all that comes to hand in the house, remembering that while loose structures of wood, such as furniture, cupboard doors, &c., are likely to catch fire or aid in a conflagration, the same materials jammed together and hung with wet blankets make good barricades, and are not very inflammable. The barricades should be six feet high at least, so as to cover all men in the rooms. Cut also a ditch in front of the door, so that an enemy close to it will be well below the height of the defenders at that point, and cannot use the defenders' loopholes. Use the earth to cover planks laid over cellar gratings. Open loopholes in the barricades of the doors, and of the windows also if they are filled up completely. Bring earth and water into the house to protect against fire.

You are now in a position to repel sudden attacks, and may go on to mask all the windows in the upper stories by mattresses or even blankets. Loophole upper floors and make openings under the eaves of the roof, through which men can fire downwards. Place chairs, forms, or improvised erections for your men to stand on when firing.

The next matter of importance is to clear the ground near the house, cutting down all fences which obstruct a full view of an approaching enemy, but generally leaving those which radiate from the house and tend to separate the forces advancing against you.

At this stage you are pretty well prepared, but there are still dangers which should be guarded against. The enemy may run in under cover of smoke or darkness, and accumulate close to the walls between the loopholes, with the intention of setting fire to the house or blowing holes in the walls with gun-cotton, dynamite, &c. To prevent this, if you have time, provide flank defence by loopholing any projecting porches and outbuildings.

Further, if you are even to resist artillery and hold your ground as long as possible, cover the floors with earth or manure, and place upright beams to support the different floors.

Possibly you may have to hold out for a long time, therefore accumulate ammunition, water, and provisions, and occupy your men in organising and preparing interior defence step by step. Prepare every door for fast closing, and loophole all the walls.[1] Remove the staircase, and place ladders which can be drawn up when the ground-floor is taken. Make holes in the upper floors to fire through.

If retreat is allowable, the ladders may be used to slip away by, and the direction of retreat, together with a rallying-place, should always be thought of.

---

[1] It has often happened that an enemy has entered a house and a long combat has ensued between the attackers in one room and defenders in another, with an empty room or passage between them.

Any form of obstacle may be employed outside in defending a house, but, in a general way, obstacles will only be employed in defence of strong buildings, or those which form part of a general line of defence, outside farms or villages. Wire entanglements are best.

The necessary garrison for a house may be put at two men for each window, door, or loophole.

DEFENCE OF A FARM.

Under this head may be included all buildings or small groups of buildings which have outhouses, yards, or gardens surrounded by walls or strong fences. They form much better defences than ordinary houses, and are constantly utilised even on great battle-fields. In considering this subject we already enter on the defence of positions, and begin to require a larger number of men and more tactical knowledge in the commander.

Principles.—The leading principle of their defence is to organise them in two parts :—

1. The outer existing defences strengthened by art.
2. The inner buildings or groups of buildings placed in state of defence as houses; all which are not useful for this purpose being destroyed.

Exterior of first importance.—In the case of farms, the exterior defences come first in order of importance, and the great principle of the defence should be to place the troops *outside* the buildings, which should be reserved as rallying-places, one in particular being organised at the 'keep' or last refuge of the defenders.

Details.—All the means previously detailed (Chapter V.) may be used in defence of a farm. Ground cleared, obstacles placed, flank defence assured, and communications made. Buildings prepared as houses. Take care to get rid of those old inflammable structures so common in farms; but if evacuation is permitted, and there are a few minutes to spare— as, for instance, in rearguard delaying actions—pile a heap of combustibles in the keep, and set it on fire when marching out.

DEFENCE OF HOUSES, FARMS, AND VILLAGES.

A farm prepared for defence is a kind of weak and temporary fort. It can be held for some time against artillery, unless there are many guns, even if the intention is to retreat eventually, and much longer if the defence is to be at all risks and hazards. A farm well prepared as an advanced post in a line of battle will of course be flanked by artillery fire, and is then very difficult to take. In such a case the rear should be left open to prevent the enemy establishing himself in the place, and to facilitate recapture. For example of a farm in condition of defence see Plate XIII.

Garrison.—Two men per yard of the outer defences will supply an ample garrison, and allow for a reserve, which should be placed at first *behind*, not in, the buildings.

Use of shelter trenches.—Always remember that houses and walls cannot be occupied as they used to be if there is a concentrated fire of artillery bearing upon them. Trenches in the open, not liable to enfilade, are better in the early stages, and can be protected from sudden attack by abatis, hedges, &c.

Second line of defence.—In every case where it is possible form a second line of defence. Nothing but this saved the little garrison of Rorke's Drift.

Defence of Villages.

Effect of changes in modern weapons.—The value of prepared villages has been the subject of much controversy since 1871. All tacticians who have had much experience in modern war agree in two points, which may be considered as beyond question.

First. The fire of field artillery is much more destructive than it used to be at all comparatively long ranges—say from 1,000 yards upwards; and concentration of fire from long range is more possible than it used to be. This favours the attack.

Second. The range and intensity of infantry fire have also increased, and a thin shooting line under cover can now produce as great an effect as a close line used to do, while that effect can take place at a longer distance. This favours the defence when the enemy's infantry comes into action.

Prominence of artillery.—The combination of these two ideas produces also a general agreement that artillery plays a much more important part in the attack of villages and small towns than it ever did before.

Pros and cons.—But here the agreement ceases. On one side there is a party which, quoting the frequent evacuation in 1870 and 1871 of villages and even fortified towns under artillery fire only, asserts that the useful defence of villages is a thing of the past. The other extreme party replies that, so far from losing, the defence has gained on the whole; because a brave garrison will know how to find shelter from all long range fire, and, at short ranges, the intensity of infantry fire will prevent the advance of the enemy's guns to close quarters, thus getting rid of their fire at the most critical moment.

The truth probably lies between the two extremes, and as a matter of fact the actions of the Franco-German war afford numerous examples both of successful and unsuccessful defence of villages. Plevna is out of present consideration. The works there constituted an entrenched camp.

We have also to remember that villages exist, and will certainly be used by one side or the other. They are not like forts which have to be built. Moreover, they are always to be found on main roads, sometimes on other places, but always on main roads which will be required for artillery and transport to travel on. It may be said at once that mere assemblages of slight and thatched wooden huts are indefensible under artillery fire. The whole place would be set in flames shortly after the commencement of the attack. The remarks to be made will only apply to solidly built villages with houses of brick or stone, and we are to suppose that the inhabitants are expelled.

Actual cases.—Now if we examine carefully the numerous cases which presented themselves in France during the German invasion, we shall be struck with the perpetual recurrence of certain causes and effects. Villages fell when they were severely bombarded by artillery for a long time, the garrisons remaining in them, and they resisted when attacks were made without such bombardments.[1] Again, the exterior defences and edge of a village sometimes fell, yet a prolonged defence was made in the interior. The Germans entered Bazeilles without a fight. Seven hours elapsed, and nearly a whole army corps was engaged before they succeeded in making their way out of the other end of the village. Le Bourget was the scene of a capture by the Germans, and a repulse of the French by the Germans at a later time. In both cases the village was entered easily by an enveloping force. The French unsuccessful defence of the interior lasted three hours, and the German successful defence about as long. It is evident that if defended villages can do nothing else, they may interpose long and perhaps vital delays to an enemy's movements.

The preparation of villages for defence does not necessarily imply that the army which uses them must act on the defensive. While their employment is almost certain in all defensive positions of modern civilised war, they have constantly been of great value in offensive campaigns. If the whole art of tactics consists in bringing a superior force against an inferior force of the enemy at the right time and place, it will often be necessary to leave one part of the field comparatively weak in men, so that a concentrated attack may be made with heavy forces in another part. The weak part must be held against an enemy's counter-attack and fortified accordingly. Again, villages often occur at fords or bridges over rivers, and may facilitate the crossing under an enemy's fire, acting as bridge-heads. If under the head of villages we class, as we must for simplicity, unfortified towns, then the number of instances in which they have been useful becomes very striking. For example, Pont-à-Mousson and Orleans in 1870.

It may be said, then, that whether the defence of villages has become easier or more difficult since the modern develop-

---

[1] Yet the number of men killed and wounded by such bombardments was remarkably small, because the troops were sheltered behind houses.

ment of firearms, there is no doubt that it must continue to form an important feature in campaigns, and to be used both by the defensive and offensive sides.

The first danger.—Now let us see what is the first danger to be provided against. Clearly, in most cases a bombardment by artillery; and the guns may be at all sorts of ranges, therefore their projectiles will fall at different angles. The weight of the projectiles for field guns has about doubled of late years, and the number of guns the fire of which can be concentrated on a given point has also quite doubled itself. Therefore, without entering into the relative effects of infantry and artillery fire at different ranges, it must be and is acknowledged that the attack on villages can bring a vastly more powerful artillery fire to bear than used to be possible. Then, if we assume that the defensive power of modern rifles has increased, it becomes clear that not only *can* a heavier artillery fire be brought to bear before the attack, but it *will* be, if possible, because it would be madness to send infantry to attack without preparing their way.

Bombardment by artillery.—How does artillery fire act on a village? Let the German official account of the war of 1870 answer in the two cases of the second attack on St. Privat (the first, unprepared by artillery, having been repulsed), and in the German attack on Noisseville, which had been carried by the French. St. Privat was solidly built and surrounded by walls. The words of the official account are—

'Walls and buildings crumbled under the crash of shells, and columns of fire rose in several places above the ruins of the village.'

And of Noisseville it is related—

'The combined fire of the German batteries . . . produced an effect far above what could have been expected. The village was in flames, the brewery buildings riddled with shot.'

The result as that the French abandoned the village without a struggle. There were many other similar cases, but these may suffice.

Reply by outer shooting line.—The result of this experience is found in a reversal of principle. Formerly the first and main line of defence was placed *inside* fortified houses. But as these have become precisely the most dangerous of all places during the artillery bombardment, the principle now is to place the first line of defence *outside* the village in shelter trenches, &c., about fifty yards from the houses, so as to avoid the danger of splintered fragments of stone or brick. We shall carry this principle somewhat further in speaking of the actual attack and defence. For the present it is enough to lay down the first principle—

If artillery is likely to be brought against you, place the first line of defence outside, not inside, the village.

Let this be called 'the shooting line.'

Inner defence by garrison.—When the artillery has done its work as far as possible, the attacking infantry will advance. Their bullets will make no more impression, practically speaking, on walls and houses than those of Brown Bess, for neither could penetrate, and 'a miss is as good as a mile.' Therefore *at that moment* a second line of defence delivering a fire from houses properly prepared, as already explained, will be most useful. We pass for the present the question of how the troops of the second line are employed during the artillery bombardment. Let it suffice that a second line must be prepared in houses, yards, &c., and must be ready to repel the infantry attack. In fact, to this portion of the force should be allotted the defence of the whole interior of the village, including interior barricades and different posts bearing the same position to portions of the village that the 'keep' does in a farm.

This is the place and duty of the second line, which may be called 'the garrison,' and will have a reserve of its own to support yielding troops and hold the main keep.

Outer Reserve.—But since the garrison is liable to be overpowered at one point by superior numbers, while the other portions are too much engaged to furnish support, it is necessary to have a special reserve. As a principle, all reserves should be kept out of fire as long as possible. Therefore the place of the main reserve is outside the village, and in rear of it. Its functions will be to support any portion of the garrison which needs help, to assist in the defence of the main 'keep,' but, above all, to be ready to deliver counter-strokes.

Artillery on flanks.—With regard to the artillery of the defence, it will be generally placed on the flanks of the village as of old. There may be cases where a couple of guns might be useful inside, but such cases are few, and the guns would always be liable to capture. The function of the artillery is to fire at the enemy's artillery at first, but, if overpowered, to withdraw into comparative safety, and be ready to act again, *at any risk*, against the attacking infantry of the enemy, when advancing on the village or when retiring after repulses. During the infantry struggle inside the village there is little that guns can do, and their absence is generally preferable. Machine guns would, however, be useful inside the village.

We can now sum up the principles of village or small town defence.

Infantry force employed, about three men per yard of exterior defences. Divide the force into three equal parts, and post them:—

1. One part as 'shooting line' in shelter trenches about fifty yards outside the buildings.[1] Its supports should be not behind but with the shooting line, in emplacements specially prepared for them.

2. A second part as garrison, to be used only when the enemy's infantry attacks, for defence of houses, barricades, and keep or keeps.

3. A third part as reserve out of fire, probably behind the village, to act as support to the garrison when required, and for counterstrokes.

4. The artillery in prepared positions, on the flanks first, to engage the enemy's guns, but not to its own destruction. Later, to engage the attacking infantry at all risks.

Before entering into the details which will be found in

[1] But see Chap. VIII. for first keeping infantry out of fire.

the next chapter, it should be stated that there are many different cases, each of which requires different treatment from the rest. Something will be said of these various cases hereafter, but, for a general study of defence and attack, it seems better to suppose a village, the defence of which is to be carried out as long as possible. Such a case might occur if an important road were to be blocked during the concentration of troops on a selected battle-field behind the village. The object would be to gain time for the army to collect its scattered divisions, and the sacrifice of a brigade would be of little importance compared with the strategical result to be achieved if the village can hold out for at least a day. We are to suppose that reinforcements are not far off and might be sent for if required, but are not to be demanded except in case of absolute necessity.

CHAPTER VIII.

DEFENCE OF VILLAGES (*continued*)—DETAILS AND THEIR REASONS.

Individual soldiers important—Different shapes of villages—Circular best—Arrangement of successive defence—First position of defenders—Delaying action of artillery—Noisseville—Infantry to be kept back at first—Under cover from bombardment till enemy's infantry advances to assault—Second position of defenders—Artillery on flanks, infantry in shooting line—Garrison still under shelter—Division of village into independent sections—If enemy carries a point, isolate it—Enemy sure to envelop —The principal keep—Machine guns—The reserve and its functions—Counter attack—Rules deduced from modern instances and progress of weapons.

(*Plates XII., XIII., XIV., XV., XVI.*)

N.B.—This chapter supposes the case of defence under the ordinary conditions of everyday warfare, and without the aid of skilled engineers.

Individual soldiers important.—We may now proceed to some details of the preparations for defence, bearing in mind the principles stated in the preceding chapter, and that mainspring of all success in action—the support of the moral force of your own troops while undermining that of the enemy. No kind of fighting tests the worth of the individual soldier more than attack and defence of villages and towns, because at the time of hardest fighting within the place there can be but little control by commanders, and superior forces cannot easily make their numbers felt on account of the confined nature of the field of action. Under no circumstances is the individual soldier less a machine. How important is it, then, that his stock of nervous energy should not be wasted in the early stages of the combat, which may in some cases last not for hours only but for days! During the famous siege of Saragossa in 1809, the breach was carried by the French on January 27, and on February 21 the assailants had not advanced more than about 400 yards into the town, with the loss of 3,000 killed and wounded.

Shapes of villages.—Villages may be said to be of two shapes—oblong when standing on a single road, roughly circular when standing on cross roads or surrounding a bridge over a river. Then the advance of the enemy may either be towards the end or the side of the oblong. An oblong village end-on to the enemy is weak against direct attack, as it can only develop a small front of fire, and the main street will be liable to be raked by the enemy's artillery and rifles. If the oblong village presents its broadside to the enemy, it is strong against the first attack, but has little power of resistance when the first line of houses, walls, &c., is carried; moreover, its flanks are weak. A circular village is the best, being equally strong everywhere, and suitable for division into sections capable of separate defence. Obviously, therefore, as a general rule, artificial defences of oblong villages should be arranged so as to make them as nearly circular as possible. Thus, if end-on to the enemy, strengthen and extend the flanks; if broadside on, make the most of any buildings in front and in rear, counting them as new sections if possible.

Let us now take a fairly natural village, and see how it arranges itself roughly for defence (Plate XVI. Fig. 1). Here we have a rather long village to begin with, changed into circular form by leaving out a portion of it, which should be razed to the ground if there is time. By using the wood on the left a greater frontal fire will be established, and it will be connected with the shelter trench at *m* by a line of abatis. The main shelter trench will be fully 50 yards on an average from the outer buildings, and the enclosed village will be divided into three or four sections, according to the amount of available garrison. The central church will furnish a keep, and the stone wall which surrounds it will make it very defensible.[1]

[1] The village is taken from General Brialmont's *La Fortification du Champ de Bataille*, but the defences are modified to suit the stage at which the student is supposed to have arrived.

FIELD WORKS.

Outposts will be established on the usual principles, as fully explained in Col. Wilkinson Shaw's 'Elements of Tactics.'

First Position of Defenders.

Since it is agreed by all tacticians that the attack will first endeavour to bring a heavy artillery fire to bear on the defenders, during which the infantry of the defence would have little or nothing to do, two principles are dictated by common sense.

First. Keep the enemy's artillery at a distance as long as possible.

Second. Keep the defending infantry concealed from the enemy's artillery fire.

Delaying action of artillery.—To carry out the first principle the defence should be active; that is to say, any good positions well to the front of the village should be occupied at first by the guns, which should attempt to delay the enemy's advance as long as possible, prevent his artillery from posting itself within range of the village, check his reconnaissances, and force his infantry to deploy earlier than it wishes. A village is not a fortress, but the troops assigned for its defence may by their early activity and later stubbornness hold three times their own numbers engaged for a whole day, and block the road for that time at any rate. The German defence during the battle of Noisseville, when Bazaine attempted to break out of Metz, may be studied with advantage. The French advanced in great force against a thin line of defence established by the Germans, which included the villages of Failly, Poix, Servigny, and Noisseville. The movement began in the early morning, and possessed the advantage of a concentrated attack on a weak line which could only be reinforced after considerable time. The best game for the Germans was to delay their adversaries, and for this purpose ten batteries were sent forward 800 to 1,000 paces in front of Poix and Servigny. The fire of the guns sweeping the gentle slopes kept the French back; the batteries suffered severe losses, but held their ground for two precious hours, and only retired when the French skirmishers had quite outflanked them by pushing up the hollow in which Noisseville stands. The artillery line then retired in echelon without losing a single gun. During those two hours the German infantry were in peace and comfort, well out of the fire, while the French infantry were suffering that trial to the nerves caused by an advance under shell fire. In their case the stock of nervous energy was being exhausted; in that of the Germans it was being recruited. Time was gained for the advance of reinforcements hurrying up from all sides, and the result was that the French were foiled, at a sacrifice of men and horses by the artillery, it is true, but the sacrifice was wisely offered. Such lessons on a large scale are not often seen, but the principle is the same for small forces.

Therefore, *if possible, delay the enemy, and force him to show his hand, by pushing some guns out to advanced positions; but do not allow them to be lost by obstinate adherence to these positions.*

Infantry out of fire.—Secondly, during all the early stages of the fight keep the bulk of the infantry well out of fire, within or behind the village; and encourage the men to eat, smoke, and even sleep. In short, *nurse their nervous energy as long as possible*; they will want it all later on. Fussy commanders will find this difficult. They will wish to be jogging the men's elbows and exciting them. Nothing could be more fatal. Such officers have mistaken their profession. Wellington went to sleep at the critical moment of crossing the Douro. His brain had done its work, and for the time he could do nothing better than recruit his vital energy.

A few of the infantry may be needed for escort of the advanced guns. They should then retire with the guns to the prepared artillery positions on the flanks of the village, and finally join the reserve. Neither guns nor escort should retire directly on the village.

The bombardment.—When the advanced guns have retired, the next action of the enemy will be bombardment. If he is strong in artillery he will fire both at the guns of the defence, which should be well protected by emplacements, and at the village. While this action is taking place the infantry of the defence should still keep under cover, except a few sharp-shooters told off to annoy the enemy's gunners, to distract their aim, and so to delay their work of preparation for the infantry attack. Let these men and all possible observers watch for the coming of the assaulting infantry. For this purpose do not neglect the church tower, as the Austrians did at Chlum during the battle of Königgrätz in 1866.

Second Position of Defenders.

The advance of the enemy's infantry will generally be preceded by greater intensity of his artillery fire, and then a cessation of fire on the point which is to be attacked. Probably the artillery of the defence will have had to retire or to cease firing. These signs, and the reports of observers posted in commanding positions, high trees, church towers, &c., will determine the moment for the defending infantry to take its place in the shelter trenches, outside the village, where the men will be aligned—about 400 to 500 yards of frontage to 1,000 men including supports, which are to be in emplacements studded along the shooting line. As for the troops entrusted with the inner defence of the village, they should be ready to post themselves rapidly within the outer edge of houses, hedges, walls, &c., as soon as the enemy's infantry is near at hand or about to attack. Each commander of a section of the village will decide the right moment for himself, and accept complete responsibility for the defence of his section from this time forward. The fire of these inner troops from the houses,[1] combined with the fire from the shelter trenches, will probably repulse several attacks, and may check the enemy altogether.

[1] It is hardly necessary to say that, while troops in the upper stories of houses can, at this period, give valuable aid by furnishing a second or even third tier of fire, infantry posted behind low walls, hedges, or barricades, must not attempt to fire over their comrades in the shelter trenches. They must be ready to act in case the shooting line is driven in.

Inner Defence.

Isolate captured points.—But as villages are not constructed with a view to defence, there are sure to be weak points in front or flanks, and we must suppose that at some time of the day the enemy seizes one of these points, and plants his foot within the edge of the village. Then will be shown whether there has been good organisation for interior defence. The shooting line must have been driven in, at least partially. It should have retired by entrances specially prepared for it, and be now available to strengthen the interior defence by joining the inner reserve, which will be able to reinforce whatever section needs help. All now depends on preventing the enemy from pushing his advantage, and this is best done by isolating the point he has carried. Here, then, we see the value of organising each section of a village or town into sub-sections capable of being isolated from one another. Even one side of a building may be isolated from another, as shown in the siege of Saragossa before quoted; but an officer with a good tactical eye and some knowledge of fortification will easily find means of cutting his section into parts, each of which is more or less independent of the rest, and of making communications which shall be so under fire from the garrison that the defenders can retreat by them, but the attackers cannot advance without coming under fire from other houses, or walls, or street barricades.

Village enveloped.—In French and English books on fortification it is usual to speak of organising one '*line* of defence' behind another. But the recognition of the fact that attacks on villages are sure to be enveloping is very general. The later German writers meet this by organising the defence by '*sections*' rather than by lines; and the nomenclature, as well as the leading idea, is used in this book. It is awkward to learn in the midst of an action that one's 'line of defence' is turned. The anxiety is not so great when men only hear that a certain section has been entered by the enemy, if their own is still intact.

The principal keep.—It is evident that the enemy can turn

the sections if he can pass along the principal streets, and the value of a central keep commanding those streets is evident. If there is no such central position, something of the kind can be formed by barricades, and here, whatever be the nature of the post, will be the place for machine guns if any are available. The value of these weapons in the open field has been much exaggerated in popular estimation, but it is almost impossible to over-value them for street fighting, provided that they are light, manageable by hand, and so mounted that they can be taken into and out of houses without difficulty. Their place would be in the keep, and behind barricades. All writers agree that there are occasions when field guns may possibly be of supreme value during the interior fighting. At Bazeilles a house defended by the French held out stoutly for a long time. Two Bavarian guns were brought up within seventy paces of it, and the defenders were quickly driven out; but later in the day the same two guns lost nearly all their men in the attempt to repeat the success against another French post. Besides, the guns cannot be in two places at once, and they will generally be of more use outside. The general rule, liable to exceptions, should be: *Let the defenders keep their field guns outside and their machine guns inside the village.*

The outer reserve.—This reserve will be held in hand for two purposes:—

To reinforce any point which is in serious danger, or prevent an enemy's success anywhere from compromising the rest of the position.

To deliver counter-attacks, either at the moment when an assaulting force has accumulated near at hand, and is just on the verge of its advance, or when it has been repulsed. There is always a moment, when the men have come up as best they could under much suffering from fire, when they are mustering courage for the rush which they know will be fatal to many, and when their commander has made up his mind for a particular stroke: if at that moment the attackers find themselves attacked—perhaps in flank—the result is at least a complete upsetting of plans, possibly a hurried retreat. And again, when they have failed to deliver a successful stroke, and have turned their heads to fly, a sudden aggressive blow from their adversaries will act on their imagination with added power. It is the business of the chief commander to seize the right occasion and act with vigour. He will be more useful here than in fussing over details, and interfering with the responsibility of his subordinates.

We shall enter still further into details when giving examples hereafter (Chaps. IX. to XIV.), but the discussion hitherto enables us to formulate certain definite rules for the organisation of the defence.

1. Make it clearly understood by all ranks that, while every effort must be made to repulse the attacks of the enemy outside the village, the capture of the exterior line of defence, and even the entrance of the enemy within a portion of the village, need not prevent a prolonged struggle, or even a final repulse, though it is easier to keep an enemy out than to turn him out when he has gained a footing.

2. The first object to be achieved is to delay the enemy's march, and force him to deploy prematurely, by occupying advanced positions with field guns, which should not, however, remain long enough to run the risk of capture. The guns should act as if in a rearguard.

3. If the time for preparation be short, the first work should be blocking approaches by obstacles, and the construction of shelter trenches and other defences outside. All available hands should be set to clear the ground, and, at the same time, to prepare emplacements for guns on the flanks. The next work will be the preparation of the outer houses, then the communications, and the keep or keeps.

4. The outer or shooting line should be about fifty yards from the buildings, and contain cover for the supports of that line. The supports are to supply losses and strengthen points menaced by the enemy. *It is no part of the duty of this line to make serious counterstrokes.*[1] Outlying houses and

[1] This does not mean that the shooting line is never to issue from its trench. There may be times of hesitation on the part of the enemy,

farms should not be included in the defence, unless a close flanking fire from the trenches can protect them against being enveloped by the enemy. Otherwise they should be razed to the ground.

5. The shooting line of defence should be strongly occupied. If you may decide for yourself the strength of your force under average conditions, have at least one man per yard, including supports, for the shooting line; an equal force for the garrison; and again the same number for the exterior reserve. If a less number is available, subtract rather from the garrison first, then from the outer reserve, leaving the shooting line strong.[1]

6. The inner defence should be organised on the following principles:—

Complete preparation of strongest houses for prolonged defence one after another, in flank and rear, as well as in front.

Division of the village into definite sections, each under a separate command; the officers commanding to have full responsibility, and arrange for their own house-garrisons, communications, reserves, and minor keep, if they have suitable buildings.

Organisation as far as possible of a central reserve under separate command. This inner reserve should hold the main keep, give instantaneous support at weak points, man barricades in the principal streets, and sweep those streets with the fire of machine guns or musketry. It has nothing to do with the shooting line outside, or with the enemy be-

when the shooting line might leap up with a cheer and decide the affair for the moment by a short charge. But even this is rather risky, and in no case should the shooting line pursue.

[1] *The Text-book for Woolwich* gives only two men per yard altogether including reserve, but does not contemplate a shelter trench outside. The French, two to three men per metre without reserves. German writers even higher numbers of men. Captain Thival (French) gives two men per metre if the village is organised and supported in rear, three if it is not. Clearly much must depend on circumstances. The proportion given in the text above may be considered as an average garrison for prolonged defence.

fore he penetrates. In fact, the inner reserve may well be formed of part of the troops which have been driven back from the shooting line.

Arrangement of communications, *not by the streets*. The enemy may know the form of the village itself. He should not know your artificial communications.

Great care to be taken that every man should know his own place under different conditions of the fight. For this purpose, if there is time, practise the troops in occupying the different posts, and moving by the artificial communications, along which guides should be posted at intervals. Every officer should understand the complete plan of defence. Whatever may be the chances of keeping troops under one hand in a general action, there is none whatever in village fighting.

7. The outer reserve will be kept out of the village, under cover, at first; and the officer in command of the whole force should be with it as soon as the enemy's infantry begins the attack. On him lies the duty of deciding when and how to make counter-attacks, and which of the demands for assistance that he will surely receive should be granted. He should beware of committing the reserve to interior work unless it is absolutely necessary, for, while inferior numbers can hold out long against superior within a village, there is hardly any limit to the number which may be swallowed up either in attack or defence. And troops once committed to interior defence can hardly be withdrawn without danger of leaving some points undefended.

Each case will present its own chances, but the two principal opportunities for counter-attack[1] are—

The critical moment when the attacking troops are screwing themselves up for the assault.

[1] The author, after reading a paper on Modern Tactics at the Royal United Service Institution, was criticised because he did not lay down as a fixed principle at what stage of a fight counter-attacks should be delivered. It would be as easy to say how all cases should be argued in a court of law, or all books written, or all pictures painted, or games of chess played. Let officers acquire the spirit of tactics and then act in accordance with circumstances, as they certainly will in accordance with their own individual characters.

The moment when the assault has failed of full success, and the attackers begin to look behind them to see the way out of their difficulties.

If the commander fails to avail himself of the first of these opportunities, the second may never come, because the assault may succeed. Above all let him attack, if possible, unexpectedly.

8. As a general rule, keep the infantry out of all danger till the men are required for their own work, and take care that they go to that work well nourished, warm, and rested. The cellars, &c., of the houses are commonly used as safe resting-places during the bombardment, but in that case great care must be taken that the enemy does not capture the men there by a sudden success over the shooting line. Remember that he will keep up the bombardment till the last possible moment.

9. The technical part of the preparations will include most of the various forms of artificial defences referred to in previous chapters. The clearing of ground will furnish materials for abatis and the rest. Bear clearly in mind the main principles which govern all defence.

First, increase the effect of your own fire.

Second, decrease that of the enemy.

You will increase the effect of your own fire if it is delivered by men in good heart, at least partially protected, resting their rifles on low parapets, loopholes, &c., perfectly knowing the range of various points which the enemy must pass, firing here and there in more than one tier, having free communication along their lines and with the rear, and able to concentrate their fire against broken-up parts of the enemy's formation.

You will decrease that of the enemy by forcing him to advance over open ground, and to stand, checked by obstacles, under your full fire. Your preparation of the ground should leave him no cover from your fire, but retain such hedges and walls radiating from your position as to embarrass his movements, prevent free communication, and forbid his making a concentrated attack on any part of your position. Force him,

DEFENCE OF VILLAGES. 107

if you can, to disperse his troops when assaulting. It is at that moment that masses tell.

Each case must have its own measures. For instance, if there are woods close to the village, you have to take care that they do not furnish cover to the enemy. If you are not strong enough to hold the far edge of the wood, at least hold the near edge and clear a zone in front of it. Of all forms of obstacles wire entanglements are probably the best. You must do something with trees cut down; they will form palisades or abatis. Low walls will of course come into the shooting line if there are such available, and hedges prepared for defence. Make the ground in front of the line as smooth as possible, placing your abatis in hollows if you can. In short, do everything to make your own fire free and to embarrass that of the enemy, but do not forget that solid means of defence, such as walls or banks of earth, may be turned to the advantage of the enemy when the first line is carried unless they are flanked or overlooked by the houses behind them. It may be better to decrease your own cover in the shooting line rather than allow the enemy cover when that line is carried. Walls have also the objectionable feature of splintering under the fire of artillery.

10. All the usual measures will be taken against fire,[1] and for the provision of everything required. Intelligent men should be selected to carry messages and orders by the artificial communications. The provision of ammunition should be lavish. There should be a distinct plan for firing the village if it can no longer be held.

11. If there are specially important points on the line of retreat or lines of communication, such as bridges, let them be occupied strongly by parties with orders to hold them till they receive permission to withdraw. Do not give these parties any other task, or they might be out of the way when wanted for their own work. You cannot define responsibility too closely, or be too careful not to interfere with arrangements when once made.

---

[1] Nothing is more important; many a village has been lost from this precaution not having been taken.

CHAPTER IX.

DEVELOPMENTS OF DEFENCE OF VILLAGES—QUESTION OF REDOUBTS.

Different cases arranged under three headings—First, to cover detachments—Second, advanced posts in the field—Third, posts in the line of battle on front or flanks—These cases detailed—Opinions of Frederick the Great—General Brialmont's opinions—The three cases considered as to their treatment—Special differences—Illustrations from wars — Necessity for information — Typical cases considered (Plates)—Treatment of defences with regard to nature of village—Front defences—Flank defences—Rear of village—Supplementary defences—Spaces—Freedom for counter attack—Barricades—Supports to outer line—Interior reserve—Keep—Defence of houses—Exterior reserve—Retreat of shooting line—Counter attack—Prolongation of front—Same details in other typical case—Notes to General Brialmont's remarks—The question of redoubts: their use and abuse, and whether they should be occupied by both infantry and artillery, discussed in conversation between A. and B.—Summary of opinion—New type of British redoubt.

(Plate XVI.)

HAVING given in the two preceding chapters general ideas on the defence of villages and the details in a general way, it is now time to distinguish between different cases; and here it seems that almost all conceivable cases may be grouped under one or other of the three following headings:—

CASES FOR DEFENSIVE POSTS.

1. *To cover detachments.*—This includes all posts established out of cannon range of an army, whatever the reason may be—either to extend the action of the army, to give warning

of the enemy's approach, to stop his advance for some time, especially on the flanks, or to hold an important communication. Other objects for detached posts may perhaps occur to the reader of military history.

Under this heading may be placed the various substitutes for regular closed works in such cases as protecting a line of operations or depôt of provisions, arms, and ammunition, or out of the way on the flanks of an army, or to protect cantonments, or to hold permanently the passage of a river.

In all these cases the post is left to its own resources for defence, and according to the amount of time it is required to hold out, so must the art of the engineer be applied to it. It will be closed all round and treated in every respect as if it were a fortress. Shelter trenches may be developed into field works and forts erected. There is no limit to the work which may be applied to them, except the amount of garrison available.

2. *Advanced posts in the field.*—These include all such posts as are established in front of a position, within a few hundred yards of and protected by the troops of the main body. Their purpose is to hinder the enemy's reconnaissances, to delay his attack, especially on the flanks, to menace the flanks of his attacking columns, or even for the minor purpose of bringing under fire some slope or watercourse not commanded from the main position, or to occupy a hill so that the enemy may not seize it and turn it to the disadvantage of the defenders. Such cases are very numerous. The farms of Hugoumont and La Haie Sainte at Waterloo may be noted as instances, and that of St. Hubert at Gravelotte.

3. *Posts in the line of battle.*—These may be either part of the general front or on the flanks. They are generally called pivots, because troops may rest their flanks on them though changing front into new directions. St. Privat was such a post as this, and there are few great battles in which some village or other is not so used. In old wars it was considered bad tactics to fight without having one or both flanks resting on such posts. The result was a growing

immobility of armies. One great general after another acted on this knowledge, and used his own mobility by neglecting a great part of such positions and bringing the main force to bear against one point, driving in the flank or line there, and afterwards capturing the village or whatever it might be at his leisure. General de Brialmont quotes this as a reason for having only small garrisons in villages, lest they should be surrounded and captured. Certainly the garrison should not be unnecessarily large, and posts in the front line will not require such large garrisons as those on the flank. But the main consideration for the defenders is to win, and the later method of defending villages outside at first requires more men ; while, on the other hand, such posts should be able to hold out longer.

The chief lesson to be learnt from such successes as those of Marlborough and Frederick the Great is that armies, even on the defensive, should be as mobile as possible, and, while resting on strong pivots, put their faith rather in counter attack than in pure defence. At the battle of Kolin Frederick's flank march and attack in oblique order miscarried to a certain extent, but the main failure took place on the Austrian right, where the village of Kreczor resisted so stoutly that Hülsen required almost all his power to take it ; and he failed to carry an oak wood, which was the real flank of the position. The wood held out against Ziethen, with 10,000 cavalry and two battalions of infantry, because the Austrians had four battalions in it beside Croats.

Frederick always spoke against entrenched positions because he had confidence in his power of handling a mobile army ; yet, when weak in numbers during the campaign of 1761, he formed an entrenched camp at Bunzelwitz for the defence of Schweidnitz, and the united Austrians and Russians feared to attack him there. It is unfortunate that we have no example of an active defence by his master hand, but the battle of Rossbach may give us some idea of what he might have done. His genius would have led him to deliver some grand counterstroke, using his fortified posts as pivots and stalking-horses. It is the inactivity of an army in defensive positions which causes posts to be lost, and this is the great danger of all fortified positions. They conduce to inactivity. It is important to understand this. Frederick wrote,—

'Our principle being to attack, and not to defend, we should not garrison such posts (country seats, cemeteries, &c.) except when they are in front of the line or the flanks. They then protect the attack of our troops, and hamper the enemy during the battle.'

This only means that, as the Prussians would not remain in their first position, it would be of no use to fortify it; but posts in front would help the army in its manœuvres. For instance, Frederick would not have shut himself up in Plevna, or, if there because of exhaustion, would have taken an opportunity for marching against a weak point in the enemy's lines. It is also to be remembered that the villages among which he fought were wretched constructions of wood and thatch, easily set on fire. Besides the case given above, Frederick used entrenched camps at Neudorf in 1741, Czaslau in 1742, Schweidnitz in 1745, but these were all before his most brilliant period.

General Brialmont considers defensive villages as hurtful to the army taking the offensive, and even on the defensive prefers in many cases such buildings as we have classed under the head of farms to the best village. But he qualifies his assertion by requiring that they should have 'a free field of fire, secure communications with the main body, buildings not liable to catch fire, enclosures and entrances easy to defend, a solid building for a keep on the side away from the enemy, and, finally, be not much exposed to the long range fire of artillery.' The preparation of such a post for defence requires little time and men, and the enemy must master it before attacking the line of battle as certainly as if it were a fortified village; yet he adds a little further on that in future such posts will always be rendered untenable by a concentrated fire of guns.

We would here remark that in most battles, even offensive, some portion of the army will want to refuse itself, and this can best be done *behind* fortified villages, while posts of some sort must fall within the line of battle. Since they are there they should be made use of in either position.

Case 1.—To Cover Detachments.

According to the position of the detachment and the time available must be the amount of work done. For instance, if a flank has to be defended by holding in the first place a village through which a turning force must pass, as that of Chenebier on General Von Werder's right flank when covering the siege of Belfort in 1871, there will be a detachment of the three arms unsupported, and the defences must be closed except such passages as are required for final retreat. In such a case the amount of work will only be limited by what is possible, and special attention must be paid to the flanks. In the case of a depôt on the line of communication there will be danger of attack anywhere, and the whole must be made self-supporting. Skilled engineers should therefore be called in; but the principles will be those given in the preceding chapter, the works to be developed if there is time by redoubts in the shooting line, or even by detached redoubts. In this case it is allowable to place guns within the defences. They stand or fall with the garrison.

Case 2.—Advanced Posts in the Field.

Here we have, by definition, the power of supporting such posts by the artillery of the general line. The chief feature is, therefore, that the flanks of the post will be well swept by fire, and should be as free as possible from all that would conceal an enemy after the capture of the village or farm, and the rear should as a rule be left open, both to facilitate retreat and to make the place untenable by the enemy if he carries it. Closed redoubts should be avoided for this reason, and means should be accumulated for burning the village unless the smoke would blow back on the main body of the defenders. Generally speaking, such posts have to be prepared hastily. The first part to be prepared is that which fronts towards the enemy, by barricading roads, and preparing enclosures. Later, if there is time and no fear of presenting fatigued men to a fresh enemy, abatis and shelter trenches may be constructed, and the rest of the arrangements already described may be carried out. The artillery will be advanced temporarily from the main body, and, as usual, retire on the flanks, taking care that no works shall be built for it which could later afford cover for the enemy.

Remark that in this case development of frontal fire is most important, and the flanks may be left weaker than in the first case. Great care must be taken to leave the rear open for retreat.

It will often be that villages in this position will need little more than barricading roads and organising the houses and streets.

Case 3.—Posts in the Line of Battle.

These may be again divided into two :
    A. Posts in the front line.
    B. Posts on the flanks.

A. *Posts in the front line.*—These may be treated in a similar manner to those in Case 2, only the defence of their flanks will be confided to the second line of the army.

B. *Posts on the flanks.*—In this case the probability of a flank attack by the enemy has to be provided against, and such a flank attack is sure to be enveloping. It is, therefore, necessary to close the village or whatever it may be completely, and to develop the defences on the outer flank.

Here we have one of those instances in which defence pure and simple becomes not only right, but necessary. The force holding the post is of comparatively little importance so long as it succeeds in holding it. Offensive returns (counter attacks) must be provided for by the masses of troops outside, and the post should continue its defence even if the enemy has succeeded in surrounding it. There may come a moment later on when it will be of the utmost importance whether such a post remains in friendly hands, and troops driven in upon the flank of their own army are not only useless but hurtful, for they cause confusion among the reserves, who are trying to restore the fortune of the day.

On this subject the battles of the Seven Years' War are particularly instructive, especially those of Prague, Leuthen, and Kolin. In the first Frederick made a flank march and attacked the right of the Austrians, which stood slightly thrown back from the rest of the line. It was driven in, and great confusion ensued, followed by the loss of the battle by the army on the defensive.

At Leuthen the same fate overtook the Austrian left flank, again leading to a terrible crush and utter disaster. 'The troops could not deploy, and stood from 30 to 100 deep, played upon by case-shot from the guns, and by the fire of Prussian infantry at close quarters.'[1] There is hardly any worse case for troops than being thus piled together in a mass, and the defenders of a post will be better employed in continuing to hamper the advance of an enemy than in helping to swell such confusion.

At Kolin, as has already been said, the defence of a wood on the Austrian right flank saved the day at a critical moment, and in the end, conjoined with other causes, led to the defeat of Frederick.

General Brialmont puts the other side of the question, and dreads the loss to the defenders of so many men if a post is strongly occupied. But it cannot be stated too often that the main idea of a general should be to win a battle, and that less men will be lost in a captured village—supposing only a strong garrison to be present—than in the retreat of a beaten army. Attacks in flank will now be the rule rather than the exception, and it is most important that posts arranged there for defence should hold out with tenacity, so as to give time for the general in chief command to design and carry out new

---

[1] *Military Biographies,*—' Frederick the Great,' by Colonel C. B. Brackenbury.

manœuvres. *The garrison of a post on the flanks should therefore be exceptionally strong, and the defence tenacious, from house to house if necessary.*

But the enemy may march completely round the village unless prevented. Therefore the line of defence should be thrown back at an angle and occupied by guns, which should be covered as far as possible from the first bombardment of the enemy. If they are driven in by a turning movement, they should retire to another position selected beforehand, whence they can flank the village and defend its rear. General de Brialmont would place these guns in redoubts, but reasons have already been given why guns are out of place there except in detached positions. One of the most useful faculties of field artillery would be lost—namely, mobility. We are not speaking of strong works for permanent, or at least long defence, but of a position taken up by an army in which to fight a battle.

We have then a post—say a village—fully closed, garrisoned, and prepared as explained in Chapter VIII., with further positions thrown back from its outer flank. But this system should be placed beyond reach of rapid attack, not to say surprise. If the country is easy and open, completely traversable by troops of the three arms, detachments should be thrown well out to front and flanks to watch for and report any turning movement on the part of the enemy. If, on the contrary, the approaches are narrow and difficult, each one should be occupied by a small post well in advance and to the flank of the main position. These will fall under Case 1 (page 112). Under any circumstances cavalry will be needed as scouts pushed well out, and in favourable country advanced guns will be useful to delay the enemy and force him to deploy prematurely.

With regard to the works to be carried on in preparing the village, destroy bridges near at hand, barricade roads outside and inside, create a shelter trench outside, and organise the whole village completely. Remember that if the enemy knows his business he will bring up many guns for the first bombardment, during which the garrison both of trench and village should be held back out of fire. You have also to provide against the post being set on fire by shells. Abatis and, if possible, inundations should certainly be used, and fougasses in front of barricades, &c., where the enemy must be held in check for a while. Inner lines or keeps will be especially useful, because they are not so much exposed to destruction by the enemy's artillery fire.

TYPICAL CASES.

It may now be interesting to the student to give two typical forms taken from the work of the most renowned engineer of the day—General Brialmont, 'La Fortification du Champ de Bataille.' And if some criticisms are appended in the form of notes, it is to be understood that General de Brialmont treats the question from the point of a great engineer who has at his command all the means and engineering talent required, rather than according to the ideas of this book, which is intended more for the use of the other arms of the service, and even militia and volunteers. For instance, the Belgian engineer makes free use of redoubts when, by the nature of our studies, we cannot contemplate anything which requires heavy working parties at particular points, and plenty of engineer officers and men.

General Brialmont considers two cases which, he believes, contain within themselves the assistance required by the student for nearly all instances (Plate XVI., Figs. 2 and 3). His explanations which follow are given in nearly his own words.

First Case.—Plate XVI., Fig. 2.

A village situated in a plain. The villages which cover the front of an army often meet this case.

Nature of village.—The village which has to be fortified stands on ground nearly level. It has great length in the direction of the road A, perpendicularly to the line of battle, and its flanks have no solid combinations or walled enclosures which could serve as elements in a part of the *enceinte.* Between x and y the buildings are fewer; those which exist should be burnt or demolished, so as to diminish the extent that has to be occupied, and to clear a zone open to the action of musketry fire and case.

Front defences.—The road A will be enfiladed beyond the point Y, and the flanks of the small group of houses, &c., Y Z, will be swept by means of redoubts[1] 1 and 2. Between these redoubts a trench will be constructed. In the centre of this trench a battery for four guns[2] will be built, with the object of defending the front of the village conjointly with the artillery of the two redoubts (1 and 2). Redoubt 1 enfilades the road D, and redoubt 2 covers with oblique fire the road C.

Defence of right flank.—The right flank will be protected by the line of defence 7, 8, 9, with zigzag trace.

Defence of left flank.—The left flank being covered by a small wood of well-grown trees, a line of abatis should be established.[3] It will be watched and defended by the infantry in the redans 3 and 4. Care must be taken to leave a free space of at least a hundred yards between that line and the interior edge of the wood to facilitate the movements of troops and the play of musketry.

Rear of village.—The rear of the village will remain open.

Supplementary defences.—If there are not, in the line of

---

[1] The redoubts supposed to be used are 'closed,' that is, defended in rear by a parapet and ditch with a mere opening for entry and exit of the garrison—that opening to be well guarded. For the question of the use of redoubts see the latter part of this chapter.

[2] I cannot agree that this is a place for guns. Houses are left standing in front of them at less than 150 yards. Those houses would interrupt their field of fire when the enemy is still distant, and when he is near the guns would be exposed at very short range to the fire of individual riflemen under cover. Every round fired by the enemy's artillery against them would strike the village somewhere. The guns would be better placed well forward at first, then retiring to a position on a flank. For the question of guns in redoubts see the latter part of this chapter.

[3] Unless it is supposed that the greater part of the wood has been cut down for abatis, its outer edge should be occupied.

battle, redoubts and batteries which thoroughly protect the flanks and gorge of the village, redoubts 5 and 6 should be constructed, and an epaulment established at F to enfilade with two or three guns the road A, which is the chief exit from the village. These redoubts and the battery F will form besides excellent supports for the exterior reserve, destined to arrest the enemy when attempting to issue from the village.[1]

Space behind outer line.—In order that the defence of the trenches and redoubts which compose the exterior line of defence should be efficacious, there must be a free space between these works and the agglomeration formed by the houses, hedges, and other enclosures.

Freedom for counter attack.—It is necessary to satisfy the important condition of not hampering the march of the columns when it becomes necessary to take the offensive. For this purpose the road A, which debouches on the head of the village, and the road D, which debouches on the right flank, may be left free. As for the road C, which debouches on the left, it can be reached, without traversing the village, by passing along the line of abatis.

Barricades.—All the communications, except roads A, B, and D, will be barricaded.

Supports to outer line.—To reinforce when necessary the shooting line in trenches or retrenchments, supports must be placed *in the trenches*, or behind the first houses and walls of the enclosures situated in proximity to the points where those supports are to go in case of attack.[2] The retreat of the supports will be facilitated by opening communications across hedges and enclosures, as shown in the plan by dotted lines. These communications should lead to the position of the interior reserve.

Interior reserve.—In large villages the interior reserve will be divided into parts.[3] In the present case it will occupy the

[1] See latter part of this chapter for question of redoubts.

[2] Better *in* the trenches when the enemy approaches to assault, but not distributed at first.

[3] And partly assigned to the sections into which the village will be divided.

cemetery of the church *b* and the open space *c* outside that building.

The keep.—The walls of the cemetery will be loopholed, and in the left angle will be placed two pieces of artillery,[1] to enfilade a part of the road A. The church will be put in a state of defence. When it has to be evacuated, the troops which occupy it will retire by the road B, in order not to mask the fire of the battery *f* enfilading the road A.

Defence of houses.—In order to arrest the enemy as long as possible in the principal street, the most solid houses should be occupied by infantry, and a quantity of material should be accumulated close to them in order to form barricades rapidly.

Exterior reserve.—This, composed of three battalions of infantry and four squadrons of cavalry, will establish a part of its force behind the village and a part behind the little wood.

Retreat of the shooting line.—When the troops occupying the trenches can resist no longer, they will retire behind the hedges and enclosures which form the outer defences of the village itself, and there, joined by their supports,[2] make further resistance, retiring finally by communications through the farms, and joining the inner reserve, which will defend itself post by post with the greatest obstinacy.

Counter Attack.—The outer reserve will intervene at this moment,[3] either to repulse the troops which will attack the redoubt, or to arrest the columns debouching from the village, or to attack in flank those which endeavour to turn it.

Prolongation of Front.—If it is considered advisable to increase the importance of the frontal fire, the head of the village will be widened by the shelter trenches *i k* and *l m*, or even trenches for riflemen may be constructed in front of the redoubts.

[1] Again artillery doubtful, but machine guns very useful.
[2] The supports should have already fought in the shooting line.
[3] This seems a little late, but better late than never.

Second Case.—Plate XVI., Fig. 2.

A village traversed by a stream of water, and commanded on the enemy's side by dangerous heights. To this category belong sometimes the villages which serve to strengthen the flanks of an army, and those which form the outer line of winter quarters and cantonments.

Nature of village.—Let us suppose that it is required to prepare a village traversed by a stream, which forms the line of defence to winter quarters. The ground beyond the stream rises steeply to the plateau M N, which commands the group of buildings.

First principle.—It will be recognised at once that no defence of the village is possible unless the plateau is strongly occupied.

Works on plateau.—Redoubts 1 and 2 [1] will be constructed with their faces so disposed as to cover with their fire roads A and B and the slopes of the ground. The trees bordering the roads will be cut down and used to form a line of abatis, the approach to which will be defended by redoubts, and entrenchments between the redoubts.

Right flank.—The right of the village will be covered by a trench, 7, 8, 9, 10. The branch 7-8 [2] will receive three or four guns, to play upon the declivity of ground on the left of the road B. After the salient at 7 the trench traverses the valley of the stream. At the point h a dam produces an inundation up to the contours 4·00, and makes the road C impracticable.

Left flank.—The left of the village will be protected by similar entrenchments. On account of the importance of road D, and to bring under fire that road and the crest of the plateau to the left of redoubt 2, [3] another redoubt, No. 3, will be constructed. To right and left of redoubt 3 a line of

---

[1] See discussion of redoubts later on in this chapter.

[2] Would not these guns be better placed behind the inundation? The difference in range would only be about 150 yards, and they could hold their ground much longer.

[3] See discussion of redoubts later on in this chapter.

abatis will be formed with trees cut from the small wood near at hand. This line will be flanked by redoubts 3 and 4.

Defence of gorge.—Redoubts 4 and 5, and the trenches *r s t* which unite them, will defend the gorge of the village. Though the portion situated beyond the stream is the more exposed, yet, because the army is far off, the enemy might send one of his columns to the other side to attack the gorge, while the bulk of his force was directed against redoubts 1 and 2. For this reason the gorge must be entrenched with as much care as the flanks.

Communications.—The usual communications for the retirement of the shooting line and defenders of the first houses will be made; but there is a marked difference as to the general communications between Case 1 and Case 2. In Case 1 the village, being in the front of a line of battle, should be covered by a line of works with large intervals, which render easy the exit and entry of columns. For the same reason the principal streets remain open. In Case 2, where the village is occupied by a detached part which is intended to dispute the ground as long as possible, the same precautions are not needed. The most exposed parts will be covered by a continuous line of obstacles, and all the streets will be barricaded. Openings should only be left at the part where succour might arrive.

Keep.—The choice of the keep requires some remarks. The church, *b*, is too near the point of attack to constitute a good redoubt. The town hall, situated in the market-place, *c*, would be more suitable, but it would fail to command the two bridges which are necessary for the defence. It is therefore preferable to prepare the factory *d*, which commands one of the bridges, and the group of houses *i i*, which commands the other.[1]

Even then, if the enemy, as must be expected, has artillery to support his attack, these two posts cannot resist long. Therefore it is proposed to create a redoubt, stronger and

---

[1] If the village is divided into sections, the church and town hall will form the keeps of two sections.

easier to defend, by uniting redoubts 4 and 5 with a retrenchment, *u v w*, commanding the interior of the village.

After giving these two cases, General Brialmont proceeds to remark that they would undergo important modifications if villages had to be fortified which, as in the suburbs of Paris (or commonly in England), have close to them country seats and parks surrounded by strong walls. In that case such buildings, when situated on the flanks or in the rear of the village, would be used as part of the main defences, because they are least exposed to the enemy's artillery fire. These defences would be connected and strengthened by trenches and abatis; and only those buildings would be absolutely given up as useless which are situated in full front of the village, where, General Brialmont thinks, earth entrenchments supported by redoubts should be used exclusively.

The Question of Redoubts.

The question of the use of redoubts has been much discussed of late years, and perhaps the best way of putting it is by imagining a conversation between two officers who may be called A. and B.

A speaks. Let us first, as skilled soldiers, agree to clear the ground in front of our positions, and I hope we may find that in so doing we shall soon be able to come to decisive opinions, even though we may agree to differ in the end.

B speaks. Willingly. If you will be so good as to begin, I will call a halt when I can go no further with you.

A. Well, then, we probably agree that most of the old systems of lines, with their angles, their bastions, and their curtains, and even the later modifications of these—in short, the proposals of such writers as Rogniat, Laisné, and De Pidoll—are not suitable for the present day.

B. Agreed; I will even go further, and say that a simple shelter trench as nearly as possible fronting the enemy with guns at commanding points would form a better defence in our days of breechloaders than any of these elaborate systems based on the idea of a bastioned trace, which is now as dead as Queen Anne.

A. May we also take for granted that the frontal fire of good infantry, partly covered and resting their rifles on something which steadies them, requires no flanking so long as the enemy cannot approach without being seen?

B. Agreed.

A. And that artillery can defend its own front against infantry advancing from a distance, provided the ground be open?

B. Yes. It is only in England that the fact is ever disputed, probably because they have never known what it is to be under the fire of a line of rifled guns well served, nor have they ever used in action more than a battery or two of rifled guns at a time against troops in the open field.

A. It follows, then, does it not, that, provided we can strengthen its flanks sufficiently, a straight line of infantry and artillery can make itself practically invulnerable to frontal attack over open country in a few minutes?

B. Yes, provided you can find ground really open.

A. Now we begin to approach points of contention. Will you admit that one of the special features of field artillery is its mobility, and that we should beware of sacrificing freedom of movement unless for some great and unquestionable advantage?

B. Admitted without demur, provided you admit also that a 'great and unquestionable advantage' the other way may be stronger than the advantage of mobility. For instance, in a fortress the guns have not much mobility.

A. Quite so, but we are talking of armies in the field, not of fortresses.

B. But field forts or redoubts are of the same nature as fortresses.

A. That is why I am inclined to object to their general use.

B. To bring us closer still, I will give up the forts with their flank defence, but I cannot give up redoubts. They would be of great value in covering the front and flanks of a line of battle.

A. Before discussing that point please give me your ideas as to what the redoubts should be exactly.

B. The first of all considerations is that they should be closed works, because otherwise an enemy who had penetrated the general line could carry them easily at the gorge, and it is just when such penetration has occurred that redoubts are most required to fire at the enemy in flank and rear.

A. Pardon me for interrupting you for a moment, but is it not a little dangerous to fire rearwards, considering that the range and power of modern weapons might cause them to do the same damage to your own troops which they are expected to do to an enemy's supports and reserves?

B. There is something in your objection, but at least the flanking fire remains, and that has great effect. But to resume my ideas on redoubts. They should be of considerable size, to hold not less than half a battalion; they should be as flat as possible in outline, so as to give a heavy frontal fire; and I disagree with those modern tacticians whom I admit to be a majority, and whose opinion is that artillery should not be placed in redoubts.

A. If redoubts are to be freely used I agree that they should be large, although by that means you seem to shut up many troops who will all be captured unless the army rolls back the attack before long, and the redoubts will soon become useless if the retreat is rapid. For that reason I should use them very sparingly, to avoid locking troops up in works which, if carried by a rush, are not only completely lost with their garrisons, but become capable of strengthening the enemy against a counter attack. I agree in objecting to sharp angles, but I am at one with the majority of modern tacticians in desiring to keep the guns outside except in rare cases. And first, with regard to the general use of redoubts, I hold that they present themselves as special features on which the enemy can concentrate his attention, and that unless much time and trouble can be taken to establish bomb-proof cover, a long range artillery fire will render them untenable. When Plevna is quoted, which was not a line of battle but a fortified camp with works all round, held by an army more numerous at first than that of the Russians, people forget with what comparative ease other Turkish redoubts were carried. At the very beginning of the war the Shipka works fell after a comparatively feeble defence, and towards the end Skobeleff stormed the entrenched camp at the foot of that pass, even without a previous bombardment. In Asia positions were captured by assault continually. Kars fell to a night attack, and if Plevna resisted long on account of its favourable situation and gallant defence, the works on the road to Sofia were captured by General Gourko. Gorni-Dubnik had four redoubts armed with guns; they were carried by assault. Telisch, again, was occupied by from 4,000 to 5,000 Turks and three guns. The Russians brought 72 guns to bear on it, and the garrison capitulated. Another fortified position at Dolni Dubnik, after two hours' bombardment, was abandoned by the troops which occupied it; and if Plevna itself held out, it was only because it was made into a closed series of strong works which shut the Turks in a trap, and caused their final capitulation. It is true that they held out longer than Mack at Ulm, but his fate was theirs at last. The point is that if you fortify an army with redoubts and so on, you destroy its mobility. Unless your redoubts and lines are tremendously strong they will fall to bombardment or assault, or the enemy will turn your position. If you encircle yourself, as at Plevna, you may resist longer, but your whole army will at last be taken prisoners.

B. But surely your argument would go to prove more than you wish. If you object to a free use of redoubts on an ordinary battle-field, how can you accept the preparation of posts as part of your programme?

A. To begin with, the farms, villages, and so forth are there, and half an hour's work makes them begin to be defensible; while redoubts, to be really strong, require hard work for some days. Feeble redoubts are quite useless. Shelter trenches with no pretension would be better. Then to fortify a position is to anchor your army instead of keeping it mobile, and you leave all the initiative to the enemy. Frederick marched on such positions and attacked their flanks obliquely. Napoleon sometimes produced his moral effects by sending a corps or division in rear; but all great generals have chosen the part of aggression if they felt at all strong enough. The whole moral tone is altered if you sit down and fortify. But, as I said before, the villages and houses are there, they give comfortable quarters to the troops at all times, and if you don't use them the enemy will.

But I admit that there are cases for redoubts, such as lines covering a capital and with flanks secured, or possibly to defend the flanks or one flank of an army; in short, wherever permanent fortifications would be useful if you had time to construct them. For instance, if England were invaded or likely to be invaded, London ought to be surrounded by a chain of redoubts to save it from a *coup de main*; but if the whole system of defence were based on defensive positions and field redoubts instead of a mobile army manœuvring in the field, I should consider the game as good as lost.

B. Perhaps we do not differ so much as you think. We will sum up this branch of the question afterwards. Meanwhile I understand you to object to placing field artillery in redoubts where such exist. Will you say why?

A. The first objection is that the action of the two arms is different, and that when one is at its best, relatively, the other is at its worst, so that to bind the two always together is to sacrifice one to the other at all ranges.

B. But you will admit that if the artillery has overhead cover, it also can work with effect at short ranges?

A. Certainly; but, at close range, infantry occupying the same space would deliver quite as telling a fire, and would be better able to repel assault by mounting on the parapet.

B. We have our inner reserve for the hand-to-hand work.

A. Yes, but if infantry will do as well, why take the guns from their movable work? They cannot fire when the infantry is on the parapet in front of them, and might be of much more use a thousand yards off on the flank crushing the enemy's supports and reserves. And at least you will allow that, at long range, the infantry will be suffering unnecessarily from the fire drawn on them by the action of the artillery.

B. I do not propose that the artillery in the redoubts should engage the enemy at long range, but only when he is near and the infantry is engaged.

A. Then you lose all those guns in the redoubts for the early combat of the artillery lines. You will perhaps say that a few guns matter little, but I am of a different opinion. If once you allow the enemy's artillery to have a distinct preponderance over yours, you are in a fair way to lose the position. And in that artillery combat every gun tells. Thus you are sacrificing artillery power at the early stages for a very doubtful advantage at short range.

B. Surely you admit the moral support which guns furnish to infantry? I have heard you say that they serve to anchor the infantry.

A. True, but the infantry are here anchored by the redoubt, and would be better pleased to see the artillery fire flanking them and sweeping the enemy from the front at the most critical moment, than to find the guns ceasing fire during the assault.

Another point I wish to make is that, though the fire of an artillery line is terrific, the action of three or four guns, or even a battery of six, is comparatively insignificant, and produces very slight effect. The same guns joined to a mass outside would be of far more service. Or if the particular spot is small, and you wish to occupy it with artillery, then I should say place your guns in a special battery, and let them be protected by infantry outside, in shelter trenches or rifle pits.

B. It is part of my design that if there is to be any long range firing of the artillery, the infantry will for that time be outside, as you say, but return to repel the final assault.

A. It will not have a very good moral effect on them to watch the redoubt suffering from a concentrated fire of shells, and then be called to retire from their own lines and enter that dangerous place. If you keep them in rear it would be different, but I would far rather have emplacements for the guns; let them take their share of knocking about, and then, at the critical moment, bring the infantry up, not into the gun emplacements, but on the flanks, or even in front, provided they do not mask the guns. By this means the fire will be turned away from the artillery, and if the affair is evidently lost it will have a chance of getting away to take up another position and protect the retreat of the infantry. If it is in a redoubt with the infantry, it can never get away at all.

B. I think there is not much more to be said on the subject, or at least we have skimmed the cream of the controversy. We are fairly agreed that redoubts may be abused, but that there are certain uses for them, and that artillery should only be placed in them occasionally. General Brialmont, who is the great advocate for the double occupation, against the general opinion of tacticians, states certain cases in which artillery may occupy redoubts with infantry. Shall I give them?

A. Yes, please; state them one by one, and I will see if I agree.

B. First—'When the redoubt occupies an important point near which artillery cannot find a suitable position for its batteries.'

A. If there is a redoubt and artillery ought to be on the spot, and cannot be anywhere else near at hand! Why, that is as much as to say, 'If artillery absolutely must be there, then it must;' but the great engineer would still have to show that the infantry must be there, and nowhere else.

B. Second—'When it serves as support to the flank of a position, and can see clearly the ground over which the enemy must advance to attack or turn that flank.'

A. Again an excellent reason for artillery being at that spot, but no proof whatever that infantry should be in the same work.

B. Third—'When the redoubt is established in rear or on the flank of an important village which has to be defended foot by foot.' And General Brialmont explains, 'In the last case, if the redoubts only contained infantry, they could neither hinder the enemy traversing the village nor establishing himself there. The presence of two or three guns in a closed work will then oblige the assailant to carry that work before going further, which will augment the difficulties and duration of the action.'

A. Here I am agreed. The redoubt will not be exposed to long-range bombardment, and the whole defence is of the same nature as that of a fortress on a small scale. There is here no question of manœuvres, and the artillery which must stand or fall with the place will not suffer by being shut up.

B. Fourth—'When a redoubt has to be established far from the line of battle, either to command a fold of ground or an important approach, or else to guard a defile, or perhaps to flank a slope which the enemy's troops must pass over before attacking the position.'

A. Should such a case occur, and guns are required for the purpose, they should be placed in a work and protected by infantry; but I should be sorry to say that I see any special reason here why infantry must necessarily be within the same redoubt as the guns. In many cases the best spot for the artillery would not be best for the infantry. Let each support the other according to the characteristics of its own arm.

B. Fifth—'Very often, also, it will be useful to establish some pieces in the redoubts, which serve as supports to that part of the position which the enemy has most interest in forcing (whether because it commands the field of battle, or because, from there, the troops deployed right and left can be taken in flank or reverse).'

A. There is here no proof whatever that the guns would

not be better employed in the general artillery line, or in flanking such redoubts from outside.

B. Well, the fact is that I have been all along using the arguments of General Brialmont, and, perhaps, in a half-hearted way. He should have been here to speak for himself.

A. He deserves every respect, but, if it came to ranging authorities, I should have on my side almost all the best men who have fought in the wars of the last twenty years, and should leave them to fight their own battle with him.

New Type of British Redoubt.—To meet the cases where redoubts for infantry are necessary—for instance, in positions for battle-fields when there is time for their preparation, or for defence of a city which has no permanent fortifications—the Royal Engineers have designed a new type, which seems to meet most of the objections to the old forms, and is certainly the best pattern which I have yet seen. It offers little target to an enemy, requires no flank defences, has no 'dead' spaces, affords plenty of opportunity for concealed obstacles, and has good bombproof cover. The following description is taken textually from the professional papers of the Royal Engineers, with the kind permission of the writer. It will be observed that no guns are provided for within the redoubt, though it may protect the flank of a line of guns, long or short.

SEMI-PERMANENT INFANTRY REDOUBTS.

BY MAJOR G. R. WALKER, R.E.

(*For section see Plate XIX., in pocket.*)

'It having become desirable to design works of a semi-permanent type, which might be constructed in a short time, to occupy positions for which permanent works, though designed, had not been commenced, or where something less than permanent works were considered to be sufficient to meet the necessities of the defence, it was decided to seek for the solution of the problem by the construction of purely musketry redoubts, commanding at close range batteries of siege type in which the defenders' guns should be mounted.

'The conditions to be fulfilled were considered to be—

'(a) The greatest possible development of musketry (including machine guns) fire from the redoubts, combined with the best possible obstacle to assault, efficient cover for the defenders, and the minimum of exposure of the work to distant view and fire.

'(b) The maximum amount of protection for the batteries outside, both by musketry fire from the redoubts, and by the provision of an obstacle sufficient to protect them from assault.

'The fulfilment of condition (a) was sought for by—

'(1) Tracing the redoubt in the form of a long and narrow oblong, with the corners rounded off; the length, in any particular case, to be adapted to the proposed garrison; the whole of the parapets, unencumbered with guns, being available for musketry fire; the width so designed as to afford, in plan, as small a mark as possible to the enemy's fire, while allowing sufficient space for the bombproofs required to shelter the garrison. The section given in the Plate shows the least depth that is considered suitable. The cover for the garrison, constructed as shown beneath the parados, is primarily intended for the shelter of the men in action, but it also affords cover from the inclemency of the weather. In winter the casemates may be temporarily closed in rear with any materials which are available, and stoves might be added; but no attempt has been made to provide permanent barracks fitted with all the requirements of civilisation. The troops would, as a rule, live in tents, or otherwise, outside the work, in rear, and the work need only be fully manned when attack was anticipated; and as for such a position an outer reserve would be indispensable, this arrangement would present no difficulty.

'(2) The profile is arranged so as to get rid of all dead spaces in the ditch, and to bring the material obstacle to assault under direct fire from the parapet while effectually covering it from the enemy's artillery fire. The section will show that this is done by prolonging the superior slope of one-sixth to the front (in the form of a glacis), until it reaches a depth of about ten feet below the natural level of the ground, and by placing in the ditch thus formed an iron palisade, leaving the counterscarp at the natural slope of the earth, and constructing a small glacis, to increase the cover for the palisade. Inside the work there is good shelter behind the front parapet. The parados, which is of the same height as the crest, and has a gentle slope in front, affords cover to the bomb-proofs, which are protected against high angle fire with iron rails, two feet of concrete, and about five feet of earth; the rear parapet is kept as low as is consistent with its obtaining a view of the ground in rear, in order to make the most of the protection afforded by the parados.

'The command of the whole work is reduced to the minimum consistent with the defence of the ground in front by musketry fire, with the object of rendering it as inconspicuous as possible.

'The fulfilment of condition (b) includes—

'(1) The protection of the batteries by the fire of the redoubt. On this point it is only necessary to say that their defence, supposing the maximum development of musketry fire from the redoubt to be attained, depends solely on the full exposure to fire from the redoubt of the batteries themselves, and of the approaches to them, and is therefore simply a case of judicious adaptation to the ground for any given site.

'(2) The protection of the batteries, by means of an efficient obstacle, against sudden assault seems to be of sufficient importance to demand, not only the preparation of field obstacles, as far as may be possible, when the necessity for defence arises, but also the extension in front of the batteries of the iron palisade proposed for the redoubts, and this more especially in positions where natural obstacles do not exist, and the means of creating abatis, &c., are not at hand.

'A design for the occupation of a given position at one of our fortresses has lately been prepared on the principles sketched above, and has been partially carried out; and as the matter has excited some public attention, and been made the subject of comment, both in the public press and also in the "Corps Journal," a description of the work and of its construction may be found of interest to the corps.

'The position to be occupied is on the left of a line of defence, where its rests on a large river, forming a secure flank, the ground selected for the site being a tolerably well-defined spur running down close to the river, and about at right angles to its direction. The frontal space available is about 600 yards, and the ground in front of the position is open and well exposed to fire. For this position the approved design takes the form of two distinct musketry redoubts of the form described above, and of sections similar to the typical one shown in the Plate attached. Each of these redoubts is completely surrounded by the iron palisade which forms the chief material obstacle to assault, and commands a full view of the ground on all sides, including the ridge about 400 yards long between them, upon which both can cross their fire. In rear of the crest of this ridge it is intended to cut out of the natural ground the batteries for the heavy guns which may be required to oppose the enemy's siege batteries. The guns are intended to fire just over the natural crest, the artificial parapet being reduced to a minimum for guns, and being altogether absent in the case of howitzers. The fall of the ground to the rear of the ridge is suitable for this construction, and batteries thus formed will be quite invisible, and in the duel between them and the besieger's first position batteries the latter will only have the advantage of the knowledge of the probable positions on plan occupied by the defence batteries. In order to secure these batteries from assault, the front ditches of the redoubts are connected by a similar ditch, with iron palisade all along the front of the batteries, this ditch being defended by musketry fire from the flanks of the redoubts, and from trenches between the batteries. The batteries are thus only assailable by parties passing round the flanks of the redoubts, and taking them in rear, as long as the palisade remains intact, and it is thought that it will be very difficult to breach it. On this point, however, experiments are being carried out this year at Lydd. The group of works is designed for a garrison of half a battalion of infantry, exclusive of the men required for working the heavy guns.

'Such being, in brief, the design, it was decided to have the left redoubt executed by civil labour, as an experiment to determine the possibility of getting such works thrown up, on an emergency, by civil contractors, with but very slight supervision from the Royal Engineers ; the supposition being that a large number of hasty defences might have to be erected simultaneously when, owing to other contingencies, but few officers would be available to superintend, and there would be no soldiers to execute the works.

'The contract for the redoubt was given to the district contractor, the conditions being that the work was to be completed in one month from the date of giving the order. The iron palisade was supplied directly from the makers, Messrs. Morton and Co., and the rails for covering the bombproofs were provided by the War Department.

'The work was commenced in June last, and was completed according to contract in exactly 31 working days. The men worked in two reliefs of eight hours each, and about 150 per relief was the maximum number employed on the excavation of which the bulk of the work consisted. The bombproofs were completed on the 21st day.

'Without going into details it may safely be asserted that the work could certainly have been constructed in 21 days, if not in a shorter time ; but to ensure this being done by a civil contractor a large bonus will have to be paid, as the cost of the work increases very rapidly with the speed of execution.

'The contractor, who took the job at a lump sum of 1,800*l*., states that he spent 2,300*l*. in wages alone, which excess was due to the high pressure at which the work was carried on. The greater part of the work was done with hand-barrows, horses and carts being used to a small extent, but no steam-power.

'Time was lost by not carrying out the excavation simultaneously on the whole circuit of the redoubt ; but to do this would have necessitated shifting some of the earth twice, and would therefore have caused extra expense, which from the contractor's point of view was undesirable. In times of real emergency the way to get such work done rapidly would apparently be to increase the rate to be paid in a high ratio for every day saved.

'Looking at the section, it seems possible to complete the whole of the work in 14 working days.

'It should be noticed that the position of this redoubt offered the greatest possible facilities for supply of materials and for carrying on the works, as it is close to a railway station, with good road and water communication near at hand, and within a short distance there is a large town. There was also a sufficient supply of water in a well on the site, and the soil throughout was exceptionally easy.

'In situations where these facilities do not exist the time stated above might be found too short, but proper provision being made for the timely supply of stores and materials, and with efficient organisation and supervision of labour, a month should be sufficient for the construction of such a work in this country in all possible cases.

'If, however, a number of such works had to be constructed suddenly in one locality, the problem becomes much more difficult, and more time would undoubtedly be required, owing to the difficulty of accumulating, at short notice, the large amount of materials and labour which would be necessary.

'The provision of the iron palisade would take longer than this, as Messrs. Morton took six weeks to provide the quantity required for this one redoubt.

'The whole cost of such a work as the one described, for a garrison of 200 men, may be taken roughly at 2,900*l.* if constructed under high pressure, and at 2,250*l.* if carried out in the ordinary time allowed to civil contractors.

'The advantages which may be claimed for this design are as follows: those which belong to semi-permanent works in general—viz. comparative cheapness and rapidity of construction as compared with permanent works, with the strategical advantages which follow, and which need not be discussed here, being already well known; *plus* those which are due to the design of this particular work, the essence of which lies in the fact of the security of the redoubts from distant fire, owing to their inconspicuousness, and from the flatness of the exposed slopes, and their suitability for the development of musketry fire, combined with security from assault, which guarantees the efficient protection of the heavy gun batteries between them.

'That they possess the special advantage of inconspicuousness is a fact that any officer can see for himself, it being quite impossible to distinguish the work already built from the surrounding ground at 1,000 yards.

'The difficulty of injuring flat earth-slopes of this kind by artillery fire is so well known as to need no argument here.

'The plan of the work, and the allotment of the whole of the parapet to musketry, insures a large development of fire, while the section equally assures its effectiveness (there being no dead ground); the security against assault due to the iron palisade, supplemented as it would be, in time of war, by every device of the engineer, may be considered very efficient, though no doubt inferior to a properly concealed and flanked escarp.

'It cannot be doubted that the heavy guns mounted as proposed will be more difficult to hit than if placed in the necessarily limited well-defined space of a fort, permanent or semi-permanent, and they will be as effective; the only question then is, are they sufficiently protected? This again, in the long run, reduces itself to the old question of money *versus* men. If the works, of whatever design, are made perfectly secure against assault, the number of the defenders can be reduced, but the cost of the works, and the time required for their execution, must necessarily be largely increased. The use of works of this type will necessitate larger garrisons for fortresses than in the case of permanent detached forts similarly designed.

'Whenever the ground occupied by field works is not too

steep (and steep ground should, wherever possible, always be avoided) the suitability of this type of section seems to be obvious, as it gets rid of the hitherto insuperable difficulty of the defence of the ditches of field works. The semi-permanent section given in the drawing would, of course, be much too large for ordinary field works, but there would be little difficulty in designing a section, on suitable ground, for which the labour would not be excessive.'

CHAPTER X.

ATTACK OF HOUSES, FARMS, AND VILLAGES.

Reconnaissance: its methods, and points to be observed—Means of procuring information—Best way to deal with fortified post is to let it alone if possible—The attack of advanced post—Example faults at Tashkessen—Always have strong advanced guard to deal with advanced posts—First action of artillery and first artillery position—First infantry advance—At what range commence fire—Question of long range infantry fire discussed—Points of agreement and disagreement—Cases in modern war—St. Privat checked but did not rout Prussians—Gorny Bougarovo, Turks repulsed and ruined at short range—General principle, use artillery to save infantry both in defence and attack—Therefore avoid long range fire—Formation of the attack—General principles—Modern attack formation—General Dragomirov's modification for attack of work adopted here—Avoid lifeless formulæ—General rules for details of attack—Artillery fire—First infantry advance—Further infantry advance—Chain closes to about 200 yards—Main body over it—Vulnerability of different formations—Attack pushed home—Destruction of obstacles.

THE principles of the formation of troops in their deployment and first advance will be treated hereafter (Chap. XI. *et seq.*). In this chapter we shall suppose that the posts to be attacked are isolated, or, at any rate, that they do not form part of an extended line of battle. The movements of the attacking force previous to its arrival near the post will only be indicated generally.

Reconnaissance.—Though liberties may sometimes be taken with an enemy of known physical, moral, or intellectual inferiority, it is never wise to do so, be it only for the bad habits thus taught to officers and men. In no case should a chance be thrown away from mere carelessness. It is the more necessary to insist on this because, curiously enough, the English army has always had a reputation for neglecting those small carefulnesses in war which have great effects on the successful choice of plans, and especially on the losses suffered in actions. The first step towards successful attack is to learn as accurately as possible what has to be attacked. The knowledge will be gained partly by spies and country people, partly by reconnaissance.

Selection of Officer.—It is the business of the Intelligence Department of an army to secure such information as can be obtained from outside, and to supply maps, but there will hardly be a case in which it will not be wise to supplement this information by inspection on the spot. The officer selected for the duty should be well trained and of keen intelligence, so that he may be able to deduce reliable conclusions from signs which would tell nothing to the outer world. Such training ought to be among the most prominent features of education at Staff colleges, and for purposes of examination nothing would better test the completeness of an officer's knowledge.

General Hints.—This is not the place to enter thoroughly into the conduct of a reconnaissance, which is a thoroughly tactical question.[1] But one or two hints may be given. If the post to be reconnoitred lies in a hollow, you may expect to meet with outposts or, if the post is very small—a farm or house—with patrols at least, *on the horizon*. Perhaps they may be avoided if there is time by making a wide circuit. The skill of the officer will be shown in avoiding contact with these or in laying an ambush for a patrol if prisoners are required. The reconnoitring party should be as small as is consistent with the execution of the task. If streams or other obstacles intervene which can only be crossed by bridges, it will be necessary to take in addition the men required to hold such bridges or defiles, to facilitate safe return. In broken country it has often happened that

[1] For some details on this subject see *Elements of Tactics*, by Lieut.-Col. Shaw, the second volume of this series.

a single officer with an orderly has obtained the fullest information. Night covers movements, but sounds are more easily heard. Sometimes, with good fortune, and under cover of darkness, officers have approached so close to works as actually to measure distances and depth of ditches, but this can never be counted upon as more than a hazardous chance. It is to be remembered that all arrangements of the defenders to intercept small reconnaissances take time and may generally be disconcerted by rapidity of movement. If various routes are open, do not return by the way that you advanced. As a rule, avoid fighting and especially the discharge of firearms. Let all your movements be based on the idea of doing exactly what the enemy is not likely to expect. If you have reason to think that you are seen in an exposed position, hurry away from it in a direction which you do not mean to take afterwards. Send information when you can, and especially before attempting any specially dangerous movement. Let your observations be known to others as well as yourself, so that, if you are captured, there may be someone to tell the facts ascertained. If you are cut off by greatly superior forces and cannot get through; if in short you see no hope for your party, disperse: somebody may succeed in escaping.

Strong reconnaissances.—If the required information cannot be obtained by means of small parties, the enemy's outposts must be driven in and the positions they have vacated used as vantage-ground for observations. In that case the officers in command of artillery and engineers will select first positions for guns and observe the weak places for attack, the engineer taking account of all things necessary for the preparation of the working party.

POINTS TO BE OBSERVED.

A house or farm.—As a defensive house is best situated in a hollow, concealed from artillery fire at medium range, ascertain—

Positions from which it can be bombarded at short range, especially with the idea of enveloping it if possible.

The strength of its walls, and whether they are loop-holed.

The time taken by the defenders to prepare it. This cannot be ascertained by sight only.

To what distance from the walls the ground is cleared.

The obstacles either pre-existent or created during the preparation, where and what are they?

Strength of the garrison and reserve if any.

What support has it from other troops?

Nature of shelter-trenches, &c., round it, and best positions to enfilade such trenches.

How infantry can best advance under cover as long as possible.

A village or other large post.—As in this case a larger number of troops are to be engaged and the fighting will be of a serious character, a good reconnaissance is specially needful, and more than one party should be sent out. The chief points to ascertain are—

The position of the outposts and what dispositions have been made by the defenders for action at a distance from the main post. Is there a line of defence weak or strong well in advance of the post? If so, what is its nature and can it be turned so as to cut off its defenders?

The nature of the ground over which the troops must advance. What cover is there, and how near the post itself? How can it be enveloped?

The nature and extent of the post, in regard to earth-defences, woods, streams and other features. Whence can lines of defence be enfiladed? What salients are there to attack? What dead angles? Are there any forts, where, and closed or open?

Nature and place of obstacles, and how far they can be overcome by artillery fire. What part of this destruction must be left to working parties?

Amount of artillery possessed by the enemy and where its prepared positions are established.

If possible, ascertain how the interior defence is organised. Whether in lines or sections. Where is the principal keep?

Strength and composition of the garrison. Its distribution. Strength and position of the outer reserve.

What support has the post from other troops, either within range or at a distance? Ascertain where they are.

It is not to be supposed that every detail can always be discovered, but officers should carry in their heads what they wish to know, and if their eyes and ears are open much knowledge may come to them from unexpected sources, as the following incident will prove.

The author of this book joined the Headquarters of Prince Frederick Charles at Orleans late in 1870, and, though treated with every courtesy and consideration, was refused all information as to the positions of the different units of the force which then stood on the defensive against the armies of Bourbaki and Chanzy. One day, shortly after his arrival, he accompanied a friend to a photographer's and happened to glance at the book of addresses to which portraits were to be sent. The number of German officers who, having received leave to visit Orleans for a day, had spent part of their time in being photographed appeared prodigious, and they had all left their full addresses, regiment, brigade, division, and locality. Late the same evening the author returned to the photographer's and after much trouble succeeded in obtaining permission to look over the book for an hour or so. Having already made out a tabular form nothing was simpler than to set down its proper place for each unit, and there were no discrepancies. At that very time a French officer was, to the knowledge of many non-combatants, living unrestrained in plain clothes in the town of Orleans, and he escaped shortly afterwards. Of course the author felt bound in honour neither to betray the French officer to the Germans, nor the information he had obtained to the French officer, but the incident may serve to show how vain it is to imagine that silence on the part of a Staff will prevent information leaking out. The first requisite for an intelligence officer is to have definite ideas as to what information he wants, the second to keep his senses awake.

It is not likely that all the points mentioned above will

be completely settled by the preliminary reconnaissances: well-trained officers should therefore accompany the first advance of the troops or a reconnaissance in force should be made. To guide the attacking troops scouts should always be sent in advance.

It may be said of any fortified post garrisoned by good and well-armed troops that the more you look at it the less you will like to attack it. A good rule is to turn it without attacking if possible. There will be many cases where it will be better worth while to detach a force to observe a post than to use a larger number of troops in attacking it with the necessary waste of life. Plevna is a case in point. If the Russians had possessed an army as large as it ought to have been and might have been for such an invasion, they could have masked Plevna, pushed over the Balkans by the Shipka Pass, already in their possession, and dictated peace at the gates of Constantinople. There is not the slightest question that in the attacks on Plevna, and the defence of the Shipka Pass with an insufficient force, they actually lost more men than would have sufficed to hold Osman Pasha's army in check. If, as seems likely, the defensive power of the new arms should lead to an abuse of fortified positions, we may yet see a general arise who will base his strategy on neglect of such positions, only leaving a force large enough to keep the garrison in check and prevent it from executing attacks on lines of communications or other important points of objective. Of this more will be said hereafter. For the present we have to suppose that a post—namely, a strong village—has to be attacked, and that it is prepared for defence as has already been explained. We suppose the attacking force to have considerable superiority over the defenders and to have obtained a fair amount of information as to the garrison, the works and the ground in the neighbourhood. We are also to suppose that the village is isolated, that the attacking troops have nothing to fear from flank attacks, and that the action is to be by daylight.

Advanced position.—The cavalry pushed on in front reports that the defenders have occupied a position evidently in advance of the village, say a hill 2,000 yards from the post —with both guns and infantry. It would be easy to develop force enough to turn such a position and then advance on it by an enveloping attack. But two difficulties might arise.

First. The enemy in the main post might attack the flanks of the turning column; or—

Second. The defenders might hold the advanced position long enough to cause all the delay required for the turning columns to reach attacking distance and then withdraw rapidly under cover of fire from the main post, having drawn the attacking columns out of their proper road, and thereby caused a great delay.

For a practical instance of this second difficulty take the admirably conducted action by Baker Pasha at Tashkessen, minutely described by him.[1] He occupied a small hill in front of a main position and held the hill till it was turned on both flanks. The effect shall be given in his own words.

'The error made by the Russian right and left divisions, which I had noticed in the morning, had done us excellent service. They had endeavoured to turn both flanks of our false or advanced position and now found themselves jammed in front of our real line, with the power of outflanking nearly lost, and, as yet, the impossibility of forcing it by front attacks.'

Time was of great importance in this as in nine-tenths of isolated defences, and, in face of very superior numbers, General Baker just succeeded in holding out till night fell, and his small force retired under cover of the darkness.

In anticipation of having to attack advanced positions, and to drive in the outposts, *the main columns should always be preceded by large advanced guards*, which will also act as strong reconnaissances. They should be accompanied or followed by the bulk of the artillery and enable the guns to occupy their first positions before the main columns arrive. The action of a superior force of artillery combined with the manœuvres of the advanced guard and its skirmishing lines will generally be sufficient to carry the advanced posi-

[1] *War in Bulgaria*, vol. ii. chaps. ix., x., and xi.

tion, and by these tactics there will be the least possible loss of time, and no exposure of the force of the attackers or the nature of their plans.

First action of artillery.—With regard to the first action of the artillery we are on firm ground. There seems to be no difference of opinion among serious tacticians that the guns should take up their position as early as possible and in full force, that they should first subdue the defenders' artillery fire, and then turn their attention to the shooting line, enfilading trenches if possible ; or, if the defenders are out of sight, which, we have previously argued, they ought to be at this stage, at least the attacking artillery can commence the destruction of obstacles.

First artillery position.—The features of the ground will generally determine the choice of the first position of the guns, but, if not, the usual rule is that they should be placed out of reach of the enemy's infantry fire, but near enough to make their preponderance felt over his artillery—say roughly 2,000 yards from the village or less if possible. If the defenders are energetic and well managed they will push out some small bodies of infantry to act as skirmishers or in groups against the attacking guns. These should be met and kept back by similar detachments from the advanced guard. Do not waste artillery ammunition upon them. If the position for the guns has been well chosen, a very few minutes will suffice to gain cover against rifle bullets. We have then as the first principle—*The artillery begins the action by crushing the defenders' artillery (supposed to be inferior) or at least reducing its fire. It then begins to bombard the outer line whatever it may be.*

First infantry advance.—The decision being made as to the direction of the different attacks—true or feigned—which should be converging, the attacking infantry begins to take up its early positions and to close in as soon as the defenders artillery is silenced. The object is to gain a footing inside however small, and some, at least, of the attacks will be directed upon such weak places as salient angles, gaps in obstacles and so on. But it is important to conceal the real intentions as long as possible so that the element of surprise may produce its moral effect. A shooting line should, therefore, envelop the village, driving in any detached parties of the defenders, and the action between the two shooting lines will soon open. The greatest point of debate in modern tactics is now before us.

At what range should the infantry of attack and defence open fire?

QUESTION OF LONG RANGE INFANTRY FIRE.

Points of agreement.—In studying this question let us begin by stating the few points which are agreed upon by the whole world of tacticians, and then examine those on which they differ.

Cases of good effect.—It is agreed that there have been cases of long range infantry fire producing very great effects, when the troops advancing against it were in rather massive formation and were possessed of inferior weapons, and when the defenders, much better armed, had either not been brought under the fire of artillery for a long period or had been completely sheltered from it. The only case of which I am aware when long range fire of infantry, mitrailleuses and a few guns obtained such dominion over an advancing enemy as to stop the attack before close range was reached, was during the first attack of the Prussian Guards on St. Privat in 1870. We shall come to it directly. In other cases the long range fire, however well nourished and however efficacious, did not stop the attack, though it must have aided in the final repulse by beginning to shake the nerves of the attackers at an early stage.

Cases of better effect at short range.—On the other hand, it is agreed that there have been many cases in the latest wars when an attack was met by complete silence of rifles till the enemy was within close distance and was then repulsed almost instantly and with comparatively slight expenditure of ammunition by a vigorous series of volleys, sometimes combined with independent firing.

Long range never drives troops out of cover.—I cannot find a record of a single case where a defensive line under shelter, however trifling, has been compelled to abandon that shelter and retire under pressure of long range infantry fire, though there are innumerable cases of successful frontal attacks driven home after preparation by artillery fire, succeeded by that of infantry at close range.

It is also agreed that there is a very remarkable difference between the effect of infantry fire on the practice-ground and the effect in battle. Also a great, though not so great, a difference between the fire of infantry under cover and their fire in the open.

Disagreement.—But there is a profound and deeply-rooted disagreement as to the general rules to be drawn from a study of the examples furnished by modern wars. The armies which have made most use of infantry long range fire are the French and the Turkish, both of which, be it observed, were finally unsuccessful. But their adversaries, Germans and Russians, had in the late wars very inferior weapons and could not have attempted a contest at long range even if they would. To-day all armies are fairly equal in small arms. The Russians are much more in favour of long range than they used to be or than Germany is now. There is a strong school in England which advocates long range fire as a regular practice, but it is remarkable that nothing of the sort was used in the Soudan.

To avoid mistakes, it may be as well to explain that all nations and armies and all schools of tacticians recognise the occasional use of a few picked men firing as sharpshooters at long range. It is only the general use of long range firing by bodies of troops which forms the subject of controversy. Let us now sketch briefly two instances for and against, and try to draw from them something like a fair conclusion.

Cases in Modern War.

St. Privat.—The first and most important is undoubtedly the repulse of the Prussian Guards in their first attack on St. Privat, August 18, 1870. About a quarter to five in the afternoon the Prince of Würtemburg ordered the 4th Brigade to advance from St. Ail. It did so accordingly, moving towards the corner of St. Privat, to the right, as seen by the brigade. This point was called Jerusalem. The Prince then joined the 1st Division which was at St. Marie aux Chênes and directed it also to march on St. Privat. General Pape who commanded the division remonstrated, saying that the columns entrusted with the turning movement were not yet in sight, that the batteries were not firing on St. Privat but on Roncourt, further towards the French right flank, and that, as the defenders of St. Privat had not been yet shaken by a serious bombardment, it was impossible to attack with any chance of success. We may add here that the ground over which the attack must be made was a smooth gentle slope, admirably adapted for being swept by rifle fire, and that the effective range of the Prussian needle-gun was only about one-half that of the French chassepôt and mitrailleuse. As the 4th Brigade had already started towards Jerusalem, the warning was disregarded and the two brigades of the 1st Division moved forward, the 1st Brigade towards the south-west angle of St. Privat in a dense formation, a regiment of the 2nd Brigade in support of it at about 600 yards distance. The Saxon batteries were still firing at Roncourt, the batteries of the Guard against the French batteries and troops south of St. Privat. But the St. Privat position was quite unshaken when the 1st Division of the Guard took the offensive.

The French infantry and mitrailleuses were established on the boundary of St. Privat, behind walls, hedges, garden fences, &c. They commenced to fire at about 2,000 paces, the Guard artillery being still engaged with the French guns. The Prussians were quite unable to reply, as their rifles were inaccurate after about 600 paces. In many instances the French soldiers kept under cover and fired without aiming. At any rate there was a great expenditure of ammunition, which told against them afterwards. But for the moment it was successful. The masses of the Guards moved only to destruction, leaving many dead at every step. In half an hour they had only arrived at about 800 paces from the

French position, still outside the accurate range of their own rifles. They had lost 6,000 to 7,000 men, about a third of their strength, and were obliged to seek shelter in a fold of ground from the death-dealing shower rained upon them.

The Prussian batteries then took up the combat, directing a violent fire against the outskirts of the village. Meanwhile the Saxon turning movement had been developed, and later on, from the north, some 30,000 men poured upon the village, which was then almost in ruins, caused by the artillery fire. The French too had exhausted their ammunition; and under these circumstances the combined attack of the Guards and Saxons carried St. Privat. It is important to remember that General Canrobert's corps, which held that part of the position, was not supported by other troops as a flank corps ought to be, especially as there was a reserve both of French Guard and artillery which could have been used. It had also no entrenching implements nor engineers, the engineer park having been left at Châlons. And, when it yielded, the village had literally been smashed by shells and was on fire in several places. Up to a late hour there was hand-to-hand fighting in the streets, nor did the definite retreat take place till after nightfall. No doubt these were admirable troops.

In this case, without any question, the principal fire directed against the first attack of the Guard was at long ranges—2,000 to 800 paces, and chiefly from chassepôts and mitrailleuses; it caused immense losses and stopped the attack. It was proof of what may be done under certain circumstances, especially against an enemy who in this case was as helpless at long range as Zulus or Arabs.

But on the other side it may be said that the effect was only arrived at by a great expenditure of ammunition, which brought about grave difficulties later in the day, and contributed seriously towards producing the final disaster. In the series of battles which occurred at that time there are numerous cases of French columns being completely stopped by Prussian artillery fire alone; and it is impossible not to question whether that attack of the Guards, in an antiquated formation against an unshaken enemy, would not have been stopped much more cheaply and with equal ease by a line of guns fairly protected and firing shrapnel, or by infantry at short range with much less expenditure of ammunition. If so, then the repulse of the Guard by long range infantry fire may prove what can possibly be done by sheltered troops, unshaken, against an enemy advancing in masses; but it does not present us with an example for our imitation. Upon the infantry must ultimately fall the decision of the combat. How important at that moment will be their fitness in every particular for a desperate struggle! Well rested, with plenty of ammunition and unshaken by previous excitement and fatigue, they will have the best chance when all depends on their vigour and steadiness. Wearied by toil, exhausted in nervous energy, and already thinned by unnecessary fighting, is it fair to expect from them that they shall be at their best?

Gorny Bougarovo.—Now take an opposite case where the defending infantry awaited their assailants, and we may remark that a large number of such cases could be quoted. The fight of Tashkessen occurred on December 19, 1877, and on the same day the column of General Veliaminof, consisting of five infantry battalions, six guns, and a brigade of Cossacks, took up a position at Gorny Bougarovo, entrenching themselves there. Next day, the 20th, the position was attacked by a Turkish force from Sofia, consisting of twelve to fifteen battalions, with six or eight guns. The Turks advanced against the front of the Russian position, at the same time enveloping the left flank, and presently the right flank also. Let us tell the tale in the words of General Gourko's report:—

'Although their bullets reached all parts of the position, and the situation of the column became more and more difficult, the brave soldiers of the regiments Pentza and Tanibof only replied feebly to the excessively violent fire of the Turks, keeping their cartridges for later on.

'Encouraged by the slowness of our fire, and seeing the relative weakness of our detachment, the Turks proceeded to the attack after having prepared it by a fire the violence of which attained the highest possible limits. But our detachment continued to respond but feebly even to that infernal fire. On the other hand, when the Turks, with shouts of "Allah!" approached within 100 paces or less from our trenches, our brave soldiers received them with consecutive discharges, and, after several well-directed volleys, leapt from their works and threw themselves with the bayonet upon the enemy, who was seized with a panic, in presence of the enormous number of killed and wounded which he had lost in a few seconds, and took to flight as soon as he found himself subjected to that counter-attack.

'The Turks suffered enormous losses in this affair. More than 1,600 wounded were carried to Sofia, and more than 800 dead remained on the field of battle. Our losses were 243 men killed and wounded. This fight produced a strong impression on the Turks and destroyed their moral force.'

Now, if we take these two opposite cases as typical of complete effects of long range and short range fire, we see in the St. Privat case a bloody repulse indeed, but no demoralisation, for the Guards attacked again when the Saxons came into action; whereas in the other case the Turks not only lost heavily but were routed, driven from the field and so demoralised that the result affected the remainder of the war. Reverse the actions and suppose that the Russians had fired at long range and wasted their ammunition. Might not the Turks have attacked again and again till the position was carried? And if the French at St. Privat had waited till the Germans were at short range, who can doubt that the repulse would have been more demoralising, and a well-pushed counter-attack might have broken the German left and changed the fortune of the battle of Gravelotte?

General principle for the defence.—In view of the numerous instances in favour of the short range action of infantry, and the extreme rarity of great effects at long range, we may lay down the following principle as applicable to the action of troops in formed bodies, leaving out the use of a few picked shots:—

Infantry being the final force upon which the fate of the day must inevitably depend, it is wise to nurse and preserve it giving it nothing to do that can be done as well by artillery; instead of fatiguing its body and nerves by giving it strains to bear which could as well be borne by other arms in the early part of the combat. It will then be ready, not only to repulse the enemy, but to demoralise and destroy him.

For the attack.—And if this can be said for troops in defensive positions, how much more is it true for an attacking force? Surely it should approach as long as it can without firing a shot, always preceded by a thin chain of picked sharpshooters who are trained to take advantage of every bit of possible cover, and, enveloping the position, to distract the attention of the defenders as much as possible. This chain should not be considered as the fighting line, but as skirmishers pure and simple, questing over the ground, discovering the enemy's weak points and preventing him from adding to his external defences. It will also discover natural obstacles of all sorts and so prevent the troops from being embarrassed by them. The men of this chain may be called scouts.

Formations of the Attack.

We now come to the formations proper for the attacking troops. Everybody knows that the object to be attained is to bring to bear eventually, on the point or points selected, a body of men in good heart and not over-fatigued, strong enough to overwhelm the resistance of the enemy. Considering the advantages possessed by a line of infantry under cover and the severe losses which any force advancing in the open must experience, the conclusion is irresistible that *no attacking force can reach charging distance from a line of defenders under cover in such condition as to hope to carry the position by means of the first line only.* We may go a step further, and add *nor by the second or any other line only.*[1]

The object of the commander must, therefore, be to bring up

[1] The reader is requested, once for all, to understand that the troops are supposed to be equal in courage, discipline, armaments, &c., on the two contending sides. Every commander must judge for himself what allowances to make for any differences which there may be. For instance, Lord Wolseley's attack on Tel-el-Kebir.

eventually an overwhelming force in such formation that it may storm the enemy's position by an attack made, not like the waves of the sea on a beach, where one recoiling wave checks the advance of the next, but rather as a river in flood accumulates against an obstacle, piling up fresh force at every moment.

It is true that, unless the forces are in actual contact—body to body—which seldom happens, no weight of physical force is brought to bear ; but there can be an accumulation of moral force caused by a great preponderance of numbers on the attacking side, if only the numbers can be brought to bear at the critical moment. The object of the attack must be to pour a stream of men against the same point with as little loss as possible both actual and moral. If flank attacks can be made so much the better, but we speak here of a frontal attack. How is the stream to be formed?

Modern attack formation.—In old days, the heavy column answered the purpose, and it was preceded by a thin skirmishing line. But the increased range and accuracy of fire have made it certain that no heavy column would ever reach the enemy. At the same time the action of a line, thicker than skirmishers, but thinner and less stiff than a line shoulder to shoulder, has become almost as powerful as the line itself would be, and every nation, including England, has adopted a formation for attack which includes first, a shooting line, second supports, third reserves or main body, whichever it be called. These three together constitute the first line. Behind it will be a second line ; but what we have to deal with for the moment is this first line with its three parts, which constitute virtually an idealised column. Speaking generally, the work of the shooting line is to engage the enemy's attention and partly subdue his fire ; the supports feed the shooting line ; the reserves ward off flank attacks, make flank attacks or, finally, become absorbed in the shooting line and strengthen it. This is the general principle, but, as General Dragomirov was fond of saying to his pupils, 'You put the chain in front, do you? Say, then, when you would put it behind. Answer, or you are only a Dourak,' which here means a 'muff.' It has been proved by much practice in war that, when an advancing force lies down within close range of an enemy, no power can raise it again intact for a charge, and this is especially the case with the chain which has borne the brunt of the fighting hitherto. The same General Dragomirov, who is one of the best officers of the time, who led the division which effected the crossing of the Danube and afterwards defended the Shipka Pass; showed in June 1886, at the camp at Krasnoé, how he would effect an advance against a field redoubt. His main principle is to push on the chain as rapidly as it can go to within about 200 yards of the work, there to lie down and fire when and how it can. The supports may be supposed to become absorbed in the chain, but the reserve acts more independently. Instead of keeping at a regulated distance, it allowed the chain to precede it by an advance of 500 or 600 paces, which it then made up at one rapid movement, so that *at 600 paces from the work, the distance at which the defenders were first instructed to open fire,* the reserve was only about fifty paces from the companies in first line. At that point the supports began to enter into the chain, which then rushed on swiftly to a distance of 200 paces from the work and lay down, with the intention of remaining as a crouched shooting line. Then the reserve came up with great rapidity, passed over the chain, and flung itself into the ditch there to take breath and prepare for the storming, the chain meanwhile keeping the defenders behind their parapet by as rapid a fire as could be delivered. All this was done in complete silence. The hurrahs only came when the final assault was delivered. No doubt, in such a case, the men of the chain would take advantage of every little mound and even turn up with their spades a sod or two for shelter, as the Turks did in several of their attacks.

In our present case there would be no ditch to take shelter in, but on the other hand, the defenders, already prepared to retire, would begin to look over their shoulders by the time that the chain arrived and lay down, and retreat on seeing the rush of the reserve coming. The reserve, now the storming party, would try to close with the retiring enemy, and gain ever so small a footing in the village. The chain would assist by its fire as long as possible, then close up and occupy the deserted shelter-trench, making it available for their own side with their spades. The duty of warding off counter-attacks from the flanks must be confided to battalions not engaged in the actual assault.

We are now in a position to lay down something like principles for an attack of this sort, first praying the reader, if a student, to remember that there are no rules without exceptions, and that if he be worth his salt as a soldier, he must be ready to devise new plans for special circumstances. The craving for a formula is only too prevalent. Let him contradict and argue against the one here vaguely laid down as much as he pleases. To turn the subject over again and again in his mind will do him more good and better prepare him for service than the best possible formula.

General Rules for Details of Attack.

1. *Begin with artillery fire.*—Get the artillery well established, taking care that the senior artillery officer knows exactly where you mean the final assault to be delivered. It will then be his business to see that all the guns can be brought to bear on that point some time before the assault. The artillery will first silence the enemy's guns, and it may be well to prevent those guns from being able to take part in the subsequent struggle, by either capturing the emplacements or commanding them at short range so that their guns cannot return to them. If your guns are annoyed and suffer losses from the enemy's sharpshooters, the proper reply is not to retire the artillery, but to send forward sharpshooters of your own to engage the enemy's attention. It is on occasions like this, that the fine shooting possible now, may find its most legitimate exercise. Your guns should of course endeavour to act on the prolongation of the enemy's trenches or, at least, obliquely. Act at decisive range as soon as possible.

2. *First infantry advance.*—During the artillery action the

infantry will be getting into position with the object of making a concentric advance. Your force is supposed to be superior to the enemy, otherwise an attack on a well-prepared village would be a very dangerous proceeding, always supposing the enemy's troops to be good. The concentric advance will oblige the enemy to disperse his fire, and prevent him from knowing where the attack is to be or how to prepare for a counter-attack. The infantry will advance slowly at first, taking every advantage of ground for cover. Do not waste any ammunition by firing at long range. The enemy is chiefly under cover. Your guns will continue the bombardment, but your infantry will produce more moral effect by not firing a shot, up to as late a period as possible. The formation at this period will not here be laid down definitely, but a few hints may be given. Do not form the order of attack before it is necessary. Small columns, such as companies advancing by sections or fours from their flanks, are the most manageable as a rule, lend themselves well to advance under cover, and are rather less vulnerable on an average than the same number of troops in line, especially if artillery is not firing at them.[1] If in this way, without firing or suffering much loss, you can establish the infantry at 1,000 to 900 yards from the enemy's position, you will have done well. Your artillery will still be bombarding the trenches. Give it fair play.

3. *Further infantry advance.*—It is not very likely that the enemy will allow you to advance much within the range of 1,000 yards without opening fire. If there is cover, move as long as you can in shelter, and postpone the attack formation lest the troops should get out of hand. But suppose that the ground is pretty level, form for attack at about 1,000 yards, or before if you suffer heavily from fire. You will then have your chain, supports and main body or reserve, whichever you like to call it. But opposite the point you are about to attack, you must have reserves as strong as your leading battalions and distinct from them.

[1] The French have made some very careful experiments on the effect of fire on different formations. I accept their conclusions.

Their business will be to support the first line, but above all to guard against counter-attacks from the enemy's general or outer reserve. It is this which is most to be feared. Take every precaution, and if possible guard your outer flanks with cavalry acting chiefly as scouts. Now let your front chain, which we will not here call your fighting line for obvious reasons, get over the intervening space as quickly as it can. At this time, if the affair has been well arranged, your artillery will concentrate its fire on the enemy who hold the point to be attacked. The enemy will be too much under its influence to dispute the infantry advance very seriously. Your chain will reach, if it can, the best position it can find within short range of the enemy, the nearer the better, and do everything possible to attract attention so as to enable the main body which is to assault to come up. The action must now be hurried because the artillery can no longer keep under the fire from the trenches. Your guns must fire at the fringe of the village or upon any reserves they can see. The chain, with supports incorporated, will lie down and protect itself as well as it can. It is odd if there be not some remains of hedge, bank, or wall between 100 and 300 yards of the enemy. Get the chain there as well as you can, and force him to attend to it. Use entrenching tools if you have them.

4. Meanwhile the business of the main body or battalion reserve has been to advance as best it could to within 400 or 500 yards of the enemy, whence it will be able to advance rapidly and pass over the chain. In what formation should the advance be? This, too, must depend on the ground; but supposing it to be a level plain without cover, it may be well to know certain facts with regard to an enemy's fire against different formations. The main body will be partly shielded from aimed fire by the chain with its attractive movements and the smoke of its firing. Besides, it is always difficult to get men to attend to a danger which is far off when there is one which is near. We may therefore suppose that the fire directed against it will not be very accurate. Now a formation in line is slightly less vulnerable than that of companies by the flank in fours or sections if the fire is

carefully aimed and there is little disturbance of it. But if the fire is not accurately aimed, as in this case, the small columns are less vulnerable. All this has been settled by experiment on the Continent, especially in France. The small columns are much easier to manage and to keep under cover; therefore it would be preferable for the main body to advance by companies from their flanks rather than in line, but for the fact that only with a broad front can the attack bring its own fire to bear heavily against the enemy. At this period, probably, each battalion and company will choose its own formation, but see Chap. XI. for the newest definite scheme of attack. Another point to remember is that, while at all moderate and long ranges troops kneeling are less vulnerable than standing, this is not the case at short ranges under about 300 yards. To lie down at these short ranges is to stay there planted to the soil; to kneel is of no use. Therefore keep the men upright unless they can creep forward behind cover.[1]

When the moment comes for the final rush, for instance, if you see some of the enemy getting up or even looking back, do not stop to arrange your men in any particular formation. It does not matter a single straw how they are formed, but it does matter that you should have thoroughly explained what you want them to do, namely, to get hold of a house or two within the village, and this can best be done by entering with the enemy. If you have engineers they should be among the first to be pushed forward.

The best formation for the second line of infantry will be in echelon on the exposed flank, so as to be able to form to front or flank as required. Moreover, it is less vulnerable there when it comes into the zone of fire.

Getting rid of obstacles.—In all this nothing has been said of the enemy's obstacles, which have already been de-

---

[1] I confess to some anxiety lest young officers should take this to mean that the astoundingly stupid, unthinking stiffness which used to prevail in many infantry regiments is right or even tolerable. Men should be constantly trained to advance under cover, which is a very different process from taking cover and sticking there.

scribed as such formidable additions to his defensive strength. If they exist, special efforts must be made to destroy them, first by artillery fire—the largest common shells attainable, with bursting charges of one of the new high explosives—and second by means of working parties sent for that particular purpose. It will be necessary to keep down the fire of the enemy while these parties are at work with explosives, fire, or the axe. It is rather curious that this, one of the most important of all the operations, is less practised and has less certainty about its details than any other. Shells will cut up abatis, especially by enfilade fire; or a little paraffine, tar, or other combustible material placed to windward and ignited will clear a large space, though leaving it unpleasant to cross. Anything in the way of holes can be bridged over with planks or brushwood. Wire entanglement, the worst of all, can be cut or partly destroyed by artillery fire, or bridged with planks, fascines, &c. Land torpedoes must be risked. They do not at any rate act twice. In all reconnaissance of a post, nothing is more important than to learn what obstacles there are and where.

Do not advance your main columns of attack till the obstacles are destroyed or in a fair way to be so. Let this duty be allotted to a body which has nothing else to do. It will be quite enough for the share of that body, and is exhaustive of nervous energy.

So far have been given general principles for the attack of a village up to the moment when an entry is effected. These principles are rather in harmony with English ideas and habits than with those of France and Germany. They aim at making the attack with the least possible loss, and are in accordance with the views of General Dragomirov, who is one of the most brilliant officers of the day. They also suppose that obstacles of one sort or another prevent the village from being carried at once by main force. But it cannot be disguised that the methods most in favour in Western and Central Europe involve a rougher and more violent attack, more quickly carried out and with heavier losses. In the next chapter the latest French attack will be given. It is supposed to be applicable to the case of the defending enemy being in the open field, but also to that of his being sheltered by trenches—in fact, to the attack of any position. It does not, however, contemplate the removal of obstacles; and a little consideration will show that, until those obstacles are got rid of, a thinner shooting line or chain, on General Dragomirov's principle, taking or making cover near the enemy, and protecting the working parties which clear away the obstacles, will probably be sufficient for the purpose, and certainly reduce the losses to a minimum. When once the way is clear, infantry must be piled on to carry any position if well defended.

CHAPTER XI.

ATTACK AND DEFENCE OF VILLAGES (*continued*).

Artillery preparation—Objects to be fired at—Ranges—Artillery defence—Further remarks on infantry attack—By front and flank—Reserves in flank attacks—Strength for frontal attack—Action by groups—New French infantry attack—Its principles—The group—Ranges at which fire is to be opened—Half sections, sections, &c.—The company—Details of formation and advance—Defence by an isolated company—The battalion—Application of its first formation—*Formation de combat*—Fighting patrols—Rules for the march—Fire effect—Dismounting of officers—Phases of the combat—First phase—Second phase, in two periods—Third phase—The battalion isolated—Defensive—Brigades and divisions—German instructions for magazine rifles—Instruction of the soldier—Instruction of the company—Instruction of the battalion—Four principal cases for magazine fire—Economy of ammunition—Artillery support.

(*Plate XVII.—New French attack.*)

HAVING given in the preceding chapter the general idea of an attack on a village, we may now go a little more into detail on some points.

Artillery preparation.—General Lewal gives in the following words the modern view on this question—a view which is universal among competent tacticians who have seen war. 'The decisive result being only to be achieved by infantry, it is necessary that, at any price, the action of that arm become possible. It is the condition which comes before all others. It will be the fundamental rule for artillery, which will press its application even as far as to sacrifice itself completely.' Most unfortunately, the view taken by some distinguished infantry officers in England is that there is some antagonism between the two arms, and that the interest of infantry should lead them to decry the action of artillery, and even keep down the number of the guns. It is the old story of the complaint of one member of the body against another, forgetting that the strength of each is necessary for the welfare of the whole. No officer possessed of common sense could doubt for a moment that the mass of an army must be composed of infantry, or that in almost every feat of war infantry must sooner or later be the arm on the action of which final success or failure must depend. But it can neither move as fast as cavalry and artillery nor act with useful effect at such long ranges as artillery. To enable it to do so would be to make it no longer infantry. Surely its position is assured enough and sufficiently recognised by those who, like the present writer, in harmony with all Continental tacticians, would make the preparation of the way for infantry, and its support even to self-sacrifice, the main duty of cavalry and field artillery. And it may be said with regard to these three arms that, while a fairly good infantry can be quickly created by a nation of free and brave men, and, having been created, can do excellent work if possessed of well-trained officers, cavalry and field artillery require much more training, and are merely a burden if not highly trained. On all accounts, therefore, the high and honourable position of being the mainstay of armies and the chief defence of nations remains with the infantry, and must ever remain. It can do more useful acts in war than any other arm, and without it no great success can possibly be obtained.

But infantry cannot do everything, and among the actions which should be done for it is the preparation of the attack of a village. Capt. Louis Thival gives lists of twenty-three cases of failures in attack for want of artillery preparation, and thirty-one cases where a good preparation caused success even when the posts were well defended. In some of the latter, previous attacks without preparation had failed disastrously. As a rule, therefore, *infantry attacks should not be made against a prepared post until the enemy has been shaken and his defences partly disorganised by the fire of artillery.*[1]

Objects to be fired at.—First, the enemy's artillery, which, being silenced, should be prevented from coming into action again, at least in the same emplacements.

Second.—The exterior defences, especially at the points chosen for attack; endeavouring to destroy obstacles at those posts. If the enemy has a shooting line established in front of the village, fire at that. If not, fire at the outer houses and endeavour to render them untenable. Fire at all flanking portions and walls, so as to produce splinters of masonry; also at roofs and towers or spires, which the enemy may perhaps be using as look-out stations.

Third.—If possible, enfilade the principal streets or any other communications, by which the enemy might move his troops.

N.B.—It is not a question how many guns you should have. Use every piece that can possibly be spared for the purpose. Do not commence fire till you have brought up many guns. Never cease the fire once commenced till your infantry have so closed with the defenders as to be in danger from the fire of the guns. Even then an opportunity may occur to support them in attack or protect them in retreat. Be ready for it.

Ranges.—The range at which fire will be opened by artillery must depend on the lie of the ground and the position of any protecting troops which the enemy may have outside. The rule is to get as near as you can with safety, and as soon as you can. First, second, and third positions, if necessary, will declare themselves. If possible, get into the final position at the very first moment.

Artillery defence.—The defending artillery is supposed to be comparatively weak. It will prevent as long as it can the establishment of the enemy's batteries, and may make play for some time, as it is supposed to have ranges accurately measured. Endeavour to draw the enemy into showing his position by opening his fire while he is still weak in guns. In

---

[1] See examples in Chapters XII. and XIII.

the early stages do not risk capture, but endeavour by all means to join your fire outside with that of the infantry inside at the time of the infantry assault by the enemy. Risks run then may pay very well.

Further Remarks on Infantry Attack.

By front and flank.—In the preceding chapter general rules were given for a frontal attack, but it is manifest that in this as in other tactical cases, advantage will be gained by combining if possible attacks both in front and by a turning movement. The essence of success lies in making these turning movements unexpectedly, and thus bringing into them the element of surprise. The smallest party suddenly attacking a flank while an enemy is being engaged in front produces a great effect on the nerves of the defenders, which is the main object. Such small attacks may be especially useful during that most difficult operation, the destruction of obstacles under cover of the fire of the chain.

Reserves in flank attacks.—A common mistake is to suppose that, because other troops may be in long line both on your side and the enemy's, therefore the part which you have to assault has no flank to be attacked. Every unit has a flank of its own which remains its own weak point, though help may be expected from other units on its right or left. But those other units have probably enough to do to look after themselves, and to attack a flank does not necessarily mean to march round it; concentrate upon it a superior force and it will perhaps show its natural weakness, especially its moral weakness, by giving way, which it will do inward, towards its centre. This creates confusion, and would inevitably lead to defeat but for the action of the defending reserves, which will here enter into the fray. *Therefore, in all attacks on flanks, hold a reserve in readiness to attack the enemy's reserve; in other words, to parry the counter-attack.*

In our present case, that of a village standing apart, there must be flanks or at least a rear on the line of communication. The attacking force is supposed to be strong enough to envelop the post, which it should do as far as possible. See the failure of the French to carry Le Bourget by partial attack (Chapter XII.). Even a salient angle is neither more nor less than the meeting of two flanks of troops and is weak accordingly. If a village or other post is wholly or largely enveloped, the defenders will always feel themselves attacked in front, flank, and rear. The penetration of any force, however small, into the heart of the defences may cause a panic.

Strength for frontal attack.—In the preceding chapter it has been shown that a successful assault must be carried out by wave upon wave of men. First the chain, with supports feeding it, are to lie down as near as possible to the enemy and not to be called upon to assault, for they would not have sufficient nervous force ; then the working party to open obstacles which have not yet been destroyed by the artillery ; then the first stormers for the assault, with reserves to protect their flanks ; then more troops from behind to carry on the impulse of the wave. The question then arises—'How many men for all these purposes?' The number is so large that I prefer to quote the work of another hand. Lieut. Mayne, R.E., in his most useful epitome of modern thought called 'Infantry Fire Tactics' has these words : 'The experience of the Franco-German war showed that the attack should have, including all troops and reserves, about twelve to fourteen men per yard of front ; this allows for the troops required to carry out the flank attack as well as those required to hold the enemy in front. This would give for the attack, after deducting the troops to carry out the flank attack and local assaults, at least one man per yard of front for the reconnaissance, two to three men per yard for the preparation, five men per yard for the advance, and ten or fifteen men per yard for the local assaults. The defence should have from seven to ten men per yard of front for any hope of a successful resistance.' The force as a whole is equal to seven lines two deep over the whole position to be attacked, or, in other words, on the frontage of a company a whole battalion of seven companies, only in a very different formation. And what Continental nations still call columns of attack would be even deeper without counting reconnaissance or preparatory chain. This is as deep as the old battalion columns, only that it extends much further to the rear and is full of gaps, especially in front.

Action by groups.—There is one more detail to be spoken of : the difficulty experienced by English officers in managing the fighting line or chain arises mainly from the neglect of the action by groups, which is familiar to every continental officer. A group means a very small body of men under the leadership generally of a non-commissioned officer. It would be about half an English section at war strength. The word group does not mean that the men are always huddled together—they may be extended or formed in any way—it simply means a very small unit which is in hand habitually, and can be sent forward to reinforce a part of a line, there to dissolve into extended order, or it can be formed pretty closely in the midst of a fighting line or on its flank. It is simply a body of men so small that it can really be held in hand by one man, who takes his orders from the nearest officer. The idea has entered into the Field Exercise, but to judge by the absence of its practical application few officers seem to have grasped its meaning. A section in a company of thirty files would make a handy group, which can be kept in good fire discipline ; such discipline we shall never have so long as commanders of battalions imagine that they can enforce it. The new French regulations of last year, 1887, refuse to allow any interference with the chain except by the corporals who command groups, and, speaking of instructions in time of peace, say, 'It is indispensable that the command be exercised in rotation of rank (*hiérarchiquement*), so as to leave to the chiefs of the different fractions that part of the initiative and responsibility which belongs to them.'

New French Infantry Attack.

The latest form of attack is that of the French, introduced by General Boulanger in 1887, and is worth careful study as being the final epitome of all that anxious examination of tactical questions which experience of war and the concentrated military mind of Europe have produced.

Principles.—Its main principles are—

1st. The offensive alone permits the attainment of decisive results.

2nd. The assembly (*rassemblement*), which means the first tactical formation from column of route, must take place in good position and time (out of fire), and be a formation containing within itself the germ of the attack.

3rd. The next formation, called the *formation transitoire*, is that through which the *rassemblement* passes to the attack formation. It must be manageable, supple, and lend itself *without manœuvre*, by a simple extension of intervals and distances, to the march across the zones swept by the enemy's artillery and infantry fire.

4th. The attack formation is developed naturally out of the *transitoire*. The resulting movements must be simple and not involve any lateral displacements; but cause a sort of necessary and almost mechanical pressure, both energetic and continuous, towards the objective.

The attack has two phases, successive and opposite in character. In the first, the object is to gain ground with as little loss as possible, by a rapid march in suitable formations, making every use of the ground for concealment. The different units here take their distances. In the second phase, the chain having begun to fire, the question of vulnerability is sacrificed to that of producing the greatest possible effect on the enemy. Distances are reduced, and the chain thickened.

5th. Fire is to be opened *as late as possible*, but when once commenced is to be carried out by the largest amount of rifles that can be used, for at this time the effect on the enemy and not on oneself is the governing idea. From the first moment the fire should assume a moral and material superiority to that of the enemy, and be kept in that condition by using supports and reserves freely.

6th. The supports and reserves push the firing line towards the enemy, and thus avoid those times of prolonged halt which cause consumption of ammunition and loss of 'go' (*élan*) in the men.

7th. In the disposition adopted there must be a force for shock distinct from that which carries out the preparation. Carefully held back during the development of the action, the shock force arrives at the chain when the rapid fire commences and carries it on to the assault. In the case supposed in Chapter X. it would pass the chain, and be itself pushed on by other shock troops from behind.

8th. The use of ground is only a temporary expedient. The object is to crush the enemy by fire and advance. A brave and well-led infantry can advance under the most violent fire, even against well-defended trenches, and can carry the position.

The group.—Now, in carrying out these principles, the whole action is based on the working of the group (*escouade groupée*), which is the half of a half section, so that in a company of about 200 bayonets in the field, where a subdivision would be 100, a section 50, and a half section 25, the group will be about 12 men commanded by a corporal. Tactical training begins with the individual soldier, who is taught how to make use of ground, what cover protects and what only conceals movements. He learns how to prepare walls, &c., for defence, and generally to take care of himself, while the idea is impressed upon him that the only way to beat the enemy is to charge him after getting the better of his fire. Part of his instruction is what he may fire at from different distances if he finds himself isolated. As the French have always been greater believers in long range fire than the Germans, it is worth while to see what practice they permit to single sharpshooters.

The soldier must not fire at more than—

200 metres	against	a man	under cover or lying down.
300 ,,	,,	,,	standing or kneeling.
400 ,,	,,	,,	mounted.
500 to 600 ,,	,,	,,	group isolated and lying down, or against a line of skirmishers.

600 to 800 metres against a { company in fighting order, whatever be the formation of the chain.

800 to 1,000 ,, ,, { compact bodies of infantry, cavalry, or artillery.

The group may either be extended or with closed files according to circumstances, the chief idea being that it is to get over the ground as best it can, paying at first special attention to cover, but, later on, devoting itself to crushing the fire of the enemy without too much attention to its own safety. The principle laid down is that the best way to avoid loss is to inflict it on the enemy. In the later firing time of the advance, the ordinary formation of the group is supposed to be in one rank, the men being only just disengaged from each other, five or six inches apart. In the marching stage, the files may be at any distance up to three paces apart ordered by the corporal, or if concealed from fire, in the formation which best suits the ground. Great importance is attached to training the men by groups, which is the basis of all instruction. If the men cannot see their corporal—for instance, if he has been killed or wounded—they regulate their movements by each other. This sounds vague, but it means that under all circumstances the men of a group cling together and constitute the final unit. Groups are practised in manœuvring against each other, the enemy being sometimes marked, sometimes represented by another group. During instruction, though all fire ceases at a distance of 100 metres from the enemy, attacks are always pushed home, sometimes even to the far side of an enemy's marked position. The enemy orders arms or collects to let the attackers pass. In training recruits, the manœuvres are first executed by trained men, the recruits looking on. Another part of the early instruction is, teaching the men what accidents of ground, such as ditches, hedges, walls, &c., cover from both sight and fire, and what others from fire only. They are taught to direct their fire especially at that part of the enemy *which will suffer most*, not at that which is well covered, even though its fire may be most annoying. They are also taught to concentrate and not scatter their fire, and to take very careful aim. All this instruction is necessary before the larger manœuvres can be executed in a workmanlike manner. Individual men are also taught to move, in the early stages, from cover to cover, keeping the general direction of the march.

Half-sections, sections, &c.—Then comes instruction of rather larger units, but always in the same sense ; when they deploy it is by groups. The half-section is under a sergeant who works his two groups, which are taught like individuals to make bold dashes, springing from one position to another. As they are supposed not as a rule to open fire in advancing till within 600 metres of the enemy, it is laid down that from 600 to 400 metres the rushes are to be of about 80 or 100 metres firing 3 rounds before each rush. From 400 to 200 metres the rushes may be of about 50 to 60 metres, and with great rapidity. At 200 metres the bayonet is fixed and a rapid fire commences, then there is a rush of another 50 metres, the magazines of repeating rifles come into play, and when they are emptied there comes the charge, which gradually increases in speed till at 100 metres the men receive the word, '*En avant —à la baïonette!*' when they charge home, right into the enemy's position, where the ranks are readjusted. Each group practises attack and defence in turn, the fire of the defending repeaters commencing when the attack begins its charge, and there is always a counter-attack. So much for the training of the individual soldier and the action by groups and small units. Then exercises of attack and counter-attack against flanks are performed assiduously until they become second nature to the men. Surely this is beginning at the right end.

The company.—Passing on to the company which, though nominally 250 strong, may for practical purposes be counted as 200 bayonets, the formation is based on the principle of a line of subdivision columns, equal to a line of English companies in column. The attack formation begins with a chain formed by the leading section of each subdivision, the other section forming the support for its leading section. This is very like the formation permitted in our Field Exercise in the second note, third section of the battalion attack, only we extend a fourth while the French extend a half for the fighting line. It is a difference in principle, for their chain or fighting line is thicker from the first than ours; and we must not forget the French arrangement by sections, half-sections, and groups.

Details of formation and advance.—The fighting front of the French company is such as would bring the whole company into line of single rank when 200 metres from the enemy, supposing it to have lost by that time one-fourth of its strength. By this rule, a company, 200 strong, should have a fighting frontage of 105 metres—that is, about 116 yards—and an English company, 100 strong, would have a frontage of 58 yards. The advance is guided from one of the flanks, and the deployment is to be by groups, with intervals equal to the front of groups. But at first the movement commences by the captain ordering, 'Attack formation! By the right [or left]! March!' The commander of each subdivision then takes command, and the rear section continues to march direct to its front. When the enemy's fire renders a more open formation necessary—say, between 1,500 and 1,100 yards—the captain gives the word, 'By half sections! March!' when the reverse half section inclines away from the guiding flank, and the captain dismounts. Later on he gives the word, 'By groups!' and the fighting line comes under the immediate influence of the sergeants and corporals, who have, of course, to look out for orders, and conform to any alteration of the general direction, as shown by the movements of the guide. At somewhere about 800 yards from the enemy, the captain orders, 'By files!' when the files open out to about eighteen inches interval; and when it is impossible to advance further without opening fire, he gives the word, '*En tirailleurs!*' which may be translated 'Commence skirmishing;' for it is the signal to begin the action always by three cartridges at a time. While this is doing, the supports continue to advance, and come gradually nearer. The supporting section on the directing flank remains

100 metres from the chain. The supporting section towards the other flank pushes on rapidly, and extends the fighting line to that flank. Thus, at about 600 metres, equal to about 660 yards, three-quarters of the company are in fighting line, and only one quarter in support. After a fire, which must be as short as possible consistent with subduing in part that of the enemy, the captain carries the whole company forward with a rush of about 100 metres, and *opens* fire again, for a short time, during which the last section comes up into fighting line on the directing flank, and by its impulse starts the chain in another rush of 100 metres or so. The company again opens fire with all its rifles in line. Further advances must be made with the help of other pressure from behind, of which we will speak directly; but, for the moment, adhering to the instruction of the company, the captain must suppose the impulses, and carry his company forward by rushes, which are intended to alternate with those of another company, and are about 50 or 60 metres, each time up to 200 yards, from the enemy, executing fire, for a short time, at each halt concentrated on the point of attack. Then fix bayonets and rapid fire at 200 metres, and, as described above, advance 50 metres, fire off magazine rifles, and charge. The company reassembles on the conquered ground as at the beginning of the manœuvres.

The isolated company acts on the same principles, but the direction is from the centre; and one section, at least, is always kept in hand to dash in at the last moment in close order, and, headed by the captain, to give vigour to the assault, dragging the rest with it. When the position is captured, the section of assault deploys into dispersed order, and pursues the enemy with its fire; while the chain, a whole subdivision, minus losses, draws together, prepared to repulse a counter-attack. Though the whole gradual deployment of a company has been given as laid down, it is distinctly said that the company must be practised in deploying a line in dispersed order from any formation whatever.

Defence by an isolated company.—One of the sections of the rear subdivision has the task of executing the counter-attack from a position concealed, if possible. The moment is supposed to be when the enemy makes his assault, and the return attack is prepared by a fire of repeaters. If the counter-attack succeeds, the defenders at once assume the offensive, with chain and one reserve section, the section which has just executed the counter-attack rallying to form the reserve. The companies are also trained to pass resolutely from defence to attack when any favourable occasion may present itself.

The battalion.—Coming now to the battalion, it must first be understood that a regiment in the field has three battalions. The normal formation of the battalion advancing before actually beginning to fight, a formation which the French call the '*Colonne pour le combat,*' is simple and flexible, and lends itself both to manœuvres and to warding off cavalry attacks. The battalion is formed in two lines of columns of subdivisions, with subdivision intervals, and double subdivision distances. In other words, if a square be drawn upon paper, the right flanks of two companies in close column of subdivisions will rest in the two right-hand corners of the square, and the left flanks of the other two companies, formed in the same manner, will rest in the two left-hand corners of the square. It will be seen at once that, by merely turning about, the formation to the rear will be exactly like that now front, or by wheeling the companies a quarter circle to either flank, there will be a front to that flank exactly like the original formation.

Application of its first formation.—By inclining the two rear companies outwards, you get a double echelon of companies, and various other easy formations can be managed. Neither exact distances nor intervals are necessary, so long as it is understood that after breaking them the old formation is restored. Either of the lines can be arranged in more open order, and even put in echelon. In this order of march the battalion advances to about 1,500 metres from the enemy, or even perhaps up to nearly 1,000 metres. It then forms the fighting order, or '*Formation de combat.*'

Formation de combat.—In the order of attack the front

calculated as that which the battalion in double rank would occupy when it had lost a quarter of its strength. On this calculation, a battalion, 800 strong, should have a frontage of about 230 yards. The formation is in three echelons. First, a chain consisting of the front sections of each of the two companies in front of the column just described. Second, supports formed by the other sections of the leading companies. Third, a reserve formed by the two rear companies. As each company had a subdivision (two sections) in front, and the same in rear, there will be four sections for the fighting line, four for the supports, and eight for the reserve. At first the supports are about 200 metres from the chain, and 300 from the reserve, and this continues till fire is opened at, say, 600 metres, when all considerations of safety are sacrificed to the imperious necessity of acting strongly against the enemy. The fighting echelon is then adopted. Supports at 100 metres from the chain, and 200 from the reserve, the total depth being now 300 metres; and this depth is gradually reduced, till it becomes only 100 metres, when the chain is 300 metres from the enemy's position. It is of course understood that the chain breaks up more and more as it advances, till it begins to thicken again near the enemy. The supports may also break up if necessary, but as they are intended to act by constituted bodies, they are held together as much as possible. If the sections have been broken up, they close when entering into line. The same rule applies with even more force to the reserve. Deployments need not be in line but in echelon; it matters not which sections are in advance.

Fighting patrols.—During the march, while the battalion is not in formation to open fire immediately, the commander sends out fighting patrols, which are generally a half section, strong and ' well commanded.' These patrols move in front of the wings, at about 200 metres distance. Their commander must never lose sight of the chain, and conforms to all its movements. One of the two groups composing the half section is deployed at intervals of about six paces; and the other group is held in hand about 50 metres in rear. When the chain deploys by groups the patrols take position and wait for it.

Rules for the march.—During a march, though the general direction, intervals, and distances must be preserved by all the echelons, the commander of each subdivision has entire liberty of manœuvre; he observes attentively the direction of fire and its effect, modifies as he pleases the formation of his men, and uses with intelligence the forms of ground, being held responsible if his men suffer losses on account of his mistakes, or want of energy. As in the case of the small actions described above, the march from 1,500 metres is uninterrupted, and as rapid as possible, up to the time when fire is opened, say, at 600 metres. The reserve companies, if under the fire of artillery, may move obliquely to right or left in place of marching straightforward; this zigzag movement is supposed to make the regulation of the enemy's artillery fire very difficult. After fire is opened, the chain advances by successive rushes, carried out rapidly and with determination.

From 600 to 400 metres the rushes are by the whole chain, and from 80 to 100 metres.

From 400 to 200 metres the rushes are made by echelon of companies, as rapidly as possible; they are from 50 to 60 metres.

After 200 metres the chain moves with increasing rapidity. The halts of the chain are used by the supports and reserves to come up and give the impulses required.

Generally speaking, the entry into line of the supports is regulated by the captains; that of the reserve companies by the commander of the battalion. But this is not to prevent commanders of fractions from acting on their own initiative if circumstances require.

Fire effect.—Concentration of fire is most important, especially for its moral effect. It is more easily obtained at mean ranges than at short, the troops being both in better formation and less excited. In each position the captains name clearly the objectives to be fired at. In principle, repeating fire is to be delivered at the moment of the assault, but captains are to use it without hesitation if the enemy's troops appear suddenly, and for a short time at convenient distances, if the captains think that they can thereby inflict serious losses. (Compare this with German regulations below, page 181.)

Dismounting of officers.—As a general rule, all officers dismount at from 1,200 to 1,000 metres, but this rule is only obligatory on captains.

PHASES OF THE COMBAT (*Plate XVII.*).

We may now put together shortly the arrangements of the fight, which is divided into three phases :—

1st. The passage from the preparatory formation to the fighting formation at about 1,500 metres, according to cirstances.

2nd. Commencement of the fight and its action from 600 to 200 metres.

3rd. Assault and occupation of the position.

First phase.—At the order to form for combat the four leading sections of the leading companies move on, inclining outwards from the centre, so as to leave in the centre of the battalion a subdivision interval. The rest of the battalion halts. The rear sections of the two first companies, destined to form supports, move off when the sections of the chain have advanced 200 metres, and place themselves in rear of the positions which they should occupy in the chain. The two companies of reserve advance when the supports are at 300 metres distance. The movements of each fraction are then regulated as before described.

Second phase.—The second phase comprises two periods. First, from 600 to 400 metres the two companies of the chain are alone in action. The movement is carried out by rushes of the whole chain, each rush being from 80 to 100 metres. Second period, from 400 to 200 metres the companies of reserve enter into line. The march is by company echelon, the rushes are from 50 to 60 metres.

1st period.—As soon as it is impossible to advance without firing, the commander of the battalion orders the fire to be opened. Without further orders the different fractions close on the chain. Supports at 100 metres from the chain. Reserves at 200 metres from the supports. The greatest stress is laid upon obtaining a superiority of fire over the adversary. For this purpose one of the supporting sections of each company moves without halting at all up to the chain, which it prolongs outwards from the centre. This section, which prepares or determines the first rush, acts according to circumstances, either by fire or by immediate pressure, and carries on the chain 80 or 100 metres, *each company closing on its centre.* Fire is again opened, and at a favourable moment the rear sections of the support push up to the inner flanks of the leading companies, by which means the chain is carried on to within 400 metres of the enemy. The leading companies have now in line all the rifles which they can dispose of.

2nd period.—This period brings the reserves into action. When the last section of the support moves up to reinforce the chain, the reserve company in rear of it continues its movement up to 200 metres from the chain, where it deploys, and falls into echelon; the outer subdivision 100 metres in front of the inner. From this time the two reserve companies work alternately to push on the movement. They act successively and by subdivisions on the companies of the chain, so as to push them in four rushes up to about 200 metres from the enemy's position. Thus at each rush about 100 extra rifles come into line, *but not deployed in open order.* The reinforcing subdivision comes up behind the chain which has lately been becoming closer, and opens immediately with it a massed fire which may in some cases be three or four deep. When a subdivision pushes on in this manner the subdivision behind it closes up to about 100 metres, ready to reinforce in its turn. The captains of the reserve companies move with the first subdivision of their company which enters into line, and take the command of that portion of the chain immediately in front of them. The captains of the companies already in the chain take charge of the other half and preserve the direction of advance; taking command of the last subdivisions, which finally come up behind them. Thus, by the time the chain has arrived within 200 metres of the enemy all the reserve subdivisions are up, and the fire is on an average about three deep. Bayonets are then fixed, and the ordinary breech-loading fire proceeds.

Third phase.—One of two cases now presents itself. If the enemy yielding to the fire effect is visibly demoralised the battalion charges at once. If he still holds his ground with firmness, and the commander of the battalion judges that he cannot carry the position at once by assault, he must await the intervention of a new element. We are supposing that a regiment is in action, and the necessary element is found in the reserve battalion of the regiment which has followed the phases of the fight, ready to intervene when necessary. It comes up either in deployed line or echelon of half battalions, so as to provide against a counter-attack. The colonel of the regiment takes command, and sounds the charge with all drums and trumpets. The battalion in front executes the most rapid possible fire with repeating rifles, if it has them, and then, a fresh impulse having been given by the reserve battalion, the whole mass charges. Making allowance for losses experienced up to this time, the charging body will probably be about four deep at the least. The position being carried, it is occupied by the former leading battalion, while the reserve battalion takes up the pursuit.

The battalion isolated.—In case of a battalion acting isolated, its formation is: One company as advance guard;

two companies for fighting line, and one in reserve. The last company marches either in rear of the interval between the two companies in front of it, or on the threatened flank. The general rules for deployment are as before, only the frontage may be greater. The two companies of the chain have to carry on the combat up to 200 metres with their own resources, and must therefore delay the advance of the supports. The third company acts like the reserve battalion in the manner just described to determine the assault, and may make either a front or a flank attack.

Defensive.—There is nothing new in the defensive action of battalions, but they are directed when acting alone to prepare vigorous counter-attacks, which are delivered at the moment of the enemy's charge.

Brigades and divisions.—There is no need to go into the details of brigade and divisional work. It will suffice to say that the new regulations recognise that even the regiment with its reserve battalion may very likely not be in condition to undertake an assault. If a regiment is isolated it must form three lines of its own ; but if it is embodied in a division, the division alone possesses always a third line. If no flank attack is contemplated a single regiment will do for the third line. The battalions of the second line are reserved to give the shock of assault, while the third line remains during the preparation of the attack, concentrated, and masked behind favourable positions, which it organises defensively. But as soon as the first line closes with the enemy and the second forms for assault, the third line follows the movement. If the assault succeeds, it pushes forward generally in line of subdivision columns, and deploys beyond the captured position, either to pursue or to resist counter-attacks ; the rest of the troops reforming behind it. It is even recognised as possible that both the first and the second line may become absorbed by the time the critical point 200 metres from the enemy is reached. In that case even the third line of the division may be called upon to give the final shock.

German Instructions for Magazine Rifles.

As the introduction of a magazine rifle into the British service is already determined upon, it may be interesting to the reader to know something of German views with regard to the employment of such a weapon. The introduction of the magazine rifle into the German army took place last year in a sudden and impressive manner. The regulations with regard to it were published on February 3, and are here summarised. It will be seen that in the French Instructions sketched above the German model has been copied almost exactly.

Instruction of the soldier.—The only important point, in what may be called the drill of the soldier in the new arm, is the care taken that even when the magazine is loaded it shall not be brought into action without special orders. There are to be two words of command, namely :—'load' and 'load the magazine.' Following the first, the rifle is loaded in the ordinary way. If the word 'load the magazine' is given, the soldier places eight cartridges in the magazine, which lies under the barrel, and a ninth in the movable chamber which transfers the cartridges from the magazine to the back of the barrel. If now he placed a tenth cartridge in the chamber of the barrel all would be in order for commencing at once repeating fire, but he is not allowed to do this, according to regulation. The practice, which will become second nature, is, to shut off the communication between the magazine and the barrel before loading in the ordinary way. After this, the apparatus allows of passing from ordinary fire to repeating and back again, at any moment during the shooting.

Instruction of the company.—Volleys may be fired, either with ordinary or magazine loading. In the latter case, if the magazine is emptied and circumstances do not permit of refilling it, fire is to be continued, if necessary, with ordinary loading, as quickly as possible. The fire by single ranks had already been suppressed. The two ranks now always fire together, and may, when called upon, use repeating fire, which is, however, forbidden as a rule to fractions in close order. The chain, in dispersed order, may use repeating fire under proper conditions; so also may the supports which close upon the chain in close order when the assault is to be immediately prepared, or when it is necessary to repulse a charge of cavalry or a bayonet attack; but, in such cases the neighbouring skirmishers must cease their individual fire and join in that of the group, taking their orders from its commander. It will be observed that this principle has been carried out to its logical conclusion in the French regulation (page 176, above). More importance is attached to the steadiness and coolness of the men than to rapidity of fire.

Instruction of the battalion.—Four cases are named in which repeating fire may be employed.

1st. When the battalion in double column is obliged to deploy rapidly, the fractions which first arrive in line may use it to cover the movement.

2nd. When the battalion presses up in close order on the chain to support it.

3rd. When the deployed battalion prepares to assault. In that case the advance should immediately follow the conclusion of the fire.

4th. Against cavalry, to deliver volleys as rapidly as possible. These volleys must, however, be conducted with the greatest coolness and only opened at 300 metres. The battalion will be grouped together as much as possible.

In the prescriptions relating to the combat of the battalion, the instruction of the individual soldier is specially insisted upon, in order to secure fire discipline, the rapid loading of the arm, and passage without hesitation from ordinary to repeating fire.

'The magazine gives to the soldier a continual reserve of ammunition, by which he may at any moment be ready to fire. This reserve will be always assured if discreet and judicious use is made of it, and if every occasion is seized for refilling it. The soldier must never forget that his new arm increases the necessity for an absolute fire discipline, and that it is destined to produce, not only a superficial acceleration but a superior fire effect. . . . Officers and non-commissioned officers will take care that the magazine constitutes a reserve which is only to be used at the decisive moment. At long and medium ranges ordinary fire suffices. As a principle, repeating fire will only take place with the shortest sights. It is only in exceptional cases that it will be used between 300 and 800 metres, to profit by the momentary appearance of objects particularly favourable if there are tactical reasons for covering them with a violent fire.'

Economised to the last moment, repeating fire will facilitate the assault, on condition that it be skilfully concentrated on certain points of the enemy's position.

When the adversary retires it will still be useful to direct against him the most violent fire that can be produced.

Besides these mass fires, repeating fire may be useful to increase the intensity of the fire of a very thin chain of skirmishers. There are some cases in which the interest of the battalion is to remain in closed order and to deploy in front of it as few skirmishers as possible.

No alterations are made in the formations for attack, which are very much like those now adopted by the French, the principle being exactly the same.

Such are the French and German arrangements for the attack brought down to the latest period, and contemplating the use of magazine rifles, which the Germans now have and the French have in part. The French and Russian armies are at present rather running down the value of magazine rifles, but this is probably because they are not yet in possession of the new arm. The French are manufacturing repeating rifles of a new pattern as quickly as they can. It is not so easy to say exactly what the Russians are doing.

If the reader will compare this chapter with the one preceding, he will be in a position to determine for himself the formation which he would adopt under any given circumstances. Has he to expect obstacles which will necessarily detain his fighting line under fire for a considerable time? Let him gain ground with a comparatively weak force, and place it, if possible, under cover, close to the obstacles till they are cleared away. Should he have no reason to expect any other resistance than that of an enemy, more or less sheltered, but not protected by actual obstacles to advance, then he must make up his mind to get over all the last portion of the ground as quickly as possible, and to thicken moment by moment his fighting line till the final charge is delivered by a mass of men, receiving as it goes fresh impulses from behind, and having the certainty that flank attacks will be provided against by other bodies kept in hand for the purpose. There must be great loss of life if the enemy stands well; but there would be greater loss and no final effect if the attack were made with less decision and more thought for safety.

Artillery Support.—It is impossible to say what the artillery should do in these later stages unless the particular case is given. But, speaking generally, it should endeavour to aid the infantry by adding its fire to that of the rifles, even at the risk of suffering loss in gunners. When hostile infantry are contending, the apparition of guns on one side, the sound of the heavy reports close at hand, and the additional intensity of fire so produced, will assuredly add greatly to that moral effect, to produce which is the end, and all physical action only the means. The risk is not great, for the enemy has his attention already occupied, and if it were great, the result to be attained would justify the risk. If circumstances render close assistance impossible the artillery can at least prevent the defenders' guns from coming into action at this period. But the golden rule for artillery is to fire at that portion of the enemy's forces which is *at the time* the most important. When the infantry struggle has begun, the enemy's infantry is clearly his most important arm.

CHAPTER XII.

COMBAT WITHIN VILLAGES.

Information required—Importance of good interior defence—Defence of first houses—Counter-attacks—Interior attack—Columns of attack—Organised advance—Flanking fire of defenders—Defence not always complete—Advance through houses—Artillery in street fighting—Attack of the keep—Traversing streets under fire—House to house fighting—Underground passages and mines—Provision against counter-attack—Completion of the capture—Night work—Action of the turning columns—Extinguishing fire—Recapitulation of Defence—General considerations—General dispositions—Barricades—Artillery—Stores—Minor keeps—Land torpedoes—House to house defence—Incendiarism — Counter-attacks—Recapitulation of Attack—First entrance—Press attack—Artillery—Gradual progress—Main keep—Completion of capture—Surprises—Ought to be impossible—Outposts—Gitschin—Troops for surprise must be good—No noise—Previous knowledge—Time for surprise : Night—Precautions on the march—Night march in Balkans—Before Tel-el-Kebir—Houchard's escape—The attack—Rendezvous—Defence.

Information required.—Many a bloody repulse has been the result of attacking while in ignorance of the enemy's preparations—*e.g.* Zaatcha, Chapter XIV.—and no pains should be spared to acquire knowledge. In an enemy's country you will receive false information, but the cross-examination of several inhabitants will sift it. Threats of vengeance and taking hostages will help you with a civil population. It is neither common sense nor humanity to risk the lives of hundreds of soldiers rather than act on the nerves of the civil population. It is well understood that no form of torture is permissible. Moral pressure will generally suffice, and if it does not you can go no further. You should obtain, if possible, a plan of the village, or at least a sketch of it, showing the principal streets, the position of public buildings, open spaces where the enemy could collect in force, buildings prepared for defence, &c.; and your information should show the best routes to follow, the enemy's prepared communications, the access to important buildings, and also any secret or subterranean passages which may exist. Find out if you can the enemy's defensive organisation, both as to men and material preparations.

Importance of good interior defence.—It is evident that an attack pushed home vigorously, as has been sketched in the preceding chapter, is certain to carry the outer line of defence unless it be repulsed by a counter-attack; and even such counter-attacks are difficult. The preparation of the village for defence hampers the defenders when endeavouring to issue from it, and counter-attacks from exterior reserves will be guarded against by the attackers, who, having the initiative in their hands, will know where their weak point is, and make special preparations to guard it. If the village forms part of a line of battle, either in that line or in front of it, the flanks will be swept by artillery fire, and a counter-attack be protected in its advance. In any case, counter-attacks should be attempted, as the only means of preventing the enemy from gaining his first footing in the village. But supposing the entrance is made, and the village is to be defended as long as possible, much remains to be done before the enemy can be said to have captured it in the full sense of the word; for the defenders may still hold the interior, and till they are driven from it the object for which it is held has been achieved—that is to say, it still bars the passage of the attackers. The interior combat has now to be dealt with, premising that the rules for villages are equally applicable to large towns, within which, if a determined and well ordered defence be made, a very large force indeed of the attackers may be swallowed up. It is customary to say that if an enemy entered London the whole defence of the country must collapse. Possibly that might be the case if London were completely in the hands of the invaders. But, taking all things into consideration, it may be doubted whether a scientific and stubborn interior defence might not have more chance of success than any occupation of positions outside the city. Examples will be given later on from history. Are the English volunteers and people of London to acknowledge that they have less skill and courage than the citizens of Saragossa in 1809, or the people of Zaatcha in 1849?

Defence of first houses.—It has been said in preceding chapters that the attack must endeavour to close with the retreating defenders and enter the place with them. The defence must bear this in mind and try to prevent it, even by the sacrifice, if necessary, of part of the advanced shooting line. To this end, the moment that the artillery bombardment ceases the defenders should garrison the houses which have been prepared for defence, and which bear upon the points first exposed to attack. If breaches have been made in the walls or houses, the first precaution is to place infantry where they can concentrate their fire on those breaches, while an attempt should be made to repair them. Parties of infantry will be placed behind the portions of wall, or whatever it is, left standing, so as to take in flank an enemy attempting to enter by the breach. A heavy fire is kept up from loopholes, &c., upon the enemy's skirmishers, and especially on working parties, which will be both removing obstacles and trying to effect an entrance to the houses by hasty demolition or other means. The defenders' fire must, under the circumstances, be independent—that is, carried out by individuals; but junior officers and non-commissioned officers should control it as much as possible, by telling off some men to fire on one portion of the enemy and some on another. In this way fire discipline may be preserved, and the soldiers will have the moral support of feeling that their efforts are being directed with intelligence.

Counter-attacks.—At this stage counter-attacks may be made, using for the purpose, if necessary, the interior reserves as well as the exterior. The advance of the attack must have caused a good deal of confusion and mixture of units, which is always a source of weakness, however well trained troops may be, and it is on such occasions that counter-attacks may have a good chance of success. But, except for purposes of counter-attack, the interior reserves should be kept sheltered from the fire of the enemy. If circumstances permit, it is better to leave all the counter-attack work to the exterior reserves. The defending artillery, which is supposed to have been driven from its first position, may give valuable aid in the counter-attacks by flanking the village from retired positions, chosen beforehand. There are numerous cases in which the assistance of the guns has been very efficacious, both in resisting the columns of attack from retired positions and supporting counter-attacks. The golden rule for artillery officers should be, that, whenever there is a struggle between two bodies of infantry, the addition *of artillery fire to one side may turn the scale both by its physical and moral effect, especially if it can be brought to bear on the enemy's flank, as it often may on the side of the defenders against enveloping attacks.*

Interior attack.—Supposing that an entrance has been effected, and some houses seized, the further advance should be as rapid as possible, and an attempt must be made to press on along the main streets. But one precaution should never be omitted, namely, to prepare against the defenders the houses which are first occupied. This will, of course, be done by troops different from those intended to push home the attack. It is of the utmost importance that no time should be lost. The infantry should rush into the houses, if possible, before the defenders evacuate them, and search at once for any commencement of conflagration or preparations for explosion. The most commanding and strongest houses should then be prepared for defence against attacks from the defenders of the village, and every endeavour be made to sweep the streets. For this purpose the barricades relinquished by the defenders may often be used against them. It is evident that the troops used for making good what has been captured must be quite distinct from those who are to push on to further conquests. These latter we will call '*columns of attack.*'

Columns of attack.—The bodies of troops which endeavour to push through the streets will have two difficulties to encounter :

1st. The defence from the front and sides of the street itself.

2nd. The flanking fire of posts especially prepared for that purpose.

Even for advancing up a street there is a right and a wrong way. The worst way is to move solidly and stolidly up the middle of the street, for, if you do, the barricade defenders will have their best opportunity for fire, and the average difficulty of shooting from the windows of the houses will be at a minimum. Let the student go to a window in the room where he reads this, or to some window, and imagine an enemy coming down a street from his right. He will find that, whether that enemy advance down the centre or on either side, the defenders cannot take aim and fire at the column without exposing a great part of their bodies. Now let him imagine the enemy to be advancing from his left, and he will find that defenders from that position can see down the other side of the street for a considerable distance without any exposure worth mentioning, but must lean outwards a little to fire down his own side of the street. Apply this to the benefit of the attack, and it will be evident that the advance should be made either on both sides of the street, or, if on one side only, then by the right side from the point of view of the attack.

Organised advance.—Supposing the defence to be weak, the attackers should advance rapidly by all the streets leading from the base seized on entering the village. As far as possible the columns should work together, communicating by side streets and helping each other to turn barricades. But if the defence be strong and well conducted, and the defenders have so occupied the houses on both sides of the streets as to fire on the rear of the attacking columns, it will be necessary to secure the ground step by step, breaking into the houses either by axes and musket butts, or even by charges of gun-cotton, which should be carried for the purpose by special parties—of engineers if possible, though all soldiers should be taught the use of gun-cotton for such purposes.

Flanking fire of defenders.—A well-considered defence will have established special posts for flanking fire. These may be either in the street itself or in side streets, or in the combination of the two formed by corner houses where streets cross. In the first two cases they must be carried either by a rush or by turning them first and carrying them afterwards. In the last case, and generally on arriving at important cross streets, occupy and organise the corner houses before pushing on, unless the enemy is making such a weak defence that you can press him steadily back without delay.

Defence not always complete.—Here we may pause for a moment to remark that all village fighting is not necessarily the attack and defence of a fortified village. It may be that an enemy retiring before you leaves a portion of his rearguard in a village to delay the advance of artillery, &c., along a main road. In such a case the defence may make a great show of fire from the outskirts, and you might suffer considerable loss and delay in making a front attack. Your tactical knowledge must enable you to judge the situation, and your skill will be shown in sending part of the cavalry and infantry round by the flanks while the artillery opens on the front of the village. In most cases the enemy will evacuate it, when your main body, which will be that of your advanced guard, can push through at an increased pace. But in no case send your artillery through a village which has been occupied by the enemy without the company of other troops. A very few men remaining there might cripple your batteries for a long time by shooting the horses. In no position is artillery so helpless.[1]

[1] The knowledge of field artillery with its strength and weakness cannot be said to be quite universal in the army. When commanding cavalry and artillery at Ipswich I found it very useful to send a column on the march, and detail detachments, representing an enemy, to lay wait for the artillery in by-roads, behind farmhouses, &c. The quickening of the cavalry officers' intelligence in scouting and escorting was wonderful.—C. B. B.

Advance through houses.—It may be that the defence will be so energetic that the attack cannot make way by the streets at all after the force of the first rush is spent ; especially is this the case against well-defended barricades. It must then burrow a road for itself through the very houses themselves, a method which will cost time and trouble, but is efficacious and comparatively sparing of life. Working parties will hew their way through the partition walls, which are seldom very thick in a village. Sometimes it will be easier to work through the gardens. Organise whatever you capture against a counter-attack, and let the soldiers occupying the houses hold on to them, even if the columns in the streets have to retire. Always work on both sides of the streets, or the enemy will work on his side and paralyse you. In the next two chapters will be found examples of actual village fighting in war, and the student will remark how valuable was the practice of either defence or attack sticking to the smallest foothold left them in a village. The American slang term, 'freezing' to a thing, exactly represents the course to be pursued. What splendid opportunities there are in war for young officers and non-commissioned officers, if only they know what they ought to do !

Artillery in street fighting.—It is commonly said that artillery should be brought into the village, to act especially against barricades, houses, firing down the street, &c. There may be cases in which such means must be resorted to, and we should be the last to object to the use of the guns if they can really assist better inside the village than out of it. But take for example the case of a barricade. It is now generally recognised that a frontal attack on a barricade is one of the most murderous operations in war ; and it is certainly a question whether a turning movement through houses and gardens is not quite as short as, while it is certainly much less murderous than, the long affair of bombardment added to the final bloody attack, which even then may not succeed. If the knowledge which a good reconnaissance, a map, and examination of inhabitants can give has been secured, there is often a good opportunity for guns outside the village to assist by taking barricades in reverse. Therefore do not bring in guns which may be more useful outside. There is, however, one case in which guns are very likely to be useful, and two pieces should always be held in readiness for the purpose if required. That case is the attack on the keep, the success or failure in which chiefly decides the capture of the village or defeat of the attack.

Attack of the keep.—It has been said above that the keep should be attacked as soon as possible, but this is exactly what the defence will try to prevent. Partial and disorganised attacks on the keep should not be made. The nature of the keep ensures that it will command some open space, and probably have a large street or avenue of some kind leading towards it from the front of the attack. Here then, if at all, is the place for field guns in village fighting. The street in front of them must be cleared of troops, and captured barricades utilised as cover for the pieces. Breaches may thus be made in the keep, and the work of the infantry made easier. It is well that artillery should co-operate where it can even inside the village, but its greatest value will generally be found to consist in support from the outside. In Chapter XIII. the reader will find a case, that of Juranville, in which the French hussars carried a village by a charge, and the author was witness of the capture both of Tirnova and Kezanlik by cavalry in 1877; but we should not give an attack by cavalry as one of the regular means of carrying villages. The place of cavalry is outside, and, in most cases, that will be the place for the guns also. The keep, whether bombarded or not from inside, must be treated like any other house or farm. It should be surrounded so as to keep all the defenders employed; its fire should be subdued by superior fire from every direction, especially from the windows of neighbouring houses. A breach or breaches must be made in its walls, and it must be assaulted with the greatest vigour. Attackers and defenders will then be face to face, and the stronger will win. The details of the attack will be as given in the next paragraphs.

Traversing streets under fire.—Before crossing a street with the enemy on the other side of it take care to arrange for a heavy fire from your side. Every window should be well occupied by men sheltered as far as possible. Use mattresses, tables, anything, as detailed in previous chapters on defence of houses. Your men must keep up a fire on every nook where an enemy may be sheltered and every orifice through which he could fire. The troops which have to advance will remember that in passing up a street they take either both side pavements or the right, only keeping as close to the houses as possible. If a street has to be crossed when part of it is occupied by the enemy, make, if possible, some sort of traverse, which can be begun by throwing furniture out of windows and continued by men working behind the portion already built. Any shelter is better than none. A mere curtain hung across, tables placed on their sides, or anything which hides a man from view, will prevent the enemy from knowing when your men are crossing. A kitchen table placed on its edge and pushed along as your barricade advances makes not at all a bad mantelet to work behind. Thus, whether you are crossing an ordinary street or are working up to a keep, you can be defended from the enemy's musketry fire. When the day comes, as come it must, when artillery carries artificial shields, probably of steel, the shields will be borrowed for village fighting, and the guns themselves can take more part in it.

House to house fighting.—Suppose a street crossed, or any means taken to arrive at a house, or the keep, or whatever it may be, the next step is to make a practicable breach, or more than one, by means of explosives, which you could never do if the house were well prepared and you could not keep down the enemy's fire. Now must the attackers dash instantly through the breach, before the defenders have time to recover from the shock of the explosion. The combination of circumstances is against the moral tone of the defence, and the floor first attacked is likely to be defended weakly. For this and other reasons it is best, when working up a street or through a block of houses, to establish breaches in two floors at least. There is no fighting which rouses the savage in man so much as attack and defence of villages and towns. The struggle in the houses will be passionate and rather cruel. Little mercy will be shown, as the men cannot encumber themselves with prisoners. Every room must be searched from cellar to attic, and no resisting force must be left behind to cut your communications.[1] If all the floors cannot be breached and attacked at the same time, it is better to work through the top of the houses, both because the walls are thinner and easier to breach, and because the clearance of the defenders is easier when working from top to bottom. Make holes in the floors and shoot down through them. Take care that no enemies remain in cupboards or big fireplaces, and burn something to make a smoke up the chimney.[2] It is better to have engineers, if possible, as working parties, to create the breaches and works generally, but if you have none, tell off special parties for the purpose, keeping them rigidly separate from those told off to assault. Search for mines and preparations for incendiarism.

Underground passages and mines.—Another precaution to be taken, so as to leave no chance of enemies behind, is to search all underground passages, so numerous and large in towns which come under the generic name of ' localities,' and are attacked and defended like villages. Before exploring drains, &c., clear them out either by a salvo of musketry from end to end or by throwing projectiles with lighted Bickford's fuze down any of the openings. These underground passages may sometimes be used to obtain access to other houses, perhaps even the keep, which may be blown in by mines. Remember that gunpowder has a more wide-reaching effect than gun-cotton, though less intense at the point where it is applied. The action of gun-cotton with detonating fuze

---

[1] At Saragossa the French were careless; the Spaniards profited by the fault and closed their way of retreat.

[2] In common with all writers M. Louis Thival recommends this. Why then so indignant with General von Schmeling's '*Nun! so räuchert sie hinaus*' ? (See p. 240.)

o

is very sharp and local in its effect; it is excellent for shattering doors and breaking up obstacles.

Provision against counter-attack.—Whatever activity has been shown by the defence at earlier stages, it must deliver a counter-attack before the keep is carried, unless the intention is not to defend the village to the last. Now the troops engaged in the actual attack of the keep will have their attention fully occupied by that work, and the result of a counter-attack at this stage may be a serious check. Two precautions should therefore be taken : 1st, to have a solid defensive organisation of houses to break the counter-attack; and 2nd, to hold in hand a reserve destined for the same purpose. In the next chapter it will be shown how the Germans before Paris based their whole system of defence on a light occupation of the ground in front and the advanced part of the villages, always having outposts to give warning; and, when the French force was somewhat disorganised by its first efforts, brought up fresh troops and took the offensive with energy. The attack should beware of these tactics, and be ready to parry them by a reserve, which, to be fully efficient, should be fresh and in its proper organisation. The defenders will make a counter-attack, if only to carry off the beleaguered garrison of the keep. If there is none the enemy is beaten.

Completion of the capture.—The capture of the keep will produce a strong moral effect on both sides; and, while it is being organised by the attackers to be a defensive post for them, the attempt should be made to carry the rest of the village. The same methods should be used as before, except that the attackers, who are winning, may be rather more rapid and enterprising. Make sure that not a single house remains in the enemy's possession. Get your troops into their proper formations as quickly as possible, and organise the village for defence against the enemy. It would not be fair to call upon the troops which have carried a well defended village after long fights to pursue the success by marching forward and attacking the formed troops outside. That must be left to other portions of the army.

Night work.—Unless circumstances permit of completely surprising the defenders, a night attack on a village is not advisable, except in the possible case of its being made by troops which know the locality well against a newly arrived enemy. Taking armies as they exist, we may suppose that the attackers do not know the streets and byways, while the defenders are or ought to be intimately acquainted with them; and a village or town is a very labyrinth at night. But cases may arise where night comes on and the village is but half captured. In that case it is better to suspend operations of advance, but utilise the time by putting houses in a state of defence; improving communications, especially such as are under fire of the enemy; bringing the troops into tactical order under their own officers, which, by the way, should be first accomplished. Special houses with ample ground-floor accommodation should be told off as alarm posts, and sentries should be posted. These things done, let the men sleep, unless some peculiar work requires labour throughout the night; in which case do not count on those who are disturbed as available for much service next day. Assemble the men before dawn in preparation for the continued attack. Get any information you can during the night.

Action of the turning columns.—We have now studied the action of a force advancing directly into the village, as if it were alone. The intelligent reader will, no doubt, have perceived how much the task would be facilitated by having flank attacks made at the same time. If circumstances permit, there should always be such turning columns, and they should make flanking attacks, proceeding exactly as detailed for the main column. Not only will the work be more quickly performed because more hands are engaged in it, but the moral effect on the enemy of feeling his flanks turned may, and probably will, cause his retirement from positions which he might have continued to hold. He will fear that his retreat is being cut off. The turning columns will also be of great use in warding off counter-attacks, and they should keep reserves for that purpose.

Extinguishing fires.—It has been said that it may often be to the interest of the defenders to set on fire parts of the village which they are forced to evacuate. In the defence of Saragossa, for instance, the French were long delayed by fires kindled by the patriotic Spaniards. It is plain that the attack must be prepared to extinguish such fires quickly, before they gain too fast a hold. No hand-work can extinguish a burning house when once the fire has laid well hold, but such fires may sometimes be isolated by blowing up or tearing down those which are close to them.

Recapitulation.

Defence.

General considerations.—1. The defenders of a village or town should be full of courage, firmness, tenacity, and, if possible, enthusiasm for their cause. It is wonderful how many good defences have been made by irregulars, or even ordinary inhabitants fighting for their hearths and homes. Examples: Saragossa and Zaatcha. Whoever they may be, they should be taught that they must not be astonished if they hear fighting on all sides of them, and, above all, that a village is not lost so long as one house remains in possession of the defenders.

2. A centralised direction of details is impossible. The chief commander must think beforehand, arrange a general plan of defence, and take care that everybody understands it. He can also select his subordinate commanders if he thinks fit; but he must then leave them to their own initiative during the action. He should, however, insist on being informed of the incidents of the fight, and especially the progress of the enemy. Having reserves in hand, he will know best when, where, and how to give effectual help.

3. Alarming news is sure to be circulated, and all sorts of amateur advice offered. All should be rejected. Each subordinate commander has to defend his own section and nothing else. If the whole of the village besides were taken, his defence should go on in spite of it, till he is ordered to retire.

4. In an enemy's country it is absolutely necessary to expel the villagers, even if they should profess the greatest devotion. In one's own country, women, children, and all who cannot be made use of should be sent away.

General dispositions.—The organisation should be by sections, unless there is no possibility of an enveloping attack, in which case it may be by lines, which will, however, be again divided into portions. The sections will be groups of houses arranged with reference to the run of the streets. Each section should be independent and have its own organisation. All sections should be in communication between each other, and with headquarters, by connecting posts, or at least by signal. Picked shots will be placed on roofs and among chimney-stacks, especially where a long street can be seen. Observers will be placed in church-towers or other commanding positions. The inner reserves will be in squares or large courts. The squares command various communications. A strong keep will be established in a central position, to be held to the last.

Barricades.—To be established in the streets which run towards the enemy, but, if possible, only erected step by step, so as not to prevent easy communication. Have the necessary material ready at other places. Later on, barricade transverse streets on flank of enemy's advance, to isolate his columns. Clear away paving stones.

Artillery.—Better outside, and machine or quick-firing guns inside. The object is to enfilade the streets. Get head-cover if possible, as the enemy's fire will be plunging from roofs of houses.

Stores.—Accumulate ammunition and stores, such as powder, gun-cotton or dynamite, tools, ladders, ropes, in important places; also food and means for extinguishing fire.

Minor keeps.—Besides the main keep, each commander of a section should organise a keep of his own as a central refuge and point of stubborn defence.

Land torpedoes.—To be outside your outer defences and well concealed.

House to house defence.—The greatest tenacity should be shown in holding not only every prepared house, but every room in that house. If one part is carried hold on to the rest, and get back any foot of ground which you can.

Incendiarism.—If any portion of a village is being captured, and you cannot get it back again, set fire to it, provided that the wind does not blow its smoke in your own direction.

Counter-attacks.—Besides the early counter-attack to save the front of the village, deliver frequent interior attacks. Good opportunities will occur, especially when any well-prepared house or group of houses opens a fresh fire on the enemy. They will also be necessary to disengage the garrison of a keep which is being cut off by the attack, and a final one should always be made before evacuating the village.

RECAPITULATION.

ATTACK.

First entrance: press attack.—Artillery bombardment ceases. Carry and organise for defence the first houses. Try to push columns forward at once if the defence is at all weak. Flanking attacks are most important, and often make all the difference between success and failure. Try to make the enemy hear firing in his rear. If the defenders give way attack their supports at once, and try to prevent them fighting in a second position. Sacrifices made in pressing a retiring enemy, though heavy at the time, are nothing compared with those which a long day's fighting would bring. Strive, therefore, to give the enemy no time to rally. But always secure your line of retreat.

Artillery.—Do not bring guns into the village if you can help it, but arrange with those outside a code of signals by which the artillerymen will know how you progress, and can assist by their fire from outside.

Gradual progress.—If the enemy resists firmly, you will have to carry the defended houses one after another and stage by stage. *At the same time* try to push columns up the streets on the right-hand pavement or on both, firing at the opposite windows. Turn barricades if possible. A house occupied by you near the flank of a barricade will render it untenable. Establish yourself solidly in the portions taken from the enemy, and squeeze him gradually from both flanks if possible.

Main keep.—Try to gain the houses which look on the keep, and bring as much fire to bear on it as you can. Isolate it as soon as possible, and use every means to capture it, breaching its walls or doors, forming a covered way to advance against it if necessary. But this determined attack should only be made if the enemy is likely to make strong counter-attacks. If he is clearly on the wing, let the keep remain without assault. It must capitulate later.

Completion of capture.—Be sure to leave the enemy no footing whatever, even in isolated houses. (See examples in Chapter XIII.) And, unless you are moving rapidly in pursuit of a retreating force, organise the village for defence. Troops which have had a long struggle in a village are hardly fit to pursue.

SURPRISES.

Ought to be impossible.—A well-organised force exercising the usual military precautions ought never to be surprised in any position. Yet we know that such things occur in all wars, and it must be confessed that the British army, in all ages, has been over-careless about outpost duties. So has the French, but to a less degree. When troops have been marching, perhaps fighting, all day, and arrive tired in the evening at a town or village where rest and refreshment seem to welcome them, it seems very hard that some of them should have to go out at once on outpost duty. Human nature rebels against it, yet there must be something wrong about a force which neglects these precautions.

Outposts should be pushed well out.—In order to be secure from surprise, there most be no nonsense about inlying picquets and a sentry here and there close to the place. The rule must be that the enemy should be prevented from bringing the place under fire without warning; and if this is beyond the possibilities of the case, the very least that is permissible is that time must be given to the garrison after the alarm to turn out and take up its allotted positions without hurry. Of course in every case those positions must be arranged and announced before the troops are permitted to go to sleep.

Gitschin.—As an example of what may be done by the surprise of a village at night, take the case of Gitschin in 1866. That village was attacked and carried by surprise about midnight. The Austrian headquarter staff was about to issue the orders for next day, and the surprise prevented their doing so, at least with any completeness. The result was that corps commanders found themselves obliged to act on the inspiration of the moment, not even knowing how they were to retire. Thus the troops to the south-west of Gitschin were unable to gain the Miletin road. They followed a road which turned them out of their way, and the 1st Army Corps only succeeded in pulling itself together before Königgrätz on July 2, the day before the great battle. The author was himself a witness of part of this march and the resulting confusion, which had a very bad moral effect on the troops.

Troops for surprise must be good.—If the effect of a night surprise is or may be great, the operation is a serious trial of discipline and conduct. None but good troops should be entrusted with it. The night march and surprise of Tel-el-Kebir was as honourable to the present race of British soldiers as to the commander who had confidence in them.

No noise.—It is necessary to exclude every element of noise. The number of men used need not be so great as in a daylight attack, and the troops should be weeded of all men whose silence cannot be ensured. Those with colds and coughs should be excluded, and no horses allowed in the neighbourhood of the point to be surprised.

Previous knowledge.—There is no case in which previous knowledge is more important. The plan of attack should be drawn up beforehand and explained to every officer and man in the force, but only just before the attack is to take place, lest they should talk about it.

Time for surprise: night.—The best time for surprise is obviously the night, and the darker, noisier, and more tempestuous the weather the better. It is very difficult for sentries to keep their senses alert when they are being buffeted by wind and rain, and if they are alert they cannot hear much. It is also well to select a night when some festivity has taken place in the village, or the enemy's troops there are dog-tired with marching or fighting. The best moment for the attack is a little before daylight, because then watchers are least awake to sights and sounds, and sleepers are most profoundly lapped in slumber. At that hour, too, men's vital forces are depressed, and panic is probable among such as are roused from sleep.

Precautions on the march.—During the night all marches should *as far as possible* be confined to roads or marked paths. The columns should be led by experienced and trusty guides. The troops should not be fatigued, and on no account should they be allowed to lie down when halts are made.

Night march in Balkans.—In crossing the Balkans with General Gourko's advanced guard in 1877, a curious fact was observed by the author. The troops had been marching since early dawn, with the exception of a four hours' rest in the afternoon. The infantry had been on its legs some sixteen to eighteen hours, toiling up the slopes of the mountains, and some helping to drag the guns in difficult places. Night fell as the head of the column crossed the ridge and disappeared in a ravine. Riding down that ravine past midnight, the way being along the bed of a stream, the author, who was with the headquarter staff, saw, in the all but total darkness, curious forms which seemed to be rocks. On touching one of these, it proved to be a Russian soldier, and the author perceived that not only the sides of the stream but all the rocks in its bed were covered with soldiers fast asleep, their feet being for the most part in the water. A check had occurred somewhere. All the men in the rear had sat down and fallen asleep almost instantly. It must have been a difficult task to rouse them. Yet, if the Turks had been at all careful, that narrow pass with its sheep track would have been watched, the advance discovered, and the sleeping column annihilated.

Before Tel-el-Kebir.—During the night march before Tel-el-Kebir a slight deviation from the direct line very nearly brought the two wings of the force face to face. But for the care of the officers and the excellent discipline of the men, a collision would have occurred, and perhaps fighting, under the impression that the enemy had been met with.

Houchard's escape.—Many other cases might be mentioned. In 1793 General Houchard owed his escape to the fact that one of the Prussian columns sent against him in the night wandered altogether out of its way. And like cases are numerous; for instance, General Heimann's failure to carry the eastern forts of Erzeroum (see Chapter XVII.).

It is, therefore, important to allow for very slow movement, to have well-trained officers leading the columns, which should constantly communicate with each other, and to have a recognised system of signalling.

The attack.—The attack should be made by different columns at the same moment, certainly in front and from both flanks. Advance as quickly as possible, and assume the air of a conqueror, calling for immediate surrender. Act with the greatest vigour and even apparent rashness. So will you dominate the spirit of the defenders, and an inferior force may even take away a village from one that is superior in number, but not in that yet stronger force—moral tone.

Rendezvous.—If victory has crowned your efforts, it will be necessary to reassemble before anything more can be done. If the attack fails, everyone should know where to go to. Therefore, appoint places of rendezvous for either case. It is, perhaps, superfluous to say that the village should at once be put in condition of defence against those whom you have lately turned out.

Defence.—After what has been said it will be evident

that the main duty of the defence is to make surprise impossible. If there are troops enough, proper outposts should be thrown well to the front, watching especially the roads and main paths, as it is most unlikely that the enemy will advance across country if there are roads. The least that should be done is to patrol well out, and establish near the village small ambuscades to snap up the patrols or advanced parties of the enemy, using the bayonet. Sentries should also be established with a system of signals agreed upon. A good precaution is to have materials laid for fires, which can be lighted by the advanced posts both as signals and to show the columns of the enemy. If the attack still comes, it ought to meet you ready and with your defence well prepared. In that case there is no surprise, and a night attack is almost sure to fail.

CHAPTER XIII.

EXAMPLES OF ATTACK AND DEFENCE OF LOCALITIES IN MODERN WAR—CAMPAIGN OF 1866 AND 1870-71.

Campaign of 1866—Austrian defects—Affair of Podol—Night attack—Battle of Königgrätz (Sadowa)—Village of Chlum unprepared—Farm of Rosberitz also—They become turning-points in defensive battle—Battle of Custozza—Farm of Cavalchino—Campaign of 1870-71—Battle of Weissenburg—Château of Geissberg—Description of château—Prussian attack bloodily repulsed—Arrival of artillery—Garrison yields to bombardment—Battle of Wörth—Elsasshausen—Fröschwiller—Battle of Spicheren—Stiring Wendel—Battle of Gravelotte—St. Marie aux Chênes—Farms of St. Hubert and Moscow—Position of St. Privat (see Chap. X.)—Lessons of St. Privat—Blockade of Metz—Battle of Noisseville—Villages of Noisseville, Servigny and Poix—Attacks and defences—Lessons—Affair of Peltre — Design—Failure—Affair of Ladonchamp—'Aggressive spirit'—Marshal Bazaine—Lesson to us in English defence—Battle of Sedan—Bazeilles—Bavarian attack repulsed—They organise centre of village—Struggle in main street—Turning movements—Final street fight—Lessons of Bazeilles—Army of Orleans—Châteaudun—Coulmiers—Ladon—Beaune-la-Rolande—Capture of Juranville by cavalry—Lesson that all arms should work together—Patay—Blockade of Paris—Basis of German arrangements—Affairs of Chevilly, Thiais, and L'Hay—General principle of defence—Would not suit all cases—French attacks—On L'Hay—On Thiais—On Chevilly — All repulsed—Remarks — Affair of Clamart, Bagneux and Châtillon—Attack on Bagneux succeeds—That on Châtillon fails—Remarks—Le Bourget—Its importance—First capture by French—Their preparations for defence—Disposition of garrison—Ineffectual bombardment—German attack on October 30—Capture of the entrance—Inner attack and defence — Faults of defence—Capture by Germans—Their preparations for defence—French preparations to attack—Attack of December 21—Failure of attack—

Remarks — Lessons of other village fights — Champigny — Villa Evrard — Buzenval — Bapaume — Villersexel—Questions raised by civilisation.

(*Plates XVIII. in pocket.*)

THE very complete and interesting work of Captain Louis Thival[1] affords to the student a large number of excellent examples, and we propose to quote freely from it, only compressing the material and adding to his criticisms such others as may occur from time to time. With the exception of Zaatcha and Saragossa, which have peculiar features of interest, it will be better to confine these examples to such as have occurred since rifled artillery and small-arms have been introduced.

CAMPAIGN OF 1866.

Austrian defects.—The great Seven Years' War was marked by a series of attacks by Frederick the Great on Austrian defensive positions, and the campaign of 1859 had much the same features, only varied here and there by a brilliant stroke by Benedek, who at the end of it remained the only general in whom the people of the dual Monarchy had any confidence. The voice of the people, therefore, called him to the command in 1866. He said to the Emperor, 'Your Majesty, I am no strategist,' and wished to decline the chief command. But, for political reasons, he was told to do his best, and that his staff would do his strategy for him. I went through the campaign by his side, heard him on one occasion say hotly to his disputing staff, 'For God's sake, do something!' and remarked with amazement that while the strategy was to be essentially defensive against the Crown Prince and offensive against Prince Frederick Charles[2]—a very questionable de-

[1] *Rôle des Localités à la Guerre.* Par Louis Thival, Capitaine au 1ᵉʳ régiment du génie. Paris, Dumaine, 1880.

[2] The following facts were some time afterwards related to me by one of the actors in the scene. After the battles of Nachod and Trautenau the second officer of the Intelligence Department examined all the prisoners, and obtained clear information of the whereabouts of all the columns of the Crown Prince, then struggling through the

cision—the villages between the Crown Prince and Josephstadt were not placed in condition of defence, nor the passes through the mountains fortified. A conversation with a staff officer left on my mind the impression that, because Austria had formerly failed through over-use of the defensive, theorists had now determined to throw aside the shield altogether; and, at a time when the great object of containing one Prussian army and defeating the other was obviously the only strategy worth talking about, to neglect the advantage of time which the resistance of villages against the Crown Prince would give, and meet the new breechloader by wild and harebrained charges in the open. Both strategy and tactics failed, and, in the end, the Austrian army fell into its old habit of taking up a defensive position only half prepared, with the old weakness of the *crochet* and the old result—defeat, great loss of guns, demoralisation, and destruction of military power. A few words on the defence of villages during the campaign may be useful.

Affair of Podol.—The village of Podol formed a sort of bridge-head to the railway and ordinary bridges which here cross the Iser. It was not completely prepared for defence, but had a farm with barred windows in advance to the right of the road, and the houses of the village were occupied during

---

mountain passes. He wrote his report and took it to the officer who had been sent to Benedek to decide the strategy of the campaign. At that time several Austrian corps were close by. The General looked at the paper and had all the facts explained to him. He then dismissed the Captain, who, however, remained and said, probably in that tone of distrust which prevailed, 'Now, Herr General, I have shown you that the Crown Prince can be beaten in detail if attacked by our great force within half a day's march; may I ask what you propose to do with the Austrian army?' The General replied, 'I shall send it against Prince Frederick Charles.' The Captain put his hands together in an attitude of supplication and said, 'For God's sake, sir, do not,' but was ordered out of the room. I did not know this fact when Benedek said, the day after the defeat of Königgrätz, 'Did you ever see such a fine army so thrown away?' But he died, unprotesting, a few years afterwards. To have proclaimed the truth might have had serious political effects. Poor Benedek! After all he deserved well of his country.

the fight by Austrian soldiers, who fired through the windows. They had six battalions, and the street was barricaded both at the entry to the village and further back. The effect of the breechloader was not yet known.

It was evening when the Prussian skirmishers appeared, some 800 yards from the village. The outposts, driven in, aligned themselves across the road, resting on the farm, which kept up a steady fire—always with muzzle-loaders. A vigorous attack by the Prussians drove back the defenders, who posted themselves behind the barricade at the entrance to the village. It was now dark. The combatants fought almost close to each other, only lighted by the flashes of the rifles. For the first time the Austrians found what it was to be opposed to the needle-gun, which inflicted astonishing losses. At last they drew back from the barricade into neighbouring houses, where they fought on with great bravery. Every house, barricaded with beams torn from its woodwork, was energetically defended. Two barricades in the streets cost the Prussians heavy losses. At one time the defenders were so closely pressed together in a side street that they could not use their ramrods to load. They were gradually driven back, and some of them cut off by a Prussian battalion which turned the village by the east. About midnight, by the light of the moon, the Austrian rearguard deployed in front of the two bridges, the enemy doing the same, and the two sides firing at close range. The Prussians, increasing in number, charged with the bayonet, but could not prevent the Austrians from tearing up the rails on the railway bridge. The defenders made a last stand at an isolated house some 300 yards on their side of the river, but finally retreated at about one o'clock in the morning. The difference of arms had told. The Austrians suffered a loss of 543 men, the Prussians of 113 men. The attack was always superior in number. No guns were used on either side.

It will thus be seen that the village was held for the best part of a night in spite of the needle-gun. Had the arms been equal, the passage of the Iser would have been still further delayed, and might have seriously influenced the campaign.

Trautenau and Skalitz.—Trautenau was the scene of a severe struggle during the first battle of that name, but there were no peculiar features. The village first checked the Prussians, was then taken by them with much difficulty, and retaken by the Austrians, who remained masters of the place. Skalitz was the scene of the first serious Austrian defeat. It covered the passage of the Aupa, and was defended house by house, though insufficiently prepared. The fight occurred the day after the occurrence related in foot-note, p. 205. On riding out from Josephstadt to the sound of the guns, the author passed heavy masses of Austrian troops bivouacked within easy reach of the battle, but they were never employed. It was on that day, after the fight, that Benedek, seated on a bank by the side of the road, exclaimed to his staff, 'For God's sake, do something!' Nothing was done, and no energy shown. The opportunity was allowed to slip, and from that moment any experienced soldier could tell that the only chance for Austria was to make peace.

Battle of Königgrätz (or Sadowa). Village of Chlum.—The Prussian successes caused a marked demoralisation in the Austrian army. Clam Gallas had been steadily thrust back by Prince Frederick Charles, and defeated at Gitschin. The Crown Prince was out of the mountains and across the Elbe after a small action at Königinhof. The Austrian staff arrived at last at a decision, which was the wrong one. A vigorous offensive of the whole army against either of the Prussian armies, especially that of the Crown Prince, might even then have saved the campaign. But the decision was to fall back on that old resource of weakness now advocated by some officers for the defence of England—namely, to await the enemy in a prepared position. Unmindful of the lessons of the Seven Years' War, the Austrian army was drawn up with its front to the little river Bistritz, its right flank thrown back at an angle to face the Crown Prince, and with the river Elbe in its rear. It was attacked there on July 3 by Prince Frederick Charles along the line of the Bistritz, while the Crown Prince made all haste to arrive on the field, marching on Benedek's right. Several villages played parts of more or less interest in the battle which ensued, and were captured and recaptured, but generally remained in the hands of the Prussians. The line of the Bistritz was abandoned, and the army concentrated on the prepared position, which, as before explained, was in the form of an angle, or *crochet*. Behind the apex of this angle stood the village of Chlum. Lipa was near the angle, but to the left of it. The engineers had been allowed three days to prepare the battlefield, and had made many entrenchments and earthen batteries. Besides entrenchments, there were eighteen batteries along the left face, ten along the right, including three in front of Chlum looking towards Prince Frederick Charles. But unless an army is made of engineers, they cannot do everything. A few battalions, with officers knowing no more than can be found in this little book, could have put all the villages in an excellent state of defence; yet those on the right face were almost neglected. The village of Maslowed, which commanded all the batteries erected with so much care on the right face, was apparently forgotten; Chlum itself, the key of the position, was not prepared for defence, nor was there even a watch set in the church tower of this dominant position on the day of the battle; Nedelitz, on which the right flank of the army rested, was also unprepared, save for a slight abatis on the road.

From early morning to midday a heavy battle raged between the whole of the left wing and Prince Frederick Charles, during which he made good the passage of the Bistritz, but, with failing ammunition and wearied men, might have succumbed to a concentrated attack supported by the reserves, could but the Crown Prince have been contained by the right wing. But the lack of steady village defence allowed him to march on; and now occurred one of those accidents which may be assumed as certain at some time or other in all passive defence except of regular fortresses. All the morning an action had been proceeding in a wood near Benatek, in front of the *crochet*, but far beyond the prepared position. Nothing absorbs like a wood, and gradually more and more Austrian troops were drawn into it, till the important angle was broken, and Chlum left uncovered, at a time when the Prussian Guard were actually taking its tower as the object of their march. There was no watch in that tower, and the Prussians easily captured the village, unprepared for defence.[1]

During the latter part of the fight Benedek had received messages as to the progress of the Crown Prince. I speak from personal knowledge, unmindful of the hearsay evidence laid before military historians. The Austrian General was, with his staff, on the hill above Lipa, having lately returned from visiting Chlum and the reserve corps near it; and a general advance against Prince Frederick Charles was being ordered, when an officer arrived in hot haste, and made a report which I did not hear, but Benedek replied, 'Impossible!' I asked a staff officer what the report was, and he said, 'that the Prussians are in Chlum.' Benedek and his staff then galloped to Chlum, and were saluted at 100 yards or so distance by a hot fire proceeding from its enclosures. The staff retired down the hill; but as I stopped to help Prince Esterhazy, whose horse had been killed and himself wounded, I saw the Austrian battalion which had been driven out of Chlum being rallied and urged to retake it, which it failed in doing. Following the staff, I found them near the farm of Rosberitz, which had also been unprepared for defence, and out of which some of the Prussian Guard were then firing. Here the Archduke William was wounded. Chlum and Rosberitz, if properly prepared for defence, must have cost the Prussians hours to take and heavy losses. Yet, for want of prevision, these two places, behind the very centre of the Austrian army, were in the hands of the enemy,

---

[1] I not only saw what is here related, but a few months afterwards, when dining in London with Prince Frederick Charles and some members of his staff, I met one of the officers of the Guards who had been the first in Chlum. He assured me that my view of the case was perfectly correct. The Guard marched on Chlum as a definite point easily seen, without knowing its importance, and arrived there without any opposition worth naming. Other parts of the Guard may have had heavy fighting; this had not.—C. B. B.

whose fire now seemed to come from all directions. The reserves, which ought to have dashed at Chlum at once, lost time in parade movements, marching 'like a wall,' but executing such elaborate preparations to get their front rightly to the foe that they were too late. I saw those movements, which, like the etiquette which allowed a king to be burnt because such a string of orders had to be given before the right man could be told to put out the fire, were magnificent, but not war.

In the case here given, one of the decisive battles of the world turned on the question of proper village preparation for defence. It is a great lesson, and should surely teach us that every officer, before pretending to lead men in war, should at least be an adept at this branch of his profession. There is far too common a tendency to treat such simple work as a study only for engineers. Is, then, every officer who finds himself with a company in a farmhouse under critical circumstances to need the dry nursing of an engineer?

Custozza.—In the same year the Austrians and Italians fought the battle of Custozza. The village of that name was the scene of some active fighting of an important character. The farm of Cavalchino stood about 1,300 yards to the north-east, and was occupied by the Austrians on their march to Custozza. An Italian column attacked them there, but was repulsed by the fire from the windows. In a second attack the Italians penetrated the farmyard, but were driven out by a cross fire from windows and barns. The third attack was led by Prince Amadeo, who fell, wounded in the breast. This attack was not only repulsed but scattered. In a fourth attack the yard was carried, and even the lower story of the house, where two officers and thirty men of the Austrians were captured; but the upper floor was held till a fresh Austrian force coming up surrounded the farm and took the Italians prisoners in their turn.

Campaign of 1870–71.

In this campaign there were many village fights, both when the posts were parts of a prepared position for battle and when they stood comparatively alone, as in some of the cases round Metz and Paris, as well as when they were isolated.

Château of Geissberg.—At the battle of Weissenburg, which opened the campaign on the French right, the defence of the town itself had no striking features, and does not appear to have been particularly well conducted, and the Germans were overwhelming in number. A stand was made by the French on a hill called the Geissberg, with their right resting on the château, whence had already proceeded a fire very annoying to the German batteries. It was decided that the château must be carried.

Description of the château.—The château was in its essence what we have agreed to call a farm; that is to say, there was a solid house of two stories with outbuildings. There was an inner and an outer court, the latter surrounded by a strong wall some sixteen feet high. Only one gate, on the north, gave access to this court; on the east there was a kitchen-garden, and at rather more than 200 yards to the north a hop-garden stood on both sides of the Altenstadt road.

Prussian attack.—The attack was made first on the hop-garden, which was easily carried, but all advance on the château was stopped by a heavy fire proceeding from all openings, right up to the roof. The Prussians retreated with heavy loss. Strongly reinforced, they advanced again, but were handsomely repulsed and obliged to find shelter in the dead angle of a hollow road, not far from the foot of the wall. While this was proceeding some companies managed to turn the position and penetrate as far as the court, where the fire of the hidden defenders still searched them out.

Arrival of artillery.—Artillery was then sent for, and the guns were dragged with great difficulty up the steep sides of the Geissberg. They opened fire at about 900 yards. First twelve, then eighteen, and finally twenty-four pieces bombarded the château. The doors were driven in, walls breached, windows became impossible to occupy. There was an awful circle of fire, and behind it German reinforcements accumulating every moment. The garrison yielded, and turned out to be 200 strong. It had put twenty-three officers and 329 men *hors de combat* out of the royal regiment of Grenadiers, and caused a long and confusing delay. No doubt the château would have fallen sooner if the guns had been brought up at first, but consider how well employed 200 men would be who could attract to themselves many times their own number of the enemy and twenty-four guns.

Battle of Wörth. Elsasshausen.—At the battle of Wörth the little hamlet of Elsasshausen was the scene of furious struggles. It was taken and retaken. Under cover of its fire the French made a vigorous counter-attack, which was only checked by the German artillery firing case. At one time no less than forty-eight German guns concentrated their fire upon it.

Fröschwiller.—The large village of Fröschwiller played an even more important part. One hundred and ninety-two guns plied it with shell from different directions in groups of fifteen, ten, and seven batteries, while 75,000 men advanced concentrically upon it. The attack was made from north, east and south, but everywhere received by a well-nourished fire of rifles and mitrailleuses. Resistance was continued to the last on the borders of the flaming village, the French standing or lying behind hedges, loopholed walls, and in gardens. After suffering great losses the Prussians succeeded in attacking the three sides at once, though suffering horribly. Then the French, finding themselves turned, retreated, disputing barricades and houses, and finally escaped towards Reichshoffen and Niederbronn.

Stiring Wendel. Battle of Spicheren.—The village of Stiring Wendel closed the gap between the forests of Spicheren and Stiring. Upon it rested the left of Frossard's Corps, the right of which was strengthened by the village of Spicheren. Stiring Wendel closed the railway to Metz and other important communications. The defensive preparations showed many defects. There were shelter-trenches and batteries in the neighbourhood to prevent a turning movement. The French were always great at engineering work of that kind during the war, but the north-east salient of the Stiring wood was left unoccupied; and, more important still, isolated houses near the village were not destroyed. Of course the Prussians penetrated the wood at the neglected salient, but were repulsed from the village. Reinforced, they then occupied a neglected house to the north of the village, and made it a starting-point for future operations. Another attack on the village was repulsed, but again isolated houses left standing, such as the Custom House, the Baraque-Mouton, and another, were occupied by the Prussians, who, creeping under cover of the railway, succeeded, after a hard struggle, in carrying some outlying posts. At six o'clock the French, being reinforced, took the offensive, and drove back the Germans to some distance, but could not carry the Baraque-Mouton, and were in their turn driven back on the village, which continued to resist till eleven P.M. Its fall exposed the left of the French army, and orders were sent to withdraw it.

Stiring Wendel was in a valley, was not well connected with the right, being flanked in that direction by steep and broken ground. The village was commanded by the wood on its left, too large to be completely defended, and opened to the enemy by its defective preparation. The Germans concentrated on it great efforts, and were assisted by the fault of the French in leaving, outside, buildings which should have been demolished. Yet the village resisted all frontal attacks, and was captured at last by troops which had turned it. *The chief lesson is the fault of leaving external houses to become points of vantage to the enemy. Another, almost as important, is the habit of the Germans to concentrate towards the critical point of a battle.*[1]

[1] 'But for the conviction that everyone should march to the decisive point of a combat, it is probable that this victory would have been changed into a defeat.'—*Troop Leading*, by Colonel Verdy du Vernois.

EXAMPLES OF FIGHTS FOR LOCALITIES. 215

Battle of Gravelotte. St. Marie aux Chênes.—St. Marie aux Chênes resisted the first attack made on it by two German columns, but was brought under a very heavy artillery fire, which set it in flames, and the German advanced troops entered one end of it as the French evacuated it at the other.

Farm of St. Hubert.—This farm consisted of a main building and two other erections, which were situated west and north. The western side of the *enceinte* (direction of attack) was not pierced with any place of issue. The eastern face along the road had openings which were not barricaded. The garden belonging to the farm was closed by a wall, which was, however, breached on the north, either by the fire of the guns at Gravelotte or by some other means. At first the farm was brought under a heavy fire from the guns in front of Gravelotte, but the battalion which occupied it twice repulsed infantry attacks made on it. About four o'clock seventeen German companies (= four and a quarter battalions) attacked on all sides at once, and penetrated the building on the west, and through the breach on the north into the garden. The defenders fought for a time, but eventually fell back on the farm of Moscow. Here we have an undefended breach.

Moscow.—After the capture of St. Hubert the Germans attacked the farm of Moscow, but were often repulsed, and at one time fell into something like a panic. The infantry were sweeping away the gun-detachments in their rush to the rear. The German artillery, however, held its ground for a considerable time when completely deserted and without escort. In the useless attack on these farms the Germans lost immense numbers, as shown by the tombs thereabouts.

St. Privat.—This most important of all the attacks and defences has already been described (Chapter X.), which the reader of these examples will do well to consult at this stage. It illustrated many principles, such as:

    1st. The grave error of attacking in close formation troops behind walls, &c., and unshaken by the fire of artillery.

    2nd. The rashness of making a frontal attack without

waiting for a flanking movement which was even then in preparation by the Saxons.

3rd. The necessity of keeping troops supplied with plenty of ammunition.

4th. The plain duty of supporting by reinforcements the troops which are at the time engaged in the most critical part of the battle. Bazaine had the Guards, who had not been engaged, and large ammunition columns under his hand. The Germans had not succeeded anywhere along the front, but were turning the French right flank. He sent neither ammunition nor reinforcements to that critical point.

Battle of Noisseville.—Some remarks will be made on this battle hereafter, when speaking of attacks on large positions. The preparations and execution of the attack are full of lessons on 'How not to do it,' unless, as the French decided at Bazaine's trial, that officer did not wish to succeed. In that case the lessons go to show, 'How to fail if you wish to do so.' Three villages were attacked and defended—Noisseville, Servigny and Poix, which were advanced posts to the main position of St. Barbe.

Noisseville, Poix, Servigny.—The villages had all been put in a state of defence with shelter-trenches, loopholed walls, &c. Noisseville had to the south, whence the French attack partly came, a brewery which was also prepared for defence. *Remark how often an outside building not destroyed is harmful.* The battle ought to have been begun at the first streak of dawn, but, by many delays, it was past five o'clock in the afternoon before the French attacked Noisseville, and quickly carried the brewery, after a short but violent struggle. They then combined a fire of artillery from outside and infantry from the brewery upon the village, which fell about six P.M. The Germans at 8.15 opened upon it artillery fire from their batteries, and made two attacks upon it without success. At about the same time the French 4th Corps attacked Servigny and Poix, while the German artillery was attacked in flank by skirmishers from the valley in which Noisseville lies. In that part the guns had to retire, and the French penetrated

Servigny, but the Germans held on to the far end of the village. As the artillery still held its ground near Poix, its fire, combined with that from the shelter-trenches, prevented the French from capturing that village. A Prussian brigade now availed itself of the retention of the rear houses in Servigny, and, aided by a heavy artillery fire, drove the French out completely. At nine P.M. Aymards's Division was brought quietly to attack Servigny again. The Germans were again driven back from the first part of the village, but retained possession of some loopholed houses and an enclosure, using which they made a strong counter-attack a little later, and finally got rid of the French, who, though making three attempts, could not recapture Servigny.

Next morning — September 1 — the line Failly-Poix-Servigny was in the occupation of two German divisions, with six brigades of infantry and three of cavalry in support. The French held Noisseville and Montoy, with their flanks prolonged through those villages. At 5.45 A.M. the Germans opened with artillery fire. Two batteries between Poix and Servigny fired down the road, while two others placed on the slope south-east of Servigny cannonaded Noisseville. At seven o'clock they attacked Noisseville on all sides with five battalions and a brigade of landwehr in reserve. They succeeded in penetrating on the east and north, but the interior resistance stopped them, and an offensive movement of the Brigade Chinchant drove them back out of the village. Finding the nut too hard to crack they fell back on their unfailing resource, field artillery, and concentrated a fire of 114 guns on Montoy, Flanville and Noisseville. This was at about 9.30, and at eleven A.M. another attack was made on Noisseville, which now offered very little resistance.

Lessons.—We may observe here the great use made of the artillery in masses by the Germans, and with regard to the attack and defence of the villages, *an obstinate tenacity in holding even one or two houses so as to retain a footing.* This turned out well for them on more than one occasion, and is a valuable lesson. Also remark the vigorous counter attacks made by the Germans after they had lost a village or part of one. Noisseville presents us with one of many examples of the difference between attacking before or after a good artillery preparation.

Peltre.—Though the blockade of Metz is generally characterised by a strange sloth and inactivity foreign to French character (compare Chap. XIV., the Arab defence of Zaatcha), the many weeks were not altogether devoid of interest and initiative. One episode, though a failure, shows what might have been done had an energetic and patriotic leader made the most of his quick-witted soldiers. The incident which follows was the work of General Lapasset, not of Marshal Bazaine.

The design.—The plan was to attack the German position of Mercy, which was to the left of the railway line, as the French faced; and to push two trains along the double railway line, the first carrying troops (one battalion chasseurs) to attack Peltre, which was on the line, while the second, which consisted only of an engine and an armoured carriage with twenty-five picked men, should dash through Peltre during the action, go on to Courcelles, hook in to some provision trucks known to be there, and carry them back with all speed to Metz.

Failure.—On September 27 a regiment marched on Mercy and attacked the fortified château there, which was in a thorough state of defence, including a shelter-trench round the village. One battalion attacked in front, the others on the two flanks. The post was carried with some loss. General Lapasset meanwhile opened an artillery fire on Peltre. The trains started as intended, but found, as every soldier who reads this will expect, that the railway line had been cut in front of the village. The chasseurs were met with a sharp fire, but managed to disperse the Germans and to seize some provisions. The French assert that the secret of the operations had been sold, and they certainly arrested, condemned and shot a supposed spy whom they found in the village. It seems very strange that the Germans should need the assistance of a spy to teach them that a railway line running from the enemy through a defended village in their own occupation ought to be cut in advance of the village, and even also barricaded. But, in any case, the example remains as a proof of the necessity of so doing.

Ladonchamp.—On October 2 the château of Ladonchamp was attacked and carried by 'some companies' of the French during the night, and it is particularly interesting and instructive to observe how the Germans were not able to drive them out again, though they attacked twice next day. On the 7th the French again took the offensive, and captured the farms of Les Tapes and Saint Remy. The former was retaken after a struggle by the Germans, who again bombarded and attacked the Ladonchamp château, but without success. Marshal Bazaine says in his *L'Armée du Rhin* that his object in ordering these operations was to awake in the army the aggressive spirit. Yet it was the last operation attempted, and he surrendered himself and his army on the 28th, after nearly nine weeks of astonishing inaction, varied only by such abortive enterprises as have now been given. Compare this inaction with the offensive defence of the Germans during the battle of Noisseville. While regarding with all respect the admirable qualities of the German soldiers, worthy of all praise, it is impossible not to be struck by the fact that the French troops never had a fair chance of displaying the best side of their character as soldiers, which is their gallantry in attack. The system of organisation prevented them from being ready to invade. A poor strategy allowed their armies to be beaten in detail, and they fought defensive battles, difficult to all troops, fatal to French habits of mind. The student of war will do well to observe as he pursues his course how often the side wins which takes a bold initiative, and *how fatally demoralising is a passive defence either on a great or a small scale.* To volunteers this question is specially important, seeing that their duties in an invasion of England seem to be confined, in the opinion of some of their would-be friends, to the occupation of positions, where, anchored to heavy position-guns which can hardly move, they would inevitably see their front neglected and concentrated attacks made on their flanks, if indeed the enemy found it necessary to attack at all, and not to contain so unwieldy a force while turning its flank and marching on London. On this kind of question more will be said hereafter. The present lesson from all Bazaine's failures in great and in small things is, *cultivate the spirit of the offensive in war.*

The battle of Sedan. Bazeilles.—The army of Marshal MacMahon failed in the mad attempt to give its hand to Bazaine, then shut up in Metz, and, too late to retire on Paris without a battle, stood before the antiquated little fortress of Sedan. The stream, the Givonne, was in front of the army, which had its left on the wood of Garenne and its right resting on Bazeilles. Behind Sedan was the Belgian frontier. The German army, superior in number, in marching and fighting power, and in moral tone—for the French were much demoralised and were crying 'Treason!'—took upon itself the difficult but decisive task of surrounding the Emperor and his army, and so, it was hoped, ending the war. The duty of the Bavarians was to assist in holding the French fast by attacking the village of Bazeilles.

Description of the village.—Bazeilles—see Plate XVIII.—was about two miles S.E. of Sedan. It was solidly built and surrounded with numerous gardens. Two roads, to Sedan and Douzy, met at an angle about the centre of the village, and divided it into two parts. The northern part was the larger, and contained the market-place with a stone church in the middle; behind it was the park of Monvilliers, with its English gardens, lawns, clumps of trees and walled orchards. A strong bridge, with ditch in front of it, bounded the north-west face. Everywhere else the park was surrounded by a high wall with only one opening at the entrance of the avenue. The Givonne, a fordable stream, watered the grounds. On the previous day Martin de Pallières' brigade had occupied the village, and, finding that the southern part of the village was commanded from outside and exposed to artillery fire, or for other reasons, decided to give it up and hold only the northern half, which was organised for defence. The Villa Beurmann was the main keep, but some other isolated buildings were also prepared as strong points.

Bavarian attack repulsed.—At daybreak there was a thick fog, soon broken by the sound of the Bavarian artillery bombarding the village. But the action of the guns was all too short. Without giving time for the bombardment to produce any serious effect, two Bavarian brigades passed the Meuse on bridges constructed the previous evening, and marched on the village, the left column attacking the south of Bazeilles, where there were no defences, the right column turning the place and attacking the northern boundary. At first the southern column found no difficulty in entering or passing up the village, but presently found themselves with a well-defended barricade in front and exposed to fire from the houses on each side. The men took refuge in the side streets, where a fierce close combat raged. The other, or turning, column reached the northern boundary, where it came under a very heavy fire and failed to get in. The Villa Beurmann was attacked with no success, and some companies which penetrated the north-west gardens were met by so intense a fire that they could not advance, and even remained exposed to reverse fire from the houses already passed. This northern attack was well repulsed, and the whole west of the village was cleared by a vigorous offensive movement on the part of the French.

Bavarians organise centre of village.—The Bavarian troops, unable to clear the defenders out, then organised for defence and occupied the two houses which form the angle of the main street with the Douzy road. The French occupied two rows of houses beyond that point, which thus became the centre of the action. For a long time neither side could force the enemy to give way. The French attacked the houses occupied by the Bavarians, and the latter attacked a large house held by the French, but were repulsed until they brought up two field guns to within seventy paces and bombarded the house, so that the French had to abandon it. The Villa Beurmann was also attacked, and after severe repulses the two guns were dragged there by hand through a side street. But this time the guns had no success. The

French riflemen across the street and under good cover shot down the gunners and forced the guns to retire.

Struggle in the main street.—The Bavarians were constantly reinforced, and the struggle proceeded hotly in the main street. They pushed their way into the market square, where the fighting was from house to house. The Germans carried the church, which the French, in spite of tremendous sacrifices, failed to retake. Reinforcements now reached the French, who once more took the offensive. The fight swayed backwards and forwards; the village was on fire, and there is little doubt that many wounded were burnt in the houses where they had crawled or been carried. At last heavy French reinforcements drove back the mass of the Germans to the Meuse, but some still held out in the houses.

Turning movements.—Meanwhile, outside the village, other work was in hand. Bavarians and Saxons combined attacked in great force the village of La Moncelle and carried it; they soon placed seventy-two guns in that neighbourhood, which brought a heavy shell fire to bear on the French regiments. The park of Monvilliers was attacked by Prussian infantry, which had not yet been engaged; the two French regiments at first retired, fighting desperately, then made a counter attack against the German left, driving back some of the guns from which they were suffering. But at this moment a reinforcement of Saxon artillery arrived, which crushed the defenders and drove them to retreat in the direction of Balan.

Final street fight.—The village was now surrounded by German infantry and artillery, almost filled with German troops, and on fire in several places. Yet there remained some hundreds of the French, animated with the courage of despair. The few houses which were still in their hands had to be forced from them one by one. At last their hold on the village was reduced to the occupation of one poor inn on the Balan road. Barricaded in this slight shelter, the little garrison held out for two hours against all attacks from a whole regiment. Guns were brought against these brave soldiers, who belonged to the marine infantry under the

Commandant Lambert. The roof, the doors, the windows were all dashed to pieces by the projectiles. Still the gallant fellows defended the post until at last their ammunition failed. Even then the soldiers wished to make a sortie and clear a way for themselves with the bayonet or die fighting; but it would have been of no avail, of no military usefulness. Their commander forbade the sacrifice, and they became prisoners of war.

The fall of Bazeilles made the turning movement of the German army easier. A ring of artillery was formed round Sedan and the French army, which, much disorganised and without sufficient provisions, could neither issue from the town next morning nor hope to defend it. Accordingly the whole army surrendered, and the Emperor himself was a captive.

Lessons at Bazeilles.—It was clearly a fault to restrict the defence to the northern part of the village. The advanced boundary should have been organised as a first line of defence, and, beyond that, the passage of the Meuse should have been disputed. No doubt it would have been carried, and probably the edge of the village also. But the advance of the enemy would have been delayed, and one of the avenues to Sedan would have been kept longer closed. This point has been insisted upon more than once in former chapters. It is most important to adopt any measures which may delay the enemy and gain time, whether it be hours or only minutes. As it happened, the morning mists would have helped by preventing the full action of artillery and concealing the French weakness in numbers. But if this was an accident, we must remember that want of attention to details has the tendency to turn accidents against instead of for us. That officer will succeed oftenest whose mind is imbued with the principles of the military art so that he neglects no precautions, yet is not so wedded to forms that he cannot turn his mind nimbly to new combinations of those principles, one of the most important of which is to be active, and impart into defence as much as possible of THE INITIATIVE.

On the other hand, the tenacity of the defence within the village shows what may be done by brave troops greatly overmatched in numbers. Two thousand Germans were placed *hors de combat*, and passage through the village was denied to them for hours, during which a large German force was occupied by a small French one. And all this was done by troops which were out of heart from failures and not a little disorganised.

Should England ever be invaded, there is no volunteer officer but may hope to write his name on the roll of Englishmen who have deserved well of their country by the gallant defence of some village or hamlet, or even farm. Who knows but that by interposing delay to an enemy's march a battle may be saved and the safety of the country insured?

The whole of the imperial organised armies were now either in captivity or enclosed, but France formed new forces with marvellous speed. They lacked, however, one important—nay, vitally necessary—feature of a solid army. They had few well-trained officers and non-commissioned officers. Hence the fighting was of an amateur character for the most part, and the mistakes so many as to render careful descriptions generally out of place.

Châteaudun, Coulmiers, Ladon.—Yet Châteaudun, on October 18, was defended for eight hours against some 12,000 Bavarians, though it fell at last. At the battle of Coulmiers the village of that name and others were captured from the Bavarians, the principles of attack being well carried out—such as thorough preparation by artillery, turning movements, &c. It is true that the French had about double the strength of the Bavarians, and that the half-organised French army was unable to reap the fruits of victory by marching on Paris. All the good-will in the world will not compensate for defective organisation and lack of military skill and professional knowledge.[1] Of the combat

[1] The author once asked Prince Frederick Charles during the war what was the chief feature in the German superiority upon which he always counted so confidently. His reply was that the German army was so

at Ladon, when that village was captured by the Prussians according to the strict rules of art—November 24—a German writer has said that it was an 'elegant or classic combat,' where 'the object of the fight was not lost sight of for a single instant, and was attained, 1st, by a well-considered preparation; 2nd, by a rational use of the disposable forces; and 3rd, by seizing resolutely the decisive moment for a general concentric attack.' M. Louis Thival remarks somewhat bitterly that the words, 'an elegant combat,' remind him of the Algerian who, whenever he had to administer a severe bastinadoing to one of his co-religionists, crowned his ear with a rose and put blue bows on his wrists. He also remarks that the affair was not a complete success; for the two battalions of mobiles which occupied the village inflicted considerable losses on the Germans, made several offensive movements, and finally escaped to join the principal force before the investment was complete. But escape may or may not be the end desired by the defenders of a village. The object may in some cases be to defend a post, as the gap at Meeanee, as long as possible, dying there if necessary. In this particular case we need not judge between the rival authorities.

Beaune-la-Rolande. Capture of Juranville by cavalry.—The battle of Beaune-la-Rolande—November 28—in which the French lost 2,500 men, and the Germans 947, was chiefly an affair of village attack and defence. Its most remarkable episode occurred at Juranville. Two French brigades, part of the force advancing—too late—on Paris, began to come into contact with the troops of Prince Frederick Charles marching southwards after the fall of Metz in time to prevent

trained that, when an order was given for a movement, the officer giving it could be certain, not only that it would be well executed, but almost exactly how it would be executed; and, moreover, each portion was trained to help each other portion. Thus few and simple orders only are required. The French, on the other hand, require elaborate orders for every movement. They may do very well as long as the orders fit the case, but are at a loss when they do so no longer. They are all abroad in a second day's fight, or under the influence of the unexpect'

Q

the salvation of the city. These brigades carried Ladon, Maizières and Lorcy, then marched on Juranville, drove out the two German companies within it, and occupied the village. At 9.30 the German artillery opened fire on the place, and presently marched in force to retake it. After a severe struggle they recaptured Juranville, with a loss of 200 men, defeating the two battalions of mobiles which garrisoned it. About two P.M. the brigade Robert, one of those which had first captured the place, once more moved to attack it. The German advanced troops were driven in, and the French began to envelop, moving to right and left of the road near the southern edge of the village. The German batteries near the Juranville road to the south-east were then attacked by the French skirmishers, who even captured one gun. Thus left unsupported, the German defenders were in a state of hesitation, and at that moment a squadron of French lancers charged the village, and actually captured it.

The student who has attentively gone so far through this book will not be surprised at this feat of cavalry, for the point on which above all others we insist is that it is moral effect which always carries the day, and there is no arm which may not at a given moment assist in producing that moral effect. All arms must work together, or full use cannot be made of any of them. Cavalry is certainly not the ideal force with which to attack a village, nor are guns best employed within it. Yet we see guns successful at Bazeilles, and cavalry at Juranville. *The lesson is that all arms should work, even to self-sacrifice, to the common end, and that when one of them is checked, the others should throw their moral power into the scale with all the influence of surprise and astonishment upon the enemy.*

Patay.—On December 4, during the retreat on Orleans, the advanced guard of General de Tacé was attacked in the village of Patay by twelve German squadrons. German guns also bombarded the village, which was presently set on fire. Two battalions of mobiles garrisoned the village, having constructed barricades and some house defence. When the cavalry attacked the mobiles first received them with musketry fire, and then made a bold counter attack, killing 200 and taking forty prisoners. As the army was in motion, the village had to be abandoned, but it was not the cavalry which took it.

Villages round Paris.

The defence of Paris was better than that of Metz, especially taking into consideration that the defenders were not a regular army, nor was Paris a regularly organised fortress. By that we mean that the immense bulk of the population and the want of a spirit of discipline (the Emperor's Government having been overthrown) presented a terrible problem from the military point of view—far more difficult than that which confronted Bazaine. Otherwise, the cases were similar. A comparatively thin German line of investment right round the city, strengthened by all sorts of obstacles, and by villages in a state of defence, enclosed a concentrated mass of armed Frenchmen, who never once succeeded in passing any body of men, small or great, through the lines of the enemy. But the garrison of Paris made more attempts than that of Metz, and there were times when the state of affairs looked uncomfortable for the Germans; especially at the time when Bazaine still detained Prince Frederick Charles before Metz, and the new French army had pushed the Bavarians out of Orleans. Had Bazaine broken out during the early part of the investment, even at the sacrifice of half his army; failing that, had his defence been better than it was, had he even carried off a few days' provisions from the Germans or economised those which he had—in short, had he by any of the many means at his disposal held out a week or two longer, it is almost certain that the siege of Paris would have had to be raised, wholly or partially; and such moral effect would have been produced upon France and Europe as must at least have changed the character of the situation, and ensured a peace much less irritating to French susceptibility than that which was made after the fall of Paris.

Undoubtedly the French had to thank Marshal Bazaine's supineness at Gravelotte and at Metz for their worst humiliations. *It may happen to any officer to be some day in a position—greater or less—where his conduct of operations may become the most critical feature of the campaign.*

It is not proposed to describe all the village attacks and defences in the neighbourhood of Paris, but only to glance over most of them, concentrating attention here and there when anything specially important occurred.

The general line of German defence was based on the preparation of villages and woods. The order was that only where none such existed should redoubts be built for a company of infantry.

Chevilly, Thiais, L'Hay, September 30.—In pursuance of the orders, the Germans were solidly entrenched in these among other villages. The investment had been completed on September 19. The first offensive action of the French was on September 30, when four columns were sent to attack the position L'Hay-Chevilly-Thiais (see Plate XVIII. for plan of position, and sections of foreign types in Plate X.). On the left of the position L'Hay had been strongly prepared. The walls of the enceinte were loopholed;[1] the bank of the watercourse leading to the Vanne was used as an epaulment. Isolated houses were loopholed to fire on the road and flank the enclosures. In rear a second line of defence was prepared by the use of enclosures and houses. By it the village was also connected with Chevilly, which in its turn was connected with Thiais on the right by a defended road and some slight field works. The whole front somewhat resembled a bastioned trace, with L'Hay and Thiais as the bastions, and Chevilly a little to the left of the centre of the curtain. Plate XVIII. shows the works of all three villages better than a description could, but it is worth mentioning that in some cases—as, for instance, that of the Seminary behind Chevilly—the walls were pierced at intervals with circular holes about a yard in diameter to allow of entrance and egress for men who could be thrown out in rifle-pits or retired at pleasure.

[1] The words 'loopholed' and 'loopholes' are used as generic terms to include both holes through the structure and those cut in the top, unless otherwise stated.

These holes also formed loopholes, as it were, for several men at a time. Some of the walls had ditches in front and banquettes behind.

General principle of defence.—Now let us think for a moment how the peculiar circumstances of the case would affect the German defence. Their main object was to prevent the French from breaking out through the line of investment, which was thinner than was at all comfortable. To have placed large forces quite in the front line would have exposed the whole army every day to the suffering and anxiety which might at any time be inflicted by artillery fire from the forts or by small harassing attacks, which the French should have carried on almost without ceasing. In numbers they were superior to the Germans, and if their raw troops required a good deal of training, that might have been obtained in actual fighting. Evidently the best arrangement for the Germans was to hold the front lightly with only the necessary troops, break the first force of the French wave there, but only meet it with a direct stoppage farther back, or at least by troops which had been quartered farther back in reserve. We find accordingly in almost all cases round Paris a first French success, only partial in character; then greater and greater difficulties, leading to repulses; then a gradual gathering of German troops, who make a vigorous counter-attack and complete the collapse of the French operations, inflicting heavy losses on the besieged.

Would not suit all cases.—Now this principle, though excellent in its own place, would not suit all cases. For instance, if a village guards the passage of a stream it will be necessary to deny that bridge to the enemy, who should therefore never be allowed to reach it. Similarly, in the case stated in preceding chapters, that of a village supposed to be isolated, it is of great importance to defend the outer boundary and never allow the attack to gain a footing at all. The case of Bazeilles was one in which the exterior should have been defended, because that village was not likely to be succoured quickly, as the rest of the army would have enough to do. Therefore, though not isolated in fact, it partook of an isolated character. We have here one of the many proofs that good officers cannot be made by any body of strict rules. They must have brains and judgment, even more at their service than is necessary for other men, inasmuch as they often have to take important decisions on the spur of the moment.

French attack.—The French force was divided into four columns. On the right a brigade was to march on L'Hay; in the centre two regiments had for their objective, the one Chevilly, the other La Belle Épine; on the left two brigades were ordered to march on Thiais and Choisy-le-Roi. The forts of Ivry and Montrouge were to bombard Thiais and L'Hay respectively. But the infantry did not wait for the guns to produce any real effect. Half-an-hour after the bombardment commenced, columns of attack were launched against the three posts. There seems to have been no connection between the attacks—no general plan for detaining the enemy in one place and overwhelming him in another.

On L'Hay.—The German outposts were driven in and the first houses carried without much difficulty, also the first barricade. A French battery plied the village with fire, increasing its range as the column advanced, so as to fire on the ground over which the German reserves must advance. Several obstacles were surmounted, such as the embankment of the Vanne and another escarpment; but at that moment a terrible fire from the cemetery dropped many soldiers and forced the French to recoil. A second and third attempt were made, but in vain. Here it may be said that the front line, including the village, or at least its outer line of defence, was carried, but the French broke down before the second line.

Thiais.—Similarly, before Thiais, the outposts were easily driven in, but at 500 metres from the place a cross fire from the gardens of Choisy and a battery behind an epaulment in front of Thiais inflicted severe loss on the attack. This was a strange place for a small battery, and the fault of placing it there was punished. The French skirmishers gradually picked off the unsupported gunners. A French battery now fired on the village, and at once the infantry attacked. But by this time the Germans were gathering, and a heavy fire repulsed the French. A second French battery came up, and, inspired by its presence, a battalion rushed forward upon Thiais, carried the battery, and, establishing itself behind the exterior of the epaulment, exchanged shots with the Germans in the first houses. Now, however, the Germans were assembling in force; a French attempt to carry the cemetery failed, and a German counter attack finished the affair.

Chevilly.—Here again the attack was begun too soon. The farm of La Saussaye was quickly carried, but the assailants were checked by fire both from the front and from L'Hay, on their right flank. The 35th Regiment showed much of that dash which is the best quality of the French soldier. Though they lay down for a short time, they rose again and sprang forward, carrying the first barricade and houses and making many prisoners. The Germans fell back on their second line. Four French guns fired on Chevilly, and especially on the Seminary, to prepare the attack, but a column sent to assault was repulsed by a heavy fire. On the right a barricade was taken, and the French pushed on to the church, organised as the keep. But here the wave of attack was exhausted. The keep could not be carried; the Germans received reinforcements; their fire became hotter and more powerful. Gliding along the walls, they reoccupied the park and filled the nearest houses, which now vomited bullets from every crevice. The 35th now massed, received a volley at close range, and the startled French soldiers fled, abandoning their conquests. About a hundred of them, who had thrown themselves into an isolated farm which they had barricaded, were surrounded by the flood of Germans. They made a brave defence, covering the ground with slain enemies, but half of them were placed *hors de combat*, ammunition failed; the Germans could now approach and set fire to the doors. The little garrison made one brave charge with the bayonet and was then forced to yield.

Thus the French were now repulsed in all their attacks.

Remarks.—It seems hardly necessary to point out here that the initial artillery fire was insufficient, the infantry being in too great a hurry to attack. There was an entire want of tactical combination in the attempts, and in their hurry to get forward the French neglected to organise defensively the portions which they captured. From lack of general control L'Hay was allowed to support Chevilly by its flanking fire, and even to send its reserves round to Chevilly after its own defence had succeeded. It is interesting to find that the walls which were behind hedges or shrubberies were almost safe from the French artillery, because of deception as to the range. But then it must be remarked that even the best of the French artillery was almost inconceivably bad during this campaign, and their failures were so common that the percentage of the loss they inflicted has been the stock argument against the value of field artillery by the opponents of that arm.

Clamart, Bagneux, Châtillon.—On October 13 a somewhat similar attack was made on the position Clamart-Bagneux-Châtillon. There was the same insufficient preparation by Fort Môntrouge, the same hasty attack, the same gallantry of the mobiles, who in this case were animated by the presence of regiments of the line. They succeeded among them in fairly carrying Bagneux, which they occupied and organised. But the Germans never let go their hold. They stuck to every hedge, ditch and enclosure between Bagneux and Châtillon, and so prevented the victors at Bagneux from aiding their friends at Châtillon.

The attack on Châtillon was not so successful. At first the Germans fell back from post to post, but always seemed to gather strength as they went. The village was turned on both flanks, the sappers working chiefly through the houses themselves. The assailants arrived at the church, which was organised as the keep; but there all their efforts failed. Though Bagneux had been carried it was of no assistance, and the attack on Clamart, which was on the other side of Châtillon, was only a feint. In view of the resistance of the keep and the approach of German reinforcements, the order for retreat was issued. Still the affair was not without its compensations. The troops had behaved better and more professionally than they did a fortnight before. One village had actually been captured and the redoubtable Germans driven out of it. The French always seem to have been more fortunate in fighting the Bavarians than in attacks on the Prussians.

But on this occasion also the attack had been made too soon, without sufficient artillery preparation.

Le Bourget.—The village of Le Bourget affords a good example because it was attacked and defended by both sides during the siege of Paris, and from opposite directions. The defence of the church has also been made the subject of a popular picture by de Neuville. The final arrangements made by the Prussians were drawn carefully by Corporal Elscholz, of the Engineers of the Guard, and reproduced by M. Viollet le Duc in his memoir on the defence of Paris. The various captures and recaptures have been the theme of much criticism. On the whole it is perhaps as good an illustration as can be found of actual village fighting in modern days, especially as the French made some mistakes, as natural, considering the elements of which the garrison of Paris was composed, as they are instructive to the military student.

Its importance.—The small map plate gives the position of Le Bourget with respect to the rest of the country, the German lines being to the north of the village, the French forts and works to the south of it. At first it was slightly occupied by the Germans as an advanced post to their lines, which were some 2,000 yards behind it. It was besides more or less defended by German guns at Blanc Mesnil, Pont-Iblon, Bonneuil, on the north and north-east, Garges and Stains on the west. Its possession was important, first, as forming a sort of bridge-head among the marshy streams of the Morée, the Molette and the Crould, covering the road to the headquarters of the guard at Gonesse, and so preventing the Paris garrison from joining hands with the French northern forces. Moreover the possession of Le Bourget facilitated the construction of batteries destined to keep down the fire of forts Aubervilliers, de l'Est and Romainville, at ranges of 2,500 metres, 3,500 metres, and 5,000 metres respectively.

The village is about 1,100 yards long, the houses solidly built, and strong walled enclosures are common; it lies on the great road to Lille, and is crossed by the small stream, the Molette, the banks of which are flat and open.

First capture by French.—On October 28 the volunteers of the press, about 250 in number, dashed into the village at four o'clock in the morning. The first Prussian post was driven back in disorder, and the small garrison, pushed from house to house, made little stand till it arrived near the church, where the Prussians rallied. But the French were reinforced. Two twelve-pounders placed in front of Courneuve covered the left flank and attacked the Prussian garrison; two battalions advanced by the right of the village, one by the left. The Prussians were soon compelled to evacuate the post.

The French at once made preparations for defence. Walls were loopholed, communications made through the gardens, and *a barricade armed with two guns was erected to cover the street.* Mark what followed. *The guns were soon brought under fire by the Prussian artillery and obliged to retire.* They moved to Drancy, on the right flank of the village, whence they took the Prussian batteries obliquely and were of some use.

About eight o'clock the same evening, October 28, two Prussian companies stole unperceived close up to the walls of the village. When seen they were met by infantry fire at close range. The first groups were destroyed, and the remainder retired in haste.

The French garrison of Le Bourget—three and a half battalions, four field-pieces, and one mitrailleuse—were thus disposed: one company in the houses along the road to the cemetery, four companies with guns at the barricade and neighbouring houses, two companies on the right side of the road, and the rest partly in the glass-works and partly as a reserve near the church.

Ineffectual bombardment.—On the 28th there was no attempt at assault, but the Germans established eighteen field-pieces at Pont-Iblon, and bombarded Le Bourget. *The French kept under cover, and in six hours of firing only three men were wounded.* This shows the absolute uselessness of field artillery fire not directed to a definite object.

German successful attack on the 30th. Capture of the entrance.—At daylight on the 30th the German artillery again opened fire on the village, and sent forward eight battalions of the Guard to assault it. The infantry was in three columns and marched by the three converging roads, so as to envelop the head of the place. The central column was too solid and suffered great loss, but the left, advancing in a thin fighting line with reserves, by successive rushes, arrived close to the village, drove in the advanced French posts, and established itself within the defences on the French right. The French guns at the barricade, which for a while checked the central column, were silenced and driven back by a superior German artillery fire; the centre and left columns then pushed on; the barricade was captured after a fierce struggle, and all three columns penetrated the village. It will be observed that *there was no counter-attack, though there were troops at La Courneuve and the French held the railway.* Not even a flank defence by artillery was arranged.

Inner attack and defence.—Then began a tremendous struggle at close quarters. The French clung to the houses, and defended themselves foot by foot. The Germans had to break through the walls of the houses and enclosures, and the fight might have lasted a long time, perhaps even turned out successfully for the defenders, but for the want of any support from the reserves, which, both from the glass-works and La Courneuve, retired at this critical moment. Evidently a badly-directed defence, and, as if to crown the blunders committed, the forts of L'Est, Aubervilliers and Romainville opened fire on Le Bourget, including attackers and defenders in a bombardment which did more harm to the French than to the Germans. On the south-east, the Prussian Guard, which had forced an entry, moved northwards to join and help the other columns; houses were carried one by one. A desperate resistance was made by a handful—eight officers and about twenty men—in the church; the Germans had to climb to the windows and shoot the defenders within. Presently the whole village was carried, and remained in German hands. The German loss was thirty-nine officers and 449 men; the French loss in killed and wounded was not exactly ascertained, but they left about 1,200 prisoners.

Faults committed in defence.—Any student who has at all mastered the preceding chapters of this book could point to grave faults committed by the French : Artillery within the village, and none to defend the flanks. No counter-attack by exterior reserve. Total want of support to the defenders. Bombardment by the forts when more hurtful to their own side than to the enemy. This one action of Le Bourget would be enough to assure any competent soldier that the French would never break out of Paris.

German preparations.—For nearly two months Le Bourget remained in the hands of the Germans, no efforts being made to displace them. Their time was well spent in strengthening the defences. The surrounding ground was cleared, the railway station blown up, as well as a group of houses at the north of it, and the line was destroyed as far as Courneuve. In the interior, several walls and houses were blown up. The outer border of the village was put in a state of defence, and two interior sections of defence were arranged behind each other, as shown in Plate XVIII. No less than 500 metres of barricades were made, three bombproof shelters, 900 metres of abatis, 600 metres of trenches with traverses, a quantity of trous-de-loup in three rows and of wire entanglement, and, finally, 750 metres of covered communications. The rear section of defence extended its wings about a thousand paces to the right and left, and contained emplacements both for infantry and guns.

French preparations.—On the French side, epaulments

for batteries were constructed at Bondy on the right, and at Courneuve on the left.

French attack, December 21.—At seven o'clock in the morning on December 21 the French in heavy force attacked Le Bourget, as part of an attempt to break out of Paris by the north. The action began by the advance of bombproof carriages along the railway line to Courneuve. They were armed with guns, and fired upon the village for a quarter of an hour. Two heavy columns then attacked; one by the north and west, the other by the south. In spite of a heavy fire from the cemetery, the marines with the first column succeeded in passing the Molette—a stream which flows through the village—partly by fording and partly on fascines, near the bridge of Duguy, and attacked the flank of the village. The fire from the enclosures was terrible, and there were heavy losses, but the column carried the first barricades and a sort of blockhouse about 150 metres from the village. The French also pushed on with great courage as far as the main street, and occupied the church, carrying one by one the houses west of the street, while the defenders held the east side. At the same time the 138th Regiment, also a part of the first column, carried the cemetery, and occupied the houses on the north side of the Molette.

Failure of attack.—The second column was not so fortunate; it carried the railway station and a house beyond it, but was then checked, and a part of it, which had arrived on the railway to the left of the Lille road, found itself exposed on open ground to a tremendous fire from the long 'white wall'; it suffered here heavy losses and could not advance. At ten o'clock an attempt was made to breach that wall, but the general inefficiency of the French artillery was not likely to be improved by the poorly-trained garrison of Paris. The projectiles hardly damaged the wall, chiefly passing over it and creating consternation among the troops of the other French column. The Prussian guns at Duguy, Garges and Pont-Iblon did better execution against both French columns. Considerable German reinforcements arrived, the marines were driven out, and the French attack finally repulsed with a loss of 1,200 men. The Germans confessed to a loss of 140 officers and 398 men.

Remarks.—Here again we see a total want of military knowledge. The preparation by artillery fire was absolutely insignificant, the enclosure walls being hardly touched. Another column certainly ought to have converged upon the village from the east. It would have made a great difference, for, as has been seen, the French did actually penetrate to the west side of the main street. Had the German defenders been at that time attacked in their rear, they could hardly have held the place. So, then, the unnecessary violations of rules were: Insufficient preparation by artillery fire. Attack not converging. To these errors must be added the wretched artillery fire during the action, and we have quite enough faults to account for the failure of the French. The Germans, as usual, sent up heavy reinforcements which took the offensive, while the French neglected to check them.

Lessons of other village fights.—Sufficient examples have now been given from this war, though the list is far from being exhausted. It must suffice to mention some of the lessons which may be drawn from different cases of village fighting.

Champigny. Want of ammunition.—At Champigny, where the French attacked the Würtemburgers on December 2 and 3 with partial success, ammunition failed at a critical moment to the defenders of a garden. The men who endeavoured to procure more were shot down, and the defenders had to sally out, but few escaping.

Villa Evrard. Good French attack succeeds.—On December 21 the village of Villa Evrard was attacked as a diversion to draw troops from the German defence of Le Bourget. Curiously enough, this diversion was better conducted than the main attack. Twelve guns breached the walls. Two columns enveloped the park of the Maison Blanche, carried it, debouched in the village, and organised all that they captured. The Saxons tried a night attack, but failed.

Buzenval. Defence of wall.—In General Ducrot's final

attempt to issue from Paris, called by the French the battle of Montretout, the château and park of Buzenval became an important point, as it covered the salient of the first line of German defence. It is interesting to observe that walls only loopholed here and there were carried with comparative ease, the sappers breaching them with dynamite or pickaxes. But the wall called Longboyau, which was thoroughly prepared, could not be carried. A gallant attempt to breach it with dynamite was tried by an officer, Lieutenant Beau, and ten men. All were shot down. The wall was never carried, and M. Thival asserts roundly, '*The frontal attack of a loopholed wall is an impossible operation in these days, if the cannon has not first made a breach. Every attempt of this kind will probably fail after useless sacrifice.*' We would add, '*provided it be defended by good and unshaken troops.*'

Bapaume. Objection to bombard French village. — On January 3 the Germans, who had been driven from Bienvillers and Favreuil, held on to Bapaume, the attacks against which, made by infantry, only failed. General Faidherbe wrote : '*To dislodge the enemy it would have been necessary to destroy with artillery the shelters in which he was established, a very rude extremity when the place was French.*' In this particular case it mattered little ; but we should really be informed if civilisation dictates that a town or village in one's own country is not to be bombarded. If so, defence against invasion is indeed heavily handicapped.

Villersexel. Firing a house.—Another important question was brought into prominence during the battle of Villersexel, undertaken by General Von Treskow to ward off General Bourbaki's efforts to relieve Belfort in January 1871. It is not worth while to criticise the details of an engagement in which one side consisted of raw recruits with untrained officers, and the other largely of landwehr regiments. There is room enough to criticise both sides. But the interesting point is this. On two occasions during this fight the French were defending a house, and the Germans, by their own account, set fire to it. In the first case the French defenders held on, and the house collapsed over their heads, so destroy ing them. In the second case the château was partly occupied by the Germans, who held the ground-floor, while the French were above and in the cellars, where they defended themselves obstinately. When this was reported to General Von Schmeling he exclaimed, 'Nun! So räuchert sie hinaus!' 'Well! smoke them out!' He has since declared that he did not mean that the château was to be set on fire; and his declaration must be believed. But, not unnaturally, the German landwehr men did apply the torch, with the result that some of their own men were nearly burnt to death. In the end, larger movements obliged the Germans to abandon the village and château, so that the burning was all to no purpose, and in such a case should no doubt have been avoided.

But there is nothing in the laws of war against applying fire to drive out an enemy, and it may well be in some cases both the most humane course and the only one which will prevent a heavy sacrifice of life. If a detachment chooses to remain and be burnt to death, it should be understood upon whom the responsibility rests. The feeling was very bitter between French and Germans during this war, and each tried to fix the stigma of barbarity on the other. During the Napoleonic wars the French were great offenders. Historical monuments were burnt or blown up apparently without thought or question. Their horses were stabled in the shrine of Leonardo da Vinci's 'Last Supper,' and a portion of that famous masterpiece, painted on the wall, was destroyed. During their conquest of Algeria Arabs were not 'smoked out,' but suffocated in a cave, and some reports of their doings in Tonquin and China are hardly consistent with the idea of making war with rose-water. It would be well to settle by international conference what may and may not be done in war, since we are constantly told that a struggle *à outrance* will occur before very long between the two great antagonists whose exploits we have been studying for our instruction.

Explosive bullets below a certain size have been forbidden, though it is difficult to know why a few grains of an explosive mixture bursting in one's stomach and destroying life by the shock is worse than the hideous wounds caused by ragged pieces of shell. At any rate, some authoritative decision is required on such points as, 'If you may fire a house or village with shells, why not with the torch?' and others of a like character.

CHAPTER XIV.

EXAMPLES—ATTACK AND DEFENCE OF LOCALITIES.

Saragossa, 1809—Special enthusiasm of the people—Their commander, Palafox—Their preparations and defence—French devices for attack—Further Spanish arts of defence—Twenty-six days for 400 yards—Suburb on left bank—First attack—Second attack—Third and final attack—Observations—Zaatcha, 1849—Preliminary remarks—Description of village—First defensive preparations—Insufficient reconnaissance for attack—Attack of July 16 and repulse—Further Arab preparations—New expedition in September—Immediate assault fails—Fresh preparations for attack and siege works—Assault October 20 again fails—Arab sortie—The attack becomes prudent—Lively sorties by the Arabs—Arrival of reinforcements—New energy on both sides—Vigorous Arab sortie repulsed—Council of war and change of plans—Mines, batteries and breaches—Arab resistance—Decision to assault—Preliminary arrangements—Assault of November 26—Character of interior fighting—Final success of French—Losses in final attack—Remarks—Lack of reconnaissance, insufficient provision of means—Divided responsibility—Lesson of the final success—Conduct of the Arabs—Russo-Turkish campaign, 1877—False conclusions drawn—Turkish errors—Sistova—Nicopolis—Tirnova—Kezanlik—The Shipka Pass—Plevna and Lovtcha—Gorni Dubnik—Telisch, first attack—Second attack—Capitulation after bombardment.

(*Plate XVIII., in pocket.*)

Saragossa, 1809.—Though sieges form no part of our present subject, the interior defence of a town does, whether it occurs in the assault of an open locality hastily prepared for defence, or in a fortress, the regular works of which have been captured and, therefore, exist no longer for purposes of defence. In this aspect must be regarded the attack and defence of Saragossa in 1809.

Special enthusiasm of the people.—The Spanish race has always been eminent for patriotism, though that quality sometimes shows itself in questionable forms which arise out of ignorance. In 1809 there were circumstances which tended to quicken the flame and bring it to white heat. The people had felt themselves betrayed by their court and nobility. The regular army had been of no use, and the only checks to French aggression had been administered by the masses. Pride, honour, religion, patriotism, love of family and home—all the warmer feelings of the human mind were awake in the people of Saragossa, who regarded the French much as we did the Sepoys during the great mutiny in India, as enemies of humanity itself.

Their commander.—To use and direct such enthusiasm a special character is required; and this was found in the young Palafox, whose proclamation to the town declared that they would hold out to the last wall of the buildings. His energy kindled energy in the people; his brain not only devised means of resistance but set others doing the same; men, women and children hungered submissively and gave their lives at his word; and the name of Saragossa will go down to all time as that of a patriotic town which set a brilliant example to mankind.

Their preparations.—Having carried the breach after the usual delays of a siege, the French found themselves in the town. But in every street were to be seen barricades, the houses were thoroughly loopholed and prepared for defence; the convents and principal hotels were all turned into strong keeps. So strong were the defensive preparations that the French found themselves unable to assault, and confined to an advance step by step under cover.

Their defence.—The besiegers first brought up guns to breach the walls of the houses and gardens, but found behind them parapets made with boxes filled with earth, while lighter masks of sandbags covered the musketeers, who fired from behind them. At every step of the French advance the same difficulties were met and had to be surmounted. The Spanish women worked hard and exposed themselves to danger freely.

Some of the houses were held with such tenacity that they could not be captured and had to be mined and blown up. One isolated house near the Quemada Gate was defended till it collapsed under the fire of a battery, and even then the ruins were not evacuated. The right attack made a breach by means of a mine in the church of the convent of the Augustines, but behind the breach were Spaniards resisting with unbroken courage. They occupied the points of vantage in the nave, the galleries and the organ loft, whence they kept up a steady fire, while peasants concealed in the belltower threw down hand-grenades on the assailants. There were barricades in the corridors, and traverses made of bags of wool. In one counter-attack eight thousand men, excited by the sound of the tocsin, charged furiously and forced the French to abandon a whole street which had been won at the cost of many sacrifices. So determined and so regular was the resistance that the French soldiers devised a new method of attack, which is thus described by Belmas.[1]

French devices for attack.—As soon as a house was conquered it was entrenched and loopholed. Wide communications were opened through the partition walls in order to have a free circulation along behind the front of the house. Doors and windows were closed with sandbags, and that house became a strong starting point for future advance. If the enemy disputed the entrance to a room (having loopholed the opposite wall), loopholes were opened in our wall and a musketry fight proceeded across the empty room or passage. By-and-by the room filled with smoke, under cover of which a sapper glided in on his belly, and crawled under the enemy's muskets. Then with a crowbar he began to strike heavy blows on the musket barrels and, when the enemy drew them in, either filled up the loopholes or threw grenades through them, thus driving the enemy to seek shelter in a room further off, where a new combat was commenced.

Further Spanish arts of defence.—In some places the Spaniards let fall grenades down the chimneys. And when

[1] *Siège de Saragosse* par le commandant du génie Belmas; quoted by Thival in *Rôle des Localités à la Guerre.*

they considered further resistance impossible at a certain spot, they covered the woodwork with resin and pitch and placed fagots of tarred wood against the doors and windows; then setting the whole on fire placed between themselves and the attack a barrier of flames. While the conflagration was burning itself out, or being extinguished, the defenders had time to strengthen their position in rear and undertake a new defence. In a covered passage barricaded by the Spaniards the French fired obliquely against the arch, and the balls glancing and bounding struck the defenders while the attackers did not expose themselves. To the French mines the Spanish opposed counter-mines, and sometimes had the best of that form of fighting.

Twenty-six days for 400 yards.—Thus step by step, with insufficient food and disease very prevalent, these gallant Spaniards fought their fight to such purpose that it required twenty-six days after the breach was carried for the attack to penetrate some 400 yards into the town.

Suburb on the left bank.—Another part of the defence, though of a different character, was quite as interesting in showing how a defence can be made. The suburb on the left bank is a sort of bridge-head situated in a low and marshy plain. This was rapidly put in a state of defence by a line of palisades and entrenchment revetted with loose stones. An inundation covered the left flank. Three thousand men occupied the post.

First attack.—On December 21, at one o'clock in the afternoon, two French battalions assaulted and carried an isolated house defended by 600 men. Under cover of olive-groves and gardens the columns advanced on the Villa-Nueva road. But, taken in flank by the fire of a redoubt, they suffered much, and were thrown back to the left on the Barcelona road. In a momentary panic the convent of St. Lazare was abandoned by the Spanards. But Palafox in person rallied them, and they repulsed the French troops, who henceforth abandoned the idea of open assault and proceeded by regular approach.

Second attack.—On February 8, twenty-two pieces bombarded for two hours the Jesuit convent and made several breaches in the enclosure wall. Eight companies attacked and carried it with difficulty, and after losing ninety men.

Final attack.—On February 18, the fire of fifty-two guns was concentrated on the suburb. The walls of the garden were pierced through and through; but every hole made by a projectile was instantly used as a loop-hole by the Spanish who fired through it. When at last driven to retire within the building of the convent the Spaniards still held out for three hours, though the building was riddled with balls. The outer door of the convent of St. Elizabeth was beaten down by artillery; the Spanish peasants lifted it up and buttressed it with their arms. A new salvo of artillery once more dashed it down, and a second time the people replaced it. The assailants were actually obliged to break the pier of the arch before they could make a clear entry through the doorway. A heap of dead bodies was found behind that door, which in each of its falls had crushed those who held it up. When the artillery had thus prepared the attack, three columns assaulted, and, after a bloody combat, penetrated into the two convents, whilst other troops cut off the retreat of the defenders.

Observations.—Here we have a case of a simple enclosure wall, well defended, having a French brigade to besiege it regularly, causing the assailants to suffer considerable losses, and holding them in check for two months. It is true that the small arms used by both sides were of old pattern, but the development of the breechloading rifles is on the whole more in favour of *defenders under cover* than of the attack. It is also true that the increase of range and accuracy obtained by rifled guns with elongated projectiles admits of concentrating on a small space a much heavier fire than was formerly possible; but against this may be put the ascertained fact that troops under cover are still practically safe against the action of field artillery. Witness the remarkable defence of Plevna, and the fact stated by Captain Trotter, R.E., that in the last siege of Kars 48,000 Russian projectiles only struck 308 persons, of whom 105 were killed, at a mean distance of 3,600 metres. Perhaps the one particular in which the attack has gained considerably is in the use of convenient explosives for breaching, such as guncotton and the various forms of dynamite; yet even here there is a future for the defence in the extended use of land torpedoes of various sorts. Taking all things into consideration, there seems to be no reason why a well-built town or village should not defend itself in these days as firmly as Saragossa some fourscore years ago, and a town has many advantages over a village.

Village of Zaatcha.

The attack and defence of the Algerian village of Zaatcha is well described by Captain Louis Thival, who gives his authorities. This contest is full of instruction both in its virtues and its faults, as well as in the originality of some of the means employed, which will suggest to the intelligent reader the wisdom of fixing principles in the mind and devising details at the time of need. This is the one lesson that the author desires to bring home to the minds of young students. *By all means study what has been done, but keep your minds supple, remembering that you also may have to set original examples to posterity.*

Preliminary remarks.—The condition of France and Europe which brought about the disorders of 1848 caused the Arabs to cherish hopes of freeing their country; but, as usual in such cases—the Indian Mutiny, for instance—the actual rising took place too late for its chances of success. Among others, an Arab named Bouzian, who had been Caid of Zaatcha under Abd-el-Kader, declared himself divinely inspired to expel the infidels. A French officer with a handful of escort went to the village to arrest Bouzian, who was rescued by the people before he could be marched off. This failure determined the insurrection, and Zaatcha was in a state of revolt. The French then sent fifty horsemen to carry off Bouzian dead or alive. They were received with a fire of musketry, and retreated precipitately. These events occurred early in 1849; and in July of that year a force of under 1,600 men and six guns was sent to repress the revolt.

Description of the village.—Zaatcha (Plate XVIII.) was a mere hamlet, situated on one of five oases, and nearly in the centre of them. That of Bouchagroun is about two miles to the east; Tolga a little more to the west; Farfar, less than 250 yards on the north; and Lichana actually touches Zaatcha and forms part of it. Each of these oases has a village of its own name, and all the other villages, though sometimes professing attachment to the French, were friendly to the insurgents and helped them. The oasis of Zaatcha was formed by many palm trees planted in a hot soil which they cooled by their shade. Under the canopy grew multitudes of fruit-trees, figs, olives, apricots, &c., and a mass of creepers, which rendered passage difficult. Water was abundant, even to the extent of supplying irrigation and keeping ditches full. The village was raised on a hillock, the flat roofs of the houses afforded excellent means of communication, and lower communications were opened by means of gaps or holes in the walls. Towers flanked the outer walls of the houses at short distances apart. A little to the north-east was a Zaouïa or sacred place, containing a mosque and other buildings surrounded by a wall. This enclosure communicated with the village by narrow winding paths walled in to the height of nine or ten feet, passing through gardens which were intersected by channels of irrigation. The walls and buildings were of bricks dried by the sun. In many places the gardens were below the level of the so-called streets.

First defensive preparations.—The apparent weakness of the French gave energy and hope to the Arabs, who prepared to defend their village seriously, and in so doing to protect their chief Bouzian, whose capture became thenceforward a question of life and death struggle. That leader took the following measures. The roads leading from the country to the village were closed with walls of loose stone and arranged for defence. The houses which formed the outer line of defence were loopholed. A ditch, some five or six feet deep and twenty-five to thirty feet broad, was dug round the village.

Reconnaissance for attack.—On July 15, 1849, Colonel Carbuccia arrived before the place with under 1,600 infantry and six guns. On the 16th he made a reconnaissance, which had rather for its object to ascertain the feeling of the district than to study the military problem. Constant fighting of inferior armies teaches bad military habits to all nations, and leads to neglect of military precautions. A column was sent to Lichana round the northern boundary of the oasis. Bouzian, with some of the contingents now within the place, issued from it armed, the leader being clad in the green burnous of an emir, thus claiming descent from the Prophet, but the French march was not stayed. Albeit that a proper reconnaissance of Zaatcha was neglected, the French traversed Farfar, and confiscated the goods of many of the insurgents. The attack was decided on for the same day.

Attack of July 16.—Two columns of 500 men each were told off for the attack, the remainder of the force being left to guard the camp. At the given signal the two columns dashed forward; that of the left against the Zaouïa, which was carried, but the column on attempting to enter Zaatcha with the flying enemy found itself in front of the unexpected wet ditch not discovered by reconnaissance, as it ought to have been, while the flying Arabs disappeared towards the South. Exposed to the fire of the defenders in the houses, the column nevertheless attempted to cross the ditch, but was repulsed, and retreated behind the walls of dried brick. A mountain howitzer was brought up to make a breach in the houses; but the shells simply made a round hole in the soft material without bringing down any mass. This column therefore failed. The right column, which was directed on the west face of Zaatcha, was not more fortunate. Impeded by numerous ditches across the roads and perhaps by walls, it also found itself at last before an unknown wet ditch which it failed to cross, and there waited for better news from the other column. Night approached, the retreat was sounded, and the loss was found to be one captain and 31 men killed,

6 officers and 111 men wounded, or nearly one-sixth of the force engaged. The Arab loss was 48 killed and 89 wounded.[1] On the 19th and 20th the camp was broken up, and all attempt on Zaatcha deferred to a cooler season of the year. Those who know the quality of Eastern nations are aware how their spirits rise and fall with success or failure. Zaatcha had now resisted three attempts to capture Bouzian, and felt that heaven was on his side. Troops of allies flocked in, and more serious defensive works were undertaken.

Arab preparations.—An enclosure wall more than six feet high was erected, thus creating a *chemin de ronde* (outer protected way) round from the only village gate, terminating at the north-east angle. The ditch and the *séguras*, small irrigation channels, were dug out and enlarged. The garden walls, which might give cover to the enemy in front of the ditch, were levelled.

New expedition in September.—On September 24 General Herbillon, with 4,830 men, left Constantine for a new attack on Zaatcha. He was joined on the march by different *goums* —troops of friendly Arabs—and arrived on October 7, establishing himself within 700 metres of the little village. What follows is extracted from the diary of an officer who was ergeant-major during the attack. The diary is quoted by Capt. Thival.

Attack and repulse.—Apparently on the same day, or but little later, the French, enveloping the place with flying columns to prevent succour, made an attempt in three columns to carry Zaatcha by a *coup de main*, but failed.

Dispositions for new attack.—The walls of the Zaouïa, again in French hands, were loopholed and a sandbag epaulment for two guns was constructed, about eighty yards in advance, on the little street leading to the village. The work, though protected by the fire of two howitzers, was made with

---

[1] The amount of losses must be taken for what it is worth. The Latin as well as the Eastern nations do not pretend to strict accuracy in numbers of killed and wounded. It is a question of policy. Napoleon I. wrote bulletins distinctly intended to mislead after his battles.

difficulty, the Arabs interrupting it as best they could. On October 8 two mountain pieces opened fire from the epaulment on the east face of the village, and a battalion under Commandant Bourbaki made a fresh assault which was repulsed with considerable loss.

Fresh preparations for attack and siege works.—The walls enclosing gardens were loopholed and organised as a parallel; and traverses formed of palm logs were constructed to cover the guards of the works. On the 10th works were undertaken with a view of carrying the extremity of the Rue de Lichana so as to drive the enemy out of the gardens thereabouts. On the 11th the attack extended to the right near the North-east angle where Bouzian's house was understood to be. Without giving details it may be understood that day by day the French extended their work, using palm logs and sandbags. The Arabs replied by turning the waters on the assailants, filling their trenches and washing away their parapets. On October 12 the French were reinforced by 1,600 men. They had now about 6,500 to carry a little village defended by Arabs! From the 13th the works were divided into two attacks with the object of advancing under cover on the south-east and north-east angles of the place, which points the artillery were finally to breach. On the same day, 13th, the Arabs made a vigorous sortie and attempted to destroy the works, but were repulsed. The flying fire of the defenders from the houses and stones thrown by the Arabs on the trenches forced the French to cover the approaches with fascines made from palm trees. On the 15th the right attack was hampered by want of materials, by the inequality of the soil crossed by numerous irrigation channels, and by the numerous fig-trees and creepers which covered the ground. On the 16th they began to fill up the wet ditch by throwing stones into it over the parapets, which were chiefly made of trunks of palm-trees. The head of the works was protected by a sap roller which worked badly among the fig-trees and their roots, so that only about one or two metres per day could be gained. By the 19th after much trouble and loss of many men, especially engineers, the artillery had succeeded in opening the two breaches as designed—distant from each other about 110 yards. The saps were completed on the left to the edge of the ditch, which was nearly filled with stones —on the right to some sixteen or seventeen yards from the ditch. In spite of this shortcoming on the right the assault was ordered for next day.

Assault of October 20 again fails.[1]—' At daybreak, October 20, the artillery rained projectiles on the left breach. At seven A.M. the charge is sounded and twenty-five sappers, followed by two companies of the *élite* of the foreign legion, throw themselves on the breach. Arrived at the top, the head of the column finds itself, at the moment of entering the village, swallowed by the collapse of the ground on which it stood. Several of our soldiers are crushed. This catastrophe throws the column of assault into disorder, and it falls back towards the trenches under a very lively fire from the neighbouring houses into which the besieged had returned after the artillery ceased firing.'

' At the right attack, a detachment of sappers and voltigeurs does its best to establish a passage over the ditch by means of a cart. Again and again the wheels catch in the irrigation ditches which cross the road, and when, at last, pushed into the ditch, it turns of itself and presents its side to the attackers. A portion of the column throws itself into the deep ditch, and gets across, but arms and ammunition are soaked with water. Another portion crosses where it is shallower, the men holding their arms and ammunition above their heads. With great difficulty the slippery bank on the other side is mounted, but, just then, the retreat of the left had enabled the Arabs to concentrate against that of the right, which, in its turn, is defeated, and has to retreat leaving the ground covered with dead.'

The losses of the French were 20 officers and 35 men killed, 5 officers and 132 men wounded, total 192 of all ranks *hors de combat*. The Arab loss is stated as being about 80.

Arab sortie.—The next night an unsuccessful sortie was

[1] Quoted textually from the journal of Commandant Ribes.

made by the Arabs against the trenches. No details are given of these sorties.

The attack becomes prudent.—Like the Russians before Plevna, the French recognised at last that they must work by proper investment and slow siege operations. Reinforcements were demanded, and the works were pushed more slowly. A blinded gallery was undertaken towards the passage of the ditch on the left, in order to place a mining charge in the interior of the place. On the right the artillery endeavoured to enlarge the breach and to ruin the towers which commanded the houses of the village.[1] The various approaches were covered over with fascines and palm-logs. On October 24, the besieged embarrassed the works of the advancing blindage, the mantelet of which was often pierced by balls. The besiegers' artillery continued its fire on the village. On the 25th, the inhabitants of the oasis attacked the working parties which were cutting down the palm-trees, but were driven off by reinforcements speedily despatched. On the 27th, the right attack had arrived at the edge of the ditch, which was quickly filled with stones. A chain of 180 men between the Zaouïa and the ditch passed materials to eight sappers, who threw them over the parapet. By the next day there was a solid road about 15 feet wide across the ditch. Its top was nearly two feet above the water, and it led direct to the breach.

Lively sorties by the Arabs.—On October 31, the camp was attacked by the nomads of the neighbourhood, in combination with a sortie from within. Both attacks were repulsed. In the night of November 1 and 2, the garrison made another sortie, cut the retaining cable of the mantelet at the head of the left sap, and overthrew it. Their heavy fire prevented the French from re-establishing it; but with

---

[1] Note the extremely small effect produced by guns of low calibre. This is always the case. The remedy is to be found in screw guns, which can be put together on the spot, so that much larger shells can be used. Thin steel shells have heavier bursting charges, and the introduction of the new high explosives will add greatly to the destructive effect.

great difficulty a new one was brought up to replace it next day. During the night of the 5th, the Arabs set fire to the head of the gallery by throwing quantities of burning material upon it. The new mantelet was consumed. On the right the sandbag parapet collapsed at the same moment, probably undermined by water. On the night of the 6th, the blindage of the gallery was burnt, but it was replaced next day by a roof of palm branches without leaves which rendered them less combustible.

Arrival of reinforcements. New energy on both sides.— On November 8, Colonel Canrobert arrived with a reinforcement of 1,200 men, and on the 12th further reinforcements arrived, including two fresh guns. The night work, which had been abandoned since the assault of October 20, was then recommenced, but generally interrupted between six o'clock and midnight by Arab sorties. The blinded gallery was carried over the ditch close to the first house of the village, and covered with skins of fresh-killed cattle to prevent ignition. During the night of the 12th and 13th, the Arabs fired heavily on the advanced works, brandishing lighted torches, with which they endeavoured to set fire to the gallery, but could not. On the 13th was constructed, by the right attack, a 'place of arms,' with biscuit boxes filled with earth. This was intended to flank the head of the sap. The next day a sap parallel to the ditch was inundated by water which the enemy managed to pour upon it from the neighbouring irrigation cuts. The parapets of sandbags collapsed into the trench, and the water had to be drawn off by cutting a new channel for it. Reports among the French Arabs, and the vigour of the resistance, combined to foster the belief that Bouzian had constructed interior retrenchments. It was therefore resolved to open new breaches laterally.

Vigorous Arab sortie repulsed.—On November 16, about midday, a body of Arabs, leaving Zaatcha by an opening at the south-west of the village, escaladed at three places a garden which served as a place of arms for the left attack. Workmen and guard, taken by surprise, retreated, leaving to the enemy the material, tools, and arms. Reinforcements came up and repulsed the Arabs; but they remained for the rest of the day in the trenches and in neighbouring gardens. Finally they were driven back by throwing a great many shells among them chiefly by hand. Want of sandbags to replace those carried off by the enemy made it impossible to recommence the works at once without danger.

Council of war. Change of plans.—On November 17, it was decided at a council of war that because of the numerical weakness of troops,[1] the line of works could not be extended laterally, while at the same time it was important to hasten the fall of the place, taking advantage of the moral effect created by the success of a column of 3,500 with which General Herbillon had driven away a mass of Arabs assembled at Ourlal, some three or four miles from Zaatcha. However, it was thought that a new assault delivered against the two existing breaches would again encounter a desperate resistance. The council agreed that new breaches should be opened as quickly as possible and the assault delivered.

Mines, batteries, new breaches. Arab resistance.—On November 18, two mining charges of ten kilos were lodged at the base of the tower where the blinded gallery ended. The tower fell, to the great distress of the Arabs. At the right attack a place of arms was formed, on one side behind a garden wall, and on the other by a parapet of palm-logs and biscuit boxes. An advance was made from it by using a large gabion of planks, filled (*farci*) and probably covered with the skins of fresh-killed animals. On the evening of the 19th, some Arabs were seen on the terraces of the houses with lighted torches, but they made no attempt. On the 21st, a

---

[1] At the beginning General Herbillon had 4,830, besides Arabs who joined on the march. He had since received reinforcements of 1,600 and 1,200 men, besides an unknown number which joined on the 12th with two guns. These figures amount to 7,630 men, and if we include the unknown number of the 12th, and friendly Arabs, the total force employed cannot have been much less than 10,000 men employed in capturing a village which seems to have been about 100 yards square. The plan shows twenty guns, but perhaps some are shown in two places.

new battery was established on the right attack. It was to take obliquely the fourth face of the village as yet intact, and prevent easy issue from the only open gate of Zaatcha, the position of which was pretty well known, thanks to a yellow and green flag which Bouzian had erected there. During the night of the 22nd, the Arabs cast lighted torches into the gardens and impeded the progress of the works; but the sap leading to the third breach was advanced to the edge of the ditch, which had still nearly three feet of water, and on the 23rd, four sappers, covered by a heavy fire of small arms and hand grenades, crossed the ditch and lodged a charge of twenty-five kilos to blow up the wall of the *chemin de ronde* which could not be struck by the projectiles from the battery. The explosion opened a practicable ramp leading to the breach opened in the house by the artillery. The filling of the ditch was proceeded with as on the former occasions. On the 23rd, three mining charges were lodged on the breach amid the mass of débris from the houses. The explosion opened a street leading to the centre of the village; but, on the 24th, a reconnaissance of the breach showed that the Arabs had built a brick wall about five feet thick to block the entrance to the street. A new mine of fifty kilos destroyed the obstacle, upon which the Arabs dashed out on the extreme right of the works, and carried the battery after a hand to hand struggle with the French soldiers. The reserve of the guard however retook the battery, and, under a heavy Arab fire, the parapets which had been destroyed were rebuilt.

Decision to assault in three columns.—After this affair of the 24th, it was definitely determined to assault the place without waiting for the establishment of a fourth breach, which would not have been ready for some days. Three columns were told off, each 800 strong, under the command of (right column) Colonel Canrobert; (centre column) Colonel de Barral; (left column) Lieut.-Colonel de Lourmel.

Preliminary arrangements.—During the night of November 25, collections of sandbags and palm-logs were formed near the breaches, so that if the troops could not hold the interior of the village they might at least make lodgments on the breaches. There were also formed depôts of tools, ladders, ropes, &c., which might be useful; and, near at hand, bags of powder furnished with quickmatch to blow up houses in which there should still be resistance. The heads of the saps were arranged for the passage of the columns; the parapets of logs which closed the trenches at the left of the ditch were replaced by masks constructed of empty biscuit boxes which could be thrown down in a moment.

At daybreak on the 26th, engineer officers reconnoitred the three breaches on which were to be placed new mines to make them as practicable as possible. At daybreak also, while the columns of assault were massing in the trenches, and the artillery covered with its projectiles the ramps of the breaches, cavalry invested the oasis and drove back into the village Arab detachments which, in expectation of the attack, had been sent to seek reinforcements.

Assault of November 26.—At 8 A.M. the signal was given. Instantly the engineers threw down the masks in front of the passages of the ditch. The three columns sprang forward on the breaches led by their chiefs and gained the terraces of the first houses. The Arabs fired steadily from behind all the points which the artillery had left untouched, and from the ruins wherever they could find shelter. The head of the right column was severely shaken on the breach; four men only remained when it arrived there. The rest of the column dashed on, penetrated into the interior, and, seizing house after house, reached the gate of the village.

The centre column rapidly climbed the breach; but arrived on the terraces (tops) of the first houses, the voltigeurs found them give way beneath their feet. But the rest pressed on. Some thirty of them captured a mosque and bayoneted or shot all the defenders. The column then joined with that from the right to carry the house of Bouzian, which was the main keep of the place. The chief himself and his son were there together with a chosen band of followers. Their resistance was most gallant.

The left column also scaled its breach and arrived at last with the rest before the house of Bouzian.

Character of interior fighting.—The following passage is a free translation of the original. 'It is difficult to dislodge the Arabs from their retreats. Each house has to be besieged. We cannot descend from the terrace to the first floor without a combat. To descend from the first to the ground floor the only opening is a hole placed in the middle scarcely illumining the lower rooms. In these obscure retreats collect all those driven from the upper stories. Whoever tries to penetrate there receives a ball and knows not to whom he should return the fire. The door is either walled up or closed by débris; no openings can be seen but the loopholes, which vomit fire at every moment. It is a new siege more deadly than the assault. The howitzer cannot be conveyed everywhere. Besides, its action is not rapid enough and the fire of the enemy soon puts the gunners *hors de combat*.[1] The sappers then try to make openings with the pickaxe, but the walls though made of earth have acquired a great solidity; and scarcely are holes made when musket barrels are thrust out of the opening and deal death to those in front of them.[2] The usefulness of powder bags is then remembered. They had not been issued when mounting to the assault lest we should see repeated the sad accident which happened at Constantine in 1837; but a few moments suffice to bring them up and set to work with them. Then on all sides are heard the detonation of petards; one sees everywhere houses blown up. Masses of wall fall, and leave large openings in the sombre haunts of the natives, where our soldiers soon penetrate, in spite of the sustained fire which issues from them.

'Bouzian holds out the longest. The 2nd battalion of Zouaves is on his track; two bags of powder placed against the house which shelters these energetic defenders produce no

---

[1] Note here the desire for artillery even in its most useless position. I think I have seen almost every common phase of war, and in every one the first cry of the infantry when the bullets begin to drop and shells to burst is for 'the guns.' There is a marvellous difference in the respect for field artillery in peace and in war.

[2] See, for the same determined act of resistance, the final attack on the suburb of Saragossa, earlier in this chapter.

effect; only at the third does a mass of wall come down. Our soldiers of the different columns of assault rush in. They are received with musket-shots.

'The efforts of our fine fellows triumph at last over that heroic resistance. Bouzian, his son by his side, fights desperately, but succumbs at last. He is put to death with his son, as rough a warrior as his father, and Si-Noussaben-Amar, the old rival of Abd-el-Kader.'

The heads of these fanatic heroes, worthy of a better fate, were carried to the camp and exposed to the view of the natives, as an incontestable proof of the victory of French arms.

Losses.—The losses were three officers and 39 men killed, 30 officers and 310 men wounded. The engineers had lost a third of their effective strength *hors de combat*. The Arabs had left 1,000 on the ground, evidently killed step by step in the houses. No record in given of the loss by disease.

Now here we have the case of a small but strongly built village defying for many months the power of France in Algeria. It so happened that the defence was isolated, and nothing else depended on it but a certain tone among the Arabs which rose with its success and fell with its fall. But much more might have rested on the holding out of that mere hamlet; and any officer in the service might be proud to die Bouzian's death if he could first render to his country a service equal to that of the Arab chief and perhaps more efficacious.

Remarks on the Attack of Zaatcha.

Lack of Reconnaissance.—The first attack was made by 1,600 men on July 16, with an absolutely inefficient reconnaissance. The commander knew nothing of the difficulties to be overcome, and a considerable number of men were sacrificed to worse than no purpose, because it is most unwise to give an adversary the moral advantage of the first success. This is particularly the case in fighting Mahometans, whose faith in Allah as a God of War and belief in destiny cause them to resist or yield as success or failure seems to be attending their first actions. This must have been well known to the French.[1]

Undeterred by this first mistake, the attack of October 7 was equally careless, and begun without reconnaissance. Once more the troops hurled themselves bravely against unknown defences and again failed disastrously, thus adding to the Arabs' belief in the favour of destiny.

Insufficient provision of means.—It is astonishing that with these failures before their eyes the French failed to lay in sufficient means for the serious work which was before them. The engineers were hampered by want of sandbags, the material for which could easily have been transported. In October they were deficient even in ammunition.

An engineer officer, Le Brettevillois, wrote concerning these matters : 'The want of sandbags has always retarded the works of attack, because a great number was required to supplement the gabions which could only be made in small quantities ; and because the means provided for the works decided upon were far from sufficing for the daily requirements. Though we used in the construction of the works everything that was at hand—biscuit boxes, provision sacks, skins of cattle and sheep, and logs of palm trees (thus ruining the oasis), materials were almost always deficient. Palm wood was abundant, it is true, but wood cannot be employed for everything, besides much time was required to cut it up.'[2]

---

[1] The author was present at the crossing of the Danube by the Russians in 1877, and afterwards went forward with the advanced guard under General Gourko. At first there seemed to be no heart in the defence. Turkish battalions were driven back by handfuls of dismounted cavalry, or even laid down their arms to squadrons on horseback. But one day after the Balkans had been passed news came of the first check at Plevna, due, like that at Zaatcha, to a careless attack without knowledge of the enemy's position. A Russian officer of high rank said to the author, 'Now you will see a complete change. The Turks will fight quite differently, being persuaded that destiny has declared for them.' The event justified this opinion.

[2] At the defensive battle of Gravelotte the corps of Marshal Canrobert was unprovided with tools for entrenching, and, though it held the

Divided responsibility.—Thival makes the astonishing statement that there were actually two commandants of engineers, each working in his own way for the common object, without any unity of direction. All that was done from October 7 to 20 was purely on the spur of the moment, the attacks proceeding totally independent of each other. Nothing but this fault of organisation can explain the fact of the assault on the right being made a real instead of a feigned attack. The right breach was not practicable, and stood behind a deep ditch full of water. The result was as could have been foreseen, a perfectly useless sacrifice of brave soldiers.

Lesson of the final success.—The assault of November 26 succeeded because the proper means were used for the end desired. All the breaches were practicable. The entrance to the village was open, and preparations of powder bags, &c., had been made for blowing in the houses. But it is astonishing that during all the time of the siege, from October 7 to November 26, no underground mines were driven against the village, seeing that the attack was always so close to it. The only explanation can be that the soil was too hard and rocky, but it is odd that no reference is made by Thival to this point. *Compare the Roumanian mine against the Grivitza redoubt at Plevna with the want of similar work among the Russians, and the objections of the latter to avail themselves of the Roumanian mine.*

Conduct of the Arabs.—The energy and resource of the Arabs were very striking. During all the siege, their sorties were frequent and determined. They took every advantage of the heedlessness of the French in not completing the investment of the place. The garrison and inhabitants of other villages worked together for the common good. Fire and water were bent to the service of the place. These warlike villagers never lost heart and, even when their defences were over-

weakest part of the French line—the only flank in the air—it was allowed to run out of ammunition. History repeats itself on both large and small scale with all nations. We English have faults which recur in every campaign. For instance, carelessness in outpost duties.

come, fought desperately, making a citadel of every house. It may have been necessary for the French to *passer par les armes* the gallant Bouzian and his son, but their heads elevated before the other villages must have seemed to the Arabs trophies of their own valour as well as of the French victory.

Russo-Turkish Campaign, 1877.

False conclusions drawn.—While the campaigns in Bulgaria and Armenia were fertile in lessons as to the value of the spade, and may be said to have decided that question for the whole of Europe, they were equally fertile in the propagation of error. There was too much political heat in the minds of soldiers of most nations to allow of cool judgment; and Russian officers, annoyed at their detention before Plevna, settled questions of praise and blame to different arms in free talk, which, caught up by semi-military or half-instructed correspondents and sometimes wrongly interpreted by them, produced false impressions on students of tactics—impressions which have hardly yet been eradicated. More will be said of this later. In the meantime we may point out that the Turks hardly ever faced the Russians on anything like equal terms in the open field, that they abandoned not only villages but towns after very slight resistance, that, while in a defensive war of positions they were often driven out of such as they had taken up, they always failed when attempting those of the Russians; and that, while their defence of Plevna was obstinate and interesting, it was carried out at first against much weaker Russian forces, and finally ended in the capture of an army and the collapse of a cause. Evidently there was here no special proof of military capacity, and it would be a grave error to set too much value on a style of fighting which admitted of such astonishing faults and led to such disastrous results.

Turkish errors. Sistova.—Among the remarkable errors of the Turks was their failure at first to defend places which, though not fortresses, might have been quickly prepared for defence. Take, for instance, Sistova. It was a solidly built town, within artillery range of the point where the Russians crossed the Danube and subsequently established their bridge. If the troops in the neighbourhood had occupied Sistova, and prepared it for defence, placing beside it a few guns, the construction of the bridge must have been seriously delayed, and time gained which might have been utilised in bringing up more forces. Yet a few rounds from field artillery, which sank five pontoons during the first crossing, was all the defence offered by Sistova, which was occupied without opposition, the only fight occurring between the first Russian troops which crossed and a detachment of Turks amply strong to garrison the town, if they had retired on that small but very defensible place.

Nicopolis.—This fortified town, containing 7,000 men and 100 guns, was attacked by the Russians on the 15th, when there was some sharp fighting round the works. It was also bombarded by guns from the other side of the Danube, and capitulated on the 16th.

Tirnova.—Tirnova is a small town, eminently adapted for defence, and lies on the direct road to the Shipka Pass. English staff officers, sent to reconnoitre that country before the war, had reported that this road would probably be the one selected by the Russians, yet, with the exception of a couple of redoubts outside the place, no preparations had been made for defence. Three battalions and a battery occupied it when General Gourko reconnoitred it with cavalry alone. The inhabitants sent word by an officer who with one squadron rode near the town, praying the Russians to advance at once or they would be massacred. General Gourko took the risk, dismounted a small force of cavalry which moved straight against the redoubts in skirmishing order, while detachments of Cossacks threatened the retreat of the Turks, who abandoned Tirnova after a mere show of defence.

Kezanlik.—After crossing the Balkans with a force of some 12,000 men, about 4,000 of which were cavalry, General Gourko skirted the southern base of the hills with trifling opposition, and his cavalry, partly dismounted, partly mounted, carried Kezanlik. On this, as on other occasions, the author saw Turkish infantry retiring before an inferior force of dismounted cavalry, a battery of horse artillery hovering on the flanks. The infantry retired on Kezanlik, but before the dismounted cavalry could reach it, a mounted Russian regiment pushed boldly into the town which it had turned, and the Turks fled.

The Shipka Pass.—The strength of the position on the Shipka Pass was proved afterwards by its defence against Suleiman Pasha, by a very inferior Russian force. Yet after repulsing two assaults, one from the north, the other from the south, the Turks abandoned this important gate to the South and Constantinople.

Plevna and Lovtcha.—It is enough, for this chapter, to say that both of these places, though capable of interior defence, made none in the one case, and little in the other. Both were but parts of positions. Plevna fell because want of provision forced Osman Pasha to endeavour to break out; Lovtcha trusted to mere placed redoubts and batteries both in front and near. There was fighting in the place itself, but nothing like a serious and well-conducted defence. It is, however, germane to our present subject to remark that General Skobeleff, who directed the main attack on the most important redoubt before Lovtcha, and whose dashing character is so well known, was wise enough to bombard it with 56 guns, from 5 A.M. till 2 P.M.—nine hours. This bombardment caused moderate damage to the guns or works of the Turks, but decimated and demoralised the defenders occupying the trenches, who thereafter made a very poor resistance.[1]

Gorni Dubnik was one of the little villages round Plevna. It lay on the route to Sophia, in a valley. As usual, its chief defence consisted in earthworks on steep heights near it. There were two principal redoubts, and, about 1,500

---

[1] *Rôle de la Fortification dans la dernière guerre d'Orient*, par J. Bornecque, capitaine au premier régiment du génie. Paris, Dumaine, 1881. Lieut. Greene, however, says that 'the lines had been much injured' by the fire of the guns.

metres from their flanks, two smaller redoubts which flanked them. The whole was combined by shelter trenches with shelter pits in front of them, and covered at their extremities with wire entanglement. This line, facing southwards, covered the village, and was garrisoned by twelve battalions of Turks. After a severe bombardment, the Russians carried the small redoubt on their left about 11 A.M., the Turks making a poor defence. But then the captors found themselves under the fire of the principal redoubt, which commanded the one they had occupied. A regiment attempted to carry it, approaching under cover of the road, but suffered heavily from the rifle fire of the defenders on the right, and was repulsed. After constant efforts on the part of the Russians—twenty-four battalions of the guards—night fell, and the position was still untaken. The order was given for retreat; but, meanwhile, some of the men, taking advantage of the growing darkness, had crept along the ditch of the road, and slipped into some outstanding buildings of the village—a little house and a mill. Thence to the main redoubt was but a short dash, and a considerable body of Russians was soon in the dead angle of the ditch. The fire of the attack from other directions prevented the Turks from mounting on the parapet to repulse them; so the Czar's soldiers cut steps in the outer slope of the parapet, scaled it, and made a concentrated rush into the works. The Turkish garrison soon submitted to be taken prisoners. The capture was effected about 7 P.M. Here the neglect to place the village in a state of defence gave the Russian troops a footing which served them well.

Telisch. First attack.—On the day when Gorni Dubnik was captured it was intended to make a demonstration against Telisch, where there was a strong fort with a garrison of about 4,000 or 5,000 Turks. The Russian force of demonstration included one regiment of infantry, twenty-four squadrons of cavalry, and three batteries, that is about 5,000 to 6,000 men and twenty-four guns. About 9.30 the position was surrounded, and a heavy bombardment opened at a range of about 1,000 metres. The Russian infantry suffered heavily from the Turkish fire, which came from two advanced entrenchments. The order was accordingly given to carry them, using the two battalions of the first line. The trenches were carried accordingly, and the two battalions not finding themselves well sheltered there from the fire of the main redoubt, advanced without orders to attack it, but were received with a terrible fire and took such cover as they could find within about one hundred yards of the redoubt. The battalions of the second line also pressed forward to submit to the same check. There they held on in spite of gallant sorties by the Turks, till the Russian commander heard that Turkish reinforcements were approaching, when he ordered the force to draw back. It was not pursued.

Here we have a good defence and even sorties. It was successful. It is interesting to know that during this affair some squadrons of cavalry attacked and carried the Turkish advanced entrenchments to the south, and retained possession of them in spite of all attempts to dislodge them.

Second attack. Capitulation after bombardment.—A few days after (October 28), it was decided to capture the redoubt at Telisch, which, be it remembered, was on a hill. The position was surrounded by sixteen battalions, and fire was opened upon it by sixty-six guns. After three hours' bombardment, General Gourko sent a parlementaire to demand that the fort should be yielded. The Turkish commander complied, and thus assault was avoided. This was the first conspicuous artillery success, and the guns employed were those of the new pattern now in the Russian service. They had been issued to the guards when leaving Russia for the front and were greatly superior to those supplied to the rest of the army.

These references to different actions may serve to show how the Turks prepared to defend localities, and we are now brought to the question of attack and defence of large positions with the strategical and moral effect of that kind of fighting.

CHAPTER XV.

EXAMPLES OF FORTIFIED POSITIONS—TORRES VEDRAS AND PLEVNA.

Passive defence to be avoided when possible—Wellington and Torres Vedras—Torres Vedras an exceptional position—Troops available—Colossal works—The position and works—Elements of success at Torres Vedras—Repeated in position before Constantinople—Elements of success wanting at Plevna—First attack upon Plevna—Further preparations for defence—Second battle of Plevna—Russian errors of plan—Krüdener's attack repulsed—Schakovskoi's attack repulsed—Remarks—Turkish attack on the Shipka Pass—Feeble Turkish attack from Plevna—Application to defence of London—Operations on the Lom—Lovtcha captured—Plevna defences developed—Russian preparations and bombardment—Elaborate plans upset by accidents—Third battle of Plevna—Attack on Grivitza Redoubt—Attack near Radischevo—The redoubts on Lovtcha road—Skobeleff's preparations—Russian carelessness in reconnaissance—Skobeleff seizes Third Knoll; skirmishes follow—Position at 2 P.M. September 11th—3 P.M. attack—Checked and reinforced—Skobeleff uses his last reserves and carries works—Condition of Skobeleff's force 4.30 P.M.—Turks attack left flank; repulsed by counter-attack—Artillery and Cossacks occupy attention of Krishin Redoubt—Russians carry Eastern Redoubt—Situation at nightfall—Problem now before general staff—Want of unity in army command; Skobeleff not reinforced—General Zotof's orders—Condition of Skobeleff's troops on morning of 12th; Turkish attacks—Turks, not pressed elsewhere, combine troops against Skobeleff, who retires slowly—Losses on both sides—Observations on third attack of Plevna—On unity of command—On necessity of reconnaissance—The best troops cannot succeed without good leaders—Tactical skill necessary—Plevna a warning, not an example.

Plate XIX. (in pocket).

Passive defence to be avoided where possible.—If the remarks on general field fortifications have made any impression at all on the readers of these pages, the result will have been to bring about a wholesome disinclination for adopting a system of passive defence, and even of constructing such works as shall produce on the troops a moral tendency towards the defensive. Still there may be occasions when a pure defensive may be absolutely necessary, because something practically immovable has to be defended, and cannot be left to take care of itself. The defence of Lucknow was a case in point; the troops were hampered by non-combatants, who would have been massacred if left behind. General Gordon's protracted defence of Khartoum was another case of the same kind, and numerous others might be named besides the defence of permanent fortresses, which exist for strategical reasons, must be defended where they stand, and with which this book has nothing to do. It may also be possible that a beaten or exhausted army needs rest and recuperation, and that there is no permanent entrenched camp near at hand to contain it. Even Frederick the Great—a master of the offensive—took refuge once in the entrenched camp of Bunzelwitz; but this was in the last of the famous seven years, when both his army and his health were nearly exhausted: even then he was soon out again and attacking with success another entrenched camp. Again, we have the case of Wellington in the lines of Torres Vedras, but, with the usual blindness of humanity under the spell of a great name, we remember the grand defensive position, and forget that, if Sir William Napier is right, the English General, had he been less bent on retreat and the defensive, might have annihilated Massena. He was hampered, by political reasons especially, but here is what Napier says:—

Wellington and Torres Vedras.—'Massena's army was not then in a condition to fight—he made a flank march within reach of an enemy in position, and he abandoned his line of communication without having established another.'

'Wellington was within four hours' march of either end of the defile through which the French army was moving. He might, with the first division and the cavalry, the Portuguese regular troops, and Trant's militia, have presented twelve or fourteen thousand men at Sardao, to head the French in the defile; while the second, third, fourth, fifth, and light divisions advancing by Mortagao assailed their rear. That he did not do so is to be attributed to his political position. . . . Nevertheless, his retreat was as dangerous as such an attack would have been, and in a military view the battle of Busaco should not have been fought; it was extraneous to his original plan, and forced upon him by events; it was, in fact, a political battle, and he afterwards called it a mistake.'

The successes of the Great Duke when standing on the defensive, particularly the battle of Waterloo—about which we are apt to forget that, splendidly as the British troops held their ground, the Prussian flank attack was the decisive stroke—have profoundly impressed the English army and people, who apparently fall into a hypnotic condition whenever that great name is mentioned, instead of regarding him, like Frederick or Napoleon, as a fine soldier who committed many blunders. 'The mistakes of Wellington' would form the subject for an interesting and instructive book could we but recover from our gaping hero-worship, and rise from that attitude of mental prostration which universally prevails.

Torres Vedras an exceptional position.—But if it be once admitted that it was necessary for Wellington to fall back on Lisbon, instead of striking offensive blows at his assailants, the lines of Torres Vedras were a magnificent example of what should be done and may be done in a short time. Only we have to find the right position to fortify. Here all was favourable. The sea was commanded by British fleets, was, so to say, at that time a British possession; on the Tagus were British gun-boats which constantly patrolled it and flanked the position. There were two distinct lines of ridges, impassable at some places, and easily made so at others. A capital city supplied from the sea lay a few miles behind, and was able to furnish everything needed—men, tools, provisions, comfort for the sick and wounded, luxuries for the healthy. In front of the first line for about a third of its extent on the left flowed the river Zizandre, swollen by rains and with marshy, impassable banks. Nor were either material or men far to seek.

The troops available.—'To occupy 50 miles of fortifications, to man 150 forts, and work 600 guns required many men, and numbers were not wanting. A great fleet in the Tagus, a superb body of marines sent out from England, the civil guards of Lisbon, the Portuguese heavy artillery corps, the militia and ordinança of Estremadura furnished a powerful reserve to the regular army. The native gunners and the militia supplied all the garrisons of the forts on the second, and most of those on the first line; the British marines occupied the third line; the navy manned the gun-boats on the river, and aided in various ways the operation in the field. The recruits from the depôts and the calling in of all the men on furlough rendered the Portuguese army stronger than it had yet been; while the British troops, reinforced from Cadiz and England, and remarkably healthy, presented such a front as a general would desire to see in a dangerous crisis.'[1]

Besides all this, Wellington drew to himself 6,000 Spanish troops, and, when all were together, more than 120,000 fighting men were present, of whom 70,000 were regular troops.

The colossal works.—The defences were of a like colossal character. The sides of the hills were scarped to form precipices, and when Massena reconnoitred the ground in front of Crauford's division this is what he found:

'Across the ravine on the left, a loose stone wall sixteen feet thick and forty feet high was raised; across the great valley of Aruda a double line of abatis was drawn; not, as usual, of the limbs of trees, but of full-grown oaks and chesnuts, digged up with all their roots and branches, dragged by main force for several hundred yards, and then reset and crossed so that no human strength could break through.

---

[1] Napier's *Peninsular War*.

Breastworks, at convenient distances to defend this line of trees, were also cast up; and along the summits of the mountain, for a space of nearly three miles, including the salient points, other stone walls, six feet high by four in thickness, with banquettes were piled up.'

The position and works.—There were three distinct positions or lines of defence. The first (Plate XIX.) was twenty-nine miles long, from Alhandra on the Tagus to the mouth of the Zizandre on the sea-coast.

The second, from six to ten miles behind the first, stretched also from the Tagus at Quintella to the mouth of the Lorenza, and was twenty-four miles long.

The third was an entrenched camp with a double line of works enclosing Fort St. Julian, south-west of Lisbon, and was intended to cover an embarkation if necessary.

The original design was to make the second the main line of defence, using the first only as a series of advanced works; but as Massena delayed, the first line gathered strength, and the rains so flooded the Zizandre that Wellington found there a position suitable for his chief defensive line. On the right for five miles was a continuous and lofty ridge defended by thirteen redoubts and scarped for two miles, showing a clear face fifteen to twenty feet high. The next portion of five miles had two salient mountains, with the valley of Aruda between them, the town being at the mouth of the pass. Three weak redoubts were constructed and the Light Division guarded this section. Then came the lofty Monte Agraça, which overlooked the whole position, and was crowned with an immense redoubt, mounting twenty-five guns, three other redoubts with nineteen guns among them being clustered round it. Pack's brigade supplied 2,000 men as the garrisons. The valley and village of Zibreira were to the left front, the town of Sobral was in advance of the centre. A reserve under Leith occupied the reserve slope. This position formed the apex of a re-entering angle. All the rest of the position had in front of it the valley of the swollen Zizandre. The first seven miles of it on well-defined hills was well occupied by a large force under the immediate command of Wellington, whose headquarters were at Pero Negro, and communicated with the whole line by a system of telegraphs. The last portion of the line had on its right a great redoubt mounting forty guns, and a series of small forts commanding all approaches; but its chief defence was the unfordable and marshy Zizandre. This first line had weak points, and offered to the enemy the facility of a good paved road extending along its front, running parallel to the foot of the hills. Five roads pierced this line, and were suitable for artillery: two at Torres Vedras, two at Sobral, one at Alhandra. Two of them united after passing the first line.

The second line was even stronger, and had only four roads leading through it from the front. Much of it was from its nature practically impassable; the rest was partly scarped and partly closed by redoubts.

The system of defence for both lines was to make the hilly parts as difficult as possible by scarps and obstacles supported by redoubts, and to close the roads by redoubts and artificial obstacles.

Massena foiled and finally retreats.—Massena reconnoitred and skirmished while taking up a position in front of the first line and waited for reinforcements. He sent columns to the rear to seek provisions. Wellington drew round the French rear the militia of the north and thus enclosed Massena, who however managed to feed his army. The greatness of Wellington was shown in his resistance to complaints and the forebodings of weaker men. He strove to have the country wasted round the French with only partial success, but finally sickness and hopelessness of forcing the lines caused Massena to manœuvre and finally to retreat. The lines of Torres Vedras had effected the purpose for which they were designed.

The elements of success at Torres Vedras.—Here we have a great example of an army taking up with success a purely defensive position. It has nothing to do with our present purpose whether such strategy was the best at the time. If it was not it might have been. But the conditions for such a defensive are not common, and Massena has been much criticised for not crossing the Tagus out of sight of the British and operating on the further bank. The defence was successful because the flanks were absolutely protected by the fleet—the sea being to all intents and purposes a British possession—and because communications with home were completely open, while Massena was threatened in rear. The English force could not be blockaded or even moderately invested. The French army was to a certain extent so invested and blockaded.

Repeated in the position before Constantinople.—Now there are other important positions in which the peculiar power of Great Britain might conceivably be exercised with better effect than could be attained by any other nation, and, so long as such cases exist, will the alliance of this country be extremely valuable in war. We need only name one, the position in front of Constantinople, which has been often reported on by English Engineers, and which General Valentine Baker strove so hard to get prepared by the Turks in 1877. The position consists of a chain of hills extending from the Black Sea to the Sea of Marmora. A series of spurs commands the broad plain in front of them, and extends over two-thirds of the whole position. The flanks are even better protected than those of the Torres Vedras lines were, for they both rest on the open sea, and no force could turn them in face of the British fleet. In this case also the resources of a large city would be behind the army, and its communications with home would be open so long as a somewhat similar position near Gallipoli were also held. The sole condition of success in maintaining a passive defence and covering Constantinople would be that the operation be undertaken by a nation which holds the command of the sea. It is a remarkable fact that in 1877-78 the Turks who showed so gallant a resistance at Plevna never completely fortified and armed this position, though their naval strength gave them every advantage.

Elements of success wanting at Plevna.—If we compare Torres Vedras and the Buyuk-Tchekmedji-Derkos positions with that of Plevna, we cannot help being struck by

T

the absence of the elements of success in the last as well as in that of any entrenched camp, which Plevna was. And we must be constrained to admit that London is a capital on the approaches to which lies no Torres Vedras, nor any positions whatever having what we have found to be the elements of success. Plevna was surrounded by hills which were fortified, slightly at first but ever more and more, till approaching starvation forced the Turkish army to attempt to break out. It had eventually no flanks because it was defended all round, but there was nothing to hinder its complete investment as soon as the Russians found the futility of their reckless frontal attacks. Neither was there anything to prevent the Russians leaving a force to contain Osman Pasha, and with the rest pushing on towards Constantinople.

Plevna.—The campaign in Bulgaria was so extraordinary in character, so fertile in bad examples, and yet exercised so strong an effect on the mind of the English army and people, solely on account of their political sympathies, that no book treating of the defensive can do otherwise than examine the conditions of that campaign, and especially the defence of Plevna. It has been shown in a previous chapter how extraordinary was the early demoralisation of the Turkish army, how blundering its strategy and tactics, and how marvellously its action had collapsed. Within a few days of the successful crossing of the Danube at Sistova the Russians had captured Biela on the left and masked Rustchuk; on the right Nicopolis had fallen after a mere show of resistance, Osman Pasha with the army of Widdin coming too late to relieve it. In the centre, Tirnova had been captured entirely by cavalry and horse artillery, and Gourko with 12,000 men had crossed the main chain of the Balkans by a mere sheep-track, and, marching behind the hills, had scattered all the Turkish forces opposed to him. After assisting to capture the Shipka Pass with its great road and all the possibilities which such a capture meant, he was pushing his cavalry still further southwards, cutting railways and telegraphs and establishing perfect consternation in Constantinople. The 8th Corps was on or behind the Shipka Pass, and 40,000 men could have marched straight on Adrianople. That force, flushed with its previous successes, would probably have carried everything before it, defeating and ruining even the army under Suleiman Pasha. But at this moment came the first check, a trifle in itself, but productive of extraordinary consequences.

First attack upon Plevna.—Osman Pasha with the army from Widdin, too late to save Nicopolis, which fell so ingloriously, marched to Plevna, where he would threaten the right of the Russian advance. A few slight preparations for defence had been made, when, on July 19, General Schildner, who commanded the right of General Krüdener's Corps, which had just captured Nicopolis, came suddenly into contact with Osman Pasha, whose forces were immensely superior in number. Whether from want of sufficient reconnaissance or because of the contempt for the enemy which the disgraceful surrender of Nicopolis must have engendered in the Russians, General Schildner attacked the Turks on the 20th. His troops succeeded in carrying three successive lines of shelter trenches, which were very badly arranged on the heights beyond Grivitza. The Turks retreated into Plevna, and it is probable that if General Schildner had strengthened his position on the Grivitza heights, and, explaining that he had to do with an army, had asked for reinforcements, Krüdener's whole corps would have come up, the Turks would have retired or been beaten, and the campaign would have continued on the lines of the first design. But, though the Russian General had only about 6,000 men, and the enemy a greatly superior number, he attempted to carry the town of Plevna by main force. He was repulsed with a loss of little less than half his strength. The Turks reoccupied the trenches which had been captured, but made no attempt to pursue. Here was a case in which temporary entrenchments would have been useful to the offensive.

Further preparations for defence.—During the fight of the 20th the Turks had discovered how great was the effect of the Russian batteries placed on the heights of Grivitza.

Accordingly Tahir Pasha, Osman's chief of the staff, put to profit the position of Grivitza by commencing works upon it. A square redoubt with sides forty-five metres long was erected to the north of the Grivitza road, in order to defend the village, and cover with fire the roads from Bulgareni and Sgalivitza. The parapet was nearly fourteen feet thick, with a command of about nine feet, and with deep and broad ditches. In front and on the flanks were shelter-trenches, and rifle-pits were arranged in front of these, so that there were actually three tiers of fire. The interior of the redoubt had a huge traverse in the form of a cross and excellent shelter for the garrison. The Nicopolis road was defended westwards by another redoubt of the same nature, and formed the centre of the defences at the village of Boukova. Covering the centre of these two works an epaulment for guns flanked and commanded all the valley of Grivitza. To the east of Boukova, on the heights near Grivitza, was placed a redoubt for infantry and artillery, called the second Grivitza redoubt; a fourth work called the redoubt Hafiz-Pasha was destined to defend the heights of Radischevo and the Pelishchat road. It was covered by two batteries, and had sheltertrenches in front and on the flanks. A redoubt commanded the Lovtcha (or Lovatz) road, and another very strong redoubt, armed with siege guns and with a lunette in front of it, covered with its fire the heights between the Lovtcha road and the Tutschenitza stream; it had shelter for the reserves in rear. The west of Plevna was defended by two redoubts, arranged for artillery and infantry, and behind this front were the greater part of the Turkish reserves, held so far back from the northern and eastern faces as to be out of fire from the artillery of an attack coming from those directions. Besides these defences Osman Pasha drew to him the greater part of the Turkish troops disposable in Eastern Bulgaria and on the frontier of Servia. To secure the line of retreat, Lovtcha was occupied and works of defence constructed.

It is evident from these dispositions that the idea was to place a strong army on the Russian right flank, to sustain the shock of battle there, and to keep open communications with the south, so that either a retreat might be made in that direction or that the army of Osman Pasha might be reinforced by the other field armies.

Second battle of Plevna.—The check experienced by the Russians on July 20 placed them in a critical situation. If Osman Pasha had marched at once upon Nicopolis or Sistova the Russian communications would have been badly threatened, and all the troops in front would have run the risk of being cut off from their base of operations. A bold strategy on the part of the Turks at this moment would have created a very dangerous condition of affairs, for not only might Osman Pasha advance with his victorious army, but the whole of the Turkish forces in the quadrilateral on the other flank of the Russian advance might have marched westwards to assist his operations. Such strategy was evidently the right course to pursue, and not the adoption of the defensive absolute at Plevna, which, while it riveted the attention of Europe upon that spot for some months, ended in the loss of an army and the complete failure of Turkish defence. The Russians reinforced General Krüdener, so that by July 30 he had about 32,000 infantry, three brigades of cavalry, and 186 guns. Unfortunately for Russian success, the great mistake was made of allowing these troops to remain under a double command—Krüdener and Schakovskoi—and this error had serious results in the coming action. Krüdener reconnoitred the positions and reported that he had not force enough to attack; he was, however, ordered by headquarters to attempt the capture of Plevna.

Best method of attacking Turks.—If we ask ourselves what would have been the tactics of a great general, such, for instance, as Frederick the Great, it is certain that he would have made up his mind as to which was the weaker flank of the Turkish position, or the flank an attack upon which would be most sure to bring about the destruction of the Turks. He would certainly have concentrated his forces for the purpose, though perhaps Napoleon the First, whose tactics were exceptionally bold, sometimes apparently reckless, would have sent a division to produce a moral effect by attacking the Turkish rear.

Russian method different.—Instead of this, the Russian army was divided into two commands, Krüdener taking the right wing and Schakovskoi the left, and the attack of both wings was right against the front of the strong position already described, without any concentration on a point.

Krüdener's attack repulsed.—The morning of July 30 was foggy, and therefore all that could be desired for a movement to gain the enemy's flank. No use was made of this advantage. About nine o'clock it became possible to see the redoubt of Grivitza, which was the key of the position. General Krüdener, with the right wing, opened fire upon it with fifty guns, but, as we know, the Turks had plenty of shelter. About half-past two the Russian columns of attack were sent straight at the works. The assailants advanced with great courage and impetuosity, forced the Turks to seek shelter in their trenches, and drove them from these into the redoubts. But the Turks in the lateral trenches not having been attacked were able to bring a flanking fire on the assaulting columns, which, together with the fire from the redoubts, forced the Russians to retire, with a loss of about a third of their number. In spite of this terrible carnage, the quality of the Russian troops was such that a second and third attack were able to be made; but these were repulsed by the Turks with their three stages of fire. Night fell, and General Krüdener ordered the retreat, which was naturally somewhat disorderly. But the Turks did not pursue, and one Russian regiment actually passed the night on the Grivitza position. The Russian losses were extremely heavy.

Schakovskoi's attack repulsed.—On the left wing Schakovskoi attacked a series of batteries and trenches, two or three deep, between the villages of Radischevo and Grivitza. Here again the fight was commenced by an artillery combat, during which two small Turkish batteries were silenced and three Russian guns dismounted.[1] At half-past two (the

[1] Lieutenant Greene in his account of the war mentions that the Russian battery was withdrawn and replaced after the loss of three

same time as Krüdener's assault) Schakovskoi sent two columns, about 10,000 men, to make a frontal attack against some 30,000 Turks, protected by strong entrenchments. The gallant Russian soldiers advanced with their usual courage, drove the Turks to their trenches, and even carried two small works, but, like Krüdener's people, found themselves mere targets for the fire of other Turkish works, especially an entrenchment which commanded the whole valley. Schakovskoi sent the whole of his reserves at this formidable battery, but the Turkish reserves came up, forced the Russians to recoil, and drove them back on Radischevo with tremendous losses. As in the case of the right wing, the retreat made after the evening shadows had fallen was much confused, and continued gradually during the night; it was daylight before the last of the Russians retired. On Schakovskoi's left the gallant Skobeleff had fought brilliantly with his brigade of Caucasian Cossacks and one battalion of infantry. With these he strove desperately to prevent the Russian flank being turned and overwhelmed. He succeeded in that object, though his losses were extraordinary. His Cossacks fought dismounted in combination with the infantry. He continued his efforts well into the night, and probably saved the main body, but he lost about half his men. One of Schakovskoi's regiments lost about seventy-five per cent. of its strength in this ill-judged attack. The total losses of the Russians amounted to about a quarter of the whole force.

Remarks.—The conduct of Osman Pasha in fortifying instead of manœuvring in the field has been defended on the plea that, as a matter of fact, the Turks never attained successes against the Russians in the open field; but this is surely a bad argument for the habit of adopting the defensive as an habitual practice in war. Why were the Turks always unsuccessful in attack? Simply because their habits, their perpetual resort to digging instead of marching, and

guns. Prince Kraft in his letters on artillery points out what a grievous mistake it is to withdraw batteries simply because some of their guns are silenced.

the quality of their officers made them unfit to act as a manœuvring army, and therefore incapable of winning a campaign. If the advocates of the defensive point to these successes at Plevna the reply is obvious. They were at first superior in number to the Russians, who attacked them unscientifically, and what was the final result? It was the same as that of Ulm, Metz, Sedan, and Paris. Capitulation of a whole army and the collapse of the National Defence. On the other hand, the Russian attacks were reckless as they were made, but the headquarters staff must take much of the blame, because in response to a telegram from Krüdener, who thought the Turks too strong, the Grand Duke ordered the attack to take place. Of course there were recriminations between the two generals engaged. We have nothing to do with them, but only to point to the fact that divided command is an evil; and that to make a frontal attack upon an enemy who is well armed, superior in numbers, and heavily entrenched is about the most reckless operation conceivable in war. If there had been a thorough feeling of co-operation among the Turks, Osman Pasha could have been reinforced by one of the other armies; but even in that case no good purpose would have been served unless, so reinforced, he had been able and willing to attack the Russians.

Attack on the Shipka Pass.—The uselessness of a strictly defensive strategy was then shown by the fact that, with Osman on the Russian right, Mahemet on the left, and Suleiman in front, no combined attack was made on the Russians. Suleiman indeed attacked the Shipka Pass during the week which began on August 20. But the principle of bringing superior forces against inferior forces of the enemy, at the right time and place, was conspicuous by its absence. On the other hand, we see in the Russian occupation of the Shipka Pass a want of sufficient preparation to defend a position which was absolutely necessary to the Russian strategy, and had to be defended by a small force. But for the mistakes of Suleiman Pasha, the Shipka Pass, which might better be called the Shipka ridge, must have fallen into the hands of the Turks. The limits of this book will not allow me to give a description of this attack and defence, which may be read in the pages of Lieut. Greene,[1] or those of Captain Bornecque,[2] but one quotation from Lieut. Greene's book may be given:

'For three days (August 21, 22, 23) less than 8,000 Russians and Bulgarians had held in check the army of Suleiman, 25,000 to 30,000 strong. During this time their only food was the biscuit (about one day's ration), which they had in their pockets when the affair began; the heat was intense, but the nearest water was at a spring between three and four miles back on the road towards Gabrova, and all that the men had to drink was the little which was brought back in their canteens by the men who carried the wounded to the rear. Whenever the firing ceased for a while they lay down on the ground they were defending and caught an hour's sleep; for it was the period of full moon, and night brought no cessation to the firing. It was not only during the assaults of the Turks that the men were under fire; it was at all times, dependent only on the pleasure of the Turks; for from behind the woods on the two spurs on either side the *Turks commanded every point of the Russian position,* excepting only a small portion of the reverse slope of the Northern Hill; and even here General Darozhinsky was shot dead on the morning of the 25th by some Turkish pickets in advance of Bald Mountain. The odour of decomposing corpses was sickening, and the sight of them demoralising.

'On the afternoon of the 23rd the men had just about reached the final limit of human endurance. Then the reinforcements began to arrive, allowing the men to be relieved and have a little rest; the soup kitchens were established back, near the spring, and the Bulgarian peasants were im-

---

[1] *The Russian Army and its Campaigns in Turkey in* 1877-78. F. V. Greene, U.S. Engineers. London, 1879.

[2] *Rôle de la Fortification dans la dernière guerre d'Orient.* Captain J. Bornecque. Paris, 1881.

pressed at Gabrova, and put to carrying water and food up to the men.

'For impetuous assaults and tenacious, dogged defence, for long-continued fighting and physical endurance, this five days' battle in the mountains is extremely remarkable; but there were no skilful manœuvres of the troops on either side. Although Suleiman took possession of heights flanking and nearly surrounding the Russians, yet he persisted in dividing his forces and making the strongest attacks upon their strongest position (Mount St. Nicholas), thereby enabling them, although far inferior in numbers, to hold their ground at all points for three days until the arrival of reinforcements. Had Suleiman thrown the whole of his force into either one of his flank attacks, he would in all probability have carried the whole place. On the other hand, the Russians, during the ten days between the time the Bulgarians were driven out of Eski-Zagra, and the appearance of the Turks at Kezanlik, had remained idly at the village of Shipka, and done nothing towards strengthening their position in the pass, except to modify the original Turkish fortifications so as to turn them against the south instead of the north. The Russians in fact felt quite confident that Suleiman would either go through Slivno to Osman-Bazar, or else through the Elena Pass to attack Tirnova. This was a most natural supposition, but it hardly justified the Russians in failing to do their utmost to make the Shipka Pass impregnable. The little force of 5,000 men was not sufficient to occupy the heights on all three of the main spurs, but they might easily have made strong lines of trenches on each of the little hills on the top of the road, and been prepared to make a good defence; whereas, on the third day of the fighting (August 23), the men on the Northern Hill were firing from behind rocks and piles of blankets; there was a sad deficiency of spades and other implements actually with the troops, and there were no engineer troops anywhere in that vicinity of the theatre of war.'

This passage gives some idea of the splendid quality of the Russian troops, and also of the way in which life may be sacrificed and an army compromised by want of knowledge and skill in fortifying positions when the defensive becomes necessary. The reader should especially remark that there were no Engineer troops anywhere in that vicinity of the theatre of war. This must often happen, and it is a monstrous mistake to suppose that the details of defending positions should not form a part of the ordinary instruction given to troops of all arms.

Feeble Turkish attack from Plevna.—While waiting for the reinforcements sent for from Russia, a force about equal to that of Osman Pasha, say 50,000 men, was entrenched opposite the Turks, who made a feeble attack on August 31. This, like the attacks of the Russians, is instructive by its faults, which were especially—

1st. Bringing to bear upon the main point of attack only a feeble proportion of the troops actually engaged, or able to be engaged.

2nd. Advancing by successive movements with an interval between them, like waves which break upon a beach, one checked by the recoil of that which went before, instead of accumulating one mass upon another until they became irresistible, like the gathering waters of a flood beating against a dam, which is at last overwhelmed.

It is also remarkable that Osman Pasha deferred his attack until the Russians had fortified their positions. We may remark here how little use Osman Pasha was at this point of the theatre of war. Instead of binding to one spot, as in theory fortifications are supposed to do, an enemy's army three times its strength, he only held there a force equal to his own. It is interesting to remember that much the same failure was seen both at Metz and Paris in 1870, when the armies outside were very little stronger than those within, yet the troops on the defensive did not succeed in breaking out. *Thus defensive works are a two-edged sword, and may end by spoiling your own troops for attack while you are fixing down to one spot as many of your own troops as of the enemy.*

Lessons applied to defence of London.—Apply this maxim to the invasion of England. Some strategists advocate the placing of large forces in a single defensive position to cover London, and massing there the supposed Volunteer Artillery, consisting of guns of position.[1] What would happen? *The enemy would inevitably render this force immovable by placing one opposite it, and the rest of his troops would march on London by another route, being certain that they could not possibly starve in the largest and richest capital city of Europe, sufficient provisions for which must be brought into it, since otherwise there would be certain starvation for millions of men, women, and children. All the diagrams in the world will not alter the facts of human endurance, or the deductions which every man, whether soldier or civilian, may draw from those facts. A capital may be defended by an immense system of fortifications or by a field army, but in the latter case the field army must be strong, well organised, and trained, thoroughly able to march, manœuvre, and attack.*

Operations on the Lom.—It is not worth while to study the trifling affairs which took place on the Lom. From first to last there was no vigour at all in the proceedings, the reason probably being that Mahemet Ali, who was a European, could not get himself obeyed by the Turkish leaders under his command. Suffice it to say that his army, which was larger than Osman Pasha's, was neutralised by a force much weaker than his own. He could only act by taking a vigorous offensive, and he could not trust his army, though, in case of a check, it was always possible to fall back safely on Rustchuk or Shumla.

---

[1] Sir E. B. Hamley has been quoted as lending his great authority to this idea. I do not so read his opinions on the defence of London. He seems rather to advocate the preparation of schemes for a chain of defensive works round the capital, to be only executed in time of danger, and then manned by volunteers. This would be to fortify London in a temporary manner, and should certainly be prepared for, as we cannot have permanent fortifications. But where are the guns for the purpose?

Lovtcha captured.—When the decision was taken to cut the Turkish communication by the capture of Lovtcha, Skobeleff was sent to Selvi with his Cossack brigade (Caucasian), and there he was met by an infantry regiment and part of another. With these troops he made a model reconnaissance in force on August 6, using his small command with such skill that he forced the Turks to develop their whole strength, counted 15,000 men and 25 guns, and, besides, had excellent sketches made of the whole position: his loss was less than 200 men. The capture of Lovtcha has already been mentioned (Chap. XIV.), but only with reference to the poor defence of the town. The attack on the position was prepared on September 1, when Skobeleff, with an advanced detachment, drove in the Turkish troops stationed on the ridge east of the town, where he entrenched himself and constructed epaulments for 24 guns, establishing there the 8 which he had with him. At daylight on the 2nd he opened fire, and by the afternoon had compelled the Turks to evacuate the ridge south of the road. On this ridge he built epaulments for 32 guns, so that, when Prince Imeretinsky arrived in the evening with the main body, there were epaulments for 56 guns. During the night those guns were dragged up into position by the infantry. At 5 A.M. on the 3rd the 56 pieces opened fire, and shortly afterwards 12 more from the hill just south of Prissiaka. The Turks took the offensive against General Dobrovolsky near Prissiaka about 8 A.M., but were repulsed and driven across the river. At 2 P.M. the Turkish guns were nearly silenced, and Skobeleff was sent to attack the Red Hill and the hills north of it. The artillery preparation had been sufficient, and the resistance was feeble. The whole line east of the river was carried by 3 P.M. Skobeleff placed 16 guns on the Red Hill to fire over the town at the redoubt behind it, and followed the retreating Turks through the town. *He then placed 16 more guns on the high road just beyond the town, and gave his infantry rest while the artillery carried out a second preparation* against the main redoubt. At 5.30 P.M. the whole infantry line advanced, the Turks withdrew all their artillery, which escaped by the Mikren road. The Russian infantry then drove back the Turkish infantry from all entrenchments except the main redoubt, which was finally carried at about 7 P.M. by a hand-to-hand struggle, in which the whole of the garrison was killed or captured. This affair was excellently managed. It was one of the many proofs in the war that lines of trenches and redoubts can be carried if attacked skilfully, but it was a bloody affair. The gorge of the last redoubt taken was choked with a mass of Russian and Turkish dead and wounded in a heap six feet thick.

Plevna defences developed.—After the unsuccessful attack of July 30 the Turks in Plevna continued to strengthen their defences. In the first week of September they possessed 18 redoubts, supplemented by several lines of trenches with batteries interspersed; but Osman Pasha was always rather short of artillery. His force included only about 80 guns, though he had 60,000 men, of whom 56,000 were infantry and 2,500 cavalry. The Russian army of attack had at this time been raised to 90,000, of which 74,000 were infantry and 10,000 cavalry. There were 24 siege guns of very low velocity, 364 field guns, and 54 horse-artillery guns. Lieutenant Greene divides the Turkish defences roughly into three groups :—

1. The Grivitza works, containing two redoubts 2,000 yards north-west of the village, and a line of trenches and batteries extending north-west along the Grivitza ridge to the Bukova creek. Beyond these was a large entrenched camp on the heights of Opanitz, overlooking the Vid.
2. The middle group, consisting of eight redoubts more or less perfectly connected with lines of trenches, on the knolls just east of the tower of Plevna.
3. The Krishin group, consisting of the Krishin redoubt, on a commanding point 3,000 yards south-west of the town, and two redoubts connected by a strong trench, just outside the town, commanding the approach by the Lovtcha road.

The Grivitza redoubt was the key of the position on the north, and the Krishin redoubt that on the south. They each commanded the entire country up to a range of 3,000 yards on all sides. The middle group was on a lower level, and was itself commanded by the Grivitza ridge on the north, and the Radischevo ridge on the south. But the Radischevo ridge remained unfortified even up to this time.

Russian preparations and bombardment.—On September 7 the Russians opened fire with about a fourth of their artillery, including twenty siege guns, at ranges of from 2,700 to 5,200 yards. Most of the fire was directed on the Grivitza redoubt, which answered all day. On the 8th the guns were reinforced and brought the middle group also under fire. The reply from the Grivitza redoubt became very feeble towards evening, but its parapets—now eighteen feet thick—were by no means destroyed. The effect was that the defenders sought shelter in their casemates. On the 9th the Grivitza redoubt was quite silent, but a reconnaissance of the Roumanians was driven back with heavy loss by infantry fire. The batteries opposite the middle group were again reinforced. On the 10th the Grivitza redoubt was still silent as regarded artillery fire, and seemed to be 'knocked out of shape.' The rest of the works were little injured, though their artillery ceased firing, partly from a scarcity of ammunition. Meanwhile Skobeleff had established himself on the Green Hills (Turkish right) as early as the 7th, and still held two knolls there on the 10th. Having no spades, the men had entrenched themselves as well as they could, using copper soup-dishes, bayonets, and even naked hands to form some kind of cover.

Elaborate orders upset by accidents.—The orders for the 11th had been: General cannonade from daybreak to 8 A.M.; then a pause till 11 A.M.; then cannonade till 1 P.M.; another pause till 2.30 P.M.; then half an hour's cannonade and a general assault at 3 P.M. It was the Czar's birthday, and Plevna was to be the army's gift to him. But all this was too elaborate to be carried out. There was a dense fog in the morning, and the guns could see nothing. Skobeleff was engaged early in taking up the best position for his advance. The Turks took the offensive towards Radischevo. They were repulsed, but the 63rd Regiment, following them up, brought in its turn the 117th into action on their right. The two regiments came among the Turkish redoubts and trenches, were taken in flank by a heavy fire, and retired with a loss of half the men and two-thirds of the officers. Worse still, they were lost for all further purposes during the day. *There is a good lesson here to avoid elaborate plans which may come to nought on account of accidents. Accidents ought to be expected as a rule.* About noon the fog partially lifted and the cannonnade was carried on till about 2 P.M., when it slackened, but was renewed at 3 P.M., when the infantry advanced. By this time Skobeleff had been long in action, and had drawn to him all the reinforcements he could count upon. We will now sketch roughly the different assaults, beginning with the right of the attack.

Attack on Grivitza redoubt.—Four columns attacked the Grivitza redoubt No. 1, which had been the chief sufferer from the bombardment. A Roumanian division attacked from the north and east in two columns, of which that to the north—No. 1 column—found itself checked by the unknown redoubt No. 2. It was driven back and entrenched itself about 700 yards to the north of No. 2 redoubt. No. 2 column, the second brigade of the division, was delayed in climbing the slippery slope. No. 3 column, one brigade (Roumanian), with the other brigade in reserve, came alone against the redoubt about 3.30, and retired to the slope between the redoubt and the village. Column No. 2 then arrived also solitary, and was driven back. No. 4 column (a Russian brigade) with two field batteries attacked from the south about 4.30, at which time the part of No. 3 column hitherto in reserve advanced from the east. Russians and Roumanians entered the redoubt at the same moment, the commanders of the leading Russian regiment and of the Roumanian brigade being both killed on the spot. But in half an hour a vigorous counter-attack drove the allied conquerors out of the redoubt. The struggle, however, continued soon after darkness fell, and at 7.30 P.M. the allies were once more masters of the position. The Roumanians had lost 56 officers and 2,511 men, the Russians 22 officers and 1,305 men. During the night two Turkish attacks were repulsed. Thus on the right the allies were partially victorious, but had only carried one of the two redoubts.

The attack near Radischevo.—It will be remembered that two regiments had been practically destroyed here in the morning, namely, the 63rd and 117th. General Schnidnikoff, whose division was to attack here, sent forward his other two regiments—the 64th and 118th—at 3 P.M. Four batteries on the left of the ridge did what they could to prepare the attack. The infantry passed the right of these batteries, descended into a hollow, and then, moving by their left flank, advanced westward against the redoubt. Just at that moment Turkish reinforcements were seen to come up and deploy on the north-east flank of the redoubt. Still the Russians moved on, and at 4.30 disappeared in the smoke which overhung the ditch; their right flank slightly refused on account of the Turkish reinforcements. For three minutes 'the affair hung in the balance, then the Russians began falling back somewhat hurriedly. The Turks streamed out of the eastern angle of the redoubt, and, joining their comrades, began to follow the Russians at a run; thereupon two battalions stopped, faced about, and lay down at about 200 yards from the redoubt, and opened the hottest possible fire. The Turkish pursuit was at once arrested, and the Turks retreated pell-mell into their redoubt again. The Russians then continued their retreat rapidly, but without any running or disorder, although they were losing terribly under the murderous fire which the Turks kept up from the redoubt.'[1] A reserve battalion was then brought up, but could of course do nothing. The two regiments regained the shelter of the hollows about 5 P.M. Two fresh regiments arrived just at

---

[1] Lieutenant Greene. *The Russian Army and its Campaigns in Turkey in 1871–78.* Lieutenant Greene was present at this battle.

this time (mark the usual series of weak attacks), and advanced a little later against the redoubt. They failed to get as near as their predecessors had done, and this is to be expected when the ground is strewn with the bodies of comrades who had gone before and failed. About 6 P.M. they fell back to the Radischevo ridge. Here, then, the Russians had been defeated, and, what is worse, defeated in an attack which ought never to have been made. For if it is a mistake for the defence to extend itself, endeavouring to be strong everywhere, how much more is this a fault in the attack!

The redoubts on the Lovtcha road.—So far we have seen two unsuccessful attacks, both of which were conducted in an unscientific manner, especially in the want of concentrated power brought against the Turkish works, the frittering away of strength, and the poor use made of the reserves. We have now to study a very different style of combat, and to witness success achieved under much more difficult circumstances—a success which must have led to the capture of Plevna had Skobeleff's attack been supported properly at the time, or even early next morning.

Skobeleff's preparations.—Up to the 9th General Skobeleff, though commanding the advanced troops on the Lovtcha road, had been under the orders of General Prince Imeretinsky; but during the night of the 9th–10th Imeretinsky received an order from headquarters dividing his troops into two distinct portions, and giving Skobeleff command of the first portion, which was ordered to attack; Imeretinsky was to support him, and at the same time cover the extreme left flank with his Cossacks. This practically relieved Imeretinsky from the command, and gave Skobeleff charge of the operations. In the early morning of the 10th, Skobeleff sent forward the 8th Regiment to seize the second knoll on the Green Hills, in preparation for the next day's work. This was effected almost without fighting, and the men entrenched themselves with soup-dishes, bayonets, and naked hands, *not having any spades available.* As soon as the 1st Brigade, 16th Division, arrived, one regiment was placed on the second knoll, and the other on the first knoll in reserve. The force

TORRES VEDRAS AND PLEVNA. 291

for next day's attack stood thus (Plate XIX.).[1] In advance, on the second knoll from west of the high road to the Tutchenitza creek, there were sixteen nine-pounders in position, with the 8th and 61st Regiments on either side. In reserve were the 7th and 63rd Regiments and the 9th and 10th Rifle Battalions. Sixteen nine-pounders were sent to the east side of the Tutchenitza creek, from which they could bring a cross-fire to bear on the third knoll at 2,500 yards range. During the night of the 10th-11th Skobeleff remained on the second knoll. In front of him was a small valley, then at 2,000 yards distance the third knoll which he was to attack; then came another little valley, and then, 1,000 yards further than the third knoll, the long sloping ridge with its Turkish works extending from Plevna to the Krishin redoubt.

Carelessness in reconnaissance.—It is interesting to observe that the reconnaissance made by the Russians had been careful along the Grivitza and Radischevo fronts, but so careless on the left that the reconnaissance sketch issued to guide the generals placed the Turkish redoubts opposite Skobeleff in quite wrong positions, and the very existence of the great Krishin redoubt was unknown till September 7, though the 9th Corps had been making the reconnaissance during the month of August. The sketch map by which the dispositions for attack were made, and the direction of Skobeleff's attack ordered from headquarters, thus ignored a most vital feature. Skobeleff had fought over the ground on July 30, but at that time the Turks had not built the Krishin redoubt. Their works always seemed to rise after the enemy had shown them the value of a particular position. Since then the staff appears to have made no proper reconnaissance in this part of the field, and the map was a blank west of the Tutchenitza creek except some dotted lines to indicate Turkish redoubts in a wrong position. The orders

---

[1] See Greene's *History of the Russian Army and its Campaigns in Turkey in 1877-78*, a very valuable book from which much of this account is taken. Lieutenant Greene had special facilities given to him both during and after the war, and was intimately acquainted with General Skobeleff.

given to Skobeleff sent him, as Lieut. Greene says, 'into a funnel,' leaving commanding positions occupied by the enemy on each side of him. Far be it from us to accuse the Russian commanders of anything worse than mistakes, but if the Czar had been David, and Skobeleff Uriah, the famous instructions of the Hebrew King could not have been better carried out by Joab than they were by the Russian staff.

At 10 A.M. Skobeleff seizes 3rd knoll. Skirmishes follow.— At 10 A.M. on the morning of the 11th, during the preliminary stage which would have been devoted to an artillery bombardment but for the fog, Skobeleff advanced and carried the 3rd knoll, which was lightly held by the Turks. But his men, who had no digging implements, suffered severely under the fire from trenches in front of the redoubts. He sheltered them as well as he could behind the crest of the hill, but they continued to suffer losses even in the reserves which were in the valley behind the 3rd knoll. About 2 P.M. the Turks pushed out a strong line in dispersed order from their trenches; Skobeleff sent the 62nd Regiment to meet them. The Turks gave way, and there was then a lull in the fight.

*Position at 2 P.M., 11th.—*At this time, before the attack commenced, Skobeleff's troops stood as follows:—First line, behind the crest of the   knoll, 61st and 62nd Regiments, with the 9th and 10th Rifle Battalions in reserve; between the 2nd and 3rd knolls, 7th Regiment. Second line, on the slightly fortified position of the 2nd knoll, 5th and 8th Regiments and 24 guns. In reserve, between 1st and 2nd knolls, 6th Regiment and 11th and 12th Rifle Battalions.

*3 P.M. attack.—*At 2.30 P.M. the guns opened fire over the heads of the first line, and at 3 P.M. Skobeleff ordered the assault. The formation was: First a line of skirmishers; then two lines of company columns, with all the bands playing. This was a fairly open formation. The Turks in rifle pits at the foot of the slope gave way at once; the Russians crossed the little stream and began to breast the hill.

Checked and reinforced.—But the Turkish fire from two redoubts and a line of trenches commanding them was too hot. The attacking troops halted and began to take shelter behind the banks of the stream and wherever else they could find cover, being at this time about 200 yards from the Turkish connecting trench. Instantly Skobeleff sent on the 7th Regiment to the aid of the wavering line, and ordered up the 6th Regiment and 11th and 12th Rifle Battalions to the reverse slope of the 3rd knoll. The artillery meanwhile kept up a heavy fire over the heads of the attacking line, which was still in the hollow. The entry of the 7th Regiment into the fighting line carried the attack onward again, but still the fire of the Turks was too terrible to allow that last 200 yards to be crossed. Again the Russians lay down and opened fire at close range. Here were now masses of men, only 200 yards apart, firing—the Russians in the open, the Turks behind trenches. The situation could not last long. The Krishin redoubt on the left and the redoubts of the middle group on the right were bringing artillery fire to bear on both flanks of the Russians. Somebody must give way.

Skobeleff uses his last reserve, and carries works.—At this critical moment Skobeleff decided on making a supreme effort. He pushed his last troops, the 6th Regiment and two Rifle Battalions, into the fighting line, and threw himself into the midst of the men, leading them forward in brilliant white uniform, and mounted on a white charger, conspicuous to friend and foe, as was his custom in battle.[1] The front line received him and his reinforcements with enthusiastic cheers, sprang up again, and once more breasted the fatal slope. The shelter trenches in front of the redoubt were

---

[1] The day before the crossing of the Danube I was in the camp of the Skobeleffs, father and son. I happened to possess a pair of nearly white horses, which the younger Skobeleff was very anxious to buy or obtain in exchange for some of his stud. Not knowing his reason, I was cautious, and kept the pair for baggage purposes. I only knew him then as a most brilliant officer and thinker, apparently under a cloud in court circles.—C. B. B.

soon cleared of Turks, and thus the enemy's tiers of fire were reduced in number. Still the fight hung trembling in the balance for some time, and, but for the presence of Skobeleff, would probably have gone against the attack. It was a question which side would first give way, but presently the Turkish line began to show signs of weakness, a portion of the Russian troops pushed into the trenches between the redoubts, then turned to the left, and by this flanking movement assisted the others, so that the more westerly of the two redoubts was carried about 4.30 P.M. The attack had thus lasted an hour and a half: it had cost the Russians about 3,000 men, chiefly killed and wounded in the assault of the redoubts and trenches, during nearly an hour's close and deadly struggle.

Condition of Skobeleff's force at 4.30 P.M.—It was now found that the redoubt captured, and, of course, the trenches, were open to the rear, and afforded no protection against the fire of the Turks, who retreated, firing, to a fortified camp about 600 yards behind the captured works. General Skobeleff had therefore only driven the enemy from one redoubt and a trench, and was still exposed to fire from one redoubt at the eastern end of the trench; a second detached redoubt, No. 13, 800 yards distant on his left flank; third, the fortified camp 600 yards in front of him; fourth, the Krishin great redoubt to his left rear at 2,300 yards; fifth, the middle group of redoubts on his right flank; and sixth, redoubt No. 10, which Kriloff's troops had just failed to carry. His men had no spades, and the ground was hard and rocky. Yet he had penetrated further than any other Russian force, and was indeed close to the town of Plevna. Most of his staff had fallen, and his own horse had been killed under him. His situation was very critical, but he knew that a retreat by daylight would be more dangerous still. He therefore decided to hold on to what he had gained. It should be understood that he had, in the course of the day, drawn from Prince Imeretinsky all the troops which had been in reserve. In that part of the field there were no more possible reinforcements.

Turks attack left flank; repulsed by counter-attack.—The Turks in the camp and the eastern redoubt kept up a heavy fire, and a force of one or two battalions was seen to issue from redoubt No. 13 (west) to attack the Russian left flank. To meet this, Colonel Kourupatkin, Skobeleff's chief of the staff, and the only officer of the staff not yet killed or wounded, moved out with about 300 men to meet and drive back the Turkish flanking movement, which, we must remember, started only 800 yards off. There was a desperate struggle in the open, in which the Russians, much fewer than their enemy, sacrificed the greater part of the little force, but not in vain. The Turks retired to redoubt No. 13. Here is an example of a bold counter-attack. If the Russians had awaited the attack in their weak position, it might have been assisted by a sally from the Turks in the camp, and the moral influence would all have been on the side of the enemy. The counter-attack in the open by 300 men looked rash, but it is clear that the boldest policy was here the best.

Artillery and Cossacks occupy attention of Krishin redoubt.—At this time some of the artillery which remained in front of Brestovetz increased its fire on the Krishin redoubts, and a portion of the Cossack Brigade did good service by dismounting and advancing on foot against the same redoubt. This demonstration attracted the attention of the Turks in the Krishin redoubt, and greatly relieved Skobeleff's infantry. *A very good example of the use which may be made of dismounted cavalry. All arms must help each other as they can.*

Russians carry Eastern Redoubt.—The redoubt at the eastern end of the trench was very troublesome, and some hundreds of Russian infantry, who sortied against it from the western redoubt, nearly all perished under the cross-fire. Then Colonel Shestakoff, of Imeretinsky's staff, advanced from the 3rd knoll with three companies of the 6th Regiment, and portions of others left in reserve, picked up scattered troops as he moved across the valley, and, gathering strength as his force rolled on, fell upon the eastern redoubt with some 1,200 men, while another sortie was made from the western redoubt. This time success crowned the combined effort, and when darkness fell the eastern redoubt was in Russian hands.

Situation at nightfall.—But, with this exception, no progress had been or could be made. Skobeleff and his force were but thrust like a wedge into a hornets' nest of Turks, who surrounded the Russians on three sides, and could even fire from right and left rear. The only reserves that could be called upon were the twenty-four 9-pounders about 1,800 yards in rear, two battalions of the 8th Regiment with the guns, and two very weak battalions of the 5th Regiment, which had lost 700 men in the fight of September 8. The 3rd Battalion of the 8th was at Brestovetz, guarding, with the cavalry, the left flank of the army, and the last battalion of the 5th Regiment was employed in keeping up communication between the two portions of the force. It was clear that if the Turks could strengthen Krishin sufficiently to make an attack on Skobeleff's rear, he and his force could hardly escape. He had carried out his orders only too well unless at this critical juncture he could be strongly reinforced. He sent a message to General Zotof, chief of the staff to the army of Plevna, explaining the whole situation, saying that he would hold on as long as he could, but that he ought to be reinforced, and the Krishin redoubt attacked by fresh troops.

Problem now before general Staff.—Now let the student (this book is not written for masters)—let the genuine student test his character by thinking what he would have done had the decision rested on him as commander or chief of the staff of that army. The blunder had been made of being equally strong, or weak, everywhere. One of the Grivitza redoubts was carried, but another, equally strong, remained intact. The middle group had not been attacked, and No. 10 redoubt had repulsed Kriloff's troops. Only Skobeleff had really penetrated close to the town, and strong reinforcements would probably enable him to capture the Krishin redoubt, occupy Plevna, and so threaten the Turkish rear while seizing their supplies. On the other hand, the Russian troops had been for the most part hard worked during the day, and had suffered discouragement from the failure of their attacks. But a successful general is always one who believes in his soldiers, and Skobeleff's work both that day and the next shows how splendidly deserving of confidence the Russian soldiers were. There was a risk to be run, an effort to be made, and the probability of a grand success, while all experience had shown that the Turks were practically incapable of assuming the offensive on a great scale.

Want of unity in command of army. Skobeleff not reinforced.—But the student will be in a better position to decide than that occupied by General Zotof. We have here another instance of the evil of divided responsibility. Who was now the guiding spirit on the Russian side? General Zotof was chief of the staff to the Plevna army. Prince Charles of Roumania was in command. But again the Grand Duke was present in the field, and he was commander of all the Russian armies. He had his chief of the staff and assistant chief. The latter had come to General Zotof some days before to explain to him the Grand Duke's wishes for the attack. The Grand Duke on arrival was really in command, but knew nothing of the ground or situation, except what he could read from the wrongly drawn map. Finally the Czar himself was on the field, and wherever a Russian Czar goes he becomes chief of every action, military, civil, or even religious. It cannot certainly be said whose was the decision, but it was to the effect that the Russian army had suffered failure and must accept the consequences, even if one of them should be the sacrifice of Skobeleff and his troops, who were, so far, the heroes of the day, and would have the honour of capturing Plevna if the battle continued next morning, and the brilliant young General were reinforced. At six o'clock in the evening the Grand Duke sent an aide-de-camp, Colonel Orloff, to find Skobeleff and ascertain his condition. Orloff wandered in the darkness and only arrived about midnight, returning then to the Grand Duke with Skobeleff's explanations. The result of all is to be found in the following orders which General Skobeleff received—the first about 7 A.M., the second at 10.30 A.M.

General Zotof's orders.

1. To General Prince Imeretinsky:—'By direction of the Commander-in-Chief, I give you and General Skobeleff the order to fortify yourselves in the position which you have taken to-day, and to hold out to the last extremity. We can send you no reinforcements, for we have none.

(Signed) 'ZOTOF, *Lieutenant-General.*'

2. To General Skobeleff:—'By order of the Commander-in-Chief. If you cannot hold the positions which you have taken, then you must retreat slowly—but, if such a thing be possible, not before evening—to Tutchenitza, covering your retreat by the cavalry of General Leontieff. Send a copy of this order—which otherwise keep secret—to General Prince Imeretinsky. The Grivitza redoubt is in our hands, but, in spite of this, the attack cannot be continued, but the retreat must be slowly begun.—8.30 A.M.

(Signed) 'ZOTOF, *Lieutenant-General.*'

This second order was brought to Skobeleff by the same Colonel Orloff who had come to him from the Grand Duke during the night. Let us now see what condition Skobeleff's troops were in to 'hold the positions' without reinforcements.

Condition of Skobeleff's troops on morning of 12th. Turkish attacks.—For some thirty hours these brave men had been struggling against the depressing influence of rain and fog, and against that process of nervous exhaustion which has been so often referred to in this book as the greatest of all dangers. Ammunition was running short. The Russian soldiers had carried certain positions, but only to find themselves still under fire from fresh entrenchments in front and on both flanks, even to the right and left rear. During the night the Turks had made two attacks, once from Krishin and once from the valley between them and Plevna. In the latter attack the Turks, mistaken in the darkness by the wearied troops for their own people, came within 100 yards before the defenders opened fire. At six o'clock in the morning the Turkish redoubts surrounding Skobeleff's position opened fire with artillery; the entrenched camp in front played on the Russian troops with musketry, and shortly afterwards a strong column advanced from the Krishin redoubt to attack the exhausted remnant of Skobeleff's force. Only at 300 yards was this column repulsed. This was just before the young General received Zotof's first despatch. Again, at 10.30 A.M., just as the second despatch came telling Skobeleff to hold on if possible till evening, though the retreat of the army was to be carried out, a third vigorous attack was made by the Turks on the Russian left flank, and, this time, though the enemy was again repulsed, Skobeleff detected that ominous sign—the dropping back of soldiers one by one towards the rear. He was then on the third knoll. He 'rode over and expostulated, threatened, ordered, and encouraged the men, and got them back into the redoubt again.'[1] Clearly the stock of nervous energy was nearly gone, and the only force left was the immense moral influence of the gallant young General, in whom the soldiers had implicit confidence. And all this time Skobeleff knew that there were troops on his right which had not been engaged since dusk the evening before, and might easily afford to reinforce him. Even an attack made at another point of the line would at least occupy the Turks and relieve him of some pressure and some danger. Between the Grivitza village and the Tutchenitza creek were eleven regiments, five of which—the 121st, 122nd, 119th, 120th, and 20th—had not been engaged at all. Not one of these was sent to help the General, who in obedience to orders was now in the heart of the enemy.

Turks, not pressed elsewhere, combine troops against Skobe-

---

[1] Greene's *Campaign in Bulgaria.*

leff, who retires slowly.—As the day advanced, and the main Russian force made no sign of activity, Osman Pasha began, as was inevitable, to mass heavy forces within his lines for a concentrated attack on Skobeleff. He at least had the sense to reinforce his troops at the critical point. Altogether about 12,000 men were sent partly into the Krishin redoubt, and thence against Skobeleff's left flank, and partly by the Tutchenitza stream, and then up the bank to attack the third knoll, and thus finally cut off the Russian retreat. Still the orders were to hold on as long as possible, and Skobeleff did his best to obey them. The attack on the third knoll began to develop itself about 1 P.M. Skobeleff ordered up the two battalions of the 5th Regiment, which had hitherto remained with the batteries on the second knoll. They succeeded in checking the Turks. But in the western of the two captured redoubts the men were suffering much from the Turkish fire. Two of the four guns which had been placed there were dismounted, and the other two had lost all their horses and gunners. To replace them Skobeleff sent forward three of the eight guns which he had kept on the third knoll. These also were soon dismounted by the Turkish artillery fire, and a limber was blown up by a shell in the midst of the men. Again there were signs of retreat, and Skobeleff once more rushed forward to the redoubt just in time to see the Turks from the Krishin and from No. 13 undertake their fourth assault with the fresh reinforcements. The Russians had no ammunition to spare and did not open fire till the enemy was within 400 yards. They then fired volleys, the Turks halted and took cover. Every attempt to attack was repulsed by Russian volleys with tremendous loss, and the enemy finally retreated to No. 13 redoubt. Skobeleff now returned to the third knoll and heard, to his great relief, that the 118th Regiment was arriving, having been sent by General Kriloff on his own responsibility, he having heard long and heavy firing on Skobeleff's front. This was one of the regiments which had attacked No. 10 redoubt on the previous afternoon: it still numbered 1,300 men. Not long afterwards, at 4.30 P.M., the Turks, heavily reinforced, made their fifth assault, both from Krishin and the camp. The nervous energy of the Russian troops was by this time fairly exhausted. They fired at the Turks with the little ammunition they had, and then began to drop to the rear in small groups. Even then there remained in the western redoubt some 200 men, who with their brave commander Major Gortaloff fought hand to hand with the masses of the enemy as their forefathers had done at Zorndorf, and were cut down to the last man. Still the men in the eastern redoubt and in part of the trenches held their ground, but there was no hope in further resistance, and to save their lives Skobeleff sent them an order to fall back: to cover their retirement, he led the fresh 118th Regiment to an attack on that part of that line between the two redoubts now in possession of the Turks. Under cover of this attack the exhausted Russians retired to the third knoll, and thence, covered by the fire of the twenty-four guns and two battalions of the 8th Regiment, fell back to the second knoll. Most of the wounded had been carried off; the dead were left on the field. Skobeleff then drew back his forces to the first knoll and remained there all night and all the day of the 13th. That night he returned to Bogot.

Losses on both sides.—Skobeleff's losses in this affair were about 8,000 men out of 18,000, an enormous proportion. Osman Pasha stated after his surrender that he lost more men on the Lovtcha road than Skobeleff did. The total Russian losses were between 18,000 and 19,000 men, of which nearly half had to be counted as dead, for few, if any, of the wounded who fell into Turkish hands were suffered to live.

Observations on Third Attack of Plevna.

On unity of command.—This third attack upon the position of Plevna was so famous, and has exercised such an influence upon the minds of soldiers, especially in England, that it is important to examine its features and see what its lessons really were. We have already seen how unfavourably the want of unity in command affected the operations.

In a previous chapter has been shown how the siege of Zaatcha was affected by the same mistake. The first lesson therefore is *the absolute necessity for unity in command and undivided responsibility.*

On necessity of reconnaissance.—Next we see that from want of thorough knowledge of the ground Skobeleff was sent to perform a practically impossible task, and from the same want of knowledge he was neither reinforced nor directed to withdraw in time. It is impossible to accept the hypothesis put forward by some writers at the time that Skobeleff was designedly sent to death or failure. Besides we know that the map on which the operations were based did not show the most dangerous of all the Turkish defences, namely, the Krishin redoubt. The second lesson, then, is that *no attack should be made on a great fortified position without a previous, and very careful, reconnaissance.*

The best troops cannot succeed without good heads.—It will have been observed that Skobeleff made excellent use of both his infantry and artillery, while even the cavalry did its part by dismounting men to threaten the Krishin redoubt at a critical moment. Skobeleff also made admirable use of his reserves, always keeping a force in hand when he could, but not hesitating to use it at critical moments. On the other hand, in the general use of the Russian army, we see that reserves which might have been of vital importance, and if used in assisting Skobeleff, have very likely captured Plevna, were not employed at all. Only a little more than two-thirds of the troops—that is to say, 72 battalions out of 103—were actually brought into action. General Zotof's assertion, in his first despatch, 'We can send you no reinforcements, for we have none,' was extraordinarily inexact. The following troops were never actively engaged: The reserve division of the Roumanians (16 battalions), and of the Russians the 1st Brigade, 31st Division (6 battalions); 2nd Brigade, 30th Division (6 battalions); 20th Regiment (3 battalions). The fact seems to be that divided counsels, and perhaps the presence of the Czar, brought timidity to the commanders; and in the anxiety caused by the check they really did not know amongst them what troops they had disposable. The third lesson is *that no bravery of troops, and not even the exceptional gallantry and talents of subordinates, can counteract the evil effect of want of skill in a commander.*

Tactical skill necessary.—The tactical conduct of the battle was as faulty in its inception as in its conclusion. One of the commonest errors in tactics, whether offensive or defensive, is the want of decision as to the point at which the greatest efforts are to be made. It is a common weakness, almost inherent in the defensive absolute, but it is only generals without character or without knowledge who can thus blunder in attack. The third assault of the Plevna position offers a remarkable example of this particular blunder—just as the French arrangements for defence of their frontier did in 1870. If the Russians had held the whole line by weak forces sheltered behind trenches and concentrated very heavy forces on either of the wings, they would probably have succeeded in capturing Plevna. *To attack a fortified line with equal strength everywhere is a grave mistake,* but it was committed by the Russians on other fields besides Plevna. Under these circumstances Osman Pasha's successful defence is to be ascribed rather to the faults of the Russians than to any virtue inherent in a fortified position. The same errors were committed by the Russians, on a small scale, in the individual attacks on particular redoubts. They were repulsed because made by a series of isolated assaults, which were all beaten in detail. A study of General Skobeleff's management of his troops will show that he was more successful than other Generals, though under more difficult circumstances, because he managed his forces as a whole, sending forward a fighting line in fairly open order, reinforcing it, *before it failed*, with fresh troops, and, as these in their turn began to be checked, bringing forward the reserves under his own dashing leadership. He has been much criticised for his display of a somewhat over-reckless gallantry, but he carried his point, and at the end of an operation, unsuccessful because of other people's blunders, remained a sort of hero of romance in the eyes of his own soldiers, who had lost nearly half their strength, and in the estimation of all his countrymen. This prestige of character had an enormous effect for good on the whole of the following Russian operations. The fourth lesson is *that all successful action must be based on proper tactical principles, and that when a brain endowed with military knowledge is combined with the burning heart of a true soldier, the combination is almost irresistible in war. Nothing but such a force can supply the stimulus which is especially needed at the moment when the process of nervous exhaustion is setting in among men.*

Plevna a warning, not an example.—If the description here given of the attacks on Plevna be attentively considered, it will appear that the advocates of the defensive have little of real force to urge against the theory that the Turks would have been more likely to have succeeded if, instead of keeping Osman Pasha sitting idle at Plevna, the different armies had combined for a strong offensive movement against the Russians. Plevna is rather a warning than an example.

CHAPTER XVI.

EXAMPLES OF FORTIFIED POSITIONS—ARDAHAN, ZEVIN, AND ALADJA DAGH.

Russian plan of campaign in Armenia—Operations of third column and of second column—Capture of Ardahan—Operations of fourth column—Position of Zevin—Detailed description—Outposts—First line—Right wing—Centre—Left wing—Second line—Principles of construction for whole—Russian attacking force—Unprepared frontal attack—Russian advance—Left column—Right column—Artillery—Retreat and losses—Turks fail to pursue—Remarks—Violation of principles—Effect of the battle on the campaign—Battle of Aladja Dagh—Previous movements—Russian plan of attack—Distribution of troops—Movement of turning column—Orders for attack—Attack on Avliar—Lazareff's attack on Vizinkioi—Attack on Aladja Dagh—General result and losses—Remarks.

Plate XIX. (in pocket).

THE battle of Zevin in Armenia affords another good modern example of a fortified position attacked without much skill. It also shows how success in the defensive tends to be of little value because the defending troops are not usually prepared morally or tactically for pursuit. In such a case the mere repulse of the enemy with loss constitutes what may be called an indecisive battle. A few words may be said of the operations which led to the battle of Zevin.[1]

---

[1] Almost any respectable map of Asia Minor will give all that is required to understand the strategy of the campaign, if the reader will only remember that almost the whole country is composed of irregular hilly masses with the usual streams formed by drainage from their flanks.

x

The Russian troops advanced from their frontier on April 24 in four columns.

1. The Rion detachment, 20,000 men, marched on Batoum and had nothing to do with the operations to be touched upon.
2. The Akhaltsyk detachment, 15,000 men, under General Devel, marched on Ardahan.
3. The Alexandropol detachment, 30,000 strong, under General Loris Melikoff, moved on Kars.
4. The Erivan detachment, 20,000 strong, under General Tergoukassoff, marched on Bayazid.

The whole of these forces were nominally under the command of the Grand Duke Michael, but were practically commanded by General Loris Melikoff.

The plan of campaign was to capture Ardahan and Bayazid, invest Kars, and then march on Erzeroum with Columns 2, 4, and part of 3. I may add that Lieutenant Greene gives as the total strength, omitting the Rion detachment, 55,000 infantry, 10,000 cavalry, and 210 field and mountain guns, but there appears to be some error in calculating the number of guns.

On the Turkish side Moukhtar Pasha had about 70,000 men and 108 field guns, but no cavalry worth the name.

Operations of 3rd Column.—On the 28th Loris Melikoff established his force at Zaim, ten miles North-West of Kars, thus cutting the communication between Kars and Ardahan. Moukhtar Pasha took 5,000 men from the Kars garrison, leaving 15,000 men, and fell back to the Soganli range, some forty miles from Kars, and later to Zevin. On May 8 Melikoff captured a Turk with despatches from Ardahan, telling the weak condition of the place and garrison. He formed the idea of carrying Ardahan by assault, and accordingly detached a force of about 8,000 men to be marched on the 10th under General Heimann to reinforce No. 2 Column.

Operations of 2nd Column.—General Devel reached Ardahan on the 28th, reconnoitred, and sent back for siege artillery. The weather was extremely bad, and the siege guns had to pass over difficult mountain roads with an ascent of 7,000 feet. They arrived, however, on May 15, two days after the arrival of General Heimann's detachment, which was accompanied by Loris Melikoff in person. On the 16th a bombardment took place with very great effect, not only on the works but on the garrison, which suffered heavy losses and was considerably demoralised. On the 17th the bombardment was recommenced, and the effect observed was so great that Loris Melikoff determined to assault the same evening, though he had originally intended to continue the bombardment all the next day. The attack was completely successful, and Ardahan was in Russian hands at 9 P.M. on the 17th. Now here is a case of a fortified town, surrounded by six casemated forts of strong profile, the commanding hills around being also fortified; yet the action of the siege guns so shatters the works and demoralises the garrison that an assault is fully successful. The Turks lost 3,000 men (of whom 1,000 prisoners), that is about half the garrison. The Russian loss was only 550 men, because of the demoralisation which caused the Turks to abandon some of the works without defence. There were 92 guns in the place, the majority being Krupp four-inch siege guns. All accounts ascribe the result chiefly to the action of the Russian artillery. Lieutenant Greene says: 'The losses of the Turks were occasioned almost wholly by the Russian Artillery, which seems to have been admirably served.' What a contrast between this and the feeble bombardments of Plevna! May we not say that in Artillery, more perhaps than in any other arm, high training and skill are needed to lift it over the last obstacles to its full power. *There are plenty of instances in which reckless dash or stubborn determination have carried infantry to success—witness the early fights of the French revolutionary levies or the 'soldiers' battle' of Inkermann; but a half-trained or badly directed artillery shall obtain no successes. It is a mere hindrance to the rest of the army.*

A small force was then sent to Olti, which it occupied on June 1, the Turkish garrison retiring to Erzeroum. Loris

Melikoff returned with Heimann's detachment to the neighbourhood of Kars.

Operations of 4th Column.—General Tergoukassoff arrived at Bayazid on April 30, and occupied it; the small Turkish garrison fleeing to the mountains and dispersing there on his approach. Leaving a small garrison there—about 2,000 men [1]—Tergoukassoff marched westward down the valley of the Euphrates, drove a detachment of 3,000 to 4,000 Turks out of the village of Kara-Kilissa, occupied the town of Alashkert, and went westward till, at Daiar or Daghar, only fifteen miles from the junction of the Bayazid and Kars roads, he found himself confronted by large bodies of the enemy. He halted there and sent back reconnaissance parties to discover if it were true, as he heard, that the Turks from Bayazid had re-formed in the mountains and were sweeping together a horde of Kurds to attack the weak Russian garrison in Bayazid. He was attacked by the Turks at Daiar on June 21, but held his own with a loss of about 400 men. He had sent to Loris Melikoff for reinforcements, but that General preferred to attack Moukhtar Pasha at Zevin as a diversion, and before that battle occurred Tergoukassoff was already retreating, encumbered by an immense number of Armenian fugitives, and knowing that the garrison of Bayazid was surrounded.

Position of Zevin.—Loris Melikoff having decided to attack Moukhtar Pasha, and having seen the extraordinary collapse of Turkish defence at Ardahan, fell into the usual Russian mistake of undervaluing the enemy. He took with him Heimann's Grenadier division, marched west of Kars to the Erzeroum road, and thence along that road over the Soganli range towards Zevin. The Turks had spent a month on fortifying the position and the whole design was one of the best instances of their manner. A sketch of their works [2]

---

[1] Greene says between 2,000 and 3,000; Captain Bornecque says 1,600; the number is quite unimportant for our present purpose.

[2] This sketch and much of the description of the affair is taken from Captain Bornecque's *Rôle de la Fortification dans la dernière guerre d'Orient*; but it appears probable that Captain Bornecque under-esti-

will be found on Plate XIX., but a few words of description may serve to make the details clearer. The position commanded the shortest communication between Kars and Erzeroum; its right flank could only be turned by making a long détour; in fact by that movement which Frederick the Great practised successfully more than once—for instance, at the battle of Prague—namely, marching past the enemy's front, then making an oblique movement to throw the main force against the flank. The left flank was difficult to attack on account of the ground, while troops attacking the centre must cross a deep valley with steep sides, under the fire of commanding and flanking positions. Either flank could easily be reinforced. Thus the wings, though not so safe as if resting on a sea in the defenders' occupation like the lines of Torres Vedras or near Constantinople, had unusual advantages. It would also be possible for the defending force to take the offensive and strike at the communications of an attacking army which should attempt a turning movement. The position was capable of utilising the whole of the troops which occupied it, about 15,000 men, and a whole month had been spent by the Turks in creating and developing the works.

Detailed description. Outposts.—The line of outposts was on a chain of heights which hung over the river. They were posted in shelter trenches and rifle pits with huts for shelter. Behind this outpost line the ground sloped very steeply to a ravine, then rose again also very steeply to the first line which commanded the outpost position.

The First Line.—The first line was situated on the crest of a chain of hills, 4,000 metres in length; it was separated from the rather lower hills of the outpost line by a deep ravine with steep sides. The position itself was naturally divided into three separate parts between which were depressions giving opportunity for roads which ran through

mates the Turkish strength. He gives them only fourteen battalions. Lieutenant Greene credits them with 23, and the latter figure seems more suited to the size of the position. Captain Bornecque gives 9,500 men, Greene 15,000.

them from the front to rear of the position. We have therefore three posts distinctly marked out for right wing, centre, and left wing.

The Right Wing.—The right covered the road from Kars to Erzeroum, and had two battalions to defend it. One company occupied the open work D, placed in the hollow to bar the road. The rest of that battalion was in the shelter trench and little wood in front of the work C, and in that work itself. To the right of the line one battalion occupied the strong shelter trench B.

The Centre.—Defended by six battalions, according to Bornecque, and six guns. One company held the work F, which assisted D to bar the road. Then came a strong parapet with wide and deep trench behind it for the supports. This extended all along the front, broken only by two (or 3?) epaulments for one gun each. On the left was an open battery made to receive four guns, but it is a question whether one of the four was not actually used in the centre epaulment. About fifteen yards in front of the long parapet were built up a number of stone parapets for riflemen with numerous traverses. These little works were arranged to suit the ground and swept the whole of the ravine with cross fire.

The Left Wing.—A system of shelter trenches arranged in terraces with traverses and an epaulment for two mountain guns, together with a work in the form of a wide-splayed lunette L formed the left wing. The lunette was constructed for infantry, but with emplacements for two field guns. This was called by the Turks the Bastion Horum-Duzu.

Captain Bornecque says, 'The right wing defended an extent of 1,500 metres with 1,500 men, the centre, 2,700 metres, with 3,600 men and six pieces, the left wing, 1,200 metres, with 1,200 men and four pieces.' I am inclined to think that the force was larger.

The second line occupied a shelter trench, E E, about 2,700 metres long on the reverse slope of the plateau, which was about 1,200 metres across. The work was more for cover from projectiles ranging too far than for fighting purposes, and was constructed accordingly. It kept in shelter as a reserve two battalions and six guns. Behind the wings of this line were two fortified hills A and K, each occupied by a battalion. The hill K also appears to have had an emplacement for three guns.

Principles of construction.—The design of all these works, in their relation to each other and the ground, was excellent for a pure defensive. On the crest of the heights the trenches had a mean depth of about 4 feet, and a breadth at bottom of about 2 feet 6 inches, with a strong parapet of stones covered with earth. There were occasional intervals as issues for a sortie. Wherever the slope was too steep, a horizontal strip was created, and a stone wall completed a defence like that of the trench spoken of above. There were traverses 10 feet high every ten paces or so, formed of mixed materials —stones, earth, &c. The epaulments for the guns were roughly made with, as a rule, no outer ditches on account of the difficulty of excavation in that rocky soil.

The reader will do well to study this position thoroughly, and the way in which it was fortified. Plevna grew up by degrees, and was after all only a circle of works round a spot where an army chose to remain until starved out. With such advantages of ground as Osman Pasha had, the task was comparatively easy against enemies who made so many mistakes. Besides, every attack taught the Turks their weak points. The case of Zevin was different. Certainly the Turks had a long time for preparation, but then the difficulties of soil were great. The point that causes Zevin to be especially interesting is that the position was created in advance; there was an attack and defence, after which Zevin remained at ease as a witness of what had been.

Russian Attacking Force.—Loris Melikoff advanced to attack this position with Heimann's division only, which had already taken part in the capture of Ardahan and other fights. It had originally sixteen battalions, which were now much weakened. Bornecque puts his force at fifteen battalions; Greene estimated it previously at 8,000 men. One thing is perfectly certain—it was weaker than the Turkish body which it came to attack. It is easy to criticise long after the event, and to say that Loris Melikoff ought not to have attacked. But if every general is to count his enemies, and to decline battle if they are stronger than his force, war would become an absurdity, and England, at any rate, might sheath her sword for ever. We hardly ever know what it is either to attack or defend without heavy numerical odds against us. Frederick attacked and carried Austrian positions, or manœuvred and inflicted defeat, when the odds were two to one against him, and the capture of Ardahan on such easy terms may well have encouraged the military pride of the Russian commander. No one has a right to condemn him for attacking a superior enemy even if fortified, but it may fairly be said that he should not have despised his enemy to the extent of attacking in what may be called a nonchalant manner without due precautions. Let us see what he did.

Unprepared Frontal Attack.—It does not appear that the Russians made any careful reconnaisance of the position, otherwise they could hardly have attacked as they did. The artillery preparation was insignificant. It is true that General Heimann put nineteen guns in position near the village of Zevin about 11.30 A.M. and cannonaded the Turkish position, and that about one o'clock this line was reinforced by five more guns; but the Russian field guns at that time were of little power, their muzzle velocity being only about 1,000 feet per second, while the Turkish works extended over three and a half miles, and part of their armament consisted of heavy guns, nearly all of it being superior to that of the Russians, which had, therefore, little effect. About mid-day the Russians attacked and carried the outpost line, and Loris Melikoff thought to follow up this minor success at once. He, therefore, gave the order for a frontal attack of the main position, thus throwing away the chance of success which might have been afforded by a concentrated attack on a flank. About two o'clock P.M. the troops advanced in two principal columns, deprived of their cavalry and two batteries, which had been sent to make a demonstration round the Turkish right flank against Chorassan in the vain hope that an army, which above all things always clings to its entrenchments, might be induced to break up from Zevin to succour Chorassan. The left Russian column of attack, composed of four battalions and a battery, marched upon Arab Tepé and the road which wound round the foot of that hill. The right column, six battalions and a battery, attacked the centre with the object of occupying the road which passed between the Turkish centre and left wing. A regiment and three batteries were to support the movement.

Russian Advance.—As soon as the Russian troops showed over the outpost ridge they came under a tremendous fire from the whole front, as might be expected. Still, with their usual gallantry, the men pushed on, hoping to find in the ravine some shelter where they could form for the attack. The slope was so steep that the soldiers slid down it, using their fixed bayonets like alpenstocks to control their descent. Arrived at the bottom they found themselves in even worse case; for, as we have seen, the whole bottom of the ravine was exposed to a cross fire from the small advanced works disposed for that purpose. It was impossible to re-form the ranks, but these brave troops, now under little guidance, decided to push on up the steep face of the hill against the works and deliver the assault. Let us take the columns in order.

Left Column.—One battalion, turning the Turkish right, attacked the trench B, where, as we have seen, the Turks had also a battalion. But, checked at first and finding some shelter, the men began to exchange fire with their adversaries without advancing—a fatal sign in an assault—and, as the Turks made no sortie, the combat languished till the evening, when, supported by the cavalry which had been sent for the demonstration, an attempt was made to get altogether round the right flank of the enemy. The effort was repulsed with heavy loss, but the fight did not cease till 9 P.M. Another battalion attacked Arab Tepé, and even reached the border of the little wood, though after suffering terrible losses, the wood having been regularly prepared for defence with abatis and shelter trenches. The other two battalions of the left wing, reinforced by a battalion from the reserve *after* they had suffered heavily, tried to force their way up the road though the defile D F. They also managed to carry the border of the wood nearest the road, but were twice repulsed in their efforts to penetrate further through the defile. They, like Skobeleff's column at Plevna, were in a funnel held on all sides by the enemy. Still they fought till 5 P.M., when they had to retire.

Right Column.—The chief effort of the right column was to carry the Top-Dagh, and thus force the defences of the road. Several times did these heroic troops press on to the assault under a concentrated fire from three sides, and once, reinforced by two battalions from the reserve, succeeded in reaching the work G which barred the road. The Turks had to call upon their reserves in E E, which came up and attacked gallantly with the bayonet not a moment too soon, for already, seeing the success achieved, the Russian commander had ordered the advance of the whole second line in the direction of Top-Dagh. The dash of the Turkish reserve, with nervous energy still intact, paralysed the weaker, because more exhausted, energy of the Russians, and caused the precipitate flight of these brave but used-up men. All cohesion was lost, and the battalions only re-formed about half-past six in the position from which they had originally advanced.

Artillery.—It has been said that nineteen guns, afterwards reinforced by six others, were placed in the neighbourhood of Zevin, and bombarded a position nearly three and a half miles long, their fire being answered by heavier Turkish pieces. About three o'clock, just as the infantry wanted help sorely, the batteries had to slacken and almost cease fire for lack of ammunition. But this mattered little, seeing that, as soon as the infantry advanced, the artillery fire was directed a little in rear of the Turkish main line *against supposed supports and reserves which did not exist there*. The whole of their projectiles were absolutely thrown away because of disobedience to the golden rule that *artillery should never fire except at a known object*.

Retreat and Losses.—Loris Melikoff ordered a general retreat, covering the movement by an attack on the Turkish left made by his last reserves. As was to be expected, this attack failed, and at 7.30 the fight was over, and the whole force withdrawn except the one battalion which had tried to turn the Turkish right, and remained in action till 9 P.M. The Turkish loss was about 700, the Russian about 3,000.

Turks fail to pursue.—The usual effect of defending a position long prepared was now seen. There was but little cavalry, and that bad, while the infantry, fixed by habit to their favourite lines, did nothing by way of pursuit. Thus the battle was not decisive; but Moukhtar Pasha reinforced the position strongly on the 27th, and Loris Melikoff retired. Moukhtar had been on his way to attack Tergoukassoff, but found that he had gone.

Remarks.—Any student who has once read this book through carefully will know the chief faults which were committed at this battle of Zevin. The Turks planned their defences very well, but it was for the defence absolute, and in consequence of this, and the habits so engendered among the troops, they failed to destroy the inferior force which attacked them so audaciously. On the other hand, the Russian general might have known the demoralising effect of the defensive absolute, and counted upon it to the extent of not fearing to transfer the bulk of his force to one of the Turkish flanks. A thin line of troops distributed under slight cover along the old outpost line would have been quite enough to contain the Turks, while the main force might have attacked the Turkish right, where, as a matter of fact, one battalion succeeded in holding its own all the evening. Frederick the Great won such actions with even more disproportionate forces in the Seven Years' War, and there are no better examples of attacking a more or less immovable force in position than are to be found in his campaigns. They are the best possible instructors for a general who has to fight a dull and slow though brave enemy who assumes by preference the defensive. But even supposing some other point of the line selected to be attacked, after careful and capable reconnaissance, it is of the very essence of success that the attack should be concentrated, not distributed. The universal maxim to be superior to the enemy at the right time and place is absolutely reversed if scattered attacks are made against which the enemy can concentrate his fire.

The Russian general began by violating Frederick's maxim not to make detachments on the eve of a battle, for he deprived himself of his cavalry, sending it round towards Chorassan, by way of inducing the Turks to evacuate Zevin. He might have known that their character and training rendered it extremely improbable that they would budge an inch on account of feeble demonstrations. The Russian fault of distributing instead of concentrating their attack was repeated on a smaller scale by waiting till the columns had suffered so heavily as to be practically beaten, before reinforcing them. And what are we to say of an artillery which distributes its fire from the first, and, when the infantry are in difficulties, gives them no support, but fires blindly into a fortified position at imagined supports and reserves which have no existence? Seeing that there was so little time for the preparation, the commanding general should have chosen his main point of attack, set the artillery to bombard it, and then the batteries, taking care that their ammunition was plentiful, should not have slackened fire till the actual closing of the infantry obliged them to cease. In this case it would have been difficult for them to have joined the infantry until one of the roads was cleared. After that some batteries should have been pushed right into the enemy's position, as the British batteries acted at Tel-el-Kebir.

Effect of the battle on the campaign.—Zevin was the Plevna of Armenia, because it caused the collapse of Russian audacity. Believing Moukhtar Pasha to be stronger than he was, the whole Russian army retired to its frontiers, retaining nothing but Ardahan, and a strip of territory in front of it. Though this book has nothing to do with strategy, I cannot but remark that strategy and tactics have practically the same ends, and the same maxims apply in principle to the two divisions of the art of war. A general who makes the particular technical mistakes which we have seen at Zevin, will commit just the same faults in his strategy, and we accordingly find dispersed action, instead of concentrated, among the great bodies of troops, exactly as it was with the columns at the battle of Zevin. The tactical errors caused the loss of a battle, the strategical that of a campaign. It is a curious sequel to all these mistakes that Moukhtar Pasha did not pursue with vigour because he was under the impression that the Russian force was stronger than it actually was, and the Russians crossed the frontier because they overestimated the strength of Moukhtar Pasha's army.

Battle of Aladja Dagh.—One more example, and that a very important one, shall be given. It differs essentially from any of the preceding, both in the circumstances and the method of attack. Its conception was more in the manner of Napoleon than Frederick. The Russians ran a great risk in order to obtain a great result, and might have been punished heavily had their opponents been a little more far-seeing and a little less stolid.

Previous movements.—The Russians had lost, in one way or another, about 10,000 men during the campaign which was concluded by the battle of Zevin. Moukhtar Pasha was raising and drilling new levies, and it was necessary to reinforce Loris Melikoff's army before it could take the offensive again. Troops were sent to him from long distances —1,000 miles railway, and 200 miles march. Knowing what took place in the case of reinforcements for the army before Plevna, it seems probable that some examples of field guns of a newer type were sent also. At any rate the artillery played a much more important part at the Aladja Dagh than it did at Zevin. The column under Rion remained unavailable, engaged in a series of combats of various kinds on the coast. Tergoukassoff also remained out of the way with his force; he had been strengthened by General Devel, but was held in check by Ismael Pasha. The only Russian army confronting Moukhtar was the old centre column, still, for all practical purposes, under Loris Melikoff, though the Grand

Duke Michael, commanding the whole army, was with him. The strength of this army as reinforced was 55,000 infantry, 8,000 cavalry, and 228 guns. Moukhtar Pasha had, including the garrison of Kars, about 36,000 infantry, a large force of very poor cavalry, and 150 guns. The original position taken up by Loris Melikoff before he was reinforced had been (see Plate XIX.)[1] in front of the Kars River, facing south-west, with right at Kuruk-Dara, near the road from Alexandropol to Kars, centre at Kizil Tepé, and left at the ruins of Ani, on the River Arpa, with a front of about fifteen miles. Moukhtar Pasha at first was on the northern slope of the Aladja Mountains, his right opposite Ani, and left (including part of the Kars garrison) thrown out into the plain at the two hills called Great and Little Yahni, near the Kars-Alexandropol road. The result of various minor fights was that the Turks had carried and held Kizil Tepé and Subotan, for which success Moukhtar obtained from the Sultan the title of Ghazi, that is Victorious. Later on the Russians evacuated the Great Yahni hill, as their flank there was in the air, and water was hard to procure. So far, Moukhtar Pasha had done well; but on the night of October 8-9, snow having already fallen, he appears to have supposed the campaign at an end for the year, and evacuated Great Yahni, Kizil Tepé, and Uch Tepé, concentrating in a fortified position on the heights of Vizinkioi, Avliar, and Aladja Dagh, that being the position occupied by him at the battle of which we have now to speak. He held also an advanced post at Little Yahni.

Russian Plan of Attack.—Now the Russians hold that the winter is of all seasons the most favourable for their military operations, because their army consists of men inured to all the rigours of frost and snow. Nothing was more unlikely than that they should give up the campaign at this point. Their plan now was to demonstrate against the heights of Avliar and the Aladja Dagh, while a strong detached force should pass completely round the Turkish right flank, wheel up in rear, and then, with the main body

---

[1] Taken from Lieutenant Greene's valuable work.

in front, envelop and crush the Turkish left, cutting off the whole of Moukhtar Pasha's army from Kars and destroying it if possible.

Distribution of troops.—The force was thus divided:—

Major-General Count Grabbe had, opposite Little Yahni, 3 battalions, 8 guns, and 15 squadrons.

Lieut.-General Heimann, 24 battalions (20,000 infantry), 8 squadrons and 104 guns of different calibres, from Great Yahni to Hadji Veli.

Major-General Kouzminski, 8 battalions (6,000 infantry), 24 squadrons, and 24 guns, in front of Kizil Tepé.

The reserve, under Major-General Dehn, 6½ battalions (5,000 infantry), 8 squadrons, and 40 guns, was posted in front of Kulveran.

The detachments of Grabbe, Kouzminski, and Dehn were placed under the general command of Lieut.-General Roop.

The turning column, which was under Lieut.-General Lazareff, had 17½ battalions (15,000 infantry), with 22 squadrons and 70 guns.

Movement of turning column.—On the night succeeding Moukhtar Pasha's change of position, Lazareff moved off, unwinding as he went a line of field telegraph, so as to keep always in touch of the head-quarters. The line of Lazareff's march is sufficiently shown on Plate XIX. to need no further description. At Kambinsk, where he recrossed the Arpa, he was joined by a regiment of infantry from Tergoukassoff's detachment at Dijom. General Tergoukassoff had also been ordered to push forward reconnaissance parties some twenty miles to the south of Lazareff, so as to discover where Ismael Pasha was; and was also ordered to prevent that Turkish general from interfering with the turning movement. Lazareff marched chiefly by night, but it is very extraordinary that either Moukhtar was not informed of the march, or took no measures to interrupt it. At some time or other he seems to have been informed, for when, after a day's rest at Digour, Lazareff advanced on the 14th to Bazardjik, he found about 6,000 Turks, under Reshid Pasha, waiting to dispute his farther progress. Part of t detachment came from Ismail Pasha, in spite of Tergoukassoff's exertions. Of course the force of Reshid Pasha was too weak, and Lazareff drove it back in the direction of Vizinkioi. Thus the movement was so far successful, and on October 14 Lazareff was fully established in rear of the left flank of the Turks, who made no effort to dispossess him. That night he telegraphed to head-quarters, and at 2.30 A.M. the Grand Duke Michael received a full report of the position he had attained and the events of the day. This is the most remarkable instance yet afforded of the value of the purely field telegraph. The re-establishment of lines has been common enough, but not till then had so large a use been made of a line paid out as the troops moved along. What would Frederick or Napoleon have thought of being able to hold instantaneous communication with a detachment right in rear of the enemy?

Orders for attack.—Immediate orders were issued. Heimann, with the Caucasian Grenadier Division and 64 guns, was to storm the heights of Avliar, while one of his brigades and the rest of his artillery was moved forward to cover the road from Vizinkioi to Avliar with shrapnel fire in case the Turks attempted to move that way. Lazareff was to move towards Vizinkioi from the rear, while Roop with part of his force was to advance on Kerchané, and, if Heimann's attack progressed well, to storm the Aladja Dagh.

Attack on Avliar.—The battle began about daylight. Heimann's 64 guns advanced gradually to within 1,500 yards of the Turkish works on the lower slope of the Avliar Hill. 'From this point,' says Lieut. Greene, 'according to all accounts, Russian, Turkish, and English, they did most terrible execution with shrapnel, which they planted on the lines of the Turkish trenches with great accuracy.' The Turks could only reply with six guns, which could, of course, effect little. The Grenadier division was lying concealed in broken ground in front and on the flanks of the hill, rather in advance of the batteries. One regiment was so far advanced that Moukhtar Pasha observed it, and sent a force from Vizinkioi to attack it about 10 A.M.; but the Turks were repulsed, partly by the Russian infantry, and partly by the fire of some long range guns placed on Great Yahni. This episode was over about noon, when Heimann decided to assault. The artillery ceased firing, and the infantry began to climb the slopes. The Turks delivered a hot fire, but not very efficacious, and abandoned the trenches as the Russians came close to them. Heimann's troops pressed on, and the Turks, demoralised by the shrapnel fire to which they had long been subjected, abandoned their position not only on the slope, but also on the crest of the hill, leaving their artillery, ammunition, and stores as prizes to the victors. Moukhtar Pasha, seeing defeat inevitable, left the western edge of the Aladja Dagh, whence he had watched the combat, and, passing behind Avliar, and just in front of Lazareff's column, escaped to Vizinkioi and then to Kars.

Lazareff's attack on Vizinkioi.—Meanwhile Lazareff had been driving back Reshid Pasha, first to the foot of the Vizinkioi Hill and then to its crest, where the retreating Turks met the demoralised and flying regiments from Avliar. A wild panic ensued, and the whole centre and left of the defensive army fled in dire confusion to Kars, pursued by the Russian cavalry and bearing away Moukhtar Pasha in the throng. Lazareff thus joined hands with Heimann near Avliar.

Attack on Aladja Dagh.—About 2 P.M. orders were sent from headquarters for Heimann to march on the Aladja Dagh, crossing the ravine and attacking from the north-west. He was to leave behind troops enough to hold Vizinkioi and Avliar. Lazareff was to attack the Aladja Dagh from the south-west, and with another portion of his force to occupy near Bazardjik all the roads along which the Turks might escape. Roop was to assault the Aladja Dagh from the north. In fact General Roop had already begun to act, for after artillery fire and light skirmishing all the morning, he saw that the Turks had begun to withdraw some of their guns from the heights as soon as they perceived the fall of Avliar. He therefore at about one o'clock sent up his troops in three columns to attack the Turkish right, supporting the attack with the fire of 28 pieces of artillery at close range, besides siege guns established on some heights in rear. At first the Turks stood and fired volleys, but soon the right gave way and began to retreat along the hill in the direction of Vizinkioi; on their way the troops met Lazareff's force advancing to attack, while, at the same time, Heimann and Roop's right, acting in harmony, drove in the left of the defenders of the Aladja Dagh. Thus, tumbled together in a heap, right, centre, and left, all intermixed and surrounded, the right wing of the army of Moukhtar Pasha was forced to capitulate.

General Result and Losses.—The army of Moukhtar Pasha 'the Victorious' was thus completely crushed. About half of it escaped to Kars, but in a demoralised condition; from 4,000 to 5,000 were killed and wounded, 7,000 capitulated with Omar Pasha on the Aladja Dagh, and the rest escaped southwards by dispersing in small bands. Heimann and Tergoukassoff took up the pursuit after the cavalry, and Moukhtar, who soon left Kars with a small force, was pushed back till he sought shelter in Erzeroum, which held out till the rigour of winter delayed operations, and the armistice put an end to them in January. The Russian loss in killed and wounded during the battle was 56 officers and 1,385 men, less than half the losses out of a total of 8,000 at Zevin. The trophies of victory were '35 guns, several thousand small arms, a vast quantity of ammunition, and such quantities of provisions that, for several weeks, they were independent of their own stores at Alexandropol.' Lieut. Greene, who—much influenced by the events of Plevna—is by no means an advocate of field artillery, says: 'The greater part of the Turkish losses were caused by the admirable employment of the Russian artillery with shrapnel.' Moukhtar Pasha himself, like Napoleon III. after Sedan, declared that he was 'beaten by the Russian artillery.'

Remarks.—But if it be true that the field artillery contributed in a high degree to the success of the day, and, no doubt, saved an immense number of lives on the Russian side, this part of the work should not be glorified as if it were the whole. If we examine the plans, we shall see shining out conspicuously the face of our old strategical and tactical principle, 'To be stronger than the enemy at the right time and place.' Lazareff's flank march was difficult and dangerous, but the circumstances, especially the curious withdrawal of Moukhtar from his positions in front, showed that the Turks were not expecting attack and might be presumed to be, as they were, careless. Every precaution was taken to make Lazareff's march a success, and it did succeed. Then Moukhtar Pasha showed himself not equal to the occasion. There were but two chances for him, namely, to force his way to Kars with his whole army, and this chance he allowed to escape; or he might have left troops to show themselves on the occupied heights and then thrown himself upon Lazareff, whose defeat would have opened the way to Kars for a portion of the force, and to Zevin for the rest. But it is said that Moukhtar had been ordered from Constantinople to take the offensive while he wished to stick to Kars, and hence his indecision. May we not also count as a heavy weight in the balance, that habit of the defensive which, like too much wealth and luxury in a nation, induces at last a sort of paralysis of energy? Whichever be the cause and whichever the effect, certain it is that the army which enters on a campaign of defending positions is a doomed army. All history confirms this statement, and I confess that when I hear Englishmen talk of defending their own soil in such fashion my heart sinks and my mind demands whether these can be the representatives of the men who fought at Crécy and at Blenheim, who drove Napoleon's marshals from the Peninsula, who with a handful conquered India, who have penetrated into the heart of Africa, and, even now, with a ridiculous dearth of men, hold Egypt for the ease of the British Empire. So paralysed was Moukhtar that when Omar Pasha, who commanded the right wing, asked leave several times to attack Heimann, and so clear the way to Kars, the permission was denied him.[1]

As a matter of detail, the works on the Avliar hill were well designed as to trace, but not in profile. The trench

[1] Captain Bornecque.

occupied by the men was too deep and the parapet too high for the ground, which sloped steeply down from the terrace on which they were constructed. The men had all the temptation to conceal themselves and thus fire high, not taking aim. This is a vice of over-fortifying, and has a bad effect on the tone of the troops. Yet, as there was no bomb-proof cover, they suffered heavily from shrapnel fire which was so directed as to enfilade parts of the trenches and take others obliquely.

But, above all, the great success with comparatively small loss was due to the good tactics of the Russians, who threw a heavy force against the flank of a weak one, and refused to engage seriously in other parts of the field till the great effort had begun to tell. It was the same idea as that which won the chief battles of Frederick the Great and Napoleon, only carried out by the Russians in the manner dictated by modern weapons and modern methods of attack.

CHAPTER XVII.

DEFENCE AND ATTACK OF LARGE POSITIONS.

Physical advantages of defence—Of attack—Moral advantages and disadvantages of defence—Of attack—Balance favours attack—Initiative the habit of great generals—Final results must be counted—Moral effect on campaigns—Comparative value of artillery—Occupation of vital points—Guns can defend their own front—Noisseville—Should be able to concentrate their fire—Infantry can act anywhere—Probably more than one position for artillery—Unity of command for artillery mass s—Preliminary active defence—Points to be occupied or abandoned—Produce the greatest fire effect possible—First line—Second line—Reserve—Zevin a useful type—Modifications of Zevin type—Choice of time for counter-attack—Cases of counter-attack—Should points be connected by line?—Particulars of average case—First line—Second line—Reserve—Flanks—Weak points of such a position—Measures if time is doubtful—The holding-back system—The attack—Principles—Reconnaissance—Preliminary—Four types: Russian—German of 1870—Frederick's—Probable coming type—General ideas—Action of field artillery—High explosives—Action of infantry—The coming type—Attack should entrench a rallying position—Question of position guns with armies in the field—Night attacks—Chain of responsibility and nature of orders.

(References chiefly to Plate XIX.).

HAVING now worked through the smallest elements of Field Fortification, having applied this knowledge to the defence and attack of localities, and examined some of the most important instances of such defence and attack; having prepared our further way by thinking over the latest and very famous battles fought in the East, between Turks who defended till they were paralysed for attack, and Russians who, except in rare instances, attacked recklessly and without sufficient care and preparation, we are now in a position to bring our studies to a close, by discussing the principles which should govern a wise use of the defensive on a large scale in war. And first let us try to get at a few facts which may be considered as so well established that they may serve as a foundation for reasonable arguments.

Physical advantage of defence.—It is generally agreed that the improvement in modern firearms used both by infantry and artillery has favoured the defensive to this extent, that if two equal forces are placed face to face, equal in all respects except that the one is shooting from behind cover, however slight, while the other is marching to attack, the defending force has a greater physical advantage than used to be the case under the same conditions. That is to say, the long range and greater accuracy of modern weapons give greater chance of destroying the formation of the assailants and reducing their numbers than was the case in former times, and this in a very high degree. We will call this the physical advantage of the defence, though, obviously, it must result in a moral advantage also if the assailant advances in the manner supposed, namely, to make a frontal attack. It is also a physical advantage that the men have rests for their rifles, and are not put out of breath by rapid movement.

Physical advantage of attack.—But, on the other hand, there is a physical advantage even for the attack caused by modern improvements of arms, and one of no mean power. The long range of weapons, especially those of the artillery, and the much greater power of modern shells, both common and shrapnel, enable the attacking force to concentrate on any particular point of the defenders' line a fire of vastly increased intensity; while the improved accuracy of guns and fuzes allows of that fire being continued almost up to the moment of the troops closing, after which it may reach still further and smite the reserves on their way to reinforce the defenders' first line or to make a counter-attack.

Moral advantages of the defence.—The moral advantages of the defence are, that any kind of shelter is an encouragement to the nervous, and the mere fact of being able to rest their rifles on something in front gives confidence in the power of shooting well, which is an even greater help to the mind. The defenders also see the effect of their own fire, which may or may not be encouraging, according as that effect is great or the reverse.

Moral disadvantages of the defence.—There are also some moral disadvantages for the defence. It is oppressive to the spirit to see an advancing fate, in spite of all that one can do to prevent it, and there has always been a general consent that only strong-nerved races can endure this cool waiting, unless the men are behind cover. The British in the Peninsular War were much admired for this quality, which is not universal. The living soldiers on the defensive are tortured by the groans of wounded comrades and the sight of the dead and mangled.

Moral advantages of the attack.—The moral advantages of the attacking troops are very great. The very act of advancing impresses them with the idea of their superiority; the first line leaves its dead and wounded behind, and misses the most terrible sights and sounds. Moreover, the commanders, if they know their business, will order the attack to take place with very strong forces against the defenders' weakest point, so that the advancing soldiers feel that their power is irresistible; while the front line, which has the first dangers to undergo, is always being supported from behind and reinforced, so that it never looks weak. The assailants also see the effect of the artillery preparing the way for them.

Moral disadvantages of the attack.—Against all these most powerful moral advantages there is only to be set the disadvantage of being exposed without cover to the defenders' fire; and that has its compensation in the pride of superior daring, and in being judged worthy to advance in the open.

Balance of all these favours the attack.—If we sum up all these advantages and disadvantages, it will, I think, appear that if the physical advantage of equal forces is in favour of the defence, more and more, as time goes on, the balance is restored by the power which the assailants have of accumulating a large force against a weak point of the defenders; while the moral advantage is largely in favour of the atacking force. There is also one peculiarity in favour of the offensive, both morally and physically. It is that the defender is beaten if he does not win everywhere; the attacker gains the day if he is victorious at a single point.

The Initiative, the habit of great Generals.—There is another power, which may be called intellectual, and is decidedly in favour of the attack—the power of the Initiative. The commander of the attack may choose his own time and place of action, and his own method. He may direct his chief stroke against front or either flank or two places in combination; or he may combine the defensive in one part with the offensive in another. It is he who calls up and rides the storm. Almost all the great generals of history have believed in the offensive. Hannibal, Marlborough, Frederick, Napoleon, and a host of other great names, including the living Von Moltke, were all advocates and masters of the offensive, and if Wellington has been quoted as being on the other side, it should be remembered that he was developing the power of the inflexible line with its broad front of fire against the column, that he considered none but British troops as able to fight in that formation, and, finally, that he refused to fortify his position at Waterloo.

Final results should be counted.—On the whole, the opinion of the enormous majority of those who have taken part in the great wars of the last quarter of a century is that, while every effort should be made to combine the advantages of attack and defence on the same field, if a choice must be made, as is generally the case, the preference should be given to the offensive. To the argument that attack is likely to cause great expenditure of life, the answer is, that the greatest losses always occur in the retreat, and, therefore, a successful attack will involve less real damage than an unsuccessful defence. It is true that the Germans suffered heavily in their successful battles against the French; but we have to take into consideration the very curious fact that both Woerth and Spicheren were accidental battles occurring without the intention of the Commander-in-Chief, so that preparations had not been made for pursuit, and no calculation is just which does not take into account the final results of those and succeeding battles, namely, the capitulation of the French armies at Sedan and Metz.

Moral effect on campaigns.—Another point to be mentioned in this connection involves the principle on which this book is founded—that moral effect is the main advantage to be obtained, and that physical effects are but means to this end. For instance, the moral effect of such a dangerous movement as that of General Lazareff round Moukhtar Pasha's right flank at the battle of the Aladja Dagh (Chap. XVI.) was out of all proportion to its physical effect. It is always urged that the Turks did not fight as well as usual on that occasion. Why? Evidently because the feeling that they were outmanœuvred knocked the heart out of them, and the thought that nothing could save them but early flight brought about the commencement of that sort of retreat which ends in flight and dispersal. On the other hand, reckless, unscientific attacks like those of the Russians at Plevna and Zevin tend to reverse the moral effect and make a present of it to the defence.

Comparative value of Artillery.—It has also been shown that, while infantry is the chief arm and has the lion's share in the fighting—now as ever since the introduction of firearms, and while there have been occasions when it has been practically the only arm seriously engaged, so that it has won engagements by itself—there is no time in history when artillery was of more importance than it is now, and the General who should base his system of fighting on the principle of neglecting the power given him by artillery would be placed at an extraordinary disadvantage. It is a great pity that writers, who have before them an enormous reservoir of facts from which to draw, persist in quoting the weakness of the French artillery in 1870, with bad material and worse manner of using it, and ignore altogether that the effect of the German artillery even without shrapnel was just about five times as great physically, to say nothing of its much more important moral effect. In the same way the failure of the Russian artillery at Plevna to effect anything worth speaking of at long range and against troops buried in field casemates has been repeated *ad nauseam*, while its successes at Ardahan and the Aladja Dagh are scarcely ever heard of in England. Yet Ardahan fell almost entirely before the effect of artillery fire, and even Lieutenant Greene, who was among those most impressed by the failure of the guns at Plevna to perform what no experienced artilleryman would expect them to do, confesses that of the 4,000 to 5,000 Turks killed and wounded at the Aladja Dagh, '*the greater part of the Turkish losses was caused by the admirable employment of the Russian artillery with shrapnel.*'[1] A similar method of argument might be used with equal futility to prove that infantry are of no use to carry a fortified position because they failed three times at Plevna. The mischief of this kind of argument about artillery is that it creeps into the textbooks and discourses of Professors, so that there is considerable danger lest the British army should be trained to views and habits which are at total variance with those established in every army which has had practical experience in war. What are we to hope from our future Generals if they have been trained to believe field artillery an encumbrance? I have at this moment before me a book which shows that the students of the Staff College were taught to look on field artillery as a thing to be protected, and to make plans for the disposal of 'the infantry escort' of the artillery of the attack! From this follows naturally the idea that the artillery of the defence are to be posted somewhere as much out of the way as possible, and that while infantry are rightly taught that their best protection is to be found in good shooting and a clear field of fire, artillery, the only power of which lies in shooting, should be hidden away in re-entering angles, probably because such angles are something like embrasures.

Occupation of vital points.—This leads us to an important rule on which all reasoning as to the defence of positions

[1] *The Russian Army and its Campaigns, &c.* p. 396.

must be based. It is that the first and most vital necessity for a good defence is that all the ground in front of it, and on the flanks if possible, should be exposed to the heaviest possible fire, both direct and cross, of the defenders. The nature of the works where there are any is a secondary consideration; and it is even possible that a General standing on the defensive for a time might, like Wellington at Waterloo, prefer not to have any works at all. From this point of view such a position as Majuba Hill was a bad one, though it was high and steep, therefore not easy to climb, while St. Privat, with the gentle slope in front of it, was good, and, speaking generally, most of the Plevna position. From this follows the simple deduction that the points to occupy, whatever else you may or may not do, *are those which command the whole ground in front and on the flanks of a position.* It is an elementary idea, but one that will be found to carry us a long way.

Guns can defend their own front.—Another maxim must be accepted as established by the facts of war as well as by all calculations, namely, that well-served field artillery can defend its own front at all ranges against infantry or cavalry advancing over open ground in any formation. It is especially necessary to clear our minds of one element of confusion. The difference of range between infantry and artillery, and the greater difficulty which infantry has in judging the range, give artillery a *relatively* greater advantage at ranges of, say, 800 yards and upwards; but *the effect of artillery fire, considered without reference to the counter effect of opposing infantry, increases rapidly as the range diminishes.* While, therefore, the losses of artillery increase as the enemy's infantry draws near, the losses of that infantry must also increase in a very high proportion, while the moral effect of that increasing destruction will reduce very considerably the accuracy of aim of individual infantry soldiers. Between the thinning of the ranks and the reduced accuracy of fire, the effect produced by infantry advancing against guns must decrease as the range decreases, and perhaps compensate for the advantage obtained by them in shortening the range.

At any rate, we have the facts of war to show that infantry cannot capture guns from the front except by surprise, though it might subdue their fire and force them to retreat by taking advantage of cover, where it exists, to advance under shelter, and thence pick off the gunners by slow and deliberate fire, especially if the fire discipline be so good that the infantry concentrates its fire by groups against individual gun detachments. This is undoubtedly the weak point of artillery, and I believe that the first army which provides its artillery with portable bullet-proof shields will obtain an advantage which will throw into the shade all other improvements. The difference in an artillery duel where one side is safe from shrapnel bullets, while the other is exposed to them, would be incalculably great. Prince Kraft of Hohenlohe goes so far as to suggest that battles may now be settled by the preliminary artillery duel; the side which has the worst of that action giving up the game before suffering the tremendous losses which must occur later. But even supposing as I do that the weaker side might withdraw from action only to take up the fight again at a later stage, the advantage gained by the winners would be enormous. We must suppose, at any rate, that a defensive position has features which enable its artillery to be posted so as to have a clear field of fire at long and short ranges, and the nearer the open ground comes to the muzzles of the guns, the better will be the position.

Noisseville.—Every student of the defensive should thoroughly absorb the action of the German guns at the battle of Noisseville (official account, first part, ninth section). A line of artillery was deployed facing the French main attack, and in advance of the German infantry. 'Dense swarms of skirmishers approached the Prussian artillery, deployed on the heights, and overwhelmed it with a hail of bullets. Isolated batteries which, during the course of the struggle, had proceeded beyond the general artillery line, had, during their withdrawal towards it, to keep at bay with canister the enemy's skirmishers which pressed upon them. The steady and well-directed fire of the remaining batteries, however, held the adversary at a certain distance, so that he made no marked progress in front; but the situation of the flank batteries, which had previously been much annoyed by the skirmishers thrown forward on the slopes of the ridge, became not uncritical as darkness drew on. The whole of the ten batteries, which for two hours had steadily maintained their important posts with visible success and in spite of heavy loss, executed towards 7 P.M. in echelon, and in perfect order, the command *to retire to the infantry line of defence.*' It was a grand example, for during those two hours the infantry could rest and await their turn.

Guns should be able to concentrate their fire.—Writers who cling to the idea that artillery is a thing to be protected by an 'infantry escort,' always aim at placing it in some retired position where it can have the infantry line in front of it for the sake of protection, and they even select re-entering angles, such as the heads of valleys between hills. It may be that such backward positions may sometimes be selected for the guns, but for a very different reason, namely, that they alone can protect such places with the best effect, or that only there can they have a commanding view of the surrounding country at long range. In such cases the general infantry line may be in front. But the best rule to lay down, so far as a rule can be formulated, is to *choose for your artillery positions such ground as will give the guns the most complete field of fire in all directions, so that the fire of the largest possible number of guns can be concentrated on any point, far or near, where the enemy may make his principal attack.*

Infantry can act anywhere.—The disadvantages of artillery, as already mentioned, are not shared by infantry, which can act with equal ease in all sorts of ground, and repel the fire of scattered skirmishers by the same tactics as theirs. It matters little to infantry what is their field of fire within moderate limits, because, whatever be the range, their fire must be supposed at least equal to that of the attacking infantry. It ought to be superior, as the ranges of numerous points will have been correctly measured, and the advancing enemy must arrive at those points. It is easy for infantry to be so placed as to command all the ground near it with a cross fire, and this is its duty. It is not so easy for artillery to find positions where it can act with equal ease at long and short ranges. Therefore, to develop the special gift of artillery—its long range—and in concession to its weakness on broken ground at short range, the first duty of a commander in preparing a position will be to *choose the most suitable positions for the artillery and base the rest of his measures on this choice.* We suppose, of course, that there is a proper proportion of artillery, and I am speaking here of large forces. As the number of troops engaged diminishes, the value of artillery diminishes in even higher proportion, until with small forces and only a battery or so it would be absurd to base the arrangement of the position on the action of guns which can neither forbid approach nor defend themselves unless they form part of a general line of troops.

Artillery will probably require more than one position.— It is perhaps necessary to say that some of the old rules for choosing an artillery position have been rather superseded since the fire of infantry skirmishers in broken ground became so formidable and the range of the enemy's artillery so great. It is necessary to think what is likely to occur considering the nature of the ground, and it may often happen that the best position for the early artillery line will not be the best for stopping the attacking infantry at later stages. In the former case the best position will be that which renders it most difficult for the enemy to get the range. A thin screen of trees in front or hedges succeeding each other will often puzzle an enemy as to where your guns actually are, but these would not be favourable in the engagement with infantry afterwards. One point has not yet received the attention which it deserves. Long range means high elevation, and such a curve in the trajectory as would enable guns to fire over a hill or other object which would conceal them from the enemy. The difficulty of not seeing the hostile artillery from the guns themselves might surely be obviated by science, so long as observers can see the enemy from another point. This ought to be an advantage to defence, and the inventive ability which has produced the Watkin position-finding apparatus for coast defence, thereby rendering the hitting of advancing ships by concealed guns almost a certainty, could, no doubt, devise means for striking the assailants' artillery while denying him a knowledge of the exact position of one's own guns. In these days of accuracy it is everything to get the range, or rather the elevation and adjustment of fuze which give the best effect, and nothing could be much more demoralising for the attack than to find itself under a concentrated artillery fire from guns the position of which it cannot ascertain. For the same reason a slight change of position is often advantageous. I have myself seen a Russian battery in the open plain, when beginning to suffer, run the guns forward less than a hundred yards without limbering up, and from that moment there was not a single casualty. All the Turkish shells passed over it. Yet the range cannot have been more than some 1,200 yards or so.

Unity of Command for Artillery masses.—Of all the objects on which time should be spent in preparing the artillery positions for a large force, there is none so important as obtaining unity of command. It is impossible to say too often that the secret of all artillery power and the only means to insure success is to concentrate the fire of as many guns as possible on that portion of the enemy which is for the time most important. Battery commanders cannot know what that portion is, and the freedom of manœuvre which has been of late years allowed to field artillery would be a curse rather than a blessing if it led to independent action in the artillery line, for any series of positions occupied in the same action at the same time must be considered as an 'artillery line.' For unity of command the officer commanding the whole artillery force should have at his disposal exceptional facilities for sending messages by telegraph or signalling or orderlies, and with these last he should be particularly well supplied. He should be wherever he will be best in touch with the supreme command and with the information most likely to arrive at headquarters, and he should not be led astray by that 'last infirmity' of the British officer, the desire of planting himself in the hottest place. Such conduct may often be valuable in an infantry engagement and necessary in great cavalry charges. It can hardly ever be either necessary or expedient in the cooler atmosphere of artillery combats.

Preliminary active defence.—Having decided upon the artillery positions, the next point will be to determine the positions and contemplated action of the infantry. Here we have to deal with an arm which can do everything except move fast or make accurate practice at long range, and the first of its tasks will be to furnish such advanced troops as are necessary to hold back the enemy's skirmishers, and for the rest to keep itself untouched in nerve and limb during the artillery combat, so as to be fresh for the critical time when everything will depend on its conduct and capacity. If there is bomb-proof cover in the trenches, that will do, but at least let the men get out of the way of that hammer, hammer on the nervous system which exposure to fire in cold blood produces. The infantry will also furnish outposts, the line of resistance of which should be so placed as to prevent the enemy from establishing guns to bombard the position before the defending force is prepared for action. As half the chances of the fight depend upon having had timely warning, it will be well to push detachments forward some miles on the roads by which the enemy is likely to advance, as already explained in the attack on villages, Chap. VIII. Field artillery—preferably horse—should invariably form part of such detachments, both because of the warning given by the sound of the first gun, and because in no other way than by artillery fire is the enemy so easily forced to deploy before he intended. Such detachments must, however, be prepared to retire without compromising themselves, unless they have been specially charged to defend a locality of some sort for a long time, so as to deny a road or a bridge to the enemy. In that case it is necessary for the commander to know how far his obstinacy is to extend. The greatest military skill is shown in defending a

DEFENCE AND ATTACK OF LARGE POSITIONS. 337

locality for a long time and then escaping, but it may be that the General commanding the whole force is prepared to sacrifice a detachment to gain a little more time. There should be a definite understanding on this point.

Points to be occupied or abandoned.—In preparing the real position for defence, the first principle must be to take up only such an extent of ground as the means available will enable the defenders to occupy with good hope of success. This again sounds like a trite maxim, and a decision which any one would take. Yet nothing is more common than to see it disregarded. There is sure to be some tempting hill or village to occupy, and all defensive positions have a tendency to stretch themselves out beyond the capacity of the troops to defend them.[1] This is a fault in tactics similar to the strategical fault of Generals who try to defend equally well all the points on a long frontier line. The attempt to prevent a landing on the shores of England by placing troops at all possible landing places would be another instance of the same natural but mistaken impulse, which violates the rule to be *stronger* than the enemy at the right time and place. Strength lies in concentration; dispersion is weakness both in strategy and tactics. On the other hand, one must be careful to occupy vital points at once and to hold them at any risk. This warning is also necessary. The officers who fought under Frederick in the Seven Years' War were well trained in all kinds of fighting. Yet General Retzow, who commanded the King's advanced guard early in October, 1758, even though directed to occupy the Stromberg hill in front of Bautzen, thought he had done enough by placing cavalry on it by day and withdrawing them at night. The retreating Austrian General Wehla reoccupied the hill with five battalions of grenadiers and a numerous artillery.

---

[1] Five years' experience as superintending officer of garrison instruction, during which the author had to inspect all the garrison classes in the United Kingdom twice a year, taught him that this is the principal difficulty experienced by students. They find it difficult to make the necessary sacrifices, and, in trying to hold too much, they risk the sacrifice of all.

When the King came up he found that the enemy had the advantage over him, and, taking up an inferior position close to the Austrians, subjected himself to a surprise and lost the battle of Hochkirch. The instances of defeat from occupying too much ground for the number of troops are so numerous as to need no quotation. The last of them was the battle of the Aladja Dagh, described in Chapter XVI.

Produce the greatest fire effect.—There has been much controversy as to the best arrangement of works for the infantry defending a position, and I am certainly not about to attempt to lay down strict rules for what must, in my opinion, vary with every site and every varying circumstance. But some useful ideas may be put forward as to what to avoid and what, on the whole, to strive at. The first principle, which governs all else, is not to think of any form of works at all, but on the probable dispositions of the enemy for attack, the ground over which he must advance, and the best way of disposing your troops so that every step he takes shall be under a cross fire if possible. If this is impossible, if there are portions of the ground where the assailants must for a time be hidden, then we must arrange for the heaviest concentrated fire to be brought to bear upon them at the moment of issuing from such places of concealment. There should be no difficulty, for the ranges can have been measured accurately, and a wise commander will not rest content even with that, but will make his troops actually practise what they will have to perform, and fire at least some rounds in order to check the variations caused by appearances, atmosphere, and defects of ammunition, which last must always occur as time goes on. There are many books, where can be found by the curious innumerable dispositions of lines, theoretically furnished with flank defence, with studied intervals for the passage of troops, with redoubts at exactly calculated distances, and all the rest of it. These are generally based on the ideas of permanent fortification, and are in most cases suggested by echoes of the bastion system, so long extinct for practical purposes. Such systems have all at the back of them, however unacknowledged, the poisonous dream of passive defence —poisonous, that is, for an army in the field. When you have disposed your troops so as to produce the greatest fire effect on an advancing enemy, it will be time to think of throwing up such cover as time and means allow. This again may seem obvious common sense, but you will not find it as a rule in text-books.

First line, second line, reserve.—Following the usual rule for all fighting, there will be a first line, a second line, and a reserve, or the second line may possibly be merged in supports for the first line. The reserve is the one necessity which can no more be omitted than the first line. The strength of these parts will vary as your plans vary, but, as a sort of general rule, the reserve may be about one-third of the whole, and the rest divided pretty equally at first between first line and second line. The proportion of men to space must entirely depend on the ground and the plans of the commander. It may suit him to hold the first line weakly and then deliver a tremendous counter-attack *inside* the position, as Von Scherf recommends, or to get the enemy involved in a heavy fight with the first line, so that he may commit even his reserves to it, before undertaking a counter-attack. Or, as is most probable, portions of the line will be held strongly and others weakly. On the whole it is better to leave the point open, only insisting on the fact that to hold one's ground at any part of the field, the approach of the enemy should be visible as long as possible, and swept with a cross fire by guns from the longest to the shortest ranges, by infantry fire from 800 or 1,000 yards to the muzzles of the rifles. Different writers have estimated as widely apart as from three to fifteen men per metre, which on such very wide assumptions we may call per yard.

Zevin a useful type.—If the student will turn to the sketch of the battle of Zevin (Plate XIX.), he will find there a good example of adaptation of means to end, and we may take that position generally as showing with fair correctness the sort of work which may be done if there is time enough. The plate does not show, however, that there was bomb-proof cover for the garrison, and that the parapets were prepared in many places for troops to march over or between sections of them. If the time had been less the defence would have been less complete, but the principles would have been the same. It was an exceptionally easy position to defend, but is perhaps all the better adapted for a student's example on that account. It is taken directly from Captain Borneque's *Rôle de la Fortification dans la dernière guerre d'Orient*. Some tacticians would say that the full parapet with shelter all along the front was a mistake, and I should be inclined to agree with them unless the parapet be so made as to be easily passable by troops from behind. This could be managed by steps or otherwise. The student must not be led astray by the idea that such a parapet would 'cause confusion' in supports or reserves advancing to a counter-attack. The stiff line is abolished for the field of battle, and the ideas which suited it and its companion, the bastion trace, need not hamper the flexible formations of the present time.

Modifications of Zevin type.—The modifications of this defended position which opposite schools would make would be somewhat as follows. The Engineer school generally, which tends towards magnifying the defensive, would not be content until the hollows up which the roads run were further defended by retired works or shelter trenches closing them in front and flank, so as to turn these gaps in the hills into complete sack-mouths. They would also probably have redoubts farther back on the plateau. On the other hand, the extreme 'offensive' school, as typified by Von Scherf, would probably do away with the long trenches altogether, develop the redoubts a little, and if the enemy (they would say 'when the enemy') succeeds in penetrating the first line, they would charge him at once, first delivering a few rapid rounds, and then exterminate his force, already suffering from the difficulty of the work and the terrible fire which has been poured upon them. My own opinion is that both forms have their advantages and disadvantages. The engineer would almost certainly make the mistake of the Turks, and, while repulsing the assailants, fail to make a victory of it. The offensive school would run a greater risk to achieve a greater and more decisive success. Among all who read these lines there will probably be no general agreement, and it would perhaps be better for each commanding officer to decide for himself according to his own character. Does he prefer to do a solid bit of duty by simply denying the position to the enemy as often as it is attacked, and waiting till the moment when he is quite sure that a counter-attack will succeed—a moment that will never come—let him follow such writers as Colonel H. Schaw, late Professor at the Staff College. Is he full of fire and desire to gain a complete victory, which may change the face of the war—does he long to come to blows with the enemy, and can he inspire his whole command with his own fervour—then let him choose the methods of the offensive school; but, having chosen, he must act with vigour and determination. One thing is certain. The man who feels unequal to the occasion had better follow the ways of the Turk; for, if the defensive extreme is inglorious and comparatively inefficacious, the spirit which delays the counter-attack till it finds a case repeating what has been laid down in books had far better not attempt what will probably turn out a failure, and perhaps lead to a fall of the position. There is, however, this to be said, that, while a frontal attack ought to be easily repelled, even without a counter-stroke—though not better without it—a flank attack, which will come some time or other, if the assailants know their business, is almost sure to succeed unless the defenders deliver their return blow. As for laying down exactly the right moment for making the counter-attack, and the manner in which it should be made, or from what direction, I should as soon think of prescribing to a chess-player at the beginning of a game how he was to checkmate his adversary. There may even be several counter-attacks, some on a small scale, some on a great, or there may be none, that portion of the fight being left to the performance of other troops which may be expected to appear. Perhaps the battle of Waterloo is better known to Englishmen than most battles. Could anyone have given good advice as to 'the counter-attack' before that battle to the Duke of Wellington?

Choice of time for counter-attack.—Instead of seeking a formula applicable to all cases, the student will do well to read a number of accurate descriptions of attacks on positions, and judge for himself when the counter-attack should have been delivered, supposing the troops on both sides equal in their moral condition, which is already a removal of half the difficulty. During the Peninsular War, the habit of the English, as Marshal Bugeaud has told us, was to stand in line quietly awaiting the French onset. This was in itself a great moral triumph, especially if the British line was at the time under artillery fire. Muskets then were of very little use at 200 yards. The French columns with skirmishers advanced, and when they came within point blank range they were already half overpowered by that cold, calm steadiness. The human items which make up what we call a column began to hesitate, and just then the English line brought down the shouldered rifles to the 'Ready!' and 'Present!' A volley rang out, the column wavered, and then the British charged with the bayonet and that cheer which is really as efficacious as the cold steel. The moral ascendency was attained, the assailants gave way, and the British usually resumed their old positions. At Gorny-Bougarovo similar tactics pursued by the Russians led to similar results. A Russian force about 5,000 strong was attacked by 8,000 Turks when hastily entrenched. Though suffering a good deal from the fire the Russians lay still till the enemy were close to their front and both flanks—fifty paces, it is said. At that moment the Russian line rose to its feet, delivered some volleys with the breechloader, tearing the Turkish columns to pieces; then charged with the bayonet. The right moral effect was produced, and the Turks fled in wild confusion. The incident so affected them that Sophia fell easily afterwards. Yet this and many other examples of the same kind do not tell us always to wait till the enemy are within fifty paces, nor always to leave shelter trenches and charge after a few volleys. What they do teach is that *there is a right psychological moment for the counter-attack as for everything else, and officers commanding troops will do well to understand their men so well and be so in touch with their emotions, that the choice of the moment of counter-attack will for them be no secret, but understood and seized by a sort of instinct.*

The proper moment, differing in each case, is when the counter-attack will produce the greatest moral effect. It can never be too quickly delivered, and will often have to be undertaken without preparation, except such as has been made while the assailants were advancing.

Cases of counter-attack.—It will no doubt be said that these were comparatively small affairs, though that Russian charge by 5,000 men was a serious undertaking. Let us take what happened under my own eyes during the battle of Königgrätz, as already related in Chapter XIII. The Prussians had found their way into Chlum, behind the centre of the Austrian defensive position. By this marvellous stroke a terrible moral effect was being produced on the Austrian Army. In the neighbourhood was an Austrian Army Corps drawn up in masses. The mistake then made, as the Austrians themselves felt afterwards, was the adherence to rules which delayed the counter-attack till the troops could be got into proper formation. By that time the Prussians had been strongly reinforced and the battle was practically lost. Yet no man ever lived so wise in war as to have been able to predict beforehand when or how the Austrian counter-attack should be made that day. Take again the battle of Zevin, upon which we have dwelt so much. There were several tempting occasions for counter-attack. Since the Russians divided into two principal columns, either of them might have been heavily struck by a counter-blow when its efforts began to slacken. There was time enough to prepare such a movement by the reserve, and the two columns ought to have been separated and broken up. At the battle of Aladja Dagh we see once more a totally new condition. There, the Russians had executed a turning movement of so complete a character that 20,000 men were actually in rear of the Turks, behind the flank nearest to Kars. The way to that fortress was still open, and part of the troops necessary for its garrison were in the field with Moukhtar Pasha. The Russian army was so strong that the Turks could not long stand before it, especially in a position which was too much extended for their numbers. Here then the counter-stroke, if one may so call it, ought surely to be delivered before the Russian attack. Can anyone doubt that either Frederick or Napoleon or Marlborough or Wellington would have seized the chance of being superior to the enemy at the time and in one place; would have sent the whole force against Lazareff, and, having crushed him, would have thrown a garrison into Kars and fallen back—say to Zevin, where Erzeroum would have been covered. But no cast-iron rule as to the proper moment of making a counter-attack would have helped Moukhtar Pasha to the right conclusion—nothing but the general principle of attacking when you are superior to the enemy at the right time and place. Lazareff's line of telegraph would only have sufficed to report that he was being attacked, and he must soon have let it go. It might perhaps be urged that Moukhtar Pasha could not trust his troops. The reply would be that, in such a case, the one chance for an army is to raise its spirits by a success obtained over an inferior enemy. But in risking the dangerous movement of Lazareff's column the Russians confided in the well-known and fatal habit of the Turks, that of fortifying a position and clinging to it obstinately. It is to be hoped that, if England be ever invaded, as she probably must be in the course of time, her defenders, volunteers or otherwise, will not allow the enemy to count on their adopting the Nessus-shirt policy of a decaying Oriental nation.

Should points be connected by lines?—Another much-debated question is whether the commanding points should be joined by lines of works or not. It is generally considered as established that masses of troops on which a cross fire can be brought to bear cannot pass between strongly held posts about 1,200 yards apart, and that distance tends to increase as the range and flatness of trajectories of all sorts of firearms increase. This supposes that the defenders are not demoralised, and *have not built such high and solid defences as tend to make the troops stoop down behind them and fire high.* Turks behind parapets, and even the gallant French soldiers, have often sinned in this way, being tempted by momentary immunity from danger. For a pure defensive the best connection between posts would be obstacles to detain the enemy under fire ; and this plan may be adopted, if there is time, at any parts of the line not likely to be made points of issue for counter-attacks. It might be largely used in lines like those round Metz or Paris to keep in an army, otherwise obstacles hamper the defenders too much. It is difficult to see any objection to shelter trenches connecting the principal points, but the troops should not be placed in them until the assailants develop their attack. Moreover, as mentioned above, such trenches should be slight enough to allow troops of all arms to cross them. The defenders will then have the option of stopping the attack outside according to the common ideas, or, with Von Scherf, allowing them to break into the position and receive the counter-attack there by troops which would no doubt be held in readiness for sudden attack. Colonel Schaw seems to suppose that a counter-attack will always be carried out in regulation attack formation, with fighting line, supports, and reserves. But such formations are only for the purpose of getting over ground with little loss, and are preparatory to the real attack, in which the troops must crush forward wave upon wave. A counter-attack supposes that the enemy has suffered much in his advance, and has himself diminished the distance. The success of the counter-attack depends on its partaking of the nature of a surprise. It should be thought of and prepared for while the assailants are advancing, and then delivered with energy, in the manner of the last, not the first, stages of the legitimate attack.

Particulars of an average case.—Having discussed most of the present points of controversy and having carefully warned the student not to cling to any formula, seeing that each case should have its own dispositions, we may now give a sort of summary of an average case, which supposes a field of battle chosen, as positions generally will be, on ground which has hills and hollows, small woods, houses, farms, and villages; and we may suppose that a ridge, high or low, is selected for the defence—such a position, in short, as is common in England. I would remark in passing that, while there were hardly any village fights in the early part of the Russo-Turkish War, there were many after the Balkans were passed. The reason probably was that both the Bulgarian and Armenian villages were composed of wretched hovels, very combustible and almost impossible to defend.

First Line.—The troops of the first line, about one-third, will be placed:—

    1st. In any works which may have been constructed, occupying them if there is bomb-proof cover, keeping out of them at first where there is not; also in villages, or woods prepared for defence.[1]

    2nd. Behind and on the flanks of these fortified posts, under cover, natural or artificial.

    3rd. In trenches established near the batteries and intermediate works, and in rear of those trenches and works, always so as to sweep the ground over which the enemy is likely to advance.

    4th. It is understood that the artillery is to be given both long and short range, and that for this purpose it may be necessary to prepare for it two or more positions. It is more likely to have to advance than to retire as the combat grows hotter.

    5th. The largest forces will be at those places, generally salients, which will enable them to sweep the ground in front with cross fire; in re-entering angles less, and behind obstacles hardly any.

For this first line, including supports and local reserves, all included in the foregoing, let us allow two men to the yard of frontage. Any detached posts should be separately

---

[1] The villages which should and should not be occupied are sometimes difficult to determine. This subject has been treated already in Chapter IX.

DEFENCE AND ATTACK OF LARGE POSITIONS. 347

provided for, as explained in former chapters. Calculate roughly for them three men per yard.

Second Line.—The second line, of about the same strength as the first, will be disposed more with the idea of helping the first than of defending itself. It will be rather more concentrated, and placed behind the wings, or in support of points likely to be attacked. Its distance from the first line will be regulated by the range of infantry fire, by the opportunities for keeping itself out of fire, while retaining the power to assist the front line, either in defence or in partial counter-attacks. It should not be seen by the enemy.

The first and second lines between them should be able to repel all frontal attacks, and, by delivering counter-attacks, to drive the enemy back to his old position. In so doing, however, the first line should never leave its works or posts unoccupied, and, as a rule—subject, however, to many exceptions—should not pursue the enemy unless called upon by the Commander in Chief.

Whether there should be a second line of works will depend on many circumstances, but it is a very good plan to have a false position somewhat advanced, so that the enemy, having made all his dispositions for front and flank attack, and having despatched his turning columns with certain orders, may find the whole scheme thrown out by your change of position. But in this case the men must be well drilled to understand the manœuvre.

Reserve.—The reserve, taken here for general purposes as about a third of the whole, will be so placed as to be under the hand of the commander for heavy counter-attacks, for turning movements, to restore the fortunes of the field if the enemy have broken through, for deliberate strokes when the enemy has been intentionally suffered to pass within the position, or, finally, to advance with the second line and a part of the first to a direct attack on the hostile army, followed by a pursuit. In this last case a considerable portion of the first line should remain to hold the works.

Disposition of troops and mutual assistance.—The same principles of disposing the troops should be followed on a large scale as have been described on a small scale in the defence of villages and woods. That is to say, the defence should be divided into sections, each under a separate commander, who will make his own arrangements, examined and readjusted by the commander of the whole. The first works to be undertaken are those of the first line, and preferably the commanding or salient points, with villages, woods, &c. The second line should here assist the first, before attending to its own special defences. It is needless to say that as far as possible any works of the second line should be so disposed as to cover the flanks of localities, &c., in the first line which have been prepared for defence or specially constructed. The defenders of any redoubts or other works of the kind that may have been built should be told off in three reliefs, and, except in presence of an attack commenced or momentarily expected, only one relief at a time should be present in the work.

Flanks.—Unless the flanks are so placed that they cannot be turned, they should be partially thrown back, and here, more than in the front, are obstacles necessary. Only it must never be forgotten that no really satisfactory triumph can be obtained over the enemy except by a counter-attack, and the issue of the troops which have to make it should be provided for. As the flanks are liable to enfilade fire, something of the nature of traverses should be provided. The two most useful points in the Turkish system, so far as the defensive was concerned, were traverses and bomb-proof cover for the men. But such cover is not good for permanent occupation, as it leads to sickness. The security of the flanks should be attended to by cavalry pushed out to gain information; and any good locality may be occupied by infantry charged to delay the advance of the enemy's turning columns.

Weak points of such a position.—No student who has gone through the early chapters with any care can hesitate to lay his finger upon the weak points of a position so prepared. Any salient is a weak point, but here we have what may fairly be called salient angles at the point where the front line and its thrown-back flanks meet. Here then should the greatest

DEFENCE AND ATTACK OF LARGE POSITIONS. 349

trouble be taken, and all possible skill applied. Here also will naturally be a concentration of artillery, because the flanks will rest on the most commanding positions, whence the guns can see and search out with their fire the greatest extent of ground. There is another danger wherever a line of troops is thrown back and attacked at the angle. A good instance of that danger was shown in the battle of Prague, May 1757.[1] The danger is that, if either of the faces which form the angle advance or retire, the inner flank of the other face is exposed. If both retire together, they crowd upon each other and there is danger of confusion and rout. Hence all such angles should be as obtuse as possible, and unless in cases of absolute necessity they should be avoided, by resting the flanks on impassable obstacles which do not suffer the enemy to bombard at decisive ranges. A well-prepared wood is a great strength to a flank if it screens the position from view of the enemy.

Measures if time is doubtful.—If there is a question of time, and it is not certain when the enemy will attack, the order of importance of duties will be as follows :—

1st. Clear the ground and establish a complete system of communications. The student can see for himself the difference between this case, where the troops could fight without works at all, and the defence of a house, where the first duty is to take cover and prepare for defence.

2nd. Form shelter trenches, being only careful as to their position so as to bring all the ground in front under fire. Afterwards an increase in strength of profile may be considered and executed at some points.

3rd. During the second stage, or rather from the beginning, the most important points of vantage will have been decided upon, and any redoubts which there are to be will now be constructed, taking the place of some of the shelter trenches.

---

[1] See *Military Biographies—Frederick the Great*, by Colonel C. B. Brackenbury. Chapman & Hall.

4th. Establish cover for the artillery, which will already have posted itself on the most commanding positions.

N.B.—It is to be understood that the preparation of such localities as are selected for defence will be taken in hand from the first and proceed step by step till they are finished, as explained in the earlier part of this volume.

The holding-back system.—Another style of defence has been advocated by certain German writers. In its essence it consists in taking the first blows of the enemy with only a half or even a third of the defending force, while holding back the rest at a half-day's march in rear. When the attackers are fully committed, this rear force will march to make what may be called a counter-attack, with full knowledge of the position of the battle. Such a scheme appears to me extremely dangerous and difficult to execute. Against it is the principle which Napoleon had in view when he said, 'Generals who keep fresh troops in reserve for the day following the battle, are almost always defeated.' It violates the spirit of the rule 'to be superior to the enemy at the right time and place.'

The Attack.

Principles of attack.—The attack of posts and localities has been so largely treated in former chapters, that a study of it in detail is hardly necessary here. The examples taken from various wars must have impressed the mind of any careful reader with certain principles which may be shortly summed up.

Reconnaissance.—First of all is the necessity of careful reconnaissance. To blunder up against an enemy's position, as has frequently been done, is to give away many of the assailants' chances. Among the pieces of information most necessary to obtain, is the amount and position of bombproof cover possessed by the enemy, and the probability of his exposing his infantry or retiring them during the early action of the artillery. Of course the general idea of the defence must be mastered as far as possible, and the actual

DEFENCE AND ATTACK OF LARGE POSITIONS.

position of his second line and reserves. Note the extraordinary conduct of the Russian Artillery at Zevin, which wasted its powers by firing at supports and reserves which only existed in its imagination.

Preliminary.—We must suppose that the attack has ascertained at least the general position of the enemy's troops and works, has driven in the advanced detachments and the outpost line, and has now to make dispositions for the attack. The next step is to overcome if possible the fire of the enemy's artillery; or if, as is very likely, the defence withdraws its guns under cover without much damage, intending to use them at a later stage, the artillery of the attack should endeavour to establish itself at decisive range with two objects :—

- *a.* To prepare the assault of the infantry and cover their advance by demoralizing, as far as it can, the defenders' infantry, at that part of the field.
- *b.* To be ready to overpower the defenders' artillery, if it comes into action against the attacking infantry.

It is evident that, for both these purposes, the commander of the attack must have made his plans and prepared orders accordingly.

Four types: Russian, German, Frederick's, and coming type.—On the whole there may be said to be four general types, which might be named, though there must be an infinite number of different methods of carrying out the arrangements, which must vary according to circumstances. The four types may be named as follows :—

- 1st. The Russian type. A frontal attack, varied by demonstrations or weak attacks in flank; the frontal attack being distributed over different points in the field of battle. This may be done when the attack is equal or superior in strength to the defence, but is not to be recommended.
- 2nd. The German type of 1870. A frontal attack combined with a strong flank attack; the frontal being intended rather to hold the enemy, but often sliding into costly local attacks, as at Gravelotte. This

type would include the enveloping an enemy, as at Sedan, and relies largely on the action of artillery. The force making it should be much superior to the enemy either in number or moral force, or both. Though this was the type of the 1870 campaign, it might not be the German type now.

3rd. The type of Frederick. An oblique attack on one wing of the defenders, which involves the refusal at first of one wing of the attacking army. This form may be executed by a force inferior in number but very well in hand. It is powerful and likely to be successful against an enemy who clings to a prepared position in which he has heavy artillery. It would probably be employed against English Volunteers holding a position to cover London and armed with guns of position, but with little field artillery.

4th. The probable coming type. Frontal demonstrations aided by the spade, combined with attack in great force on one or both wings, obliquely or otherwise. If the defenders are active, this type will resolve itself into combined attack and defence on both sides. It also might be employed with advantage by a highly trained invader against a position held to cover London.

General Ideas.—To attempt to pursue all these types through their various details would require a whole treatise of itself, and we must content ourselves with a few remarks applicable to all cases. Most of these remarks will be found already scattered through the book with the arguments on which they are based, but will be all the more likely to dwell on the memory if repeated here.

Action of Field Artillery.—With regard to the preliminary action of the artillery, it is well to remember that field guns cannot be expected to have any effect at all worth the expenditure of ammunition against solid earthworks or troops under bomb-proof cover, so long as they only use their present ammunition. Neither will artillery have much effect if its action is distributed instead of massed. The ideal would be to distribute the guns while concentrating their fire, but this is practically impossible for the attack, though sometimes possible for a defence if provided with a very elaborate system of telegraphic communication. As nothing is so important as unity of command, and guns themselves are seldom destroyed, though there may be great losses in men, it is better that a large portion of the artillery should be exposed than that unity of command should be lost. The longer a line of guns *under one control* is, the more intense will be its action on any given point selected by the commander of the whole. Prince Kraft von Hohenlohe thinks that it is asking rather too much from human nature to expect artillery to fire at a point whence they receive no harm instead of against the annoying enemy in front, but he would be the first to admit that good troops may be trained to anything. Artillery is hardly ever assembled in masses during peace, yet that is the training which it most requires. The sceptics as to the power of field artillery, properly applied, would be converted at once could they but see the action of a hundred guns in line, occupying a mile of frontage, directed by one commander and transferring the whole shrapnel or shell power of the mass, now to one point, now to another, of the field within its utmost range. To gain its full power field artillery should advance as soon as possible to decisive ranges. The improvement in guns and ammunition has been so great within the last few years that 2,000 yards may now be said to be a decisive range. In the late war the Russian guns had a muzzle velocity of only about 1,000 feet per second. The British 12-pounder now being supplied to the field artillery has a muzzle velocity of more than 1,700 feet per second.

High explosives.—It has been necessary to base all our arguments on what actually exists; but there is one obvious development of field artillery which would give it greatly increased power against field works. It is quite time that chemistry should supply a much stronger explosive, for bursting charges, than gunpowder. I do not pretend to say whether roburite or melinite is yet satisfactory and safe to carry, but it seems certain that some high explosive, to be used in common or even double shells, will turn out to be the reply of the attack to the modern development of defensive field works.

Some interesting experiments have also been tried in England with machine guns. It has been proved that redoubts could be covered with a hail of bullets from machine guns by sinking the trails of such pieces in the ground, so as to give excessively high elevation. This method would, however, be of no avail against bomb-proof cover, while the light machine guns would be severely cut up by the fire of field artillery directed against them; whereas the high explosives as bursting charges for shells have been found capable of actually clearing away everything in the shape of earth-works. It is to be hoped that the British artillery may be provided with some such explosives before our next great war. In this direction, and in the use of shields for protection against shrapnel and rifle bullets, seems to lie the future progress of field artillery.

Action of Infantry.—Admirable as is the fire effect of well-trained infantry armed with the newest weapons even at long ranges when the distance is known, it is well to remember that the highest value of infantry is not to be found in any amount of damage done at long range. Its chief duty and power is shown when it approaches close to the enemy, and by one means or another causes him to retreat from the ground which is the object of dispute. Eventually, the effect is, and must be, moral; for all the talk of 'pressure' of columns and so on is mere rhetoric. Infantry never really pushes other infantry except now and then in a struggle in a house or other closed space. What happens is that from one cause or another the weaker side yields—runs away, in short—and the stronger either takes its place or runs after it. No such effect can be produced at long range, nor would the habit of trying to produce it be good from any point of view. Defenders may fire at any range which will help to check the enemy, but attacking columns will do well to reserve their fire.—See Chapter X. *et seq.* All infantry fire should have an aggressive character—two or three rounds fired as quickly as possible, then silence and time for the smoke to clear away. On approaching the enemy, if an assault is decided upon, it should be made by one wave coming on after another before the first has lost its power. After the war of 1870 the idea prevailed that first or fighting lines would do the chief work. The tendency now is in favour of a deeper formation than ever, only in very different formation from the solid column. The whole subject has been treated when discussing the attack on localities, and we have only to enlarge the scale, and to suppose a tremendous artillery fire supporting the attack till the last moment, and all that was said of localities applies as well to attack on positions. There will be the same preparation—unless the defenders are in bomb-proof cover, when it is useless; the same destruction of obstacles if they exist by long artillery fire, for which we want a better explosive than gunpowder as bursting charges; the same working parties to clear away the obstacles; the same rolling forward of the infantry; the same occupation of the position, only in this case artillerymen should accompany the column, to spike or turn backwards the guns of the defence; and some field artillery should be in readiness to occupy the ground taken and repel a counter-attack. Wherever the infantry columns attack, whether in one part of the field or several, the action will be the same as that for the attack of a village or work, only with some added features which have just been named.

The coming type.—The system which I have called the probable coming type will only make this difference, that a comparatively weak and outspread force will advance as near as it dare to the defenders, probably flanked by guns and supported here and there by firmer bodies. The men will throw up a few sods of earth or take shelter as they best can, and become a defensive force occupying the attention of as many of the defenders as possible. The defence will not know at what moment such a demonstration may be turned into a real attack by the advance at any time of columns of assault from the rear, and if the defenders should retire, their place would quickly be taken by the then line of attack. In all cases of success the defences should be organised at once against their quondam occupants.

Attack should entrench a rallying position.—It is most important that all assaulting columns should have strong reserves intended to receive the counter-attack of the defenders; and all attacking forces, great or small, will do well to have behind them some slight defence—shelter trenches and the rest—behind which to rally in case of repulse. These should be constructed, not by the men advancing to the assault, but by troops following them, because preparation for being beaten is not the best spirit to have among troops going in to win. General Brialmont says with reason, 'These entrenchments mark the limit of the retrograde movement; the troops halt there and rally naturally; confidence returns, the pursuit ceases, and if all goes well the offensive may be reassumed.'

Cavalry.—The chief use of cavalry in attack of positions will be to guard your own flanks and rear, to threaten those of the enemy, to make demonstrations by dismounted action, to bring information, and finally to take up the pursuit and prevent the enemy carrying away his heavier artillery and stores.

Question of position guns with armies in the field.—There is at the present moment a strong feeling in Europe that guns of rather heavy calibre should accompany an army in the field, for the purpose of bombarding with some useful result the works which will certainly meet them frequently, whether or not the enemy acts generally on the defensive. These guns will have powerful shells, probably filled with roburite or melinite, or some composition of like character combining safety in transport and firing with violent bursting effect. The Germans seem to be making some deliberate arrangement of the sort, and probably the French will do the same. In that case the preparatory action of the artillery would be shorter and more efficacious, but the weight of the guns would cause time to be lost. They would usually be

DEFENCE AND ATTACK OF LARGE POSITIONS. 357

in rear of the army, and would hardly be able to accompany it far after the first battles had been fought.

Night Attacks.—However well conducted the attack of a fortified position by main force may be, it is sure to sacrifice a great deal of life, and to expend a large number of brave soldiers, for it is the bravest who are apt to go first. The use of a powerful artillery will tend to save life by demoralising the defenders, and if these are already demoralised, as the Turks were after the fall of Plevna and the astonishing feat of crossing the Balkans in mid-winter, the assault may be comparatively easy without the aid of artillery. Witness Skobeleff's famous capture of the Shenova redoubts below the Shipka Pass, where that dashing General advanced his troops without firing a shot, all the bands playing, till on nearing the works the Russians broke into a run, sprang over the parapets and carried the day for once by a sheer struggle with the bayonet. It should be remembered that on the same day Radetsky and Mirsky had both carried Turkish works, though their success was not of the same brilliant character as Skobeleff's. Such cases are exceptional, and can only occur when the assailants have already achieved a moral superiority. Even then Skobeleff lost 22 per cent. of the troops which actually attacked. Where no such moral superiority has been attained the losses must be extremely heavy, and all tacticians are studying how the effect of the defenders' fire can be neutralised. One of the greatest tactical questions is whether attacks of positions can be made under cover of night. No doubt the efficacy of the defenders' fire can thus be diminished, for the assailants will not be seen approaching, and the effect on the nerves of the defenders will be very striking if the assailants can succeed in approaching without confusion or mistakes as to direction. The fortress of Kars was captured by a night attack, but the defenders had been demoralised by the battle of the Aladja Dagh, from which many of the garrison of Kars had fled in panic. One of the heights of Kizil Tepé was carried by a night attack of the Turks, and the Russians could not retake it by day. The village of Yaslar, on the Lom, also fell to a

Russian attack in the dark, and cases of a similar character occurred in the Franco-German War. I was present at one of them, the capture of Changé in the dusk of the late afternoon and a snowstorm. On the other hand, there have been awkward failures, such as that of General Heimann, whose attempt to capture the eastern forts of Erzeroum at night resulted in his two columns losing their way and arriving by daylight. The only troops which did not wander were three battalions of an advanced guard, and these carried rapidly the fort which they reached. Our own army in 1882 very nearly suffered disaster during the night march, two wings almost coming into collision, though the leading was good. This is the chief danger, but it is one not to be despised, and it would seem that none but the best troops already trained to night marches are likely to be sure of avoiding the dangerous results attendant upon such attempts. Outposts well placed ought to make night surprises impossible, and if daylight should find the columns of attack wandering and the defenders in readiness for a counter-attack, the result might be a catastrophe for the assailants. Still, the benefit of getting over the dangerous zones of fire under cover of darkness is so great that we are likely to find night attacks a feature of the next war, and both attack and defence under these conditions should be carefully practised. The chief elements of success are, a thorough knowledge of the ground, perfect silence, slow movement, and constant communication between the different columns. For the defence, the best precautions are, well placed and alert outposts, and means for covering all the near portions of ground with a cross fire, even in the dark. The assailants should not fire at all, as the shooting would be inaccurate and betray their position. The formation should be in close order.

Chain of responsibility: Nature of orders.—There is one point more which deserves a word of notice. The necessity of a proper chain of responsibility has often been referred to and illustrated. Its importance is the same either in a defended village, a small attacking column, or in the attack or defence of a great position. From this it follows that the

DEFENCE AND ATTACK OF LARGE POSITIONS. 359

nature of the orders issued should be such as to cause the responsibility for any action to rest in its proper place. If the officer commanding the whole thinks to foresee and give instructions for every little detail, he is, in the first place, attempting the impossible, and, in the next place, storing up for his subordinates a mass of difficulties by tying their hands. The commander should, before an important operation, go patiently into the intended business with the commanders of high units, and request them to take care that the knowledge is spread in their commands. The orders which he will then issue in writing should be as short as possible, merely saying generally what the higher units are to achieve, while leaving to the commanders the full responsibility of choosing how they will execute those orders. Two points should always be named, the position of the Commander-in-Chief and Headquarter Staff, and also where the trains are to remain. Everybody should read the Archduke Albert's admirable pamphlet on 'Responsibility in War,' wherein he spoke frankly of the sins of his own countrymen. I may also refer to a pamphlet by Captain Norman Bray on the framing of orders, of which he gives some interesting examples to illustrate the good and the bad. The subject is of the highest importance, and Prince Frederick Charles spoke of it as one of the chief superiorities of the German army over the French. In the German army only general orders were issued from headquarters, and those of the shortest description, but the commander knew pretty well how they would be executed. In the French army, on the contrary, the endeavour to keep everybody in leading strings resulted in a general confusion, which became worse as time went on. Besides, if commanders do not leave responsibility to their subordinates, how are these to learn their higher work? The attempt to order everything is a great vice and very detrimental to the efficiency of an army.

Spottiswoode & Co. Printers, New-street Square, London.

The borrower must return this item by
the last date stamped below. If
places a recall for this item, the bo